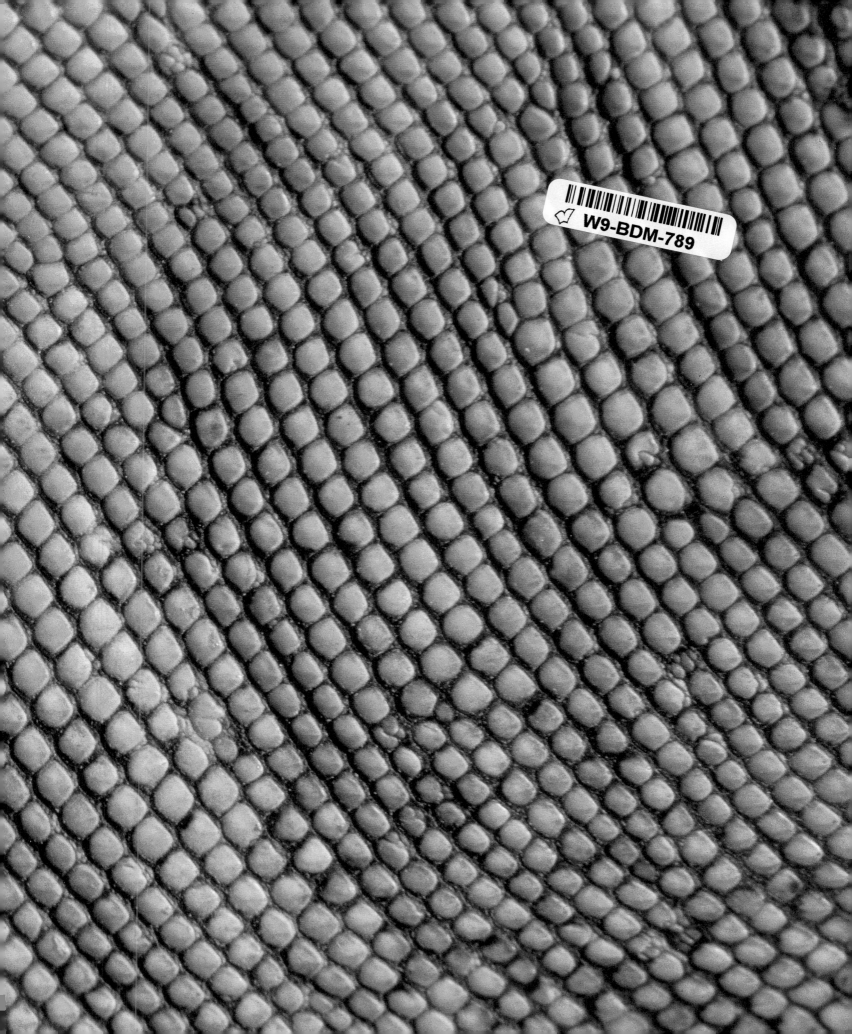

W9-BDM-789

DINOSAURUS

THE COMPLETE GUIDE TO DINOSAURS

DINOSAURUS

THE COMPLETE GUIDE TO DINOSAURS

STEVE PARKER

FIREFLY BOOKS

A FIREFLY BOOK

Published by Firefly Books Ltd., 2003

Copyright © 2003 Quintet Publishing Ltd.

All rights reserved. No part of this publication may be reproduced, stored in a retrieval system, or transmitted in any form or by any means, electronic, mechanical, photocopying, recording, or otherwise, without the prior written permission of the copyright owner.

First Printing

National Library of Canada Cataloguing in Publication
Parker, Steve
Dinosaurus : the complete guide to dinosaurs / Steve Parker.
Includes bibliographical references and index.
ISBN 1-55297-772-2
1. Dinosaurs. I. Title.
QE861.4.P37 2003   567.9   C2003-901039-2

Publisher Cataloging-in-Publication Data (U.S.)
(Library of Congress standards)
Parker, Steve.
Dinosaurus : the complete guide to dinosaurs / Steve Parker. —1st ed.
[448] p. : col. ill. ; cm.
Includes index.
Summary: A comprehensive encyclopedia of dinosaurs, including the latest scientific knowledge and fossil discoveries.
ISBN 1-55297-772-2
1. Dinosaurs. I. Title.
567.9/1 21   QE862.D5P1452 2003

Published in Canada in 2003 by
Firefly Books Ltd.
3680 Victoria Park Avenue
Toronto, Ontario M2H 3K1

Published in the United States in 2003 by
Firefly Books (U.S.) Inc.
P.O. Box 1338, Ellicott Station
Buffalo, New York 14205

www.fireflybooks.com

This book was designed and produced by
Quintet Publishing Limited
6 Blundell Street
London N7 9 BH

Picture and Project Editors: Duncan Proudfoot, Anna Southgate, Anna Kiernan
Text Editor: Monique Lamontagne
North American Editor: Françoise Vulpé

Art Director: Tristan de Lancey
Design: Jon Wainwright and Matt Sanderman
Graphic Illustration: Richard Burgess

Managing Editor: Diana Steedman
Creative Director: Richard Dewing
Publisher: Oliver Salzmann

Manufactured in Singapore by Universal Graphics Pte Ltd
Printed in China by Midas Printing International Limited

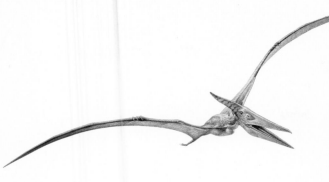

FOREWORD

Almost everyone is interested in dinosaurs at some point in his or her life – be it at the age of five or 95. Even the great fact and fiction writer Arthur C. Clarke traces his early interest in science to dinosaurs, recalling that his first exposure to these "saurians" as a boy in rural England was a series of cards his father gave him.

Why the great interest in this long-gone group? What is it about dinosaurs that has drawn our attention so intensely for so long? Maybe it has been simply because some dinosaurs are big, and nasty and, more importantly – extinct! Perhaps this ongoing infatuation is that there are so many different kinds of dinosaur.

Most of the well-known dinosaurs are from either North America, typically the west (Wyoming, Montana and Alberta), or Eurasia, for example Mongolia. More recent finds in South America, Australia, Antarctica and Alaska are not so widely known, but it will not be long before younger generations are picking their way through such new discoveries for themselves.

The latest finds of bigger and smaller dinosaurs in places like Argentina, and of a range of small but varied polar dinosaurs have combined with studies showing that many dinosaurs were anything but big, slow moving and dim-witted, to change common perceptions of this very successful group. We now know that some dinosaurs had feathers and were at least gliding if not flying. Furthermore the discovery of a variety of tough little critters that lived near the North and South Poles, suggests that some of these dinosaurs must have been warm-blooded to deal with such severe conditions.

What has made dinosaurs even more interesting in recent years are the many studies that have centered on the companions of these creatures and the environments in which they lived during the Mesozoic Era. Current research focuses on why so many of these otherwise successful animals were nearly wiped out 65 million years ago and on how they evolved from reptilian ancestors in the first place. The result, as shown here, is an extensive resource on the world in which dinosaurs prospered – and died – with as much detail on the ancient habitats as on the inhabitants themselves.

Dinosaurus cannot hope to include every known dinosaur – we would need a small library for that – but it certainly offers excellent coverage of many of the creatures that existed, their environment and contemporaries. Many of the newest dinosaurs get a mention too, giving enthusiasts a much broader understanding of the dinosaur system as a whole.

Professor Patricia Vickers Rich
Chair in Palaeontology,
Monash University

Founding Director,
Monash Science Centre,
Melbourne, Victoria
Australia

Dr Thomas H. Rich
Curator,
Vertebrate Palaeontology
Museum Victoria
Melbourne, Victoria
Australia

3 1489 00502 4755

CONTENTS

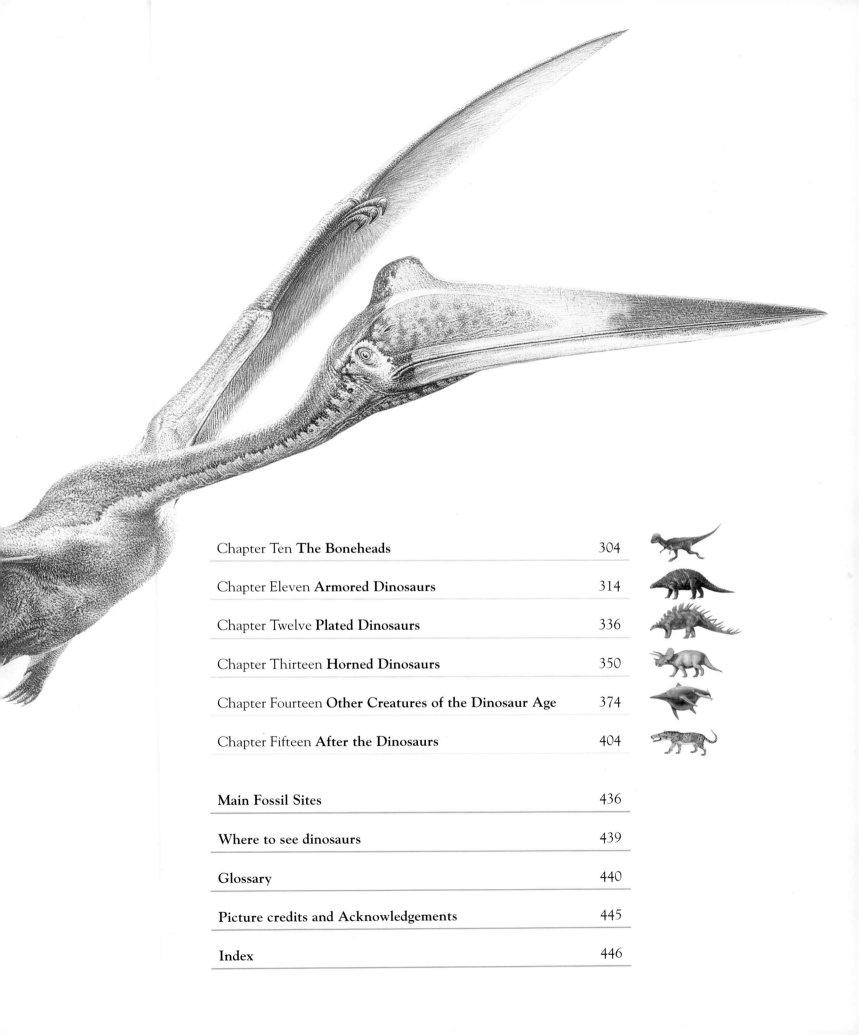

INTRODUCTION

WHEN DEALING WITH DINOSAURS, THERE IS PERHAPS ONLY ONE CERTAINTY: THE "FACTS" WILL CHANGE. OF COURSE, THE LIVES OF THE DINOSAURS AND OTHER PREHISTORIC ANIMALS IN THIS BOOK CANNOT BE ALTERED. THAT WORLD IS LONG GONE. WHAT DOES CHANGE IS OUR INTERPRETATION OF HOW DINOSAURS LIVED AND DIED. ALMOST EVERY WEEK, NEW DISCOVERIES ARE ANNOUNCED. DEBATES AND DISAGREEMENTS OCCUR, OLD IDEAS ARE REVIVED, AND NEW IDEAS ARE CHALLENGED. PERHAPS ONCE A YEAR, A FRESH FOSSIL FIND OR A NEW THEORY OF PREHISTORY CATCHES THE PUBLIC IMAGINATION. THESE NEWSWORTHY EVENTS TEND TO FOCUS ON WHICH WAS THE BIGGEST OR THE FIERCEST OF DINOSAURS, WHICH CAME FIRST, AND HOW THEIR EXTINCTION IS EXPLAINED. IT IS THE PROGRESS IN OUR KNOWLEDGE OF THESE ANCIENT ANIMALS THAT MAKES THEIR STUDY SO EXCITING AND ENDURING.

DINOSAURS IN PERSPECTIVE

The number of kinds, or species, of animals, plants and other living things in existence today likely exceeds 10 million. Insects are the vast majority. Some of the other main groups of invertebrates (animals without backbones) include around 100,000 species of slugs, snails, octopuses, mussels and other molluscs; 40,000 species of crabs, prawns, lobsters and other crustaceans; and 10,000 species of the simplest of all animals, sponges. Prehistoric versions of all these groups are shown in this book. Among the vertebrates, fish are by far the most species-rich group, at 25,000, followed by some 9,000 species of birds, 7,000 reptile species and 5,000 types of amphibians. Our own group, the mammals, trails behind, with around 4,500 species. Overall, close to two million living species from all groups, including plants, have been described, named, and cataloged by scientists. Yet more than 99 out of every 100 kinds of living things that have ever existed are no longer around. They form a vast array of life forms that have appeared and then disappeared on our planet.

Within this array, scientists have listed several hundred types of dinosaur. Each of these is a genus (plural, genera) containing one or more very closely related species. For example, *Tyrannosaurus*, "tyrant reptile," is a genus of huge meat-eaters from very late in the dinosaur age, about 70–65 million years ago. The best-known species is *Tyrannosaurus rex*, "king tyrant reptile." The differences between dinosaur species within the same genus are often complex and are much debated, depending on interpretation of tiny details on the fossils. This book describes principally genera of dinosaurs and other prehistoric creatures, with a few excursions to the level of species to illustrate certain points.

The classification of some 400 genera of dinosaurs, and of several species within many of these genera, is a terrific achievement in relation to a group of animals known only from fossils. The fossil record is very scarce, patchy and fragmentary. The chances are that it shows us only a few kinds of dinosaurs that existed. The numbers and variety of dinosaurs we do know about give some idea of the dominance they achieved over other forms of land life. Their fossils accumulated over a span of more than 160 million years.

ABOVE Fossils of the "giant armadillo" *Glyptodon*, some just a few thousand years old, litter certain regions of South America.

LEFT Staring death in the face: this fossil of *Tyrannosaurus* teeth, jaws and skull shows how detailed preservation can be.

EVOLUTION

IN ONE SENSE, "EVOLUTION" SIMPLY MEANS CHANGE. LIVING THINGS HAVE CHANGED SINCE THEY BEGAN, AS SHOWN BY EVIDENCE FROM THE FOSSIL RECORD. TYPES OF PLANTS AND CREATURES APPEARED, FLOURISHED FOR A TIME, AND THEN FADED AWAY. THE BIRD CALLED THE PASSENGER PIGEON TEEMED IN THE MILLIONS IN NORTH AMERICA BEFORE EUROPEAN SETTLERS ARRIVED, BUT WAS SLAUGHTERED INTO OBLIVION BY THE EARLY 20TH CENTURY. THE DODO, THE QUAGGA (A HOOFED ANIMAL RESEMBLING A HORSE OR ZEBRA) AND THE AUROCHS (ANCESTOR OF TODAY'S CATTLE) ALL DIED OUT WITHIN THE PAST MILLENNIUM. AND ALL OF THESE RECENT CHANGES HAVE BEEN DUE TO "UNNATURAL" INTERFERENCE BY HUMANS IN THE NATURAL WORLD. BUT ALL THROUGH EARTH'S HISTORY, SUCH DISAPPEARANCES, OR EXTINCTIONS HAVE OCCURRED ON A REGULAR BASIS. THERE IS A TURNOVER OF SPECIES TODAY, AS THERE HAS BEEN SINCE LIFE BEGAN.

BELOW Species come and go. Since humans came on the scene, other species mostly go, like the Columbian mammoth. Its demise across North America roughly coincides with the spread of people. Such changes have happened through prehistory, but at a much slower rate than today.

Farther back in time, during the Age of Dinosaurs, the same changes occurred. They were due to the pressures of living – finding food, escaping predators, sheltering from the elements, competing for a breeding partner and generally struggling to survive. If every offspring of every living thing survived, the world would soon have become impossibly crowded. No animal had a life free from

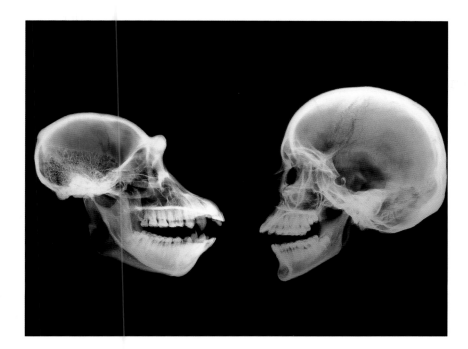

hardships or interference. Natural forces or pressures, such as trying to get food or avoid a hunter, meant that some living things died out. The survivors were, in effect, those left after selection by nature's pressures – which is what scientists mean by "natural selection."

What determined whether a living thing survived the struggle for existence? In part, the genetic "instructions," in the form of the chemical DNA, for bodily features or characteristics. Genes are inherited from parents. The way that reproduction works means that genes sometimes undergo change (mutation) or come together in different combinations (recombination) in different individuals. These are regular occurrences, and the result is that offspring vary from their parents and from each other. These variations may be small, but can be enough to tip the balance in the trial of survival. Useful features or characteristics mean that an individual is more likely to survive and breed, passing on its genes to its offspring by the process of inheritance.

Through prehistory, dinosaurs and other living things were subjected to the pressures of natural selection. If the environment had remained constant for all this time, then perhaps the dinosaurs, and life in general, would have reached a steady state or equilibrium. Conditions, however, have always changed. Climates have fluctuated, temperatures have varied, sea levels have gone up and down. Living things responded to the alterations by evolving. As they did so, living things were also part of the environment in relation to each other, causing further changes to evolve. Sometimes, evolution happened slowly and gradually, over millions of years. At other times, it occurred relatively quickly, followed by a long period of relative stability, which is known as "punctuated equilibrium" – evolution by "jumps."

Evolutionary history is sometimes imagined as a "tree of life." There were one or two types of life early on, gradually giving rise to more and more different kinds, and so on. The end-points or "twig-tips" are animals and plants alive today. However an untidy "hedge of life" might be more apt, since some species died out as others arose. Apart from life's earliest stages, there has always appeared to be great diversity and abundance.

ABOVE According to studies of fossil evidence and genetic differences, scientists estimate that chimps (skull on the left) humans (right skull) have evolved from a common ancestor about 6–8 million years ago. Both have probably changed in this time – the ancestor did not necessarily look as the chimp does now.

BELOW The dodo is a well-known symbol of extinction: "dead as a dodo." But this turkey-sized, flightless bird did not succumb to the pressures of natural selection, as dinosaurs did. Like the mammoth opposite, it was exterminated by humans, but relatively recently. It had disappeared from its Indian Ocean island home of Mauritius by about 1670.

Fossils

The principal evidence for the existence of dinosaurs and other long-gone living things comes from fossils. These are the remains of organisms, or the traces they left, which have been preserved, usually in the form of rock. The phrase "bone to stone" sums up how a fossil forms, although not only bones have been preserved, and not all fossils are in the form of stony minerals. Also, the process of fossilization is long and beset by chance events. The fossil record in the rocks, and the story it tells of life on Earth, should therefore be approached with caution.

An old dinosaur lies down on a riverbank and dies. Then the river floods and, as the waters subside, they leave a thick layer of sandy sediment that covers the animal's body. The fleshy parts of the dinosaur, such as its muscles and guts, rot away slowly. The harder parts, such as the bones, teeth, claws, and horns, are more resistant to decay. Through time, the sand is buried deeper as more layers accumulate on top. The pressure and temperature of the layers rise with increasing depth. The originally loose sand is gradually compressed and cemented by rock minerals, to become hard sandstone. The minerals seep into the dinosaur's bones, and other hard parts, too, and turn them into stone, while preserving their original shape.

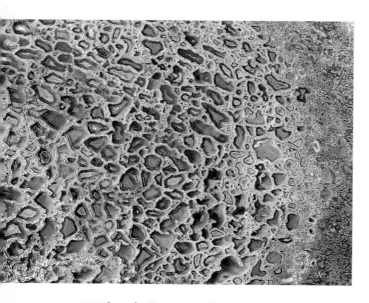

ABOVE Some fossils are prized for beauty as well as information, like this "agatized" dinosaur bone impregnated with tinted quartz.

BELOW Fossils show "frozen behavior," like a fishy meal that became a death struggle, 50 million years ago.

Meanwhile, millions of years pass. Great earth movements lift and tilt the rocks, so that they are no longer built up but worn down. Natural forces of erosion – the sun's heat by day, cold winds at night, rain, hail, frost and ice – crack and split the overlying layers. One day, the erosion reaches the layer with the dinosaur's remains, or fossils. These are exposed to view just as a paleontologist walks past.

The above story may seem unlikely – and it is. In fact, the vast majority of dinosaurs that ever lived did not form fossils. Their remains were crunched up by scavengers, or rotted away, or disintegrated in wind and rain. Vast numbers of the remains that did become fossilized did not last very long. They and their rocks were buried so deep in the Earth that they melted, destroying all traces of fossil shape and form. Many fossils that exist today are still deep in the Earth, far out of reach of our eyes or drills. It follows that the chances of a single dinosaur leaving any preserved remains at all must be millions to one.

Not only dinosaurs left fossils. Most living things, including animals, plants and even microbes, are represented in the fossil record. The great majority of preservations are hard parts, such as bones, teeth, claws, horns, shells, wood, leaf-ribs, seeds or cones. Because fossils tended to form when sand, mud or similar sediment quickly covered remains, protecting and slowing their disintegration, the greatest numbers are from marine animals that died and sank into the ooze on the seabed. As a result, the shells of crustaceans, such as trilobites, and of molluscs, such as ammonites, abound as fossils. Also, not only body parts were preserved. Eggshells, excavated nests and burrows, footprints, scratch marks, furrow-like tail-drags and even droppings or dung all left signs, known as "trace fossils." Much rarer are fossils of softer body parts, such as skin and flesh, which need exceptional conditions to be preserved (see page 23).

TOP Water-dwellers, like this fish *Lepidotes* from 150 million years ago, are more likely to be preserved than land animals, by sinking to the seabed and quickly being covered by mud-carrying water currents.

ABOVE Almost any parts or signs of animals can be preserved. These are fossilized remains from the stomach of a plesiosaur, a four-flippered sea reptile of 150 million years ago. The shells and other fragments reveal what it ate.

FINDING FOSSILS

FOSSILS OF DINOSAURS AND OTHER PREHISTORIC LIFE FORMS ARE COMING TO LIGHT EVERY DAY, AT THOUSANDS OF SITES AROUND THE WORLD. HOWEVER, USUALLY NO ONE IS THERE TO RECOGNIZE THEIR SIGNIFICANCE. EXPECTANT FOSSIL-FINDERS CAN SEARCH AND MONITOR ONLY A TINY FRACTION OF THE PLACES WHERE PRESERVED REMAINS OF PREHISTORIC LIFE BECOME VISIBLE. A KEY REQUIREMENT FOR SUCH SITES IS SUITABLE TYPES OF ROCKS AT OR NEAR THE SURFACE.

ABOVE One of the world's most valuable fossils is this specimen of the earliest known bird, *Archaeopteryx*, from about 160-150 million years ago. It is exquisitely preserved in fine-grained limestone at Solenhofen in Germany. The fossil came to light as part of quarrying operations. This type of rock has such fine grains that it was used for printing and is known as lithographic limestone.

Because of the way in which fossils were formed, only the types of rocks called sedimentary rocks contain them. These include sandstone, siltstone, mudstone, clay, chalk and limestone. They are made of tiny particles, sediments, which once drifted and sank in water or were blown by the wind on land. The sediments settled in layers, were gradually buried deeper and eventually compacted and cemented into rock, with their fossils inside (see previous page). The two other major groups of rocks, igneous and metamorphic, hardly ever harbor fossils. Their formation includes massive pressures and great temperatures, which destroy any preserved remains they might initially contain, so vast areas of granite, basalt and other non-sedimentary rocks are of little interest to fossil-hunters. Also, many suitable fossil-bearing rocks are covered by soil and vegetation, such as woods, forests and grassland, and so are hidden from the fossil-hunter's scrutiny.

To find fossils from a certain age, such as dinosaur remains from the Mesozoic era, the rocks must have been formed during that age. This greatly narrows down the choice of sites. Geological maps for large parts of the world's surface are produced by geologists, especially those prospecting for minerals and other resources such as coal, petroleum (oil) and metal ores. These maps are invaluable for paleontologists, who often work alongside geologists in surveying teams. The maps show the types and approximate ages of the uppermost layers of rocks. However, much of the globe's land surface remains to be mapped in detail. Modern fossil-hunters are also helped enormously by aerial surveys and various types of photography from planes and satellites, including both normal visible-light photographs and also images made from infrared, ultraviolet and other types of rays. These can identify potential sites in very remote areas that have been overlooked so far.

Many of the regions that contain the world's most famous fossil sites, such as the Gobi in Mongolia or parts of the midwestern USA, are "badlands." They are harsh landscapes where the rocks are exposed at the surface, and are continually worn away by the extremes of the elements. Hot daytime sun followed by chilled or freezing nights, and the occasional flood or sandstorm, crack and erode stone so that fresh layers are always being exposed. Soil is either blown or washed away, so few plants grow, and the rocks stay bare. Other excellent sites are along rocky coasts, lakeshores or riverbanks, where waves, wind and rain eat away at the cliffs or outcrops, and rockfalls regularly expose new formations. In mines, quarries, cuttings for roads and railways, and major construction projects such as dams, machines cause erosion. Such sites are regularly visited by fossil-hunters searching for newly revealed and interesting-looking remains.

ABOVE Some rocks are mostly fossils, like these "petrified" trees at Lulworth, on the south coast of England.

BELOW A dinosaur has replaced the original kangaroo on this sign at Dinosaur Cove near Melbourne, Australia. The site has yielded many amazing specimens but access and working conditions are tricky.

DATING FOSSILS

HOW OLD IS A FOSSIL? THERE ARE VARIOUS WAYS OF DETERMINING ITS AGE.
THESE FALL INTO TWO BROAD GROUPS: RELATIVE OR COMPARATIVE DATING,
AND ABSOLUTE DATING. IN RELATIVE DATING, FOSSILS AND THE ROCKS THAT
CONTAIN THEM ARE COMPARED, ONE WITH ANOTHER, TO SEE WHICH ARE
NEWER OR OLDER. FOR EXAMPLE, THE LAYERS OR STRATA OF SEDIMENTARY
ROCKS ARE FORMED IN SUCH A WAY THAT THE YOUNGEST LAYERS ARE
USUALLY NEARER THE SURFACE, WITH OLDER ROCKS BURIED MORE DEEPLY.
THERE ARE EXCEPTIONS. SOMETIMES, ROCK LAYERS CAN BE GREATLY TILTED
BY EARTH MOVEMENTS — SO MUCH SO THAT THEY CAN FLIP RIGHT OVER,
PLACING THE OLDER ROCKS AND FOSSILS NEARER THE SURFACE.

In many regions, layers of sedimentary rocks were laid down in a characteristic
sequence of types and thicknesses that is well studied. Rocks and fossils from
a small sample or extract of this pattern, perhaps just two or three layers, can
be dated by fitting them into the overall sequence. "Index fossils," or "marker
fossils," are the remains of living things that were widespread, plentiful and
readily fossilized, surviving through great time periods with continuing
evolution or change. Examples include shelled sea creatures, such as the
trilobites of Cambrian times and the ammonites and belemnites of the Jurassic
(see pages 42, 45 and 49). The changing details of their shell shapes and
patterns place them within a specific time span. This knowledge provides
evidence for dating other, less familiar fossils found with them. Tiny fossils,
such as those of aquatic organisms called foraminiferans, and the tough,
resistant pollen grains of plants, are also used for indexing.

BELOW Layering or stratification is shown clearly in this cut-
through "slice" of sandstone, which was once the sandy bed
of a shallow sea. The bands are especially clear and attractive
in this example, due to various hues of iron-rich minerals.

In absolute or chronometric dating, a fossil is assigned a specific age, usually expressed as millions of years ago, within a range or degree of error. The technique involves measuring quantities of isotopes (forms of certain chemical elements) in a sample, or the amounts of natural radiation (radioactivity) they contain. The measurements are usually done using a machine known as a mass spectrometer. Over time, specific isotopes break apart or decay into other chemical forms at a set and steady rate, like the ticking of a clock. By measuring the comparative amounts of isotopes and other substances, and projecting backward using their known decay rates, geologists can pinpoint when the rock or fossil was formed. The analysis of the amount of carbon 14 compared to other isotopes of the element carbon is commonly known as "carbon dating." However, carbon decays relatively rapidly and cannot be used for remains much older than about 75,000 years. Chemical elements that decay much more slowly, and so are useful for rocks and fossils many millions of years old, include the uranium sequence and the potassium-to-argon sequence.

Many times during prehistory, the Earth's natural magnetic field has reversed completely, so that the magnetic North Pole became the South, and vice versa. As certain kinds of rocks formed, tiny magnetic particles in them aligned with the Earth's magnetic field of the time. Magnetic reversal or switch caused rapid changes in these alignments, which were "frozen" into rocks as they formed. The full sequence of reversals is now well documented, so rock samples with very weak magnetism can be compared with the known sequence to match the sample into their time period. Generally, only igneous rock contains these tiny traces of natural magnetism – but it very rarely contains fossils. However, the technique of paleomagnetism can be used to date igneous rock layers that occur just above or below sedimentary strata containing fossils.

ABOVE Fossils are not all massive chunks of bone- or tooth-shaped rock. Some of the most important for dating, known as index or marker fossils, are as small as this o – tiny preserved seashells and other items. They are sieved and sorted under a large magnifier using forceps (tweezers) and other delicate instruments.

RECOVERING FOSSILS

SOME FOSSILS HAVE BEEN ERODED FROM THEIR SURROUNDING ROCK BY
NATURAL FORCES AND SIMPLY LIE ON THE GROUND, WAITING TO BE PICKED
UP. OTHERS ARE ALMOST FULLY ENCASED IN ROCK, WITH JUST A SMALL PART
EXPOSED THAT GIVES A CLUE TO THEIR EXISTENCE. FOR FOSSIL-HUNTERS,
THERE ARE SEVERAL FACTORS IN DECIDING WHETHER IT WILL BE
WORTHWHILE TO RECOVER A SPECIMEN. IS THE FOSSIL LIKELY TO BE RARE
AND INFORMATIVE, MAKING A SIGNIFICANT CONTRIBUTION TO KNOWLEDGE
OF THE PREHISTORIC WORLD, OR IS IT JUST ANOTHER EXAMPLE OF A VERY
COMMON TYPE, WITH THOUSANDS ALREADY IN MUSEUMS, EXHIBITIONS AND
COLLECTIONS? WHAT ARE ITS LIKELY DEGREES OF COMPLETENESS AND
DISTORTION? WILL IT BE EASY OR DIFFICULT TO REMOVE FROM THE SITE?

The location and nature of the excavation site itself are also important
considerations. It may be remote and awkward, lacking comforts and facilities,
with difficult working conditions and troublesome access, requiring a major
expedition with careful planning and great expenditure. Can permission be
obtained from the relevant authorities, which may range from the local
landowner up to national bodies such as museums or even governments? Also,
in some parts of the world, workers at the site may be at risk – not only from
hazards such as rock falls or extreme weather, but also from lawlessness, group
rivalries, political and economic unrest or even full-blown war and revolution.

BELOW Many fossil-rich sites are in "forsaken" lands like stony deserts, rocky uplands or mosquito-infested swamps. In the Siberian wastes of northeast Russia, where the Kolyma River empties into the Arctic Ocean, melting channels and gouging glaciers may uncover the frozen remains of mammoths and other ice-age creatures.

A well-organized scientific excavation or "dig" is based on taking measurements and making records. First, the site is surveyed and mapped, with measurements plotted using a grid system. Geophysical mapping techniques, such as ground-penetrating radar, may help predict what is under the surface and where the digging should begin. Stage by stage, as rocks and fossils are removed, details on the map are updated. Numerous photographs and extensive notes are taken at every phase. Sketches are also made to show or highlight certain features that a photograph may not emphasize.

Usually, rock must be removed to reveal the fossils themselves. The overlying material can be shoveled, pickaxed or jackhammered away. Mechanical diggers or even explosives might be used. As the excavation becomes small-scale and detailed, it requires hand tools, such as hammers, chisels and trowels, or, for soft, crumbling rocks, scrapers and brushes. There are frequent discussions about the direction of digging, or which part of the fossil is which, and every item is measured and labeled as the dig continues. When the identity and extent of the specimen becomes clear, there may be a decision to chop the block containing it out of the stone as a whole. It is transported back to the laboratory or workroom where conditions are more comfortable and there is a greater range of equipment at hand. Some fossils are so fragile that they are encased in plaster or resin-and-fiber for support and protection as they are lifted clear and transported back to base.

Fossil-hunting has long been an academic pursuit – and also big business. The most important fossils may change hands for millions of dollars. Hundreds of collectors around the world make a good living finding and selling specimens. Because of unscrupulous dealers, the potential for hoaxes, and the spread of "fossil rustling," the locations of some digs are kept closely guarded secrets.

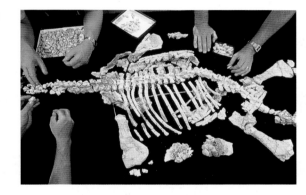

TOP Extracted fossils are usually cleaned and pieced together in the comfort of the laboratory or workroom. Rebuilding a dinosaur egg is like working on a three-dimensional jigsaw, but far more complex – the pieces for several eggs are mixed up, and many are missing or distorted.

ABOVE Expert hands position the almost complete fossil bones of a plesiosaur (predatory marine reptile) that lived some 120 million years ago. The pink color is due to infiltration of the bones by the mineral opal, during fossilization.

MYTHS AND LEGENDS

DINOSAURS ARE PROMINENT AMONG PREHISTORIC ANIMALS, IN BEING THE SUBJECTS OF MYTH AND LEGEND, TRENDS AND FASHIONS. A SINGLE FOSSIL DISCOVERY MAY BE HAILED AS REWRITING PREHISTORY, AS EXPERTS GIVE THEIR LATEST OPINIONS. THE GENERAL KNOWLEDGE OF THE PUBLIC, HOWEVER, OFTEN LAGS WAY BEHIND THE MOST RECENT SCIENTIFIC THEORIES. FOR EXAMPLE, MANY PEOPLE STILL MARVEL AT THE ENORMOUS SIZE OF THE "BRONTOSAURUS"; OR ARE IMPRESSED BY THE REPUTATION OF TYRANNOSAURUS, THE BIGGEST MEAT-EATER OF ALL TIME, PREYING ON PREHISTORIC HORSES; OR BELIEVE THAT FLYING DINOSAURS GLIDED THROUGH THE AIR ON WEAKLY BEATING WINGS; OR IMAGINE THAT SEA DINOSAURS HAD ROWS OF SHARP FANGS. YET NONE OF THESE IDEAS ABOUT DINOSAURS IS BASED ON CURRENT INFORMATION.

"*Brontosaurus*," or "thunder lizard," was christened for science in 1879 by a famous American fossil-hunter, Othniel Charles Marsh, but as time passed it became clear that the fossils he named were probably from the type of animal named in 1877 as *Apatosaurus*, "deceptive reptile" (see page 227). The rules for naming fossils say that if two or more identities are given, then the first one should prevail, so all specimens of "*Brontosaurus*" became *Apatosaurus*, and the name "*Brontosaurus*" is no longer on official lists.

ABOVE While pterosaurs like *Ornithocheirus* were probably furry and warm-blooded, with sophisticated behavior, impressions still persist of them as clumsy, dumb and scaly.

Tyrannosaurus was never the world's biggest meat-eater. The sperm whale of today is far larger, and the prehistoric sea-reptile *Liopleurodon*, a type of pliosaur (see page 396), perhaps rivaled it. *Tyrannosaurus* did hold the record for largest known land meat-eater for almost a century, but in the early 1990s *Giganotosaurus* took the crown (see page 187) – for now. Also, no *Tyrannosaurus* ever ate a horse, for all the dinosaurs had died out long before the hoofed group of mammals appeared.

Dinosaurs never flew, and never lived full-time in water, although they may have paddled or swum in emergencies. The winged reptiles mistakenly called "flying dinosaurs" were pterosaurs. They were truly remarkable animals – fast and aerobatic, with astonishingly lightweight bodies and highly evolved wings, which gave them mastery of the air. Many of their fossils show a hairy, furry or filamentous body-covering. Calculations suggest that, to pump their muscles enough to stay airborne, their bodies were probably warm-blooded (see page 377). Several major groups of reptiles were sea-going, but none were dinosaurs. Nothosaurs, placodonts, plesiosaurs, pliosaurs, ichthyosaurs, mosasaurs and others came and went in the oceans. However, they did not live entirely beneath the waves. They lacked gills and breathed air with lungs, as we do, so they had to visit the surface often, and some types probably came onto land to lay their eggs, as sea turtles do today.

Even the name "dinosaur" can be misleading. Richard Owen, a British zoologist and anatomist, coined the word in 1842, from two ancient Greek words meaning "terrible lizard" or "terrible reptile." Yet dinosaurs were not lizards, and lizards were, and are not, dinosaurs.

TOP Ichthyosaurs such as *Temnodontosaurus*, and pterosaurs (opposite) are sometimes called "dinosaurs." But they were very different groups of animals – as distinct as sharks and killer whales today.

ABOVE Snapping turtles date back to dinosaur times – the fossil above is from Wyoming. Many kinds of animals originated before the Age of Dinosaurs, persisted through it, survived the mass extinction and still thrive today.

ABOVE Giant dinosaurs are awesomely impressive – but they also have giant fossils. Each of the main preserved bones here at the Dinosaur National Monument, Utah, weighs a metric ton or more, and would take dozens of hours to excavate, transport, clean and study. Only fossils which might add important new nuggets of information end up in the preparatory room.

REBUILDING DINOSAURS

A COMPLETELY FOSSILIZED DINOSAUR SKELETON, WITH ALL THE BONES PRESERVED AND ARTICULATED, IS AN EXTREMELY RARE FIND. NEARLY ALL SPECIMENS ARE BITS AND PIECES, AND THESE ARE USUALLY CRACKED, CRUSHED AND DISTORTED DURING PRESERVATION. IF SEVERAL FOSSILS FROM WHAT LOOKS LIKE ONE INDIVIDUAL ARE FOUND TOGETHER, THEY ARE USUALLY JUMBLED AND OUT OF POSITION – AND THEN IT MAY BE THAT THEY ARE FROM SEVERAL INDIVIDUALS. TRYING TO REASSEMBLE A DINOSAUR CAN BE LIKENED TO COMPLETING A JIGSAW PUZZLE WHERE MANY PIECES ARE MISSING OR TORN INTO FRAGMENTS, OR THE BOX CONTAINS TWO PUZZLES!

In the paleontology laboratory, fossils are carefully cleaned and studied. Small drills, cutters, picks and sanders remove any bits of rock so that the fossil's surfaces and contours are revealed. This is a painstaking process. Tiny, even microscopic wear marks on fossil teeth can give valuable clues to an animal's diet, while roughened patches of bone show where muscles were attached in life, so the preparator must avoid adding scratches, gouges or any other marks. Acids and similar chemicals are used to dissolve rock to expose the fossil. Many of the dinosaurs and other creatures shown in this book are composites.

A variety of fossil parts from different individuals have been put together, to build up a picture of a typical individual. Comparisons with similar but better-studied kinds of dinosaurs can be used to fill in the missing parts. There are numerous clues from the fossils themselves that help in reconstructing a whole dinosaur. For example, the way bones fit together in a joint shows the natural position of that joint and how flexible it was. Rough patches on fossil bones, called "muscle scars," reveal where muscles were anchored and indicate their size and lines of pull. Chambers, holes and cavities in bones like the skull reveal the size and shape of parts such as the eyes and brain. Much evidence also comes from living animals that are relatives of the dinosaurs, including reptiles in general, and especially the dinosaurs' closest living cousins – birds and crocodiles. The bones, teeth, scales, soft-tissue anatomy and other details of these living creatures are related to their diet and other behavior patterns. Then comparisons are made with the fossil evidence to propose the appearances and habits of the dinosaurs in life.

In general, soft tissue, such as muscles, guts and skin, did not form fossils. However, there are a few cases where specialized conditions have allowed such parts to be preserved. The knowledge from these rare specimens of one type of dinosaur can be extended to other types. The issue of color and pattern is one major area where knowledge is lacking. Fossilized patches of skin may show the size and arrangement of scales or bony nodules, but these parts and the original skin have turned to stone, and so they are the color of that type of stone. As a result, there is no direct evidence to say whether a dinosaur was green, or brown, or striped with pink and yellow, or any other color and pattern. Usually, best guesses are made by comparing size, shape, behavior and habitat with those of animals alive today, such as crocodiles.

BELOW RIGHT Fossils such as the scales covering a fish or dinosaur are rock, and so are the color of that particular rock. In life, the scales and skin may have been vibrant colors, like those of this frilled lizard from Australia and New Guinea. As yet, no scientific techniques can suggest the living color of scales, skin or other body parts, from fossilized ones.

BELOW LEFT Exquisite details abound in these fossilized scales from the fish *Dapedium*, which lived almost 200 million years ago. The entire fish was not much larger than a human hand, and each of these preserved scales is about the size of this 0.

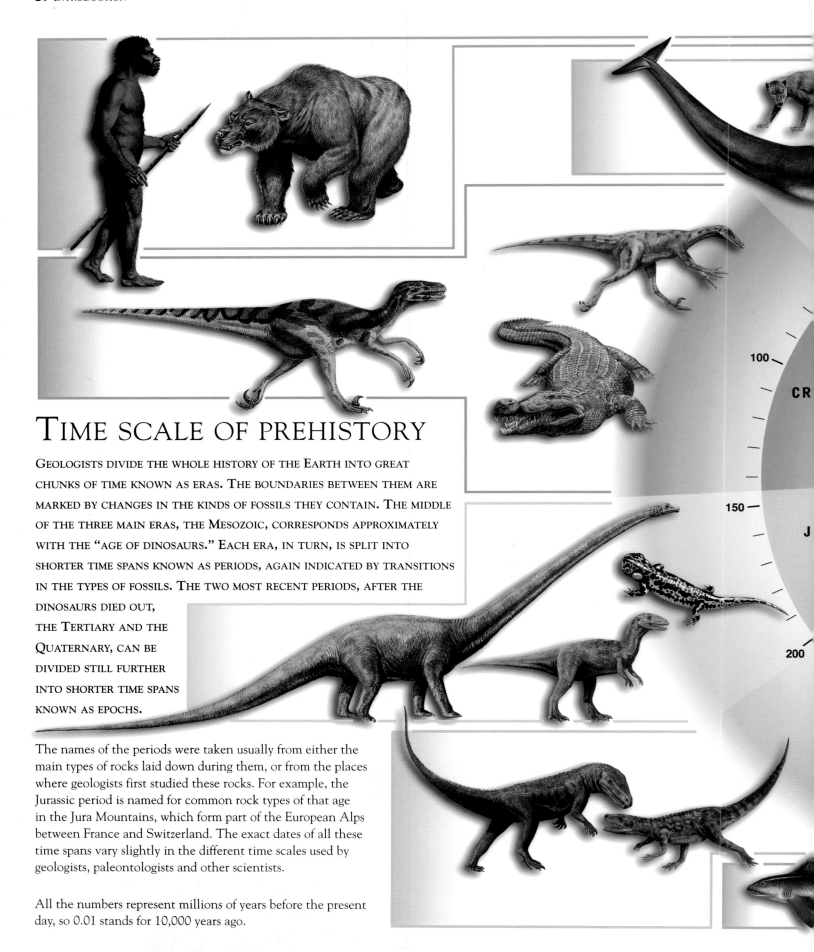

TIME SCALE OF PREHISTORY

GEOLOGISTS DIVIDE THE WHOLE HISTORY OF THE EARTH INTO GREAT
CHUNKS OF TIME KNOWN AS ERAS. THE BOUNDARIES BETWEEN THEM ARE
MARKED BY CHANGES IN THE KINDS OF FOSSILS THEY CONTAIN. THE MIDDLE
OF THE THREE MAIN ERAS, THE MESOZOIC, CORRESPONDS APPROXIMATELY
WITH THE "AGE OF DINOSAURS." EACH ERA, IN TURN, IS SPLIT INTO
SHORTER TIME SPANS KNOWN AS PERIODS, AGAIN INDICATED BY TRANSITIONS
IN THE TYPES OF FOSSILS. THE TWO MOST RECENT PERIODS, AFTER THE
DINOSAURS DIED OUT,
THE TERTIARY AND THE
QUATERNARY, CAN BE
DIVIDED STILL FURTHER
INTO SHORTER TIME SPANS
KNOWN AS EPOCHS.

The names of the periods were taken usually from either the
main types of rocks laid down during them, or from the places
where geologists first studied these rocks. For example, the
Jurassic period is named for common rock types of that age
in the Jura Mountains, which form part of the European Alps
between France and Switzerland. The exact dates of all these
time spans vary slightly in the different time scales used by
geologists, paleontologists and other scientists.

All the numbers represent millions of years before the present
day, so 0.01 stands for 10,000 years ago.

100

CR

150

J

200

QUATERNARY

Today

Million
years
ago

50

550

TERTIARY

PRE-
CAMBRIAN

CAMBRIAN

500

ACEOUS

CENOZOIC
ERA

ORDOVICIAN

450

MESOZOIC
ERA

PALAEOZOIC
ERA

ASSIC

SILURIAN

DEVONIAN

400

TRIASSIC

CARBONIFEROUS

350

PERMIAN

250

300

CHANGING WORLD

THE WORLD HAS CHANGED THROUGH TIME – MORE THAN WE COULD EVER IMAGINE. NOT ONLY DINOSAURS, BUT OTHER ANIMALS AND PLANTS HAVE COME AND GONE, AND CLIMATES HAVE ALTERED HUGELY. THE GREAT LAND MASSES OR CONTINENTS HAVE DRIFTED AROUND THE GLOBE, GENERALLY AT A RATE OF 1 OR 2 CENTIMETERS (½-1 INCH) EACH YEAR. AS SEA LEVELS ROSE AND FELL MANY TIMES, THE COAST-LINES CHANGED TOO, ALTERING THE SIZES AND SHAPES OF THE CONTINENTS. ALL TIME CHANGES ARE GIVEN IN MILLIONS OF YEARS AGO, "MYA."

1. CAMBRIAN
540–500 MYA
PALEOZOIC ERA

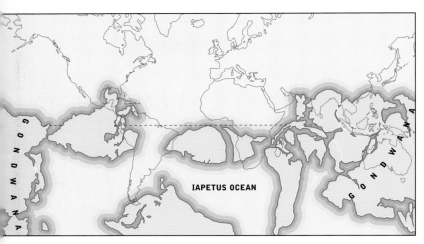

2. DEVONIAN
410–355 MYA
PALEOZOIC ERA

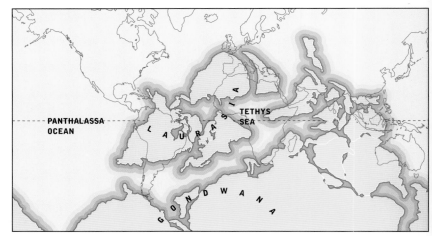

5. JURASSIC
203–144 MYA
MESOZOIC ERA

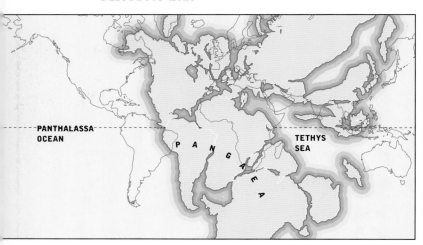

6. CRETACEOUS
144–65 MYA
MESOZOIC ERA

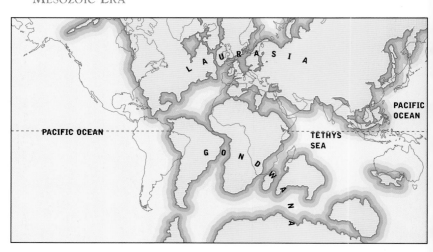

The general story is of great supercontinents that drifted as one, broke apart, and re-formed again during most of the Paleozoic era. In the Permian period, they collided to form the super-supercontinent Pangaea. This showed signs of cracking apart in the Early Jurassic. Rifts and seaways opened up as Pangaea divided into Gondwana and Laurasia by the Early Cretaceous. At the same time, each of these supercontinents was itself splitting. During the Tertiary period, the land masses moved to the positions we know from today's world map. The focus of these maps is on the Mesozoic Era, the Age of Dinosaurs; note that the Palaeozoic Era is not comprehensively covered because it was a time not populated by dinosaurs and related animals.

3. CARBONIFEROUS
355–295 MYA
PALEOZOIC ERA

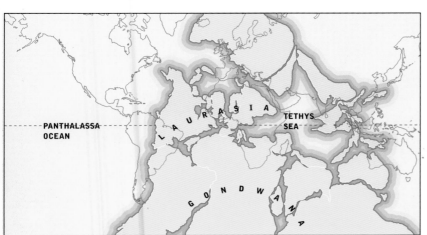

4. TRIASSIC
250–203 MYA
MESOZOIC ERA

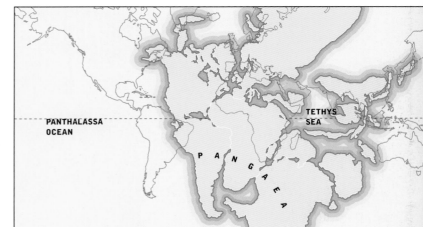

7. TERTIARY
65–1.75 MYA
CENOZOIC ERA

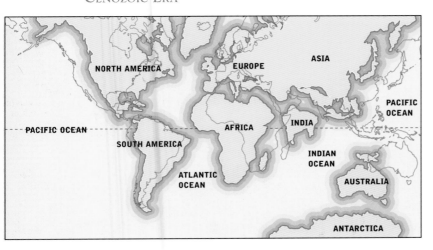

8. TODAY
1.75 MYA–PRESENT
CENOZOIC ERA

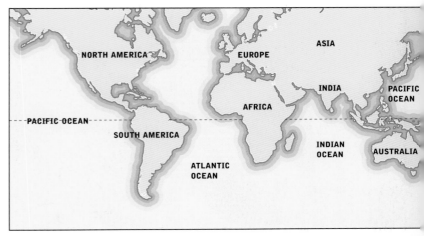

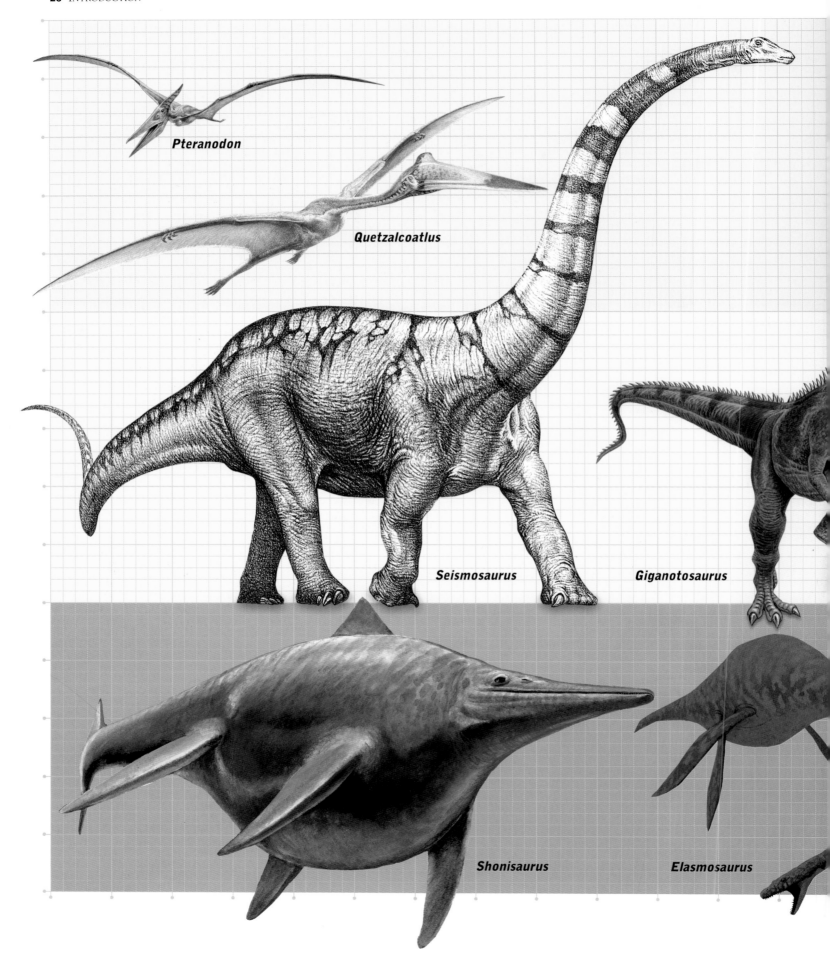

Pteranodon

Quetzalcoatlus

Seismosaurus

Giganotosaurus

Shonisaurus

Elasmosaurus

PREHISTORIC LIFE TO SCALE

6 FEET
1 METER

ALTHOUGH MANY DINOSAURS AND OTHER PREHISTORIC ANIMALS WERE INDEED HUGE, SOME WERE MUCH SMALLER THAN WE LIKE TO IMAGINE. IN THIS DIAGRAM THE SIZE OF THE ANIMALS IS COMPARED WITH THAT OF A 1.83-METER (6-FOOT) MAN.

Seismosaurus was a very long dinosaur at up to 52 meters (197 feet); the heaviest is thought to have been *Argentinosaurus* at 100 metric tons (110 tons). *Giganotosaurus* was the largest predator at 14 meters (46 feet) tall, bigger than *Tyrannosaurus rex* which had been thought, until 1994, to be the largest. *Anchiceratops* measured 4.5–6 meters (15–19½ feet), but other ceratopsians, such as *Protoceratops*, were no bigger than a pig. *Sinosauropteryx* was one of the smaller dinosaurs, reaching a maximum length of only 1 meter (3 feet). *Quetzalcoatlus* was one of the largest flying creatures ever, with a wingspan of 12–14 meters (39–45½ feet). *Ophthalmosaurus*, while not especially large, holds the record for the largest eyeballs of any vertebrate, almost 10 centimeters (3 inches) across.

Each Animal Factfile has an indicator bar which compares the size of the animal to that of a 1.8-meter (6-foot) man. If the man equals 1 and the colored bar extends to 3 for a certain animal, that animal is three times larger than man. The scale alters between chapters to allow for a range of comparative sizes. For example, the largest animal in one chapter may be about 3 times the size of the man, but in another chapter nearly 30 times the size of the man.

| 0 | 1 | 2 | 3 |

| 0 • | 5 | 10 | 15 | 20 | 25 | 30 |

Anchiceratops   **Bactrosaurus**   **Sinosauropteryx**

Kronosaurus   **Ophthalmosaurus**   **Metriorhynchus**

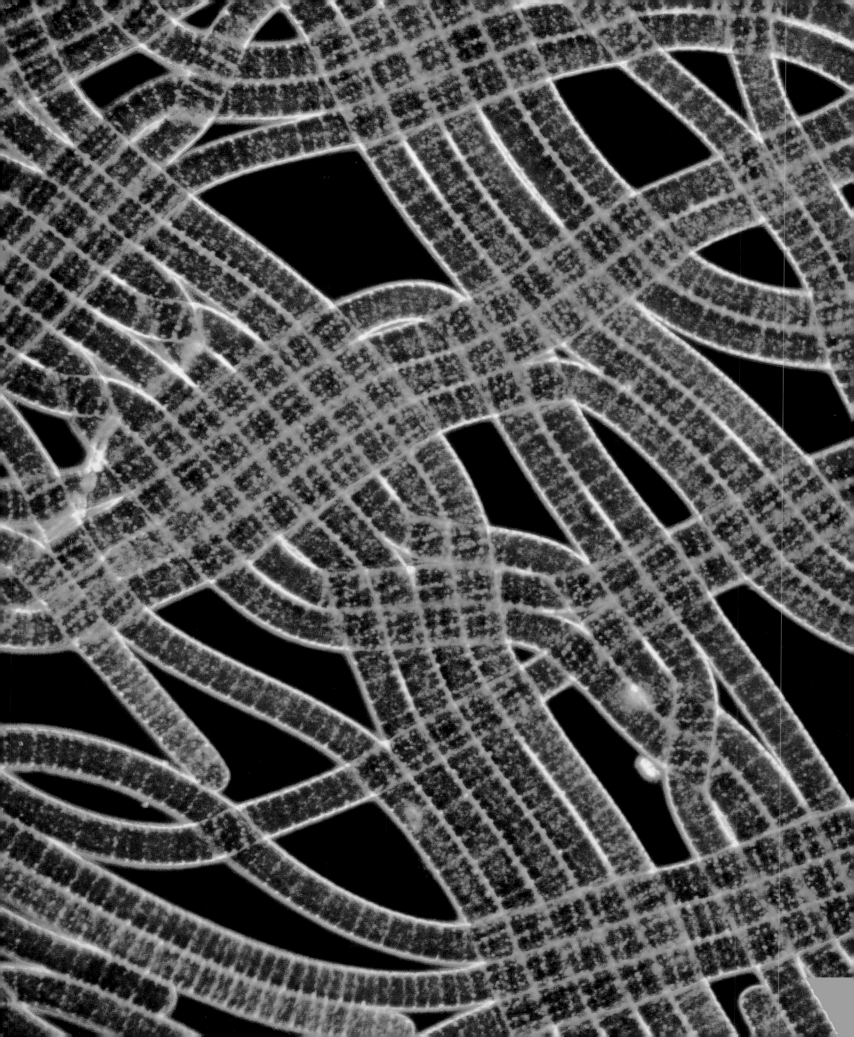

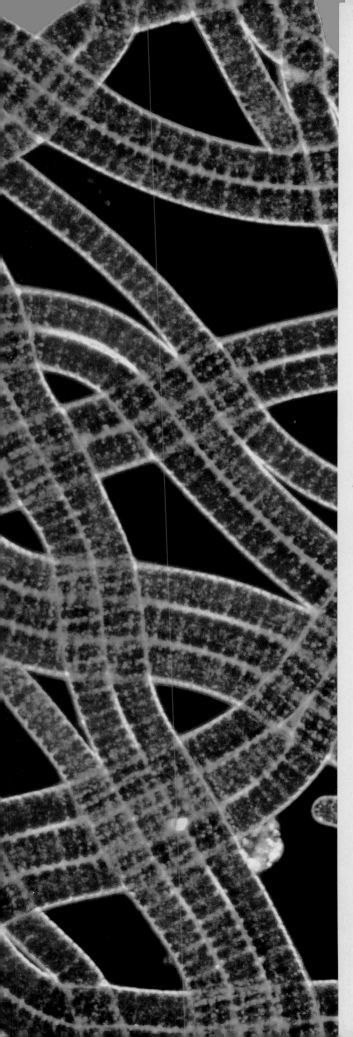

CHAPTER ONE

EARLY
LIFE

THE PALAEOZOIC ERA SAW THE EARLY KINDS OF ANIMALS THAT
POPULATED OUR WORLD, FROM WORMS AND JELLYFISH IN THE SEA
TO THE FIRST CREATURES THAT WALKED ON LAND.

How life began

THERE ARE MANY THEORIES ABOUT HOW LIFE ON EARTH BEGAN. INDEED, THERE ARE VARIOUS
DEFINITIONS OF LIFE ITSELF. MOST OF THESE FOCUS ON THE KEY FEATURES OF REPRODUCTION, GROWTH
AND ENERGY TRANSFORMATION. LIVING THINGS REPRODUCE – THEY MAKE MORE OF THEIR KIND. THE
RESULTING INDIVIDUAL ORGANISMS GROW – THEY BUILD NEW LIVING TISSUES USING NUTRIENTS AND
RAW MATERIALS, SUCH AS MINERALS, FROM THEIR SURROUNDINGS, AND THEN REPRODUCE AGAIN.
THE PROCESS OF GROWTH REQUIRES ENERGY, WHICH LIVING THINGS ALSO ACQUIRE IN SOME FORM
FROM THEIR ENVIRONMENT AND THEN USE TO POWER CHEMICAL AND PHYSICAL CHANGES.

SMALL AND SIMPLE

Some theories about the origins of life say that
it came from extraterrestrial sources (outside the
Earth), or that it was made by some kind of supreme
entity or being. Such proposals are very difficult to
test by scientific methods. The prevailing scientific
views hold that life began here on Earth, billions
of years ago, as microscopically small and simple
organisms. From these tiniest scraps of living matter,
large and more complex life-forms arose by a process
of change or modification known as evolution.
The theory of evolution underpins our entire view
of prehistory, explaining how and why organisms
changed through time.

FIRST LIFE FORMS

The Earth was formed around 4,500 million
(4.5 billion) years ago. The first signs of life are the
microfossils seen in rocks more than 3,500 million
years old. They suggest the presence of organisms
similar to organisms surviving today that are known
as archaeobacteria. They lived in the sea and may
have obtained their energy from the light of the
sun, as plants do today, by the process known as
photosynthesis. Their living relatives occur today
as cyanobacteria or "blue-green algae," which are
sometimes seen as scummy-looking layers on
ponds. Some of the earliest organisms may have
tapped energy-rich minerals found in the Earth's
outer layer, or crust. This still happens in the
features known as deep-sea hydrothermal vents,
where energy-rich sulfurs and other minerals
bubble out of the seabed, to be absorbed by simple
micro-organisms.

EARLIEST ANIMALS

For more than 2,000 million years, living things
stayed small and simple, as tiny units of life known
as unicells. Then, as some scarce and valuable
fossils have shown, cells started to group together
and form bigger, more complex, multicelled
organisms. The cells became specialized to do
certain jobs, such as support, movement, feeding
or reproduction, and worked together as larger
living units. Some of these multicellular life forms
still obtained their energy from sunlight: these
were the early plants. Others acquired their energy
by taking in, or consuming, the micro-organisms
or the plants, or each other. These were the first
animals, or metazoans, and they continued to
evolve in prehistoric seas. By the Late Precambrian
period, about 700–600 million years ago, they had
given rise to several different groups of early animals.
By extension from the simplest creatures alive
today, these primitive animals probably resembled
types of sponges, jellyfish and worms. They had
soft bodies, however, and they lived a very long
time ago, so their fossils are extremely rare, and
our knowledge of them is limited and sketchy.
Better known are the animals of the "Cambrian
explosion," when new attributes such as shells and
legs arose (see pages 38 and 46).

PREVIOUS PAGE Magnified about 80 times, these are strands
of a blue-green algae or cyanobacterium known as *Oscillatoria*.
To the naked eye they would appear as greenish, slimy cotton-
wool. The individual living cells are very simple, and perhaps
similar to the early forms of life to appear on Earth, more than
2,000 million years ago.

OPPOSITE Sea lilies or crinoids thrive on a tropical coral reef
today – as they have done for more than 500 million years.
These flower-shaped creatures are upside-down cousins of
starfish, each fixed to the rock by a stalk. The starfish group,
echinoderms, was one of the earliest main groups of complex
animals to appear.

Siphonia and Chaetetopsis

The simplest animals alive today are the sponges (poriferans). There are more than 10,000 kinds, mainly in the sea, though some live in the fresh water of lakes and rivers. They have no muscles and cannot move, are stuck to the bed of the sea, lake or river, lack sense organs such as eyes or ears, and do not have brains or nerves. However, they gain nutrition by consuming other living things, which makes them members of the animal kingdom (see previous page).

Siphonia was a common type of sponge in shallow seas around the world for 100 million years and more. It was a member of the subgroup called demosponges, in which the tissues of the body wall are strengthened with a network of tough, horny fibers. More than nine-tenths of sponge species today belong to this subgroup; earlier members are some of the first animals to be preserved as fossils,

from well over 600 million years ago. *Siphonia* had the typical sponge shape of a hollow, bag- or vase-like body, in this case raised on a stalk. Water containing tiny floating plants and animals (plankton) was sucked through small holes in the body wall into the chamber inside the body. Microscopic cells lining the chamber consumed the plankton, and the water was then expelled through a larger hole at the upper end of the body.

Chaetetopsis, which lived from the Ordovician to Tertiary periods (500 to less than 60 million years ago), was a coralline type of sponge. The stiffening reinforcement of its body wall consisted of tiny spicules, like needles or spikes, made of calcium minerals. It was more irregular in shape than most sponges, resembling a pile of overlapping, flattened plates, around 4 centimeters (1¹/₂ inches) tall.

ANIMAL FACTFILE
Siphonia

Meaning: Siphon (sucking animal)

Pronunciation: Sigh-fone-ee-ah

Period: Cretaceous onward

Main group: Porifera

Size: Length around 1 centimeter (½ inch)

Diet: Plankton

Fossil sites: Worldwide

0	1	2	3

RIGHT These fossilized sponges, embedded in their rocky matrix, are from the Cambrian period.

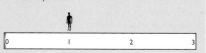

ANIMAL FACTFILE
Chaetetopsis

Meaning: Bristle face, hairy appearance

Pronunciation: Keet-ett-op-siss

Period: Ordovician–Tertiary

Main group: Porifera

Size: 4 centimeters (1¹/₂ inches)

Diet: Plankton

Fossil sites: Numerous, mainly Northern Hemisphere

0	1	2	3

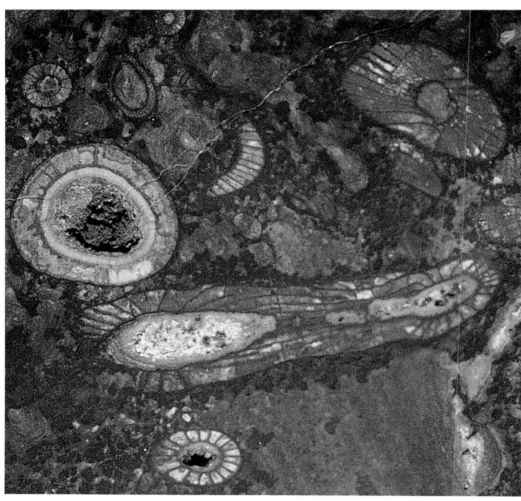

MILLEPORA AND HALYSITES

Cnidarians (formerly known as coelenterates) include a wide diversity of extinct and living forms: jellyfish, corals, hydras, sea pens, sea fans and sea anemones. They have been around since Precambrian times, more than 600 million years ago. However, fossils of soft-bodied types such as jellyfish or sea anemones are extremely rare, because their bodies quickly disintegrated. For the vast majority of prehistoric cnidarians, all that is preserved as fossils are the tubes, cups or other parts of their outer "skeletons." Reconstructions of the animals within are made using knowledge of living species.

Millepora is a fairly modern example of an ancient group of cnidarians known as hydrozoans. These tiny animals, called polyps, resembled miniature, tall, slim sea anemones. They lived in colonies and built communal "skeletons" of branching tubes made from stony minerals, which formed irregular fan- or finger-like shapes. Some polyps were specialized for feeding, while others around the outside guarded them. The polyps could become shorter and withdraw into their stony tubes for protection.

Halysites was a type of coral known as a "chain coral," and lived from Ordovician times until the Late Permian period, around 250 million years ago. Like *Millepora*, it consisted of small, elongated, anemone-like polyps, each with an upper array of flexible tentacles that could sting and grasp particles of food, mostly even tinier animals floating past in the plankton. Each polyp of *Halysites* built a tube of rock minerals around itself, and these tubes were joined side by side in an irregular pattern, forming colonies up to 10 centimeters (4 inches) across that spread across ancient reefs.

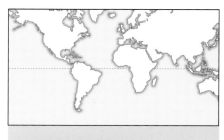

ANIMAL FACTFILE
Millepora
Meaning: Thousand pores (holes)
Pronunciation: Mill-ee-poor-ah
Period: Quaternary
Main group: Cnidaria
Size: Height up to 10 centimeters (4 inches)
Diet: Plankton
Fossil sites: Worldwide

LEFT Living coral animals or polyps like these *Dendrophyllia* resemble miniature sea anemones. They make hard, cup-shaped "skeletons" of limestone, which abound in some rocks as fossilized coral.

ANIMAL FACTFILE
Halysites
Meaning: Chain coral
Pronunciation: Hall-ee-site-eez
Period: Ordovician–Permian
Main group: Cnidaria
Size: Colonies about 5 centimeters (2 inches)
Diet: Plankton
Fossil sites: Europe, Asia

SPRIGGINA AND SERPULA

ANIMAL FACTFILE
Spriggina
Meaning: For Sprigg (see text)
Pronunciation: Sprig-een-ah
Period: Precambrian
Main group: Perhaps Annelida
Length: 4 centimeters (1½ inches)
Diet: Possibly particles in seabed mud
Fossil site: Ediacara (Australia)

All worms may look much the same, but they are actually some of the most varied of all animals. There are several major groups, including segmented worms (annelids), such as the earthworm or the seashore lugworm; and the round worms (nematodes), which live almost everywhere, including inside other animals, as parasites. Because most kinds of prehistoric worms had soft bodies, glimpses of them in the fossil record are exceptionally rare. However, several examples are known from Ediacara and Burgess rocks (see following pages).

Spriggina is an example from Ediacara, named after Reg Sprigg, an Australian geologist who discovered this amazing fossil site in 1946. *Spriggina* was thumb-sized and swam or crawled across the seabed almost 600 million years ago. It was probably an annelid worm, but, unlike today's versions, it had a tough, curved "shield" on its head. Around 80 flaps along the two sides of its body each ended in a small spine. However it may have been a cnidarian or even an arthropod.

Species of *Serpula*, which belong to the subgroup of annelids called tubeworms, still live along today's coasts. Each worm builds a spiral tube around its body, which sticks to a rock or large shell. The tube is often white, being made of limestone minerals. The worm sticks its tentacle-covered head out into the water, to catch tiny bits of food, and draws itself back into its tube if danger approaches or when the tide goes out. Fossils of *Serpula*'s spiral tubes are known from the Silurian period, more than 400 million years ago.

ANIMAL FACTFILE
Serpula
Meaning: Little snake
Pronunciation: Sir-pugh-la
Period: Silurian onward
Main group: Annelida
Size: Up to 10 centimeters (4 inches)
Diet: Plankton
Fossil sites: Worldwide

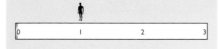

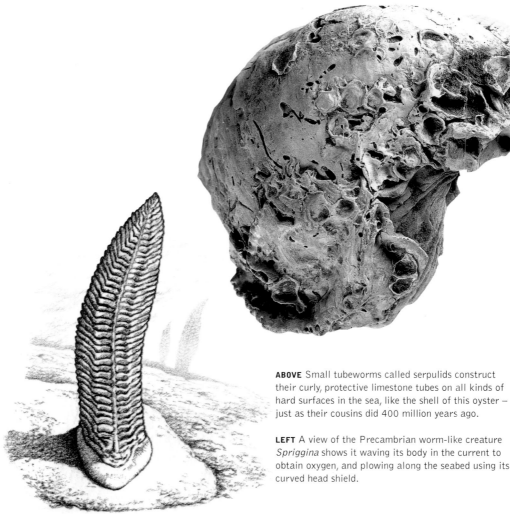

ABOVE Small tubeworms called serpulids construct their curly, protective limestone tubes on all kinds of hard surfaces in the sea, like the shell of this oyster – just as their cousins did 400 million years ago.

LEFT A view of the Precambrian worm-like creature *Spriggina* shows it waving its body in the current to obtain oxygen, and plowing along the seabed using its curved head shield.

DICKINSONIA AND CANADIA

Dickinsonia is a type of worm found in the extraordinary fossils of Ediacara, Australia. It was a relative giant for its time, with some partial specimens estimated at 60 centimeters (2 feet) in length, although most were 5 to 20 centimeters (2 to 8 inches). Fossils show a low, broad, almost disc-shaped body, with clear lines that could be the segments, or repeating body sections, of the creature. The number of lines varies from 20 to 500. However, this is only one view of *Dickinsonia's* identity. Some experts suggest that it was not an annelid (segmented worm) but a member of another major and very different worm group, the platyhelminthes (flatworms). Yet other views are that *Dickinsonia* was a type of coral colony, or even a lichen (a combination growth of simple plants or algae and fungi).

Canadia was about the size of a human finger and is regarded as a Middle Cambrian version of today's seashore ragworm. It was a type of annelid with "leg"-like flaps and bristles along its sides. Its fossils come from the Burgess rocks of southwestern Canada. If *Canadia* lived the same lifestyle as the modern ragworm, which many think is likely, it would have been an active predator. It would crawl, wriggle and even swim after prey such as smaller worms, seizing them with its strong, pincer-like mouthparts. These mouthparts are among the few hardened pieces of worm bodies, and are often preserved. They are called scolecodonts and resemble miniature saws or serrated-edged plates of various shapes. Most are smaller than this o.

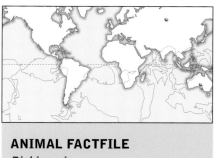

ANIMAL FACTFILE
Dickinsonia
Meaning: For Dickinson
Pronunciation: Dick-in-so-nee-ah
Period: Precambrian
Main group: Possibly Annelida
Length: Up to 60 centimeters (2 feet)
Diet: Possibly particles in seabed mud
Fossil sites: Ediacara (Australia), Russia

| 0 | | 1 | 2 | 3 |

LEFT The living worm *Tomopteris*, swimming in the open ocean, generally resembles its Cambrian counterpart, *Canadia*.

ANIMAL FACTFILE
Canadia
Meaning: Of or after Canada
Pronunciation: Kan-aid-ee-ah
Period: Cambrian
Main group: Annelida
Size: 5–20 centimeters (2–8 inches)
Diet: Smaller animals
Fossil sites: Southwest Canada

| 0 | | 1 | 2 | 3 |

THE CAMBRIAN EXPLOSION

LIFE DID NOT BEGIN WITH A DRIP AND DIVERSIFY
STEADILY UNTIL THE PRESENT. CREATURES OF
MORE THAN 500 MILLION YEARS AGO SHOWED
INCREDIBLE DIVERSITY WITH SEGMENTS, SHELLS,
JOINTED LEGS, FLEXIBLE FINS AND GRASPING
TENTACLES. VERY RARELY, FAST PRESERVATION
BY FINE-GRAINED SEDIMENTS CREATED EXQUISITE
FOSSILS, EVEN OF SOFT-BODIED CREATURES LIKE
JELLYFISH AND WORMS. TWO CELEBRATED
EXAMPLES ARE FROM THE EDIACARA HILLS
OF SOUTH AUSTRALIA (PRECAMBRIAN, OVER
550 MILLION YEARS OLD) AND THE BURGESS
PASS OF THE ROCKY MOUNTAINS IN BRITISH
COLUMBIA, CANADA (CAMBRIAN, OVER 500
MILLION YEARS OLD).

RIGHT *Anomalocaris*, rearing up in the center, was a giant
predator in Cambrian seas, at about 60 centimeters (2 feet)
in length. This arthropod was a distant cousin of crustaceans
like crabs.

CHITON AND CONOCARDIUM

The mollusc group is hugely represented in the fossil record, mainly because most types lived in the sea and had hard shells, both factors that make preservation more likely. *Chiton* is the genus name and also the group name for one of the major types of molluscs, the chitons or "coat of mail" shells (also known as polyplacophorans). They originated in Late Cambrian times, more than 500 million years ago, and thousands of kinds have come and gone since; around 550 species survive today, all on the seabed or seashore rocks. The genus *Chiton* varied in size from less than a centimeter (half an inch) to 50 times larger. It had the typical group feature of about eight overlapping plates for its body shell, fringed by a "lip" of rubbery flesh, toughened with grains or shards of minerals. Under the shell, the main body had a head end, with a mouth for grazing on the fine growths of algae that coat sea rocks, and a powerful sucker that held the animal firmly to the rock like its molluscan cousin, the familiar seashore limpet.

Conocardium was a type of mollusc known as a rostroconch. This is one of the many extinct subgroups of molluscs, although it may have given rise to the bivalves, such as oysters, clams and mussels. *Conocardium* had a cone-shaped, slightly curved shell made of two parts fused together, measuring about 5 centimeters (2 inches) across. It probably crept along on its fleshy, sucker-like foot, and fed on the tiny plants and animals that continually settle and grow on any hard surface in the sea.

ANIMAL FACTFILE
Chiton

Meaning: Skirt, girdle

Pronunciation: Kye-ton

Period: Cambrian onward

Main group: Mollusca

Length: Mostly up to 10 centimeters (4 inches)

Diet: Algae (simple marine plants)

Fossil sites: Worldwide

RIGHT *Chitons are much the same today as they were half a billion years ago, grazing on tiny growths of algae on seashore rocks.*

ANIMAL FACTFILE
Conocardium

Meaning: Cone-heart

Pronunciation: Kon-owe-card-ee-um

Period: Ordovician–Permian

Main group: Mollusca

Size: Shell mouth 5–7 centimeters (2–3 inches) across

Diet: Tiny plants and animals

Fossil sites: Numerous, mostly Northern Hemisphere

DENTALIUM AND MYTILUS

These two shelled creatures are examples of two mollusc subgroups that still survive today, but with different degrees of success. *Dentalium* was a type of tusk-shell, or scaphopod, with a shell about 10 centimeters (4 inches) in length, shaped like a slightly bent long cone or elephant's tusk. The animal was usually positioned at an angle in seabed mud, with the pointed end of the shell poking above the surface. The head end protruded from the wider, open, lower end to gather tiny edible particles from the mud with its numerous fine, thread-like tentacles. The foot end also protruded from the lower opening and was adapted for burrowing. Water to provide oxygen was drawn in and out through a small hole at the pointed end.

Tusk-shells such as *Dentalium* appeared in the Ordovician period and around 560 species are alive still today. The bivalve molluscs originated later, but they have been hugely more successful, and there are now some 15,000 species of them. Bivalves, also called lamellibranchiates, have shells made of two parts or valves, which are usually hinged, and can be closed to protect the whole creature. *Mytilus* is the common mussel. It first appeared as fossils in Triassic times, the same period in which dinosaurs began. Most types had a shell length of around 5 centimeters (2 inches). *Mytilus* attached itself to rocks and took in a steady stream of sea water, to filter or sieve tiny edible particles such as the micro-organisms of the plankton.

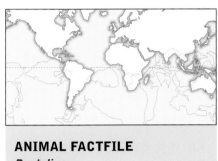

ANIMAL FACTFILE
Dentalium

Meaning: Of or for teeth

Pronunciation: Den-tale-ee-um

Period: Ordovician

Main group: Mollusca

Length: Up to 12 centimeters
  (4¹/₂ inches)

Diet: Edible particles in seabed mud

Fossil sites: Worldwide

LEFT Mussels are among the most familiar of the bivalve molluscs. Their ancient close cousins, *Mytilus*, were already established along seashores when the first dinosaurs appeared.

ANIMAL FACTFILE
Mytilus

Meaning: Mussel (also derived as weasel)

Pronunciation: Mite-ill-us

Period: Triassic onward

Main group: Mollusca

Size: Shell usually 5–7 centimeters
  (2–3 inches)

Diet: Plankton

Fossil sites: Worldwide

ORTHOCERAS AND STEPHANOCERAS

ANIMAL FACTFILE
Orthoceras

Meaning: Straight shell/horn

Pronunciation: Or-thoe-sair-ass

Period: Ordovician to Triassic

Main group: Mollusca

Length: Shell 15 centimeters (6 inches)

Diet: Small animals

Fossil sites: Worldwide

RIGHT Ammonoids can trace their ancestry back to the Cambrian, but they became truly successful during the Mesozoic era.

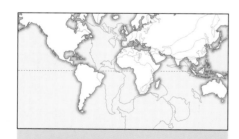

ANIMAL FACTFILE
Stephanoceras

Meaning: Crown horn

Pronunciation: Steff-an-owe-sair-ass

Period: Jurassic

Main group: Mollusca

Size: Shell about 20 centimeters (8 inches)

Diet: Smaller animals

Fossil sites: Worldwide

The creatures on this and the next two pages were cephalopods, advanced and complex members of the huge mollusc group. Today's cephalopods include octopus, squid, cuttlefish and nautiluses. They are all fast, efficient hunters, with large eyes and long, flexible tentacles that are used to grab victims. The cephalopod group probably began more than 500 million years ago, and soon thousands of types swarmed in the seas. They are known mainly from their preserved shells, which have a massive variety of shapes and suture lines (the ridges where parts of the shell joined each other).

Orthoceras was a nautiloid with a straight, slowly tapering shell around 15 centimeters (6 inches) long. The head end protruded from the wide open end, and would have resembled that of a living member of this group, the nautilus (see opposite).

Stephanoceras was a member of the cephalopod group known as ammonoids. They had characteristic shells coiled into a flat spiral, with ribs and ridges in different patterns for each of the thousands of species. The shell had cross-walls inside, dividing it into compartments for strength. As the creature grew, it added shell material to the open end to continue and widen the spiral, and made new cross-walls at intervals. The main body of the animal was in the last, largest compartment, with the head end protruding from the opening, as for *Nautilus* (opposite). The shell of *Stephanoceras* grew to around 20 centimeters (8 inches) across, but some ammonoids reached diameters of well over 2 meters ($6^{1}/_{2}$ feet). After fantastic success in the seas before and during the Age of Dinosaurs, the ammonoids became extinct by the close of the Cretaceous period.

LEFT A fossilized nautiloid shell, similar in almost every detail to one of today.

BELOW Overall design of the modern paper nautilus, or argonaut, differs little from shells of 500-plus million years ago.

NAUTILUS

The nautiloids belong to the group of molluscs known as cephalopods. Some had straight, tapering shells, like *Orthoceras* (opposite). The genus known as *Nautilus* has many species that appeared and then faded to extinction right up to the present day. The approximately six living species of *Nautilus* inhabit mainly deep Pacific and Indian Ocean waters. They are sometimes referred to as "living fossils," although of course this term has no scientific meaning. The largest of the surviving nautiluses have shells around 25 centimeters (10 inches) across, but some nautiloids from Ordovician through to Jurassic times were huge. The earlier ones, with straight shells 5 meters (20 feet) long, were among the biggest predators of Ordovician seas, just as fish were appearing.

The various types of nautiloids had horny, beak-like mouths (similar to that of an octopus), surrounded by two rings of short but profuse and non-suckered tentacles, in some cases numbering more than 60. The head had two large eyes for hunting by vision in the gloom of deep water. Like the shells of ammonoids (see opposite), the coiled shell of these nautiloids had internal cross-walls, known as septa, at regular intervals. The animal's body occupied the last compartment of the shell, but the head could not be withdrawn.

Movement was by a form of "jet propulsion," in which water was drawn in through a wide opening into a body chamber called the mantle cavity, and then squirted out forcefully through a narrower opening, the siphon (as in squid). Nautiloids could also adjust their buoyancy to rise or dive by altering the composition of gases in the smaller, unoccupied compartments of the shell. These molluscs probably hunted any victims they could overpower, including fish.

ANIMAL FACTFILE
Nautilus

Meaning: Sailor

Pronunciation: Naw-te-luss

Period: Ordovician (nautiloids generally)

Main group: Mollusca

Size: Shell around 10–20 centimeters (4–8 inches) across

Diet: Prey animals

Fossil sites: Worldwide

| 0 | 1 | 2 | 3 |

CALYMENE

Trilobites were perhaps the most numerous of all prehistoric animals, and more than 15,000 species are known from fossils. They appeared during the Cambrian period, more than 500 million years ago, and dominated the seas until fish began to evolve. Thereafter they faded, and the last types disappeared 250 million years ago, at the end of the Permian period, in the greatest mass extinction of all time. Many of their fossils are not from the actual animals, but are cast-off body casings. Trilobites grew in the same way as crabs do today, at intervals. They shed or molted the old rigid body casing, and expanded in size quickly before the new casing underneath became hardened. Some types of trilobites reached 70 centimeters (28 inches) in length. (For further information, see page 46.)

Calymene is one of the best-known genera of trilobites. Coal miners in the Midlands of England during the 19th century found so many of its fossils that it was called the "Dudley locust" for one of the towns in that region.

As in other trilobites, the body consisted of the cephalon or head at the front, bearing large eyes on either side of a central hump, and mouthparts on the underside; a middle section or thorax, which was made of a dozen or more repeating units or segments; and a pygidium, or tail, where the segments were fused firmly and so could not flex or articulate with each other, as the thoracic segments could. The main lobe along the middle of the animal is called the axis, and the two lower lobes flanking it are termed pleural lobes. They carried fringed gills along their sides. Most trilobites crawled along, and their furrow-like tracks are preserved as fossils. Some could swim by waving their paddle-like legs or even flapping the whole body.

LEFT Dead individuals and cast shells of *Calymene* are found by the thousands in some ancient rocks. It is possible that they did not live in groups, but died in scattered locations and were then washed together by tides and currents, perhaps cast up on the beach like seashells today.

ANIMAL FACTFILE
Calymene
Meaning: Beautiful cover
Pronunciation: Kall-ee-meen
Period: Late Ordovician to Silurian
Main group: Arthropoda (Trilobita)
Length/Size: 7 centimeters (2½ inches)
Diet: Small edible particles
Fossil sites: Worldwide

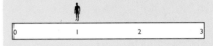

LINGULA (LAMPSHELL)

Lingula is one of the animals that people like to call "living fossils," which is just an unscientific way of saying that they have been around a very long time. Indeed, *Lingula* could claim to be the "oldest living fossil," for its kind have been around since the Ordovician period, nearly 500 million years ago, and still survive today.

With the two-part, tongue-shaped shell that gives it its scientific name, *Lingula* closely resembles the types of molluscs known as bivalves, such as mussels (see page 41). However, it is not a bivalve, or even a mollusc. It is a member of the major animal group called brachiopods ("arm feet"). This group contains around 350 surviving species, but through prehistory it was vastly more successful, with more than 25,000 known kinds. Brachiopods were so common at times that whole layers of rocks are made from their accumulated seabed remains. The way their

shell details changed through time makes them useful as fossil markers for dating rocks (see page 16).

The difference between a brachiopod and a bivalve is that, while the former has its shell parts on the upper side and underside of the body, the latter has them on the left and right sides.

Brachiopods are also known as lampshells because ancient people, including the Romans, used stone or metal lamps shaped like their shells to hold oil for lighting purposes.

Different species of *Lingula* were fixed to the seabed by a stalk, or pedicle, or were mobile and used the stalk for burrowing. The two-part shell enclosed a fringed, loop-like body part, the lophophore, which gathered tiny bits of food and passed them to the animal's mouth. Today most brachiopods inhabit the deep sea and have shells less than 10 centimeters (4 inches) across.

ANIMAL FACTFILE
Lingula
Meaning: Little tongue, small flap
Pronunciation: Linn-geu-lah
Period: Ordovician onwards
Main group: Brachipoda
Size: Shell length usually 10 centimeters (4 inches)
Diet: Tiny edible particles in sea water
Fossil sites: Worldwide

LIMBS AND LEGS

THE JOINTED LEG, WHICH HAS A HARD OUTER
CASING LINKED AT FLEXING STRUCTURES, WAS
ONE OF EVOLUTION'S GREATEST SUCCESSES.
IT IS THE FEATURE THAT NAMES AND UNITES
THE GIANT ANIMAL GROUP ARTHROPODA.
THIS INCLUDES CRUSTACEANS, SUCH AS THE
LONG-GONE TRILOBITES AND THE STILL-SWARMING
CRABS, AS WELL AS SPIDERS AND SCORPIONS, NOT
TO MENTION THE MILLIONS OF SPECIES OF INSECTS.

RIGHT A menacing eurypterid or "sea scorpion" prowls the
shallows of 400 million years ago. These formidable arthropods
grew larger than an adult human, and were the biggest hunters
of their time. Nothing like them survives today, although being
chelicerate arthropods, their distant living cousins include
spiders, scorpions and centipedes.

AMPYX AND PLIOMERA

Some of the best-known prehistoric animals were the trilobites. Their name means "three-lobed": their bodies had three parts or lobes, separated by two long grooves or furrows running from head to tail. In appearance, they resemble the woodlice (sowbugs) that live under damp bark today. Woodlice are crustaceans, cousins of crabs and prawns (see page 50); trilobites were not crustaceans, although they did make up a major part of the larger group to which crustaceans, spiders, insects and scorpions belong – the arthropods. They walked or swam with jointed legs (see page 46), and they were also the first animals to have reasonably large eyes that could, presumably, form clear images of their surroundings.

Ampyx was one of the smaller and earlier types of trilobites, about the size of a human thumb. It was lightly built, with a thin body casing that extended into a long snout at the front, and into two backswept spine-like projections from the front sides of the body. It probably sifted seabed sediments, such as mud and sand, for small edible bits and pieces, and burrowed deeper for protection. *Pliomera* was also small and also lived during the Ordovician period, around 450 million years ago. It lacked the casing extensions but its head had notched ridges, and, when the animal curled up, these clipped into the rear end of the body, so that the vulnerable underside was protected within the rolled-up body casing (see below).

ANIMAL FACTFILE
Ampyx
Meaning: Around two
Pronunciation: Am-picks
Period: Ordovician
Main group: Arthropoda (Trilobita)
Length: 4 centimeters (1½ inches)
Diet: Small edible particles
Fossil sites: Europe, North America

0	1	2	3

ANIMAL FACTFILE
Pliomera
Meaning: More monstrous
Pronunciation: Plee-owe-meer-ah
Period: Ordovician
Main group: Arthropoda (Trilobita)
Size: Up to 5 centimeters (2 inches)
Diet: Particulate matter on the seabed
Fossil sites: Mainly Western Hemisphere

0	1	2	3

ABOVE A specimen of *Pliomera* from Putilowa, Poland, shows how the trilobite rolled up to protect its limbs, gills and other parts on the underside.

LEFT Living woodlice are arthropods, as trilobites were, and although not closely related, they have the same ability to roll into a ball for protection.

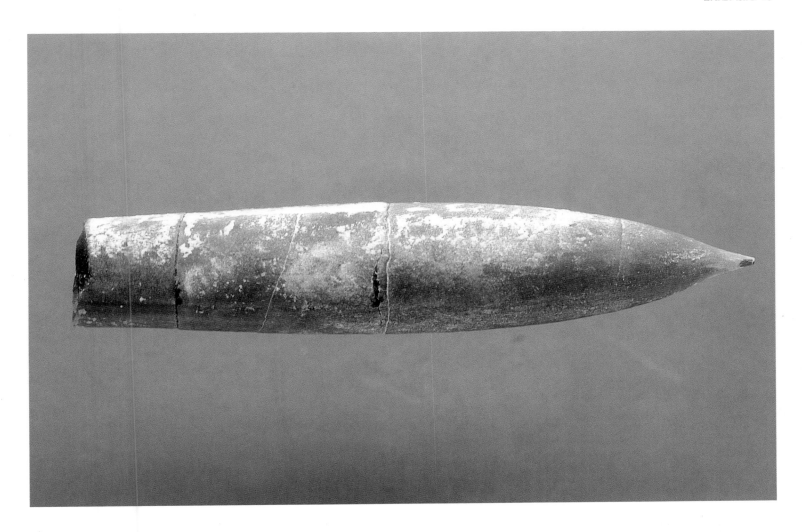

GONIOTEUTHIS

Like the big-eyed, fast-moving hunters on the previous pages, *Gonioteuthis* was a type of mollusc called a cephalopod ("head foot"). It belonged to the subgroup known as belemnoids, which exploded onto the marine scene in Ordovician times, with hundreds of different kinds. However, like the similar ammonoids (see page 42), they faded during the Cretaceous period and by its end they were all extinct. *Gonioteuthis* was an example of a belemnite from near the end of their time, the Late Cretaceous. It was relatively small, with a body length of 15–20 centimeters (6 to 8 inches), plus tentacles.

In life, belemnites probably resembled another group of cephalopods that survive today, the squid. The body was long and streamlined, with two wing- or fin-like side flaps. The head had two large eyes and a horny beak in the center, surrounded by ten long tentacles, which in some types had

hooks or suckers along their length. However, the main belemnite part that was fossilized was the animal's shell, which was wholly within the body rather than enclosing it. The shell had a cone-like forward portion, the phragmocone, in the middle of the body, and a long, slim part, the guard or pen, which extended into the animal's rear end. Some fossil sites contain thousands of these preserved guards. The shorter, wider ones are commonly called "belemnite bullets," while others are longer and slimmer, like dagger blades. Belemnoids were named after their shell shapes from the ancient Greek word *belemnos*, meaning "dart."

ABOVE Fossilized "belemnite bullets" are found in their hundreds in some locations, such as the Isle of Wight, southern England. Each is the preserved internal shell of a belemnite, found within the body at the pointed rear end. A modern equivalent is the "cuttlebone," the inner shell of the belemnite's modern close cousin, the cuttlefish.

ANIMAL FACTFILE
Gonioteuthis
Meaning: Narrow squid, slim squid
Pronunciation: Gon-ee-owe-tee-ewe-thiss
Period: Cretaceous
Main group: Mollusca
Size: Body length (excluding tentacles) up to 20 centimeters (8 inches)
Diet: Small animals
Fossil sites: Europe and elsewhere

AEGER AND ERYON

The crustaceans, or "crusty cases," are a massive group within the major arthropod group (see page 46). Today, there are more than 40,000 species and they dominate much life in the seas. Their fossil history stretches back to the Precambrian age, more than 550 million years ago. One of the major crustacean subgroups is the decapods, meaning "ten legs." This includes shrimps, prawns, lobsters, crabs, crayfish and crawfish.

Aeger was a prehistoric prawn from the Jurassic period, when dinosaurs flourished on land. Its fossils have been found in many areas, and in general its features are little changed from prawns of the present day. They still have a long pointed spike, or rostrum, on the forehead, very long antennae (feelers), a casing over the head and thorax (middle part of the body), and pincer-tipped limbs to pick up small pieces of food and any edible debris from the seabed.

Eryon was a type of spiny lobster (or langouste) from the Jurassic and Early Cretaceous periods, about 150 to 100 million years ago. It was slightly smaller than a human hand and had a broad, flattened head shield, or cephalothorax, with a jointed, flexible, tail-like abdomen behind. Its four pairs of limbs bore clawed tips, the first pair being largest, and the tail tip had a fan-like shape. When *Eryon* curled its tail down and under its body with a flicking motion, this would jerk the whole animal backward, as a means of rapid escape. It is possible that this type of creature was the ancestor of one of the last major groups of crustaceans to evolve, the crabs, which made their first appearance during the Jurassic period.

ANIMAL FACTFILE
Aeger
Meaning: Prawn

Pronunciation: Eee-jur

Period: Triassic–Jurassic

Main group: Arthropoda (Crustacea)

Length: 12 centimeters (4½ inches)
(excluding rostrum)

Diet: Small edible bits

Fossil sites: Worldwide

RIGHT This fine specimen of the fossil prawn species *Aeger tipularius* is dated to the mid-Jurassic period, 170 million years ago, and comes from southern Germany. Its bodily structure is extremely similar to its living relations.

ANIMAL FACTFILE
Eryon
Meaning: Red (animal)

Pronunciation: Erry-on

Period: Jurassic–Cretaceous

Main group: Arthropoda (Crustacea)

Size: 10 centimeters (4 inches)

Diet: Particulate matter on the seabed, carrion

Fossil sites: Mainly Northern Hemisphere

EURYPTERUS

Among the strangest and most fascinating prehistoric animals were the eurypterids, commonly known as sea scorpions. Nothing like them exists today. They were members of the great arthropod group, belonging to the subgroup known as chelicerates, named after their chelicerae (chelae), or "biting claws," which form formidable fang-like mouthparts in many species. Living chelicerates include spiders, scorpions and the horseshoe crab, *Limulus*. Eurypterids appeared in the Ordovician period, from 500 million years ago. For a time, they were extremely numerous as marine predators until bigger carnivorous fish began to evolve. The eurypterids then waned in the face of this opposition. They died out in the biggest-ever mass extinction, 250 million years ago at the end of the Permian period, but they have at least some local fame today as the state fossils of New York.

Eurypterus gave its name to the group and was a widespread genus with several species, most of which were fairly small. The head end, or prosoma, was overlain by a shield-like carapace, which covered the chelicerae on either side of the mouth, and four pairs of small walking limbs behind these. The rearmost pair of limbs was larger and paddle-like, and was used for rowing and swimming. The main eyes were large and prominent, and there were also smaller accessory eyes nearer the midline, higher on the head (as in scorpions). The second mainpart of the body was the opisthosoma, with 12 jointed segments known as tergites. Bringing up the rear was a spike-like tail, the telson. *Eurypterus* probably stalked small worms and other sea-floor prey.

ABOVE A preserved *Eurypterus* seen from above, showing the jointed dorsal plates covering its back.

ANIMAL FACTFILE
Eurypterus

Meaning: Wide wing, broad paddle

Pronunciation: You-rip-tur-uss

Period: Ordovician

Main group: Arthropoda (Chelicerata)

Length: 10 centimeters (4 inches)

Diet: Small prey

Fossil sites: USA, Europe

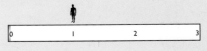

PTERYGOTUS

This fearsome predator was a eurypterid or sea scorpion (see *Eurypterus*, previous page). It was the largest known member of the chelicerate group, and also the largest-ever known creature in the entire (and massive) arthropod group (see page 46). Some specimens had a head-to-tail length of more than 2 meters (6½ feet). Added to this were the chelicerae, the massive "biting claws," which were pincer-shaped like a crab's nippers. Each was the size of a human arm bent double at the elbow.

Pterygotus lived during the Late Silurian period, 420–410 million years ago, and its fossils have been found both in North America and in Europe. It was larger than most other creatures of Silurian seas, and it terrorized them with its power. It almost certainly hunted by sight: each of its eyes was almost the size of half a basketball. It would prowl along the

seabed, crawling on its four pairs of walking legs, or wafting its paddle-like fifth pair of limbs.

Unlike the spiky telson (tail) of *Eurypterus*, *Pterygotus* had a wide, flattened telson, almost like a tail fin. It could probably swish this up and down by flexing its body, and also flapits paddle-limbs more strongly, to produce a sudden burst of speed for a surprise attack. The victim was grabbed using the chelicerae (claws) and impaled on the spikes along their inner surfaces, then torn up and the parts fed into the mouth, under the front of the head, like a giant preying mantis.

It is thought that some of these sea scorpions lived (despite the name) in fresh water, and a few even took to life on land, where they breathed by gills adapted as lungs and kept moist in a special body chamber on the underside.

ANIMAL FACTFILE
Pterygotus

Meaning: Wing- or fin- animal (one)

Pronunciation: Terry-goat-uss

Period: Late Silurian

Main group: Arthropoda (Chelicerata)

Length: Head to tail up to 2.3 meters (7½ feet)

Diet: Larger animals, such as early fish

Fossil sites: North America, Europe

RIGHT *Pterygotus* was about the same length and height as a modern Formula 1 racing car. Its massive eyes were among the largest of any animal, living or extinct, and its scorpion-like pincers could crush the hardest shellfish.

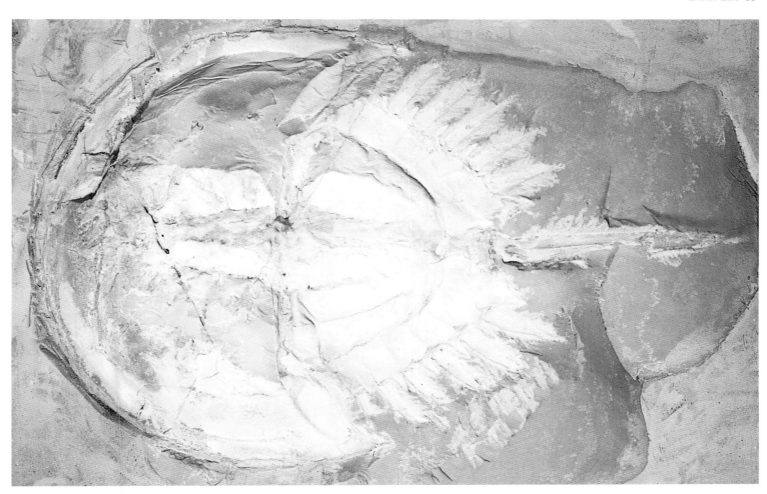

LIMULUS

Limulus, the living animal known as the horseshoe crab or king crab, has a fossil history stretching back some 400 million years. Members of its group, xiphosurans, first appeared in Devonian seas, and various types have come and gone since. They are not true crabs but belong to the chelicerate group of arthropods, as described for *Eurypterus* (see page 51 and opposite), which also includes arachnids such as scorpions and spiders. The earliest kinds of horseshoe crabs were small, only a few centimeters (1–2 inches) across, but they soon diversified into a range of shapes and sizes. The first species of *Limulus* itself are found in fossils of rocks from the Jurassic period more than 150 million years ago. They are almost identical to the living species, *Limulus polyphemus*, familiar along the coasts of North America. In spring, swarms of the creatures come into the shallows and along the Atlantic shore to breed. Three other species of *Limulus*

inhabit the shallow coastal seas around Southeast Asia.

The body casing of *Limulus* consists of a large head shield, or carapace, covering the front part of the body, the cephalothorax. There is a pair of larger eyes for detailed vision, and a smaller, simpler pair near the front. The mouthparts with their "biting claws" (chelicerae) are on the underside near the front, with another limb-like pair behind them, the palps, specialized for detecting objects by feel or touch and by scent. Behind these are four pairs of walking legs. The rear of the body, the abdomen, is hinged to the front part, and *Limulus* can swim by flexing its body at this joint. The long, spike-like tail can be raised over the body to flip the animal right side up if it lands upside down on the sea floor.

ABOVE An overhead view of *Limulus* showing the head to the left and long, sharp tail to the right.

ANIMAL FACTFILE
Limulus

Meaning: Slimy one

Pronunciation: Lim-you-luss

Period: Jurassic onward

Main group: Arthropoda (Chelicerata)

Size: Main body 5–30 centimeters (2–12 inches) (excluding tail)

Diet: Scavenger, sifting small edible bits and pieces

Fossil sites: Worldwide

PLEUROCYSTITES AND BOTRYOCRINUS

ANIMAL FACTFILE
Pleurocystites

Meaning: Rib bag/side bladder

Pronunciation: Plure-owe-siss-tite-eez

Period: Ordovician

Main group: Echinodermata

Size: Height 2 centimeters (³/₄ inch)

Diet: Tiny floating particles

Fossil sites: Worldwide

Echinoderms form a major group of animals today, with more than 6,000 species, all living in the sea. They include starfish, sea stars, brittlestars, sea urchins, sand dollars, sea cucumbers, sea lilies and feather-stars. They differ from most animal groups in having radial symmetry, which means that their bodies are basically circular, with tentacles, spines and other parts arranged like the spokes of a wheel. Echinoderms are extremely ancient, having first appeared in Cambrian seas more than 500 million years ago. (For more information, see opposite.)

Pleurocystites belonged to an extinct group of echinoderms known as the blastoids. It was very small, only 2 centimeters (half an inch) long, and lived during the Ordovician period. It was fixed to a rock or into sand by a long stalk. The main body, the calyx, was shaped like a cup. Above this were two long arms, which in some types had numerous bristles. The creature filtered the water with these arms to trap tiny pieces of floating food. *Botryocrinus* belonged to another group of echinoderms that still survive today, the crinoids or sea-lilies. They look like flowers, with a ring or crown of feathery tentacles encircling a central mouth, mounted on a tall stalk that is fixed to the sea bottom. They also filter tiny food particles from the water, as blastoids did. *Botryocrinus* lived during Silurian times and had a total height of 15–20 centimeters (6–8 inches). Some crinoids had stalks more than 1 meter (39 inches) in length and their feathery "petals" spanned more than 70 centimeters (27¹/₂ inches).

RIGHT Starfish are close cousins of crinoids and first appeared in Ordovician times, almost 500 million years ago. The first types closely resembled today's kinds, like this firebrick starfish from Australian waters.

ANIMAL FACTFILE
Botryocrinus

Meaning: Group of lily flowers

Pronunciation: Bott-ree-owe-krin-uss

Period: Silurian–Devonian

Main group: Echinodermata

Size: 15 centimeters (6 inches)

Diet: Plankton

Fossil sites: Worldwide

BOTHRIOCIDARIS AND DICHOGRAPTUS

Bothriocidaris was an early type of sea urchin from the Ordovician period. It belonged to the echinoderm group. Many fossil echinoderms are known from fragments of their body casings, which, as in today's representatives of the group, were made of tough, mineralized, almost stony plates just under the skin. In a sea urchin, these plates were fused to form a single hollow ball, called the test. However, in most cases the test was broken during fossilization, so it has been preserved as jumbled bits and pieces. *Bothriocidaris* was very small, only the size of a grape. Like today's sea urchins, it probably moved by tilting its spines at their bases, and it fed on the film of tiny plants and creatures that constantly grows on any surface in the sea, using its five-part mouth on the underside of the ball.

Dichograptus was a graptolite, a member of a group of animals that arose in the Cambrian period, spread and diversified during the Ordovician, but faded away by the Carboniferous. Graptolite animals were like very small sea anenomes or coral polyps, with tentacles that fed by sieving sea water for plankton and other tiny edible materials. Each animal, known as a zooid, lived in a tough, cup-shaped structure called a theca, and extended its tentacles from this to feed. Many thecae were joined together in rows. These have been preserved as fossils that often resemble the narrow, toothed blade of a hacksaw. Some floated while others fixed themselves to the seabed. *Dichograptus* formed a colony with eight double-chains of thecae projecting like wheel spokes from a central float.

ANIMAL FACTFILE
Bothriocidaris

Meaning: Best furrow or trench
Pronunciation: Both-ree-owe-sid-arris
Period: Ordovician
Main group: Echinodermata
Size: 15 centimeters (6 inches)
Diet: Plankton
Fossil sites: Worldwide

LEFT Present-day sea urchins, like *Astropyga,* carpet the seabed near the French coast, just as *Bothriocidaris* (which was much smaller) would have done over 450 million years ago.

ANIMAL FACTFILE
Dichograptus

Meaning: Two-branched writing, double-line marks
Pronunciation: Die-koe-grap-tuss
Period: Ordovician
Main group: Branchiotremata (Graptolithinia)
Size: Individual animals were tiny, a few millimeters in length (1/8 inch)
Diet: Plankton
Fossil sites: Worldwide

DAWN OF THE VERTEBRATES

THE VERTEBRATES (ANIMALS WITH BACKBONES)
ARE FISH, AMPHIBIANS, REPTILES, BIRDS, AND
MAMMALS. RECENTLY DISCOVERED CHINESE
FOSSILS MAY SHOW THE EARLIEST "PRE-BACKBONE"
STAGE IN A SMALL, EEL-LIKE CREATURE FROM
530 MILLION YEARS AGO. A STRIP OF STIFF
TISSUE, THE NOTOCHORD, INSIDE THE BODY
FORMED A SIMPLE "ROD" THAT THE MUSCLES
WERE ANCHORED TO AND PULLED AGAINST,
PRODUCING THE SIDE-TO-SIDE SWISHING THAT
FISH WOULD EXPLOIT SO WELL.

RIGHT This fossil fish shows the all-important backbone or
vertebral column, which serves as a bendy central support
along the body's length.

HEMICYCLASPIS

ANIMAL FACTFILE

Hemicyclaspis

Meaning: Half-round shield, semi-circle plate

Pronunciation: Hem-ee-sigh-klas-piss

Period: Late Silurian, Early Devonian

Main group: Osteostraci (Cephalaspida)

Length: 13 centimeters (5 inches)

Diet: Particles from the mud on the seabed

Fossil sites: Europe (England), Asia, eastern Canada, eastern USA

The earliest fish of the Late Ordovician period resembled their modern counterparts in general shape, but they had no true paired fins on the sides of the body (pectoral and pelvic fins), which in modern fish are adjustable for maneuvering, and no true jaws either. These first fish are known as agnathans, meaning "without jaws." They had sucker-like or rasping mouths that were either rounded or slit-shaped. There were several main groups, and species of many different shapes. Most were smaller than a human hand. Also, many types had bony plates in the skin, for protection against powerful hunters of the time such as sea scorpions. This feature has earned them the general name of ostracoderms, "bony skins."

Hemicyclaspis was just 12–13 centimeters (4–5 inches) in overall length and had a low, flattened body, which indicates that it was a bottom-dweller. It lived from Late Silurian times, from around 420 million years ago, probably in fresh water. At the front end was a semicircular bony head shield, with a sucker-like mouth on the underside to gather small edible particles from mud and sand. There were two close-set eyes on the upper part of the head and a fin-like horn projecting from each side of the lower part of the head. The main body was encased in sections or segments of narrow, curved bony plates, which could tilt slightly against each other. The tail end tapered to a point with an expanded flap below, which worked as a tail. A stiff, fin-like projection on the back gave some stability as *Hemicyclaspis* bent its body from side to side like today's fish, in a combination of wriggling and swimming, to plow along lake or river beds, or, occasionally, rise slightly above them.

PTERASPIS

Pteraspis, "wing shield," was named for the pointed, wing-like spines that stuck out from its sides. These helped this jawless fish, or agnathan, to keep stable as it swam by thrashing its rear end, which had a much larger lower tail lobe than upper one. This provided both forward propulsion and lift. Along with the generally rounded shape of the body in cross-section, and the generally streamlined profile with a sharp rostrum (nose projection) that was also angled upward for lift, these features suggest that *Pteraspis* was also an active swimmer in upper waters, as well as a bottom-dweller, as *Hemicyclaspis* was. A large, long, rear-curving spine projected from the back, with several similar but smaller spines of reducing size behind it, along the rear body and upper lobe of the tail. These prevented *Pteraspis* from rolling or tilting as it swam.

Pteraspis had a slit-like mouth and probably fed on small sea creatures that it gathered by swimming forward, probably along the seabed. Its eyes were small and were located on either side of the head, with a restricted field of vision. Like most of the early jawless fishes, *Pteraspis* was small – only 20 centimeters (8 inches) long. Its head "armor" was made of several curved plates, while the rear half of the body was covered in small overlapping scales.

After a relatively short span of success, in the Late Silurian and Early Devonian periods, the jawless fish began to suffer competition from their jawed, finned, faster-swimming cousins (as shown on the next few pages). By Permian times they had become much more scarce. Today only two main kinds survive, the lampreys and hagfishes, with about 90 species in total.

ANIMAL FACTFILE
Pteraspis
Meaning: Wing shield
Pronunciation: Tear-ass-piss
Period: Early Devonian
Main group: Heterostraci
Length: Up to 20 centimeters (8 inches)
Diet: Tiny animals such as crustaceans in surface waters or bottom sediments
Fossil sites: Europe (Belgium, Norway, England, Wales), Asia, northern Canada, USA

LEFT The shields and spines of *Pteraspis* were probably for protection or perhaps forcing a way through seaweeds – the reconstructed bodily musculature of this fish does not suggest a speedy swimmer.

CLIMATIUS AND ACANTHODES

Among the first fish with jaws and symmetrically paired side fins were the acanthodians. They evolved in the sea but soon spread into fresh water; their oldest fossils date back to the Early Silurian period, 430 million years ago. They are sometimes called "spiny sharks" because they had rows of large, sharp spines along the back and underside, which helped to hold up the thinner fin membranes, and in outline some of them were sleek and resembled sharks. However, the true sharks are a different group and appeared after the acanthodians. Acanthodians enjoyed greatest success in the Devonian "age of fish," but then faded, and they were extinct by the end of the Permian period, 250 million years ago.

Climatius was the size of a human finger. It had a blunt nose, sharp teeth in the lower of its newly evolved jaws, and big eyes to hunt prey by vision. There were two large spined fins on the back, and four or more pairs of spines on the underside, making *Climatius* a sharply prickled mouthful for any predator. The pectoral fins stuck out rigidly from the lower front of the body, with protective bony plates above them. *Acanthodes*, which has given its name to the whole group to which it belongs, was larger than *Climatius*, at 30 centimeters (12 inches) in length. It had a slimmer body, more like an eel's, but it had the same upturned tail with a fin only on the underside. It had a spine-supported fin on the back and another on the underside, both near the rear of the body. The jaws were toothless; feeding was by the gills, which had evolved comb-like rakers to sieve small food items from the water. Fossils of *Acanthodes* come from Australia as well as from many sites on northern continents including the USA (Illinois, Pennsylvania, West Virginia) and Europe (Scotland, England, Germany, Spain).

ANIMAL FACTFILE
Climatius

Meaning: Inclined or tilted fish (for its upturned tail)

Pronunciation: Klim-at-ee-uss

Period: Late Silurian to Early Devonian

Main group: Acanthodii

Length: 8 centimeters (3 inches)

Diet: Tiny mid-water prey such as crustaceans and small fish

Fossil sites: Europe, North America

ABOVE Acanthodians like *Acanthodes* earned their nickname "spiny sharks" from the sharp, rigid spine supporting the front of each fin.

ANIMAL FACTFILE
Acanthodes

Meaning: Spiny or thorny base

Pronunciation: Ak-anne-thoe-deez

Period: Carboniferous to Permian

Main group: Acanthodii

Length: 30 centimeters (12 inches)

Diet: Plankton, small animals

Fossil sites: Northern Hemisphere, Australia

ABOVE *Climatius* is shown here larger than life. In addition to the two pairs of spined fins on the underside, and the rearmost upper (dorsal) and lower (anal) fins, it had a row of thorn-like projections along the belly.

ABOVE The head end of *Dunkleosteus* is well known from fossils. The rear of the body is more conjectural, reconstructed from preserved remains of its relations.

BELOW Even the tough shells of trilobites and nautiloids could be snapped and sliced by the "teeth" which were in fact daggers of bone.

DUNKLEOSTEUS (DINICHTHYS)

Like the acanthodians (opposite), the placoderms or "plated skins" were a very early group of fish with jaws and true side-paired fins. Their name refers to the large slabs or plates of bone that curved over their heads and the fronts of their bodies, embedded in the skin. Placoderms originated in the Late Silurian period, and became some of the most successful of all animals during the next period, the Devonian. However, they soon died out as sharks and other kinds of fish spread and took over.

One of the biggest known placoderms was *Dunkleosteus* of the Late Devonian. Estimates of its length range from 3.5 meters (11^1/$_2$ feet) to almost three times this size, and it was one of the largest animals of its time. Its fossils have been found in Morocco, in European locations such as Poland and Belgium, and in the United States. The front end of the fish is well known because of the preserved bony plates that show the shape of the head,

with a huge mouth and ferocious, tooth-like blades of bone, some almost 30 centimeters (12 inches) tall, set onto powerful jaws. The main part of the skull was more than 65 centimeters (25^1/$_2$ inches) long and had a joint behind it linking to the chest plates, so *Dunkleosteus* was one of the few fishes with a flexible "neck." It could have chopped and sliced up almost any victim in the Devonian seas. The rear part of the body is less known however, presumably because it had little or no protection of bony plates or scales. It may have been tapering and eel-like, with fleshy flaps for fins, and an upturned tail supporting a fin on the underside. Perhaps *Dunkleosteus* devoured bottom-dwelling prey. Or it may have had a more shark-like shape and been a fast, active, midwater hunter. It belonged to a subgroup of placoderms known as arthrodires, or "jointed necks," because both the skull and jaws could tilt on the front vertebrae (neck backbones).

ANIMAL FACTFILE
Dunkleosteus

Meaning: Dunkle's bony fish (for its discoverer)

Pronunciation: Dun-klee-oss-tee-uss

Period: Late Devonian

Main group: Placodermi (Arthrodira)

Length: 5 meters (16^1/$_2$ feet) or more

Diet: Large fish and other prey

Fossil sites: Europe, Africa, USA (California, Ohio, Tennessee, Pennsylvania)

0	1	2	3

THE AGE OF FISHES

THE DEVONIAN PERIOD, 410–355 MILLION
YEARS AGO, SAW MANY AND VARIED FISH AS
THE DOMINANT LARGE ANIMALS IN ALL AQUATIC
HABITATS. SOME GROUPS, SUCH AS THE
ACANTHODIANS AND PLACODERMS (THROUGHOUT
THIS CHAPTER), HAVE LONG SINCE DISAPPEARED.
OTHERS, SUCH AS THE SHARKS AND LOBEFINS
(SARCOPTERYGIANS), ENJOYED HUGE SUCCESS
AND STILL SURVIVE – WHILE SOME LEFT
DESCENDANTS TO WALK ON LAND.

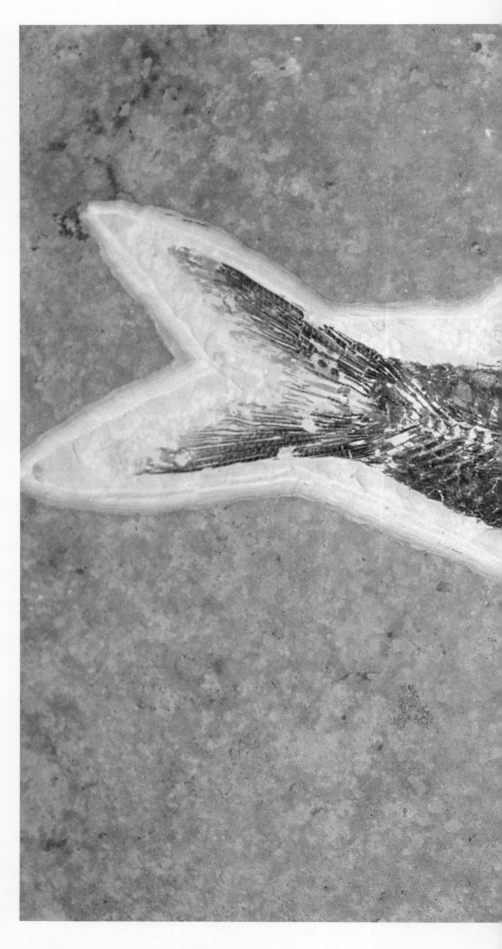

RIGHT The basic design of bony fish arose more than 400 million
years ago and persists largely unchanged today. This specimen
was found in the Green River Shale Formation of Wyoming.
Fish are by far the biggest group of vertebrates in terms of
species numbers.

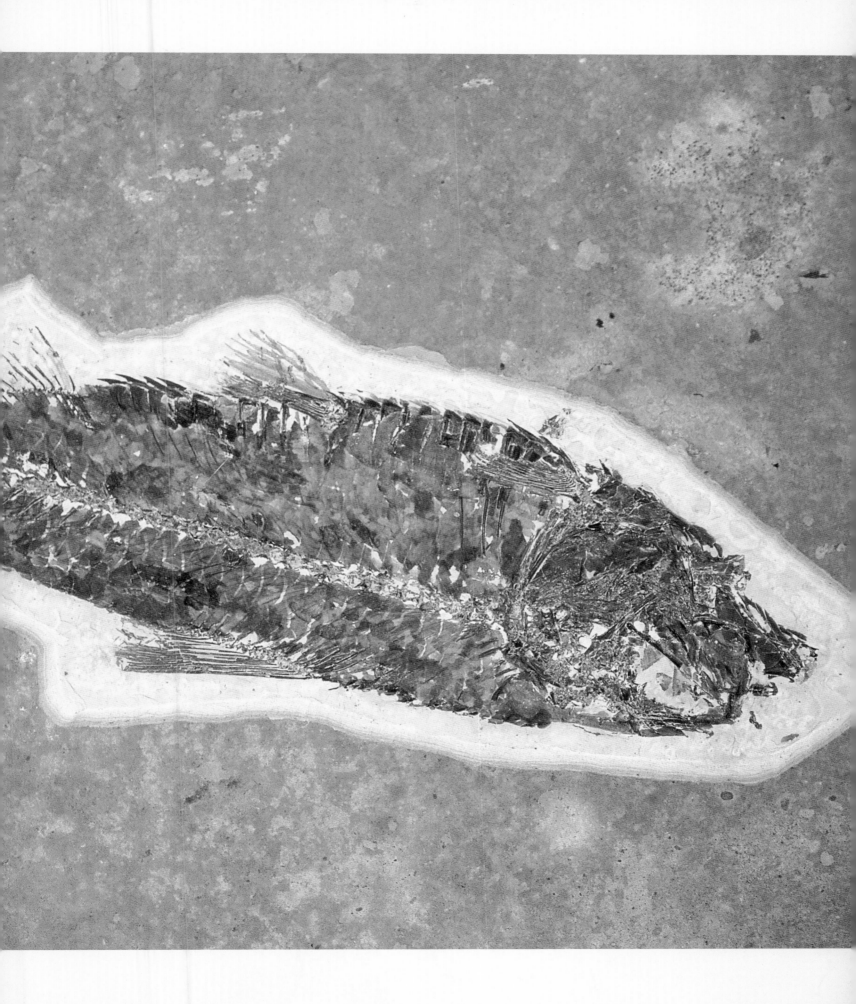

BOTHRIOLEPIS

ANIMAL FACTFILE
Bothriolepis

Meaning: Trench scale

Pronunciation: Both-ree-owe-lep-iss

Period: Late Devonian

Main group: Placodermi (Antiarchi)

Length: Up to 1 meter (39 inches)

Diet: Small food items, scavenged matter

Fossil sites: Worldwide

This fish was a member of the placoderm group, like the massive predator *Dunkleosteus*. Placoderms were among the first fish with true jaws and symmetrically paired side fins, and arose in the Late Silurian period. Like most members of the group, *Bothriolepis* lived during the next period, the Devonian, more than 350 million years ago, and it had curved bony plates protecting its head and the front of its body. It was quite different, however, from its giant cousin *Dunkleosteus*, being smaller, at around 1 meter (39 inches) long, and having a low, flattened body, with eyes almost on the top of the head. This general shape is common among bottom-dwelling fish. *Bothriolepis* probably moved along slowly, sifting and sorting any small animals and other edible materials from sand and mud with its weakly jawed mouth.

The most curious features of *Bothriolepis* were its two "arms." These were its pectoral fins, situated on each side of the lower body behind the head, as in most fish. They were both long and slim, and were formed of jointed casings made of linked bony tubes. They may have been used for "crawling" through water, but the angles of the sections making up the "arms" and their degrees of movement do not seem suited to this. The "arms" may have probed and dug in the bottom to loosen items of food. Another suggestion is that *Bothriolepis* used them to crawl over land, from one pool to another. This fish's fossils have been found in rocks that derive from freshwater and marine habitats, and fossil comparisons suggest that *Bothriolepis* may have had simple lungs with which it took in oxygen from air (see *Dipterus* page 68).

ABOVE The weird pectoral (front side) fins of *Bothriolepis* were adapted as jointed "tubes" – but for what, is unclear.

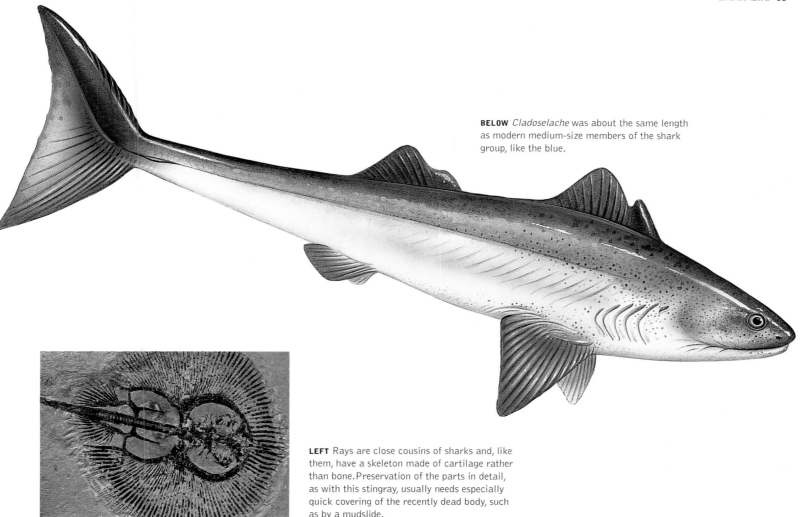

BELOW *Cladoselache* was about the same length as modern medium-size members of the shark group, like the blue.

LEFT Rays are close cousins of sharks and, like them, have a skeleton made of cartilage rather than bone. Preservation of the parts in detail, as with this stingray, usually needs especially quick covering of the recently dead body, such as by a mudslide.

CLADOSELACHE

The greatest predatory fish in the seas today are the sharks. Much the same has been true for almost 400 million years since the shark group appeared in Late Silurian seas. However, the earliest fossils of these ultimate hunters are only fragments of their denticles, or skin "scales," and teeth. Much better remains date from the Middle to Late Devonian periods, when the group expanded in number and diversity. *Cladoselache* is one of the earliest sharks known from well-preserved fossils. Some of the finest are in the rocks known as the Cleveland shales in Ohio. These fossils show traces of soft tissue, such as skin, fins, and muscles, which are not usually preserved. In fact, there is a general problem with fossil sharks, because their skeletons were made of cartilage (gristle), not bone. Cartilage is slightly softer and more susceptible to decay and disintegration than bone, so the skeletons

of sharks and other cartilaginous fish, such as rays (known as the Chondrichthyes group), are much less likely to be fossilized than the harder bony skeletons of other fish.

Cladoselache had a generally shark-like appearance, especially in its streamlined body, large but relatively stiff fin flaps, and wide mouth bristling with fang-like teeth. However, it belonged to an extinct subgroup of sharks, rather than a living subgroup. *Cladoselache* has a number of features that made it distinct from modern sharks. These included a mouth at the front of the head, rather than slung under the snout; the lack of an anal, or lower rear, fin; and an upper jaw with more extensive joints to the main skull and braincase.

Xenacanthus and *Hybodus*, described on the following page, are other examples of extinct sharks.

ANIMAL FACTFILE
Cladoselache

Meaning: Branched shark

Pronunciation: Klad-owe-see-lack-ee

Period: Devonian

Main group: Chondrichthyes

Length: Up to 2 meters (6½ feet)

Diet: Suitable-sized prey

Fossil sites: North America, Europe

| 0 | 1 | 2 | 3 |

XENACANTHUS AND HYBODUS

ANIMAL FACTFILE
Xenacanthus
Meaning: Strange spine

Pronunciation: Zen-ah-kan-thuss

Period: Late Devonian to Permian

Main group: Chondrichthyes

Length: 75 centimeters (30 inches)

Diet: Small freshwater animals

Fossil sites: Northern continents, Australia

As described on the previous page, the shark group rose to prominence in Devonian seas, almost 400 million years ago. From the outset, they were large, speedy hunters, and some types survived over huge time spans with little modification. These long-lived genera included *Xenacanthus* and *Hybodus*. *Xenacanthus* was a member of the shark group called the xenacanthids, sharks that spread into the fresh water of lakes, rivers and streams, but eventually became extinct. *Xenacanthus* was shaped more like an eel than a modern shark, with a long, ribbon-like dorsal fin that extended backward to wrap around the pointed rear end of the body and join the anal fin on the underside. On the top of the head was a long, sharp spine, presumably used for defense. The teeth were also unusual, each one shaped like a V with two points or cusps. *Xenacanthus* probably preyed on small freshwater animals,

including other fish but also crustaceans and worms.

Hybodus was much larger, more than 2 meters (7 feet) in length. It belonged to the modern shark group, Selachii, and looked very similar to the fast-swimming oceanic sharks of today, such as the blue and mako, although its snout was blunter. However, it retained a feature no longer found in the majority of modern-day sharks: fin spines. The two dorsal (back) fins each had a large, sharp, stiff spine at the front. *Hybodus* had sharp impaling teeth in the front of its jaws, and lower, broader teeth in the rear, which it used for crushing hard items of food. This was one of the most widespread and long-lived of all shark types. Fossils of various *Hybodus* species are found worldwide and date from the Late Permian to Cretaceous periods, a time span of well over 150 million years.

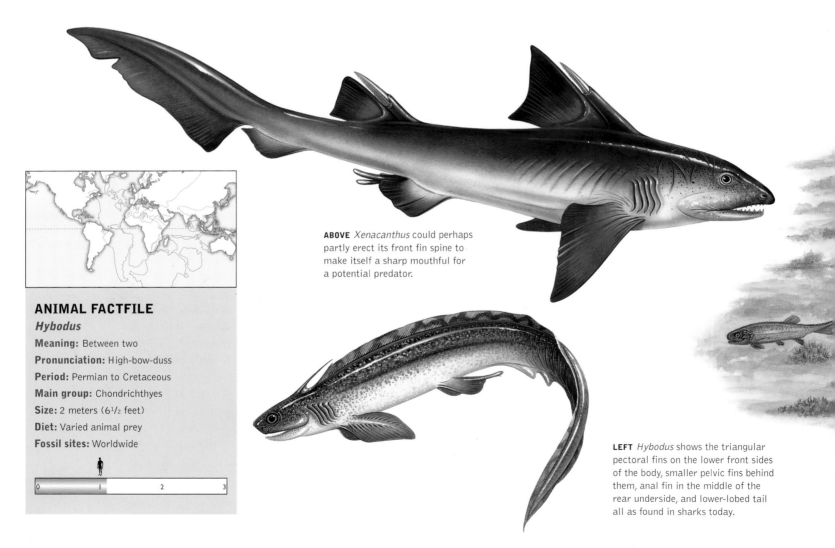

ABOVE *Xenacanthus* could perhaps partly erect its front fin spine to make itself a sharp mouthful for a potential predator.

ANIMAL FACTFILE
Hybodus
Meaning: Between two

Pronunciation: High-bow-duss

Period: Permian to Cretaceous

Main group: Chondrichthyes

Size: 2 meters (6½ feet)

Diet: Varied animal prey

Fossil sites: Worldwide

LEFT *Hybodus* shows the triangular pectoral fins on the lower front sides of the body, smaller pelvic fins behind them, anal fin in the middle of the rear underside, and lower-lobed tail all as found in sharks today.

EUSTHENOPTERON AND PANDERICHTHYS

Most fish today belong to the group called the ray-fins (actinopterygians). Their fins are supported by spine-like structures called fin rays that can fold or twist the fin into different shapes, like a flexible fan. Very few living fish belong to the group called lobe-fins or fleshy-fins (sarcopterygians). (See also the next two pages.) However, the lobe-fins were once much more common and widespread. They are of special interest because it is thought that some of their kind evolved into the first backboned animals to walk on land, the amphibious tetrapods (as described in the next chapter).

Eusthenopteron and *Panderichthys* were creatures very similar to the first land-living tetrapods. The fleshy, muscular lobe at the base of the fin, where it joined onto the body, contained the series of small bones that, in later species, became larger and formed the skeleton of a walking leg (see page 79). Other body and teeth features link these fish to early tetrapods, including the details of the skull bones, the pattern of hard enamel on the teeth, and the joints between the ribs and vertebrae (backbones). *Eusthenopteron* fossils have been found in Scotland, Russia, and the province of Quebec in Canada. *Panderichthys* fossils, from Europe, show even more similarities with the early tetrapods. This fish had no back fins, and only small tail fins, but the lobes of its four paired fins, pectoral (front) and pelvic (rear), were large and powerful. Both *Eusthenopteron* and *Panderichthys* lived in fresh water, were about 1 meter (39 inches) long, and had sharp, biting teeth.

ANIMAL FACTFILE
Eusthenopteron
Meaning: Fine strong fin, good powerful wing [fin]
Pronunciation: Yous-then-op-tur-on
Period: Late Devonian
Main group: Sarcopterygii (Osteolepiformes)
Length: Up to 1 meter (39 inches)
Diet: Smaller animals
Fossil sites: Europe, North America

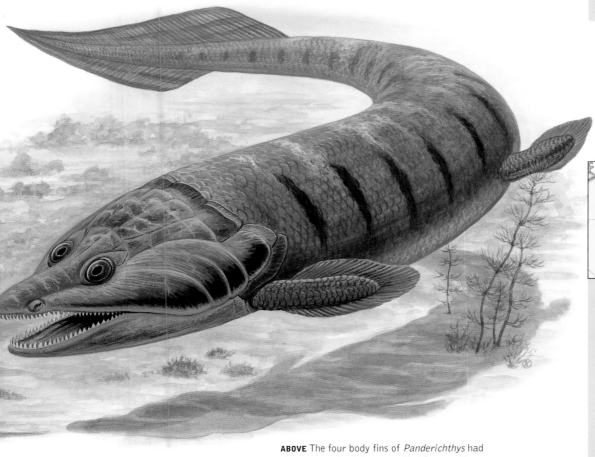

ABOVE The four body fins of *Panderichthys* had strong muscular lobes, as suited for crawling as for paddling and swimming – foreshadowing the four-legged tetrapod design.

ANIMAL FACTFILE
Panderichthys
Meaning: Pander's fish
Pronunciation: Pan-der-ick-thiss
Period: Late Devonian
Main group: Sarcopterygii (Osteolepiformes)
Size: 1 meter (39 inches)
Diet: Smaller animals
Fossil sites: Europe

ABOVE Sleek and streamlined, *Dipterus* had most of its fins toward the rear of its body, for sudden acceleration when dashing at victims.

DIPTERUS

ANIMAL FACTFILE

Dipterus

Meaning: Two fins

Pronunciation: Dip-tur-uss

Period: Devonian

Main group: Sarcopterygii (Dipnoi)

Length: 30–40 centimeters (12–16 inches)

Diet: Hard-bodied and other prey

Fossil sites: Europe (Scotland, Germany), USA (Idaho and neighboring states)

| 0 | 1 | 2 | 3 |

Lungfish are members of the fish group called lobe-fins, or sarcopterygians (see previous page). There are six living species: four in Africa, one in Australia, and one in South America. An early type of lungfish was *Dipterus*, from the Middle Devonian period, almost 400 million years ago. Its fossils have been found in Europe, including sites in Germany and Scotland, and perhaps also in North America. In overall body shape, *Dipterus* resembled modern ambush-predator fish like pike. It was long and slim, with a streamlined snout, two dorsal fins at the rear of the body, and a large tail fin behind them. This structure was suited to making sudden bursts of speed, allowing lunges at prey. *Dipterus* became very abundant by the end of the Devonian period. It lived in fresh water and had broad teeth, with which it crushed hard-cased prey. The fossilized stomach contents of other fish, such as placoderms (see page 61), show that *Dipterus*

itself was a common victim of other predators.

Lungfish were not the first fish to develop lung-like parts inside the body, capable of taking in oxygen from air. Various other fish probably developed them millions of years earlier. Also several groups of fish today gulp air into their guts, which work partially like lungs. In fact, lungfish, although they could breathe air, and had fleshy-based lobe-fins that seem to foreshadow limbs, were not a group ancestral to the tetrapods (land vertebrates). This is shown by various details of their skeletons, especially in the skull and in the limb lobes. Another group of lobe-fins, the osteolepiforms, probably gave rise to the tetrapods. But perhaps *Dipterus* could "hibernate" like modern lungfish. When their pools dry out, most lungfish burrow into the damp mud and stay there for months, even years. This condition of inactivity to avoid dry periods is more correctly known as aestivation.

MACROPOMA AND LATIMERIA

In 1938, the discovery of a living *Latimeria*, commonly known as the coelacanth, caused a sensation. The find was made in deep waters off southeastern Africa. Popular accounts of "Old Four Legs" told how the most distant living relative of human beings was a fish that had lived during the Age of Dinosaurs, but had been missing ever since. It had come out of the water and given rise to four-limbed land animals, from early tetrapods through to mammals. In the late 1990s, another species of *Latimeria*, about 1.5–1.7 meters (5 to 6 feet) long, and so around the same size as the African coelacanth, was discovered in the seas of Southeast Asia.

Popular accounts were not fully accurate, however. Coelacanths, also known as actinistians, were a group of lobe-fin fishes (sarcopterygians), like the osteolepiforms and the lungfish (shown on the previous two pages). But the group that contained the probable ancestors of subsequent land vertebrates was the osteolepiforms; coelacanths were a side or sister group to them. The earliest coelacanths are known as fossils in Devonian rocks, and they have changed little over an immense time. A well-known type was *Macropoma*, from fossils in Late Cretaceous rocks of Europe, including England and the Czech Republic. Like today's *Latimeria* (but one-third the size) *Macropoma* had lobe-based fins, a large mouth with small teeth for catching fish and other prey, and a small third tail lobe and fin between the main upper and lower tail fins. As the Cretaceous period ended, and with it the Age of Dinosaurs, coelacanth fossils disappeared from the rocks. Scientists believed the whole group to be extinct, until "Old Four Legs" resurfaced.

ANIMAL FACTFILE
Macropoma
Meaning: Big apple, large fruit
Pronunciation: Mack-roe-pome-ah
Period: Late Cretaceous
Main group: Sarcopterygii (Actinistia)
Length: 55 centimeters (22 inches)
Diet: Smaller animals
Fossil sites: Europe

LEFT A living African coelacanth, *Latimeria chalumnae*, swims in the Indian Ocean near the Comoros Islands. This carnivorous fish, nearly two meters (6½ feet) long, shelters in a cave or crevice by day. It emerges at night to hunt fish, squid and shellfish on or near the sea bed, at depths of 200–710 meters (670-2,330 feet).

ANIMAL FACTFILE
Latimeria
Meaning: For Latimer
Pronunciation: Lat-im-air-ee-ah
Period: Cretaceous to Tertiary
Main group: Sarcopterygii (Actinistia)
Size: Up to 1.8 meters (6 feet)
Diet: Smaller animals
Fossil sites: Africa, Southeast Asia

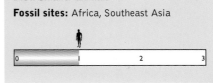

LIFE ONTO LAND

THE FIRST CREATURES TO WALK ON LAND WERE
NOT THE SPRAWLING, FOUR-LEGGED, METER
(39 INCH)-LONG VERTEBRATES, RESEMBLING
LARGE NEWTS, THAT ARE SOMETIMES SEEN IN
PICTURES OF PREHISTORY. THEY WERE SMALL AND
INSIGNIFICANT, ANCIENT COUSINS OF TODAY'S
MITES, SPRINGTAILS AND MILLIPEDES. THEY
COULD NOT HAVE CRAWLED FROM THE WATER
UNTIL AFTER SMALL PLANTS HAD PIONEERED
LAND LIFE, PROVIDING FOOD, SHELTER AND THE
FIRST SOILS.

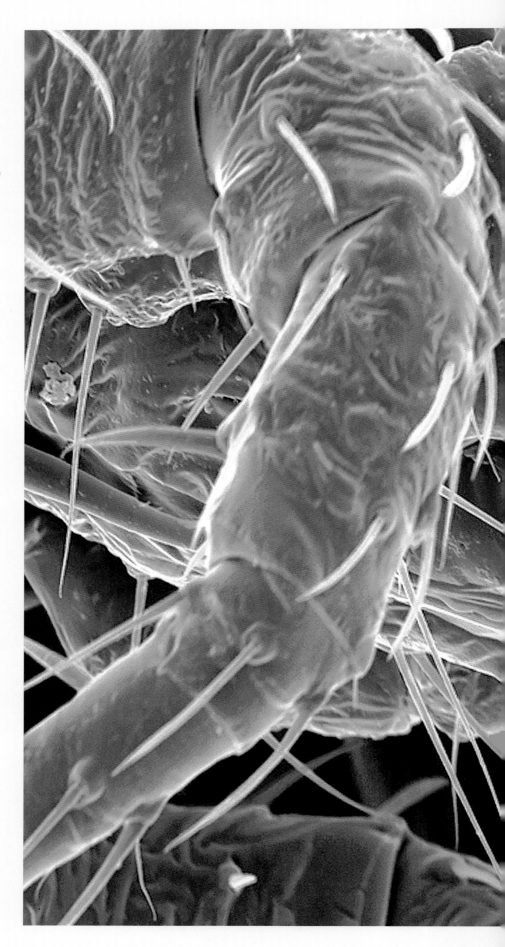

RIGHT Mites were among the very first land animals. Most
were smaller than this o. They probably began by feeding on
the living or decaying parts of early land plants. Then some
evolved into hunters, like this modern-day predatory mite,
and began to feed on their herbivorous cousins. Slowly the
first terrestrial food chains built up in miniature: plants >
herbivores > carnivores.

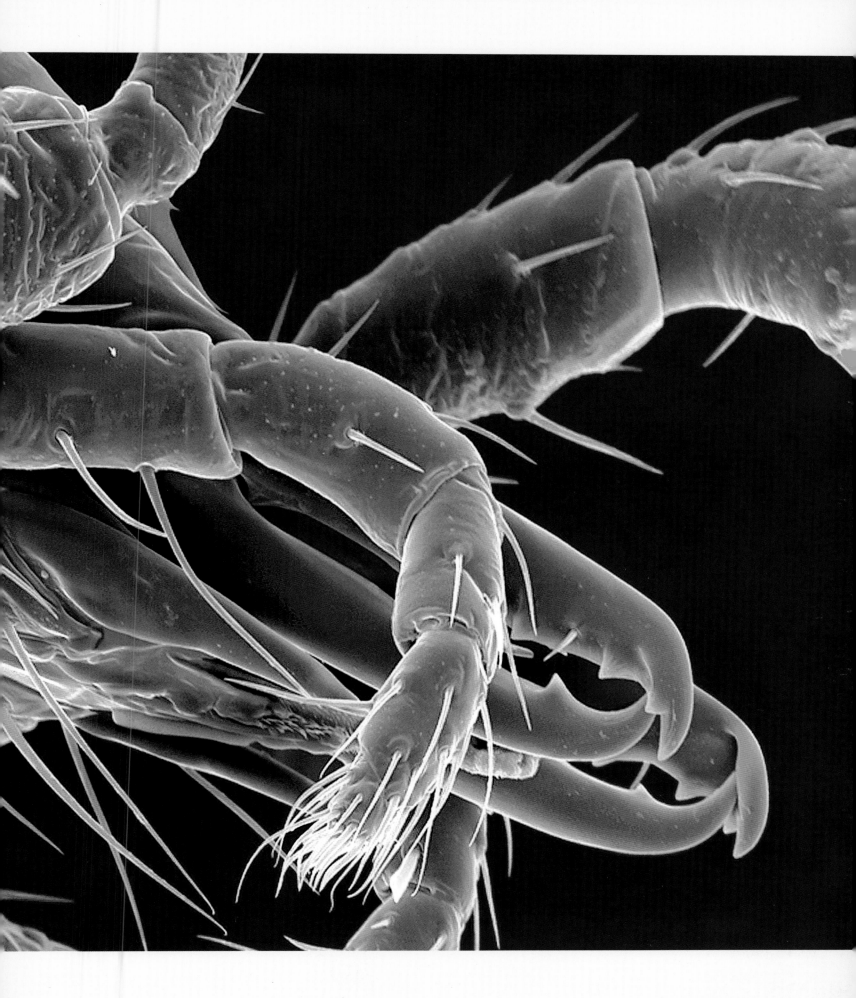

MEGANEURA

The Late Carboniferous period was a time of plentiful moisture and warmth over most of the Earth's land masses. This encouraged the rapid growth of great forests of huge ferns and other plants. The animals of the time, such as the millipede-like *Arthropleura* (see below), also reached tremendous sizes. Between the great plants flapped the largest-ever insect, *Meganeura*. It was a kind of dragonfly, from the insect group known as the odonatans. Dragonflies were among the earliest types of flying insects to appear, around 320 million years ago: they retain largely unchanged wing structures today. They have to hold the wings out sideways, being unable to fold them at right angles so they lie lengthwise along the back, as in most other types of winged insects.

Meganeura had a head and body longer than a standard ruler, and wings that measured 70 centimeters (28 inches) from one tip to the other. It almost certainly lived in much the same way as today's dragonflies. It was a fast, aerobatic predator that could twist and turn in a flash, spot and track prey with its huge eyes, and grab victims using its legs like a basket.

The prey would be transferred to the strong, biting mouthparts, and then torn up and consumed later, while *Meganeura* rested on a perch. Indeed, the legs of *Meganeura*, compared to modern dragonflies, were even longer and more powerful, almost the size of a human hand. Perhaps *Meganeura* swooped near to the ground to grab victims such as members of another early insect group, the cockroaches.

The insect group as a whole probably appeared as some of the first small land animals, more than 400 million years ago. Early types included prehistoric versions of silverfish, bristletails, and non-flying cockroaches and earwigs. The power of flight may have arisen about 350 million years ago, at the start of the Carboniferous period. Some of the most familiar insects today were relative latecomers. Bees and wasps did not thrive until the Cretaceous period, when their rapid evolution was probably linked to the appearance of flowering plants.

LEFT A fossilized Jurassic dragonfly from a genus allied to *Meganeura*, from the fine-grained limestones of Solnhofen, Germany.

ANIMAL FACTFILE
Meganeura
Meaning: Big filament [wing]
Pronunciation: Meg-ah-neur-ah
Period: Late Carboniferous
Main group: Arthropoda (Insecta)
Length: Head-body 35 centimeters (14 inches)
Diet: Flying insects
Fossil sites: Europe

ARTHROPLEURA

Among the first land-dwellers were creatures loosely known as myriapods, members of the great arthropod or "jointed leg" group (see page 46). Their representatives today include millipedes (diplopods) and centipedes (chilopods). *Arthropleura* can be regarded as an ancient type of millipede. It lived long after its kind first appeared on land, but it achieved extraordinary size. Even the giant tropical millipedes of today seldom exceed 25 centimeters (10 inches) in length, but *Arthropleura* was up to 2 meters (6½ feet) long, and also very low-set and wide, not unlike a "walking table." It lived during the Carboniferous period, more than 300 million years ago, and was the largest land arthropod of that time known to science, although it was not the equal of the fearsome water-dwelling arthropods known as sea scorpions (see page 52).

Arthropleura had a wide, wrap-over body casing made of jointed strips and edged with wide spines along the sides. Superficially it resembled the woodlouse (sowbug) of today, or perhaps a trilobite, but these were members of different arthropod groups. Under the body shield were *Arthropleura*'s mouthparts, suited to sorting and munching soft foods, probably plant matter. The Carboniferous period was a time of warm swamps and "coal forests." Giant ferns and other lush vegetation carpeted the land, providing vast amounts of food for herbivores of all kinds. Around 60 pairs of jointed walking legs, two pairs to each of the 30 body segments (as in modern millipedes), carried this heavy creature along. Millipedes are not to be confused with centipedes, which have one pair of legs per body segment compared to the millipede's two pairs, and are fierce predators.

ANIMAL FACTFILE
Arthropleura
Meaning: Jointed sides
Pronunciation: Are-throw-plur-ah
Period: Carboniferous
Main group: Arthropoda (Diplopoda)
Length: Up to 2 meters (6½ feet)
Diet: Plant matter
Fossil sites: Germany

AYSHEAIA AND RHYNIELLA

ANIMAL FACTFILE
Aysheaia
Meaning: After local mountain, Ayshea
Pronunciation: Ay-shee-eye-ah
Period: Cambrian
Main group: Onychophora
Length: A few centimeters (1–2 inches)
Diet: Possibly sponges and decaying matter
Fossil sites: Canada

| 0 | I | 2 | 3 |

RIGHT A modern springtail, or collembolan, has changed hardly at all from its counterparts which were pioneering land-dwellers in the Devonian period.

ANIMAL FACTFILE
Rhyniella
Meaning: Small beak
Pronunciation: Rye-nee-ell-ah
Period: Devonian
Main group: Arthropoda (Insecta)
Size: 1 centimeter (½ inch)
Diet: Rotting matter
Fossil sites: Greenland

| 0 | I | 2 | 3 |

The most numerous creatures today are insects: the number of known species vastly exceeds those of all other animals added together. Their origins are something of a mystery, however. Insects belong to the group called arthropods (see page 46), along with crustaceans, spiders, scorpions, millipedes and centipedes, and extinct trilobites and other creatures with jointed legs. It is possible that arthropods share a common ancestor, way back in the Cambrian period, more than 500 million years ago, and that this ancestor was a type of worm which no longer survives. A glimpse of what an intermediate "worm arthropod" may have looked like was provided by *Aysheaia*, from the fossil-rich Middle Cambrian rocks known as the Burgess Shales, in Canada (see page 38). It had the segmented body of a worm, but also twenty stubby legs in two rows. It was similar to the living creatures known as velvet worms or onychophorans, which, unlike the sea-dweller *Aysheaia*, live on land. The legs are hydraulic, flexing by means of body fluid pressure like a worm's body, and although they do not have joints, they do function as walking limbs.

Rhyniella resembled the modern insect-like creatures known as springtails, which are also wingless. In some classification schemes, springtails are regarded as insects, but in others, they form a closely related group of their own, collembolans. Springtails are found in vast but largely unnoticed numbers in many habitats, especially soil and leaf litter. They feed on scraps, and most are smaller than this o. *Rhyniella* was larger, about one centimeter (half an inch) long, but it too probably lived on decaying plant matter.

ANIMAL FACTFILE
Arthrolycosa

Meaning: Wolf [spider] with joints

Pronunciation: Arth-roe-lie-coze-ah

Period: Carboniferous

Main group: Arthropoda (Arachnida)

Size: Head-body 5 centimeters (2 inches)

Diet: Smaller animals

Fossil sites: Europe

0	1	2	3

ABOVE LEFT Living tarantulas are members of the spider group known as mygalomorphs. They are regarded as "primitive" because they share many features with their prehistoric cousins such as *Arthrolycosa*.

BELOW LEFT *Palaeophonus* would have resembled today's scorpions in most characteristics, including the large pincers, four pairs of legs, and the arched tail tipped with the pointed poison sting.

ANIMAL FACTFILE
Palaeophonus

Meaning: Ancient killer

Pronunciation: Pal-ee-owe-fon-uss

Period: Late Silurian

Main group: Arthropoda (Arachnida)

Length: 7–8 centimeters (2¹/₂–3¹/₂ inches) (including tail but excluding pincers)

Diet: Small prey

Fossil sites: Europe

0	1	2	3

PALAEOPHONUS AND ARTHROLYCOSA

The group of arthropods (jointed-legged creatures) called chelicerates has been seen on several earlier pages. Among their kind were the fearsome eurypterids or sea scorpions (see page 51). These were not true scorpions, of the kind that prowl in darkness and arch their poison stings over their heads, though true scorpions are also a very ancient group. *Palaeophonus* was one of their early representatives. It was around the length of a human finger and had large nipping pincers, called pedipalps, and powerful chelicerae, or "biting claws," with which it tore apart its prey. It also had a narrow tail-like abdomen with a sharp, thorn-like tip, which was probably used to jab venom into victims or enemies. At one time, *Palaeophonus* was thought to have been terrestrial (living on land), but it did not have the air openings for breathing found in the land types, so it probably dwelled in water.

Scorpions belong to the subgroup of chelicerates known as arachnids, which have four pairs of walking limbs. More arachnids appeared on land in the Carboniferous period: the spiders.

A typical example from that time was *Arthrolycosa*, which was nearly the size of a human hand. Almost from the very beginning, these early spiders looked much like the spiders of today, especially the pursuit-hunting types known as wolf spiders. The earliest spiders used their eight long legs to chase victims; spinning webs to catch prey was a slightly later development. The two shorter limbs on either side of the head, called palps, were mainly sensory, used by *Arthrolycosa* to feel its way.

This early spider had eight eyes arranged across the front of the head, and below them, in the center, were two fang-like chelicerae to impale victims.

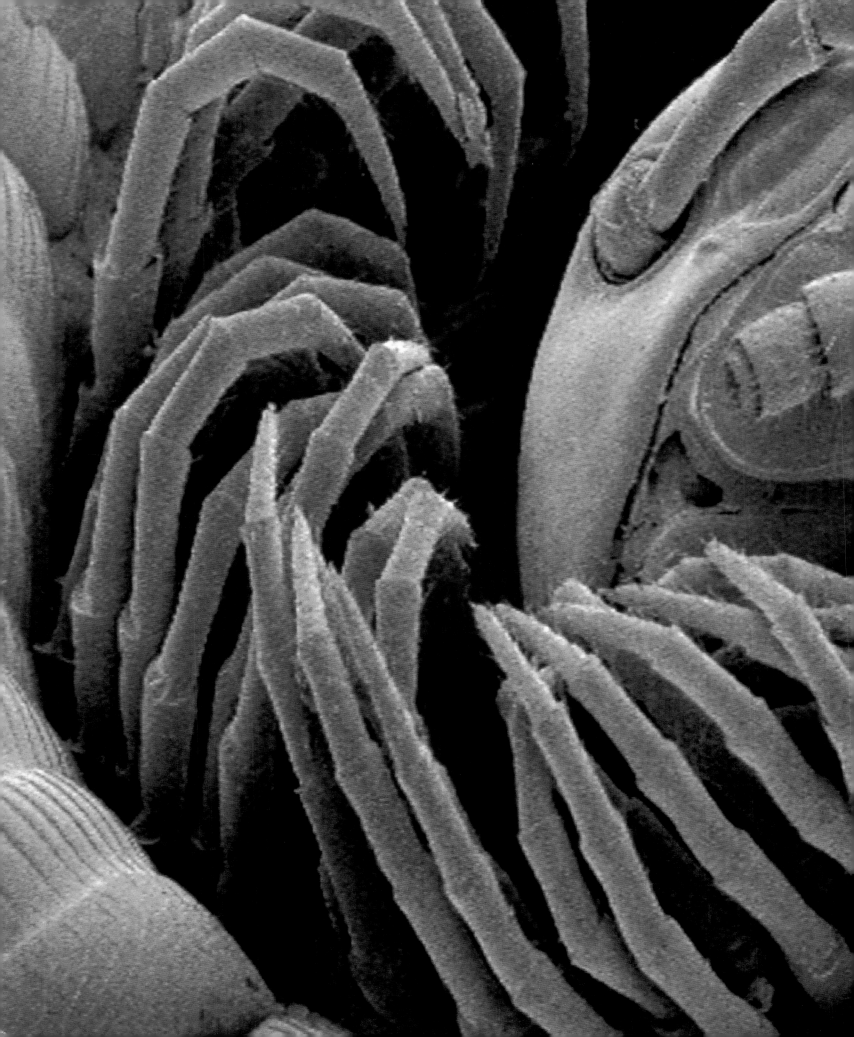

CHAPTER TWO

CONQUERORS OF THE LAND

FROM THE DEVONIAN PERIOD, SOME 400 MILLION YEARS AGO, ANIMALS BEGAN TO WRIGGLE FROM THE WATER TO CRAWL THROUGH THE MARSHES AND THEN WALK ON DRY LAND — AND BY THE PERMIAN PERIOD, 230 MILLION YEARS AGO, THE STAGE WAS SET FOR THE RISE OF THE DINOSAURS.

OUT OF THE WATER

MANY POPULAR ACCOUNTS OF PREHISTORY BEGIN WITH DINOSAURS, WHICH PERHAPS GIVES THE IMPRESSION THAT THEY WERE THE FIRST LAND ANIMALS, OR EVEN THE EARLIEST CREATURES. HOWEVER, VERTEBRATES — ANIMALS WITH BACKBONES — TOOK TO LIVING ON LAND WELL OVER 100 MILLION YEARS BEFORE THE FIRST DINOSAURS APPEARED. LONG BEFORE EVEN THIS TIME, INVERTEBRATES (ANIMALS WITHOUT BACKBONES), SUCH AS MITES, MILLIPEDES, SCORPIONS AND INSECTS, WERE CRAWLING ACROSS THE GROUND OR CLIMBING UP PREHISTORIC PLANTS. THE MOVE OF VERTEBRATES FROM WATER TO LAND WAS A MAJOR STEP, HOWEVER, BOTH LITERALLY AND FOR EVOLUTION. IT OPENED UP WHOLE NEW HABITATS, WHERE LARGER LAND-DWELLING ANIMALS COULD ADAPT — WITH LITTLE COMPETITION — TO NEW FOOD SOURCES AND ENVIRONMENTAL CONDITIONS.

FIN TO LIMB

A key event was "fin to limb" – the change from a fish's fin to a leg suitable for walking. This began in certain sarcopterygian or "lobe-fin" fish, a group that persists today in the coelacanths and lungfish (see Chapter One). Each fin had a fleshy base with bones and muscles inside, used for controlling the shape and movement of the main fin surface. In some lobe-fins, however, the base gradually became larger while the fin part shrank, as the appendage was used to push against surfaces harder and more resistant than water. The bones became longer, and the muscle more powerful, until the fin had disappeared and the lobe became a leg.

TETRAPODS

The number of limbs in the first land vertebrates derived from the standard fish pattern of two sets of paired fins, the pectoral fins and the pelvic fins. The resulting four-limbed animals are known as tetrapods (which simply means "four feet"). Some of the earliest examples, from the Late Devonian period more than 360 million years ago, are shown on the following pages. At one time, these were thought to have been fully capable land-walkers, since the evolutionary impetus for the change from fin to limb change was the need to crawl between pools as they dried out. However, newer studies have suggested that tetrapods may well have evolved in water. At first, their limbs were not legs for walking, but paddles for swimming or pushing through water plants. Only later did tetrapods venture away from their aquatic environment onto dry ground, as the paddles became legs.

LAND-DWELLING

The walking limb was only one of a whole range of features needed by tetrapods to conquer dry land. Others included lungs to obtain oxygen by breathing air, rather than gills, which filtered oxygen from water. Lungs were not especially new – several groups of fish had already evolved them, perhaps to aid breathing in warm, still pools with low-oxygen water. (Various kinds of air-gulping fish still do this today, for example the group known colloquially as "bony-tongues", which includes the world's larges freshwater fish, the arapaima.) Another need was for skin that could prevent moisture and body fluids being lost too fast in open air – in water, this was not a problem. Most of the early tetrapods are what might be called "amphibians," although in newer classification schemes "amphibian" is a loose and descriptive term for a variety of groups. One change that these "amphibians" probably did not achieve was to break free of water when breeding. Their young stages, or larvae, led an aquatic life. Full independence of the watery environment came later with the appearance of the shelled amniote egg, and with it, the beginning of the reptiles (see page 88).

PREVIOUS PAGE A colored scanning electron micrograph of a coiled garden millipede magnified about 15 times. Its major group, the arthropods, were the first creatures to live on land.

LEFT The pioneering tetrapods (four-legged backboned animals) *Ichthyostega* rest on a bank among giant tree-ferns and similar ancient plants, in the warm, dank Devonian forests of what is today cold Greenland.

Ichthyostega and Acanthostega

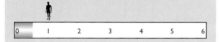

ANIMAL FACTFILE

Ichthyostega

Meaning: Fish plate

Pronunciation: Ick-thee-owe-stay-gah

Period: Late Devonian

Main group: Tetrapoda

Length: 1 meter (39 inches)

Diet: Animals

Fossil sites: Greenland

Among the first tetrapods (four-legged back-boned animals) were *Acanthostega* and *Ichthyostega*. In earlier classification schemes they were formerly both included in the group called labyrinthodonts, which were the first types of amphibians (as shown on page 78). Labyrinthodont, meaning "labyrinth teeth," refers to the folded pattern of very hard enamel on the teeth of these animals. Their teeth are one of the features that link them to the fish that were probably their ancestors – the lobe-fin fish known as osteolepiforms, a group that included *Eusthenopteron* and *Panderichthys*.

Acanthostega approached 1 meter (39 inches) in length and outwardly resembled a large, big-mouthed newt or salamander. Its limbs were probably not strong enough to support it for easy walking on land but were used as swimming paddles or for pushing through swamps. Its wide mouth had jaws studded

with small sharp teeth, and its tail had low but long fins on the upper side and underside. It had gills but it could almost certainly also breathe air.

Ichthyostega was slightly longer and bulkier than *Acanthostega*, and also dwelled in fresh water. It lived around the same time, during the Late Devonian period some 360 million years ago, and in the same region, present-day Greenland. It was more heavily built and had more powerful limbs, especially the front pair. For many years it was regarded as the main ancestor of modern tetrapods, but because of the details of its skeletal structure it is now generally seen as being on a "side branch" of the tetrapods' family tree. It had seven toes on each back foot, compared to *Acanthostega*'s eight on the front feet. Even earlier tetrapods include the recently re-studied *Elginerpeton* from fossils preserved in Scotland from almost 370 million years ago.

ABOVE Tailed, four-legged amphibians today are represented by salamanders and newts, such as this European fire salamander.

RIGHT The numbers of toes of early amphibian-type animals like *Ichthyostega* have been much disputed, ranging from four to eight per foot.

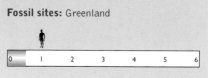

ANIMAL FACTFILE

Acanthostega

Meaning: Spine or thorn plate

Pronunciation: Ak-anne-thoe-stay-gah

Period: Late Devonian

Main group: Tetrapoda

Length: 1 meter (39 inches)

Diet: Animals

Fossil sites: Greenland

EOGYRINUS

The amphibious four-legged vertebrates known as anthracosaurs persisted for more than 100 million years – almost the same time span as the Age of Dinosaurs. Many types came and went, among them the massive *Eogyrinus*. It was one of the longest of all amphibian-type animals and one of the largest of all the creatures of its time. *Eogyrinus*, like *Seymouria* (on the following page), belonged to the subgroup that arose in the Late Carboniferous period, more than 300 million years ago, but had died out by the end of the next period, the Permian.

At nearly 5 meters (16^1/$_2$ feet), *Eogyrinus* would rival most crocodiles today in overall length. Its body shape also was similar to a crocodile's, although generally slimmer, as was its skull, with long, powerful jaws equipped with sharp teeth. Its limbs were relatively small and weak, however, and on land *Eogyrinus* may have moved by a combination of wriggling, slithering and pushing with its feet. Its tail was extremely long, resembling a modern eel's, with a long dorsal fin on the upper side. This suggests that it lived mainly in water, and swam by lashing the tail from side to side, again like a crocodile. *Eogyrinus* lived at a time of warm, humid conditions when much of the land was covered by thick forests of giant ferns and other swamp-loving "coal forest" plants. It probably preyed on victims such as fish and smaller tetrapods.

ANIMAL FACTFILE
Eogyrinus
Meaning: Dawn ring or circle
Pronunciation: Ee-owe-jiy-rin-uss
Period: Late Carboniferous
Main group: Tetrapoda (Anthracosauria)
Length: 4.6 meters (15 feet)
Diet: Medium-sized prey
Fossil sites: Europe

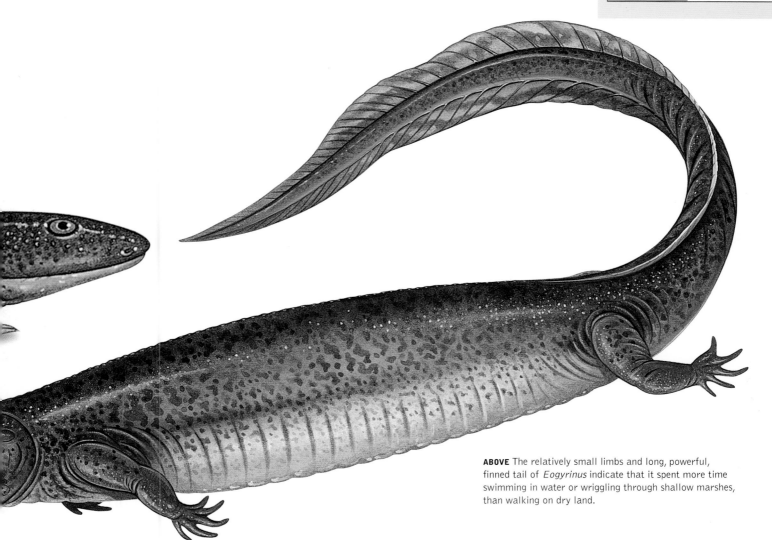

ABOVE The relatively small limbs and long, powerful, finned tail of *Eogyrinus* indicate that it spent more time swimming in water or wriggling through shallow marshes, than walking on dry land.

SEYMOURIA

ANIMAL FACTFILE

Seymouria

Meaning: Of Seymour (its discovery site)

Pronunciation: see-moor-ee-ah

Period: Permian

Main group: Tetrapoda (Anthracosauria)

Length: 60 centimeters (2 feet)

Weight: 10–15 kilograms (22-23 pounds)

Diet: Smaller animals

Fossil sites: North America, Europe

Many excellently preserved fossils of this 60-centimeter (2-foot) predator have been found in rocks in Texas known as the Red Beds. The rocks, which date back to the Permian period, have also yielded remains of many other impressive creatures, such as the "sailback" *Dimetrodon* (described later in this chapter). *Seymouria* was named after the town of Seymour, Texas, where some of its fossils were uncovered. It resembled a large lizard or even a crocodile, with a wide mouth and sharp teeth for grabbing prey. *Seymouria* was a member of the amphibious group called the tetrapods, like other creatures shown so far in this chapter. Within this main group, it is placed in the anthracosaur subgroup, like *Eogyrinus* (on the previous page). Fossils of other animals and also plants found with those of *Seymouria* show that the habitat of the time was fairly dry upland, here and there dotted with rivers and lakes. Although *Seymouria* was able to live on both land and in water, it probably dwelled mostly on land.

The scientists who first studied the remains of *Seymouria* thought that it might be a reptile. It had reptilian features, including the structure of its shoulder bones and hipbones, and the joints between the skull and the cervical vertebrae (neck backbones). However, there were small details that were not reptilian, such as the presence of lines on the skulls of young specimens. These usually accommodated the lateral line sense that detects waterborne vibrations, clearly seen as a line along each side of the body in fish. Several types of *Seymouria* are known from most of the Permian period.

RIGHT A fine specimen of *Seymouria* from Texas showing the sturdy or robust construction of the skeleton, with thick-set bones for carrying considerable weight on land.

BELOW *Seymouria* was a tough, reptilian-looking tetrapod well adapted to dry land. But it retained amphibious features such as the lateral line, seen as a stripe along length of the upper body, which detects ripples and vibrations when submerged in water.

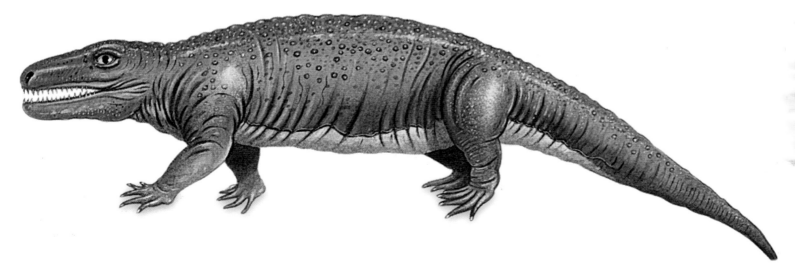

DIADECTES

The four-legged land vertebrates known generally as "amphibians" were all meat-eaters, or perhaps scavengers, until the appearance of creatures such as *Diadectes* in the Early Permian period. Its front teeth were spoon-shaped and stuck out slightly from the jaw at a forward angle, while its back teeth were broad and suited to crushing. This arrangement seems to indicate that it gathered plant matter and chewed it at length, although an alternative suggestion is that it picked up shellfish with the probing front teeth and crunched them with the rear teeth. However, the wide, bulky body of *Diadectes* also indicates a slow herbivore rather than a fast-moving predator. Indeed, it was one of the largest land-dwellers of its time, at 3 meters (10 feet) in length. Its shoulder bones and hipbones were very large, to anchor the powerful muscles that moved its four sturdy limbs. It may have used its large, strong feet, with their five blunt-clawed digits, to dig up plant matter. Its tail was relatively short and thin.

Diadectes had several reptilian features in its bones, especially in its skull. It had a partly developed secondary bony palate (the "shelf" that separates the mouth cavity from the nose chamber), allowing more convenient breathing through the nasal airways while the mouth was full of food. This feature is found in certain more advanced reptiles. At one stage, *Diadectes* was suggested as an ancestor for the herbivorous reptiles, but plant-eating was being taken up already, at around the same time as *Diadectes* lived, by reptiles, or reptile-like creatures, such as *Edaphosaurus*.

ANIMAL FACTFILE
Diadectes
Meaning: Biter-through, penetrating bite
Pronunciation: Dye-ah-deck-teez
Period: Early Permian
Main group: Tetrapoda (Diadectomorpha)
Length: 3 meters (10 feet)
Weight: Up to 100 kilograms (220 pounds)
Diet: Plants
Fossil sites: North America, Europe

LEFT *Diadectes* was one of the first amphibian-like tetrapods to take up plant-eating, at least, if the suggestion is correct that its teeth were adapted to raking in and chewing plant material.

ERYOPS

ANIMAL FACTFILE

Eryops

Meaning: Long eye

Pronunciation: Air-ee-ops

Periods: Late Carboniferous and Permian

Main group: Temnospondylii

Length: Up to 2 meters (6½ feet)

Weight: 50–70 kilograms (110–154 pounds)

Diet: Smaller animals, carrion

Fossil sites: USA (Oklahoma, Texas,
New Mexico)

Many of the large, four-legged, amphibian-type creatures which lived in Carboniferous and Permian times belonged to the very successful and long-lasting temnospondyl group. Another of its members was *Eryops*. Its name, which means "long eye," was coined in 1887 by Edward Drinker Cope, an American fossil-hunter, as he hurried to name dozens of dinosaurs and many other creatures. *Eryops* certainly had a broad, long-snouted head, with powerful jaws that bore many small, spiky teeth. The entire build of the creature was sturdy and strong, with a bulky wide body, short but well-built legs, and a medium-length, tapering, finless tail. It was probably a semi-aquatic hunter. It could have lurked in swamps, with just its eyes and nostrils (on the top of its head) showing above the water, or it might have prowled riverbanks and lakeshores for any likely prey.

Fossils of *Eryops* have been found at various sites in Oklahoma, Texas, New Mexico, and other parts of North America. Its kind survived for several million years, into the Permian period, when they faced competition from newly evolving large predators of the mammal-like reptile group. The temnospondyls, which appeared in the Early Carboniferous period, 350 million years ago, persisted for 150 million years. They became extinct by the Early Jurassic when larger meat-eating dinosaurs known as therapods began to dominate the land. However, during their long time span, some temnospondyls may have given rise to the ancestors of today's amphibians, the frogs and toads, known as lissamphibians.

RIGHT The enormous mouth of *Eryops* would be difficult to open on land, because of the weight of the head and lower jaw, the position of the jaw joint, and the need to lift the head clear of the ground. So *Eryops* probably hunted in water, grabbing prey like fish in its massive gape.

BELOW *Gerrothorax* had a strong, wide head shield, presumably for protection. Yet behind this protruded its delicate, feathery gill filaments, which it used for breathing underwater even when adult. One suggestion is that the filaments could be withdrawn under the shield.

GERROTHORAX

Amphibian animals such as frogs and toads begin life as aquatic young – as larvae or tadpoles – that breathe in water by means of gills. A few of today's amphibians – for example, the axolotl – keep their gills and continue to live underwater even when adult. The same is true for *Gerrothorax*, a 1-meter (39-inch) predator which lived during Late Triassic times, when the dinosaurs were beginning to spread and take over the land.

Gerrothorax is regarded as a member of the temnospondyl group, along with *Eryops* (see page 84, opposite). Its fossils have been recovered from several sites in Sweden, southern Germany, and other parts of Europe.

Gerrothorax looked like a tubby tadpole growing four small, weak limbs. Three pairs of feathery gills protruded from the sides of the head, just behind the animal's most distinctive feature – its strange-shaped skull. This was extraordinarily wide, and extended

into pointed "wings" on either side. Both the head and body were flattened and armored with tough "plates." Perhaps *Gerrothorax*'s most remarkable feature, its very large, close-set eyes were situated on the top of the skull, meaning that it could look only upward. It has been suggested that this ambush-predator lay in wait for prey on the bed of a swamp or lake, perhaps camouflaged by its coloring and unusual outline. It would then suddenly lunge upward to swallow its victims in its gaping mouth.

Gerrothorax showed a combination of immature or larval-type (tadpole) features in what was presumably a sexually mature body, able to reproduce. Several kinds of modern amphibians like the axolotl mentioned above also retain juvenile features in the sexually mature state. This condition is known as neoteny.

ANIMAL FACTFILE
Gerrothorax
Meaning: Chest carrier
Pronunciation: Jeh-row-thore-acks
Period: Late Triassic
Main group: Temnospondylii
Length: 1 meter (39 inches)
Weight: 20–25 kilograms (44–55 pounds)
Diet: Smaller animals
Fossil sites: Europe

Diplocaulus

ANIMAL FACTFILE

Diplocaulus

Meaning: Two stems, double stalk

Pronunciation: Dip-low-kawl-uss

Period: Permian

Main group: Lepospondyli

Length: 1 meter (39 inches)

Diet: Small animals

Fossil sites: USA (Texas)

Although its name means "double stalk," *Diplocaulus* is informally known as "boomerang head." This was yet another amphibian-type freshwater creature that is known from fossils in the Permian rocks of Texas. It is placed in the group called the lepospondyls, which were common during the Carboniferous and Permian periods, but did not make it into the Triassic period, at the start of the Age of Dinosaurs. Nevertheless, they may have given rise to the modern amphibians, such as frogs and newts.

Some lepospondyls were shaped like newts or salamanders, and are known as nectrideans. *Diplocaulus* was a nectridean too, but it was unusual in many ways. *Diplocaulus* was very flat, with a low skull, a wide, pancake-like body, and a short tail with small fins running along the upper side and underside. Its limbs were small and flat, and stuck out sideways

from the body. The large eyes on the upper side of the almost horizontal face could see upward as well as sideways. All this suggests a bottom-dweller, watching the waters above for food and danger. *Diplocaulus* also had backswept "wings" on its head, formed from an extended bone at the rear of each side of the skull, which tapered to a point. There are many ideas about the functions of these extensions. They may have made the head so wide that even the larger predators of the time could not fit *Diplocaulus* into their mouths. On the other hand, since their shape, more curved on the upper surface than the lower, is reminiscent of an airplane wing, it has been suggested that they may have been "water wings," with water flowing past lifting the head, perhaps as *Diplocaulus* swam from one resting place to another.

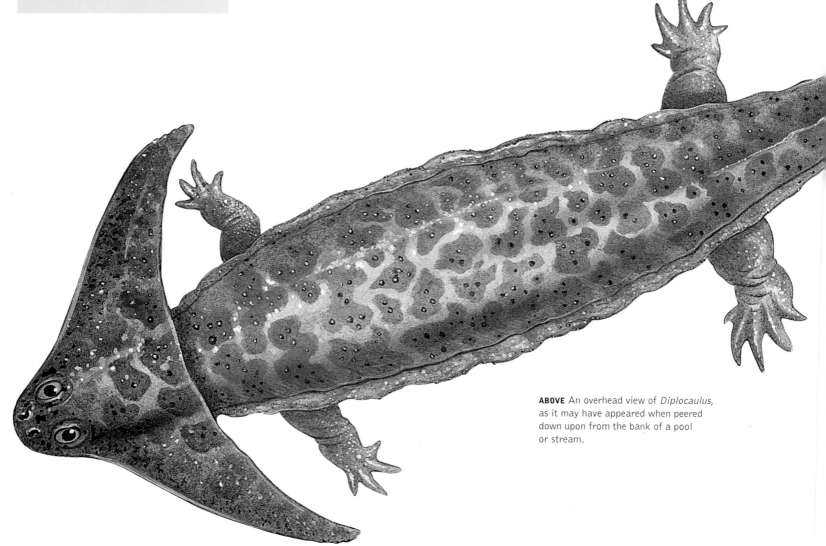

ABOVE An overhead view of *Diplocaulus*, as it may have appeared when peered down upon from the bank of a pool or stream.

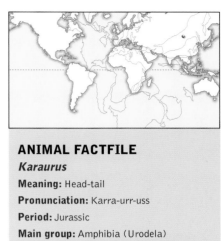

RIGHT Frogs, like salamanders, show "conservative" evolution. They have changed little in more than 200 million years and so they fit into the category of "living fossils." This specimen fossilized more than 40 million years ago.

RIGHT *Karaurus* would be difficult to distinguish from salamanders today such as the tiger salamander of North America and the fire salamander of Eurasia. It probably lived a similar lifestyle as a voracious predator in damp forests.

ANIMAL FACTFILE
Karaurus
Meaning: Head-tail
Pronunciation: Karra-urr-uss
Period: Jurassic
Main group: Amphibia (Urodela)
Length: 20 centimeters (8 inches)
Diet: Small animals
Fossil sites: Central Asia

0	1	2	3	4	5	6

TRIADOBATRACHUS AND KARAURUS

From the many and hugely varied amphibian-type creatures of prehistory, only three main groups survive today. These are frogs and toads (anurans or salientians); salamanders and newts (caudatans or urodelans); and the caecilians or apodans (gymnophiones), which are less familiar and worm-shaped. Together the three groups are called lissamphibians.

The earliest frog-like creature in the fossil record is a single specimen known from rocks in Madagascar and dated to the Early Triassic period, around 240 million years ago – before the dinosaurs evolved. This creature, *Triadobatrachus*, was just 10 centimeters (4 inches) long, including its very short tail, a feature which nearly all modern frogs lack. Its back legs were longer and more powerful than the front ones, but not greatly so. This is another feature which suggests that *Triadobatrachus* was intermediate between

modern frogs and their probable ancestors, a subgroup of the lepospondyls (see *Diplocaulus*, page 86, opposite). In many other respects, *Triadobatrachus* looked like a modern frog and probably behaved like one.

Karaurus was one of the earliest known tailed amphibians, or salamanders. It dated from Late Jurassic times and was very similar to salamanders of today, despite the intervening time span of 150 million years. It had a broad head, four strong legs and a total length of 20 centimeters (8 inches).

Karaurus was probably a small but fierce predator, preying on even smaller animals, such as insects, worms and grubs. It could most likely move about on land as well as in water in the moist Jurassic forests, keeping out of the way of the giant sauropod dinosaurs of that time.

Fossils of *Karaurus* have been found in Kazakhstan, Central Asia.

ANIMAL FACTFILE
Triadobatrachus
Meaning: Triassic frog
Pronunciation: Try-add-owe-bat-rack-uss
Period: Triassic
Main group: Amphibia (Anura)
Length: 10 centimeters (4 inches)
Diet: Insects and other small creatures
Fossil sites: Madagascar

0	1	2	3	4	5	6

FREE OF THE WATER

EARLY TETRAPODS (SHOWN ON PREVIOUS PAGES)
PROBABLY LAID THEIR EGGS IN WATER, AS TODAY'S
FROGS DO, AND SO WERE TIED TO AQUATIC
HABITATS DURING THE EARLY STAGES IN THEIR
LIFE CYCLES. REPTILES BROKE FREE OF THIS
CONSTRAINT WITH FEATURES SUCH AS SCALY
RATHER THAN MOIST SKIN, WHICH PREVENTS
WATER LOSS FROM THE BODY; AND AMNIOTIC EGGS,
WITH TOUGH, WATERPROOF SHELLS AND INTERNAL
FOOD SUPPLIES OF YOLK, WHICH COULD BE LAID
ON LAND.

RIGHT Some 300 million years ago one of the earliest known
reptiles, *Hylonomus*, stalked along the woody stem of a giant
clubmoss. Its head-and-body were not much larger than a
human finger. *Hylonomus* outwardly resembled today's lizards,
as did many kinds of prehistoric reptiles, but it belonged to a
very different reptilian group.

MESOSAURUS

ANIMAL FACTFILE

Mesosaurus

Meaning: Middle reptile

Pronunciation: Mezz-owe-sore-uss

Period: Permian

Main group: Reptilia

Length: 70–100 centimeters
(28–39 inches)

Diet: Small food items

Fossil sites: Brazil, southern Africa

0	1	2	3	4	5	6

BELOW *Mesosaurus* swam mainly with its large webbed rear feet and long-finned tail.

RIGHT The ribs of the mesosaurs were thickened to resist water pressure, and with the sturdy limb girdles (shoulders and hips), provided firm anchorage for the swimming muscles.

It may seem strange that, after reptiles had spent millions of years of evolution becoming free of the water, some returned to an aquatic life. *Mesosaurus* was one of the first reptiles known to have done this. It had features that make it seem like a combination of modern lizards, crocodiles and salamanders, although it was only distantly related to any of these creatures. It had a very long tail, extensively finned both on the upper and lower midlines; large limbs with big webbed feet, the rear pair being even larger than the front pair; and a long, slim body. Its skull was likewise slim and elongated, and the narrow jaws were full of long, needle-like teeth. The total length of *Mesosaurus* was up to 1 meter (39 inches), but, being so slim, it was a relatively small predator. It probably pursued small fish, shrimps and other prey of the same relative size. Its plentiful, spiky teeth were used as grabbing tools or stabbing weapons or perhaps

Mesosaurus gaped its mouth wide and closed it around small prey so that its teeth trapped them like the bars of a cage.

Mesosaurus has given its name to a group of freshwater reptiles, the mesosaurs, that appeared during the Permian period, more than 250 million years ago, but did not survive its end. Their relationship to other reptiles is unclear, although they are usually viewed as a companion group to pareiasaurs and other early reptiles. Fossils of *Mesosaurus* have been found in both South America and Africa. Several other fossil reptiles and other creatures show a similar distribution between these two continents. This is taken as further evidence – in addition to geological similarities, and the close "fit" between their coastlines – that these two great land masses were joined during the Permian period, and drifted apart as the Atlantic Ocean was formed at a later time (see maps, page 26).

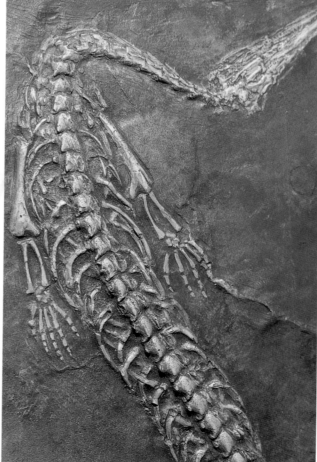

LEFT *Proganochelys* chomps on soft plants, cutting the vegetation with its sharp-rimmed jaws. Then, as today, tortoises were messy eaters – some food simply falls out of the mouth.

PROGANOCHELYS

The turtles and tortoises form a specialized group of reptiles known as chelonians. Their characteristic feature is, of course, their shell, which is made of two parts, the upper forming a domed carapace over the back and the flatter plastron covering the underside. Each part has two layers, an inner one of bony plates and an outer one of horny plates, and each layer is made of many of these plates joined at the edges, like a jigsaw puzzle. The first chelonians, known from the fossil record of the Triassic period, were strikingly similar to their modern relatives, despite a gap of more than 200 million years.

Proganochelys lived at around the same time as the early dinosaurs. It had a fully formed shell of some 60 plates, as all-over protection against land predators: it was a terrestrial chelonian, or tortoise, rather than a water-dwelling turtle. It also had a spiky tail, perhaps tipped with a lump of bone. Unlike many

modern chelonians, *Proganochelys* could not pull its head or legs into its shell for even better protection. However, it had the typical chelonian skeletal structure – shoulder bones and hipbones within the rib cage rather than outside it, and wide, flat ribs attached to the inside of the shell along with the vertebrae (backbones). *Proganochelys* also possessed the typical chelonian jaws, which lack teeth but have sharp bony edges for chopping through plant food. Fossils of *Proganochelys* come from rocks in southern Germany and possibly also Thailand. Similar creatures, also land-dwellers, are known from slightly later fossils found on other continents, including Africa, Asia and North America. (See also *Archelon*, page 96.) They and *Proganochelys* had bony lumps or knobs on the head and neck to help protect these parts, and hard lumps on the palate inside the mouth, to help squash and mash food which the sharp-rimmed jaws had cropped.

ANIMAL FACTFILE
Proganochelys

Meaning: Before lustrous chelonian

Pronunciation: Pro-gan-owe-kell-iss

Period: Late Triassic

Main group: Reptilia (Chelonia)

Length: Shell 60 centimeters (2 feet)

Diet: Plants

Fossil sites: Germany, also possibly Thailand, Africa, North America

| 0 | 1 | 2 | 3 | 4 | 5 | 6 |

HYLONOMUS

ANIMAL FACTFILE
Hylonomus
Meaning: Forest mouse
Pronunciation: High-low-nom-uss
Period: Late Carboniferous
Main group: Reptilia
Length: Head to tail 20 centimeters (8 inches)
Diet: Small animals
Fossil sites: Canada (Nova Scotia)

Hylonomus is generally regarded, if not as the first known reptile, then as one of the very earliest. It was fully adapted for life on land, with no gills or skeletal features in common with the many amphibian-type animals described on previous pages. *Hylonomus* fossils are known from rocks of the Late Carboniferous period, some 300 million years ago, at the Joggins site in Nova Scotia (eastern Canada). The total length of *Hylonomus* was 20 centimeters (8 inches), including its long, flexible tail. Its strong skull and sturdy jaws had small, cone-shaped, sharp-pointed teeth, so *Hylonomus* was probably a predator of insects, worms and similar small creatures. In general appearance, it resembled a modern lizard, but it lived long before this type of reptile appeared, and had different skeletal features. *Hylonomus* is pictured here perhaps about to become trapped as described below.

Many specimens of *Hylonomus* have been found beautifully preserved inside the old, rotten stumps of giant club mosses, known as *Sigillaria*, that grew as large as some modern trees. Perhaps *Hylonomus* was hibernating, sheltering from adverse conditions such as a drought or cooler spell. However, other creatures such as insects and millipedes also populated these sites. More probably, the club moss forest was flooded, perhaps by salty water, causing the plants to die and topple, and leaving the lower stumps in the ground. These gradually rotted from within to leave bucket-like holes. Small creatures could have fallen into these, as perhaps did *Hylonomus*; or it may have climbed in to eat them, become trapped, and eventually died. The stump interiors would then have been filled with mud during the next flood, and the long process of fossilization could begin.

BELOW This illustration shows *Hylonomus* approximately life-sized. It was slim, long-legged, big-footed and whippy-tailed, suggesting a fast, darting mover like a modern lizard. However the lizard group would not evolve for another 50-plus million years.

LEFT One of the first very large reptiles, the pareiasaur *Scutosaurus* foreshadowed the big, armored, plant-eating dinosaurs which would evolve more than 100 million years later.

SCUTOSAURUS

This massive beast was as big as a modern rhinoceros, and had a protective covering of bony plates, spikes and knobs. It therefore looks similar to some of the armored or plated dinosaurs, such as *Ankylosaurus*. It was an entirely different type of reptile, however, and not a dinosaur at all. It belonged among the pareiasaurs, which were in turn part of a larger group of very early reptiles called the parareptiles. (In some older classification schemes, pareiasaurs are included in an alternative group, the captorhinids or cotylosaurs.)

Pareiasaurs were among the first really large reptiles. They were squat, heavy plant-eaters that used the serrated (saw-toothed) edges of the leaf-like teeth in their jaws, and also on their palates, to nip off and shred large quantities of plants, such as horsetails and ferns. Their strong, pillar-like legs were angled slightly diagonally from the body, and

then downward at the joints, rather than supporting the body directly from straight underneath, as in dinosaurs.

Scutosaurus had a very short tail, five blunt curved claws on each of its broad feet, irregular conical lumps over its back, and a skull extended at the cheeks as a type of neck shield.

There were many lumps, bumps and warty growths on its head – in particular, a downward-facing spike grew from the rear of each side of the lower jaw, and small groups of lumps were set on the snout. These structures seem to have first appeared in juveniles and thereafter enlarged with age.

As in the dinosaurs later, these spikes and lumps of *Scutosaurus* may have been merely for display – signs of physical maturity and readiness to breed – or they may have been actual weapons used against rivals at breeding time, or against enemies.

ANIMAL FACTFILE
Scutosaurus
Meaning: Shield reptile

Pronunciation: Skoot-owe-sore-uss

Period: Middle to Late Permian

Main group: Reptilia

Length: 2.5 meters (8½ feet)

Diet: Plants

Fossil sites: Eastern Europe, southern and eastern Africa

REPTILES DIVERSIFY

THE FIRST REPTILES APPEARED SOME 300 MILLION YEARS AGO, TOWARD THE END OF THE CARBONIFEROUS PERIOD. THE NEXT PERIOD, THE PERMIAN, SAW A RAPID INCREASE IN SIZE, SHAPE AND DIVERSITY, AS A BEWILDERING ARRAY OF REPTILE GROUPS APPEARED — PAREIASAURS, MESOSAURS, NEODIAPSIDS, WEIGELTISAURS AND MANY OTHERS. SOME LASTED FOR JUST A FEW TENS OF MILLIONS OF YEARS, AS THEY COMPETED WITH EACH OTHER FOR SURVIVAL ON LAND AND IN WATER.

RIGHT Crocodiles are the great survivors from the age of reptiles. They arose at about the same time as the dinosaurs, at first as terrestrial predators, but most kinds moved to a semi-aquatic lifestyle. *Sarcosuchus* was a giant of the group and lived 110 million years ago in what is now the desert of north Africa.

RIGHT The huge front flippers of *Archelon* were each well over one meter (39 inches) long, and flapped up and down with a "flying underwater" motion, rather than rowing forward and backward.

ANIMAL FACTFILE

Archelon

Meaning: Ruling chelonian, ruling turtle

Pronunciation: Ark-eh-lon

Period: Late Cretaceous

Main group: Reptilia (Chelonia)

Length: 4-plus meters (12-plus feet)

Diet: Probably soft-bodied sea creatures

Fossil sites: USA (Kansas, South Dakota)

ARCHELON

Following their first appearance in the Triassic period, the chelonians – the turtles and tortoises – spread widely and soon evolved into a variety of sizes, although their overall shape was less varied. The largest chelonian that ever lived, as far as known from the fossil record, was the massive *Archelon* of the Late Cretaceous period. Its shell was 3.7 meters (12^1/$_2$ feet) long, which is twice the length of the shell of the biggest chelonian today, the leatherback turtle. The span between the tips of *Archelon*'s outstretched front limbs, or flippers, was around the same. All four limbs were greatly modified for swimming, with enormously powerful shoulder and hip muscles, and the five digits on each of its huge feet were enclosed in a large paddle-like web or "mitten." The front limbs provided most of the propulsion, flapping up and down with a motion like that of a bird's wings.

Archelon roamed the seas toward the end of the dinosaur age. Its jaws, though weak and toothless, were sharply rimmed and scissor-like, so that as in some of today's marine turtles (including the leatherback) *Archelon* fed by chopping up jellyfish and similar soft-bodied sea animals. Also like the leatherback, *Archelon* had a shell that was not a solid dome of bony plates, as in other chelonians, but comprised of bony struts with wide spaces between. In life, this scaffolding-like structure was probably covered and filled in by tough, thick, rubbery skin – hence the name of its modern relative, the leatherback. This greatly reduced the amount of bone and consequently the weight of the turtle, although its mass was usually buoyed up by water. Still, *Archelon* probably came ashore to lay its eggs, like all chelonians (and all reptiles) today. The need to move briefly on land may have limited its size.

YOUNGINA

Over half of all the species of reptiles in the world today are lizards – there are more than 4,500 different types. Their evolutionary origins are unclear and much debated. Part of the problem is that, from the outside, many prehistoric reptiles looked extremely similar to lizards, although further study of the details of their skulls and skeletons has shown that there were different types of reptiles. At one time, *Youngina* was suggested as the ancestor of the lizard group, mainly because of similarities in the rear parts of the skull. Now, however, this long, slim reptile is regarded as a member of the group known as neodiapsids, named from the two openings or "windows" in each side of the skull, one of them just behind the eye socket. Most neodiapsids lived during the Permian and Early Triassic periods. Their parent group, the diapsids, is one of the major reptile groups. The neodiapsids – but not

Youngina itself – probably gave rise to two of the greatest reptile groups of all: the squamates, including lizards and snakes; and the archosaurs, including crocodiles and dinosaurs and also the pterosaurs.

Youngina was so long and slim, with small legs and a strong skull bearing a long, low, pointed snout, that it resembled the burrowing lizards of today. Fossil specimens of several juvenile *Youngina* were found preserved in a burrow, where it appears they gathered for shelter, perhaps to escape extreme temperatures outside. *Youngina*'s sharp teeth indicate that it was a predator of worms, grubs, insects and other small creatures. But its teeth were unusual in that they grew on the inside of the mouth – on the palate – as well as along the rims of the jaws. *Youngina* was named in 1914 by Robert Broom and includes genera formerly known as *Youngoides* and *Youngopsis*.

ANIMAL FACTFILE
Youngina
Meaning: Of Young
Pronunciation: Yung-in-ah
Period: Late Permian
Main group: Reptilia
Length: Up to 50 centimeters (20 inches) head to tail
Diet: Small creatures
Fossil sites: South Africa

RIGHT The sharp claws of *Youngina* were suited to scratching in loose soil for small animal prey and perhaps to digging burrows for shelter.

Coelurosauravus and Icarosaurus

ANIMAL FACTFILE
Coelurosauravus

Meaning: Coelurosaur grandfather

Pronunciation: Seel-yur-owe-sore-av-uss

Period: Late Permian

Main group: Reptilia

Length: Head to tail 60 centimeters (2 feet)

Diet: Insects and similar small creatures

Fossil sites: Europe, Madagascar

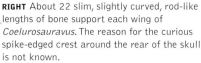

So-called "flying lizards" evolved at various times through prehistory and also live today in the forests of Southeast Asia. In fact, none of them has ever really been able to fly – they have all been gliders – and by no means were all of them lizards. *Coelurosauravus* was a member of a different reptile group, the weigeltisaurs, named for *Weigeltisaurus*, a similar glider from the Late Permian period, whose fossils have been found in Germany and England. Weigeltisaurs were diapsid reptiles, like *Youngina* (see previous page). *Coelurosauravus* had a lizard-like shape and small, sharp teeth, but its most distinctive features were its two large "wings." Each consisted of long, thin rods of bone supporting a skin-like gliding membrane. The "wings" could be extended like fans for gliding or folded along the body when not in use. *Coelurosauravus* had long toes with sharp claws

to grip bark as it scampered, jumped at take off and then landed among the trees. The wings could be tilted or changed in shape slightly by muscles at the rod bases.

The thin bony struts of the wings of *Coelurosauravus* were not connected to other parts of the skeleton. In the modern flying lizard *Draco*, they are connected. The gliding membranes of this true lizard are held out by long, thin extensions of the ribs. *Draco* glides mainly to escape enemies or to move to new feeding places. *Icarosaurus* was a similar creature from the Late Triassic period. Its fossils were found in New Jersey. Another glider of the same time and type was *Kuehneosaurus*, which lived in what is now western England. These creatures were close cousins of early lizards. Their wings were longer and slimmer than those of today, but were held out in the same way on very long, slim, extended ribs.

RIGHT About 22 slim, slightly curved, rod-like lengths of bone support each wing of *Coelurosauravus*. The reason for the curious spike-edged crest around the rear of the skull is not known.

ANIMAL FACTFILE
Icarosaurus

Meaning: Icarus reptile

Pronunciation: Ik-ah-roe-sore-uss

Period: Late Triassic

Main group: Reptilia

Length: 40 centimeters (16 inches)

Diet: Small animals

Fossil sites: USA (New Jersey)

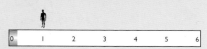

DINILYSIA

The snakes, with almost 3,000 living species, make up the second-largest group of living reptiles. They have their own subgroup, Serpentes, but are included with the lizards, Lacertilia, in the larger group known as the squamates. Some experts propose that snakes evolved from lizards, some time during the Early to mid-Cretaceous period, more than 100 million years ago. Perhaps some lizards took to a burrowing way of life and lost their limbs completely. Then some of these newly evolved snakes, in turn, gave up tunneling and lived again on the surface, up in trees or even in water. After all, a few lizards today, such as the slow worm, are limbless. Another proposal is that snakes evolved from the same reptiles that gave rise to the ferocious sea reptiles known as mosasaurs (see page 397).

The most ancient types of modern snakes are the pythons and boas, which kill their prey by suffocation – coiling around and squeezing, or constricting, the breath out of them. *Dinilysia* was perhaps a very early snake of this kind. It lived in Patagonia, in the southeastern corner of South America, during the Late Cretaceous period, when the Age of Dinosaurs was coming to an end. It was about 1.8 meters (6 feet) long and had the typical snake skeleton: a skull of loosely connected, strut-like bones; sharp teeth in its jaws; and a long body made up chiefly of dozens of vertebrae (backbones), each with a pair of ribs. *Dinilysia* had small, vestigial limb bones. Some of today's pythons and boas still retain tiny vestiges of their rear limb bones, but not the front ones, which have completely disappeared. The hip parts are encased within the muscle and flesh of the rear lower body, and what is left of the leg is just visible on the surface as a small claw or spur.

ANIMAL FACTFILE
Dinilysia
Meaning: Two lilies or flowers
Pronunciation: Die-nill-iz-ee-ah
Period: Late Cretaceous
Main group: Reptilia
Length: 1.8 meters (6 feet)
Diet: Smaller animals
Fossil sites: South America

LEFT The fossilized remains of a snake. Boas and pythons, the constrictors, were the first kind to evolve. Venomous snakes are not known to have existed until before about 30 million years ago.

BELOW *Dinilysia* wraps itself around a young Cretaceous crocodile and begins to squeeze away its breath. The modern constricting snake called the anaconda, from the Amazon region, does much the same to the living crocodiles called caimans.

SCAPHONYX

ANIMAL FACTFILE

Scaphonyx

Meaning: Canoe claw

Pronunciation: Ska-fonn-icks

Period: Middle to Late Triassic

Main group: Reptilia (Rhynchosauria)

Length: Head and body 1.8 meters (6 feet)

Weight: 40 kilograms (88 pounds)

Diet: Plants

Fossil sites: South America

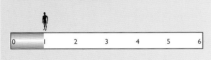

Rhynchosaurs such as *Scaphonyx* are sometimes referred to as the "sheep of the Triassic." Being reptiles and not mammals, they had scales rather than wool, but they were very numerous plant-eaters, around the same size as modern sheep, and can be imagined dotted over the landscape, munching on low-growing plants such as ferns. (There were no flowers, herbs or grasses at the time.) Also, like some sheep today, rhynchosaurs were probably occasional victims of large predators – in their case, early dinosaurs such as *Herrerasaurus* and the mainly land-dwelling crocodiles of the time.

Rhynchosaurs were related to the major archosaur group of reptiles, which included crocodiles and dinosaurs. *Scaphonyx* was typical, with its bulky pig-like body, squat but sturdy limbs, thick tail, and upper jaw that curved down at its pointed tip like a bird's beak.

(The name rhynchosaur means "beak reptile.") Some rhynchosaurs had skulls that widened in the cheek region to form small neck frills or shields. The beak probably hooked and gathered vegetation, and the many broad-topped chewing teeth were arranged in long rows in the cheek region. The lower jaws were narrow-edged and fitted into grooves in the upper jaws, so that the teeth came together with a combined chopping, shearing and crushing action.

Rhynchosaurs were very abundant, but only for a relatively short time. In some areas which are rich and varied in fossil remains, those of rhynchosaurs make up more than half of all the preserved larger plant-eating animals. They faded away at the end of the Triassic period, perhaps in the face of competition for food as herbivorous dinosaurs spread across the land.

RIGHT The narrow, hooked, parrot-like beak of herbivorous *Scaphonyx* was a recurrent plant-cropping design in prehistoric times. Several types of dinosaurs evolved very similar features, including the horned dinosaurs or ceratopsians such as *Triceratops*.

DEINOSUCHUS (PHOBOSUCHUS)

For decades, *Deinosuchus* has enjoyed fame as the largest crocodile that ever lived. But it now has a rival, discovered in 1970, in *Sarcosuchus* (see page 387). This is partly because specimens of *Sarcosuchus* discovered in Africa show that it grew bigger than was believed from its remains found earlier in South America. It is also because recent studies of the fossil skull of *Deinosuchus*, which is the only part discovered, have resulted in reduced estimates of the animal's total length, from more than 15 meters (16$^1/_2$ yards) to nearer 10 meters (11 yards). Even at this reduced estimate, *Deinosuchus* was larger still than the biggest crocodile and biggest reptile today, the saltwater crocodile of southern and Southeast Asia and Australia. *Deinosuchus* lived a few tens of millions of years

later than *Sarcosuchus*, and on a different continent, North America.

The skull of *Deinosuchus* measures more than 2 meters (2 yards) from front to back and has a broad rather than narrow snout. Its proportions are similar to the skull of today's Nile crocodile, which specializes in hunting large prey like antelope and zebra. *Deinosuchus* probably lurked in rivers or swamps, waiting for prey to come and drink from the water's edge. It would grab the victim in its massive jaws, studded with long but not especially sharp teeth, and then drag it into the water to drown, or perhaps spin around lengthwise like a top, to tear off chunks of flesh. Its prey probably included dinosaurs and, perhaps, large fish or swimming reptiles.

ANIMAL FACTFILE
Deinosuchus

Meaning: Terrible crocodile

Pronunciation: Day-no-sook-uss

Period: Late Cretaceous

Main group: Reptilia (Crocodilia)

Length: 10 meters (11 yards) some estimates up to 15 meters (16$^1/_2$ yards)

Weight: 2-3 metric tons (2-3 tons)

Diet: Large animals

Fossil sites: USA (Texas)

0	1	2	3	4	5	6

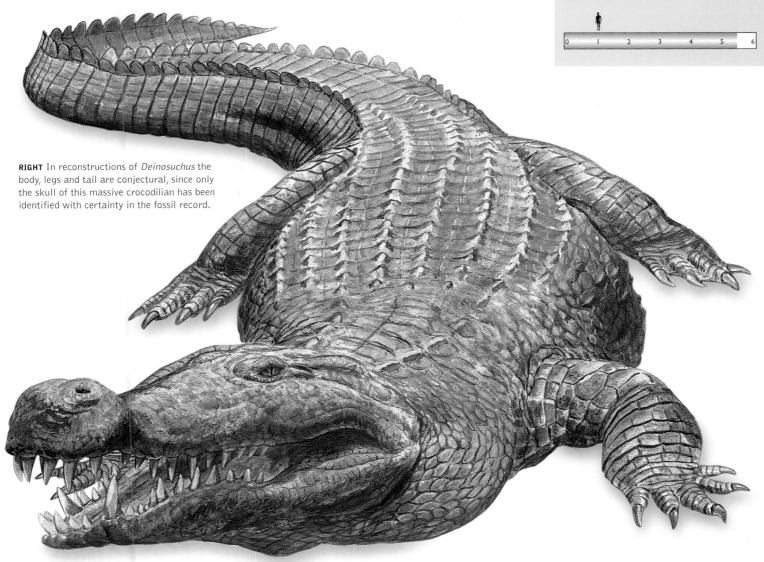

RIGHT In reconstructions of *Deinosuchus* the body, legs and tail are conjectural, since only the skull of this massive crocodilian has been identified with certainty in the fossil record.

EUPARKERIA

ANIMAL FACTFILE

Euparkeria

Meaning: True [reptile] of Parker

Pronunciation: You-park-ear-ee-ah

Period: Early Triassic

Main group: Reptilia

Length: Head to tail 60 centimeters (2 feet)

Diet: Insects and other small creatures

Fossil sites: Southern Africa

The reptiles that evolved directly into dinosaurs are a subject of huge debate. The earliest known dinosaurs were meat-eaters that walked on their two rear limbs, which were directly under the body to support it from below, rather than angled and sprawled out to the sides. These dinosaurs, which include *Herrerasaurus* and *Eoraptor*, probably evolved from creatures that were similar either to themselves or to *Euparkeria*. Some authorities place this small reptile in the group known as archosauromorphs, that is, reptiles with a form or body structure like that of the archosaurs, the group that includes crocodiles, dinosaurs and pterosaurs. Other, usually older classification schemes, however, put *Euparkeria* in a group known as thecodonts or "socket-tooth" reptiles, because their teeth grew from pit-like sockets in the jawbone, rather than from the surface of the bone. However, the thecodonts are now no longer regarded as

a true single-origin group, but as a group of archosaurs or near-archosaurs that did not evolve into a dinosaur, pterosaur or crocodilian.

Whatever the classification scheme, *Euparkeria* is not considered the ancestor of all dinosaurs, or even of some dinosaurs, but it may have been similar to those that were ancestors and so may serve as a useful guide to what a "proto-dinosaur" looked like. The fossils of *Euparkeria* come from South Africa and are dated to the Early Triassic period. *Euparkeria* was an agile, nimble predator with a relatively large head and sharp, rear-curved, serrated teeth dotted along the edges of the jaws. It probably pursued insects, grubs and other small animals through the undergrowth. The rear legs were larger and more powerful than the front pair, and *Euparkeria* could rear up to sprint at speed on them, its head and body at the front balanced by the long tail behind.

BELOW *Euparkeria* was about the size of a pet cat of today, and probably just as quick and agile when hunting, with its sharp-clawed feet and numerous needle-like teeth.

RIGHT *Ornithosuchus* was up to 4 meters (13 feet) long and one of the most formidable predators of 200 million years ago, at a time when the early carnivorous dinosaurs were spreading across the continents.

ORNITHOSUCHUS

Ornithosuchus – "bird crocodile" – was neither a bird nor a crocodile. It is now regarded as an archosauromorph (as explained opposite) or, according to older schemes, as a thecodont reptile. Whatever its exact classification, it was closely related to the archosaur group that included dinosaurs and crocodiles. Indeed, at one time, *Ornithosuchus* was regarded as a dinosaur – one of the earliest of them all. It had several features, however, that were non-dinosaurian, including the pattern of gaps or holes in its skull; the structure of the lower backbone and its joints to the hipbones; the number of digits on its feet (being five); and, especially, the details of its ankle joint: the upper ankle, called the astragulus, did not have a dinosaurian shape but instead lacked the upward projections and extension typical of most dinosaurs.

Thomas Henry Huxley named *Ornithosuchus* in 1877. Huxley was a British paleontologist who is still famous today as a vociferous supporter of Charles Darwin and of the theory, proposed by Darwin and other scientists, of evolution by natural selection. He saw features in the fossils of *Ornithosuchus* that reminded him of crocodiles and of birds.

At a glance, a reconstructed *Ornithosuchus* might be mistaken for an early theropod, or meat-eating dinosaur. It could stoop down to move on all fours and also rear up to walk or run bipedally, on its two larger, more powerful rear limbs. These grew below the body, in the upright posture characteristic of the dinosaurs. The long snout of *Ornithosuchus* housed powerful jaws with sharp teeth for biting and tearing prey.

Several similar reptiles, known as ornithosuchians, have been discovered in Europe, especially in Scotland, as well as in South America. They ranged in total length from only half a meter (20 inches) to more than three meters (10 feet), and most have similar body proportions to *Ornithosuchus*.

ANIMAL FACTFILE

Ornithosuchus

Meaning: Bird crocodile

Pronunciation: Orn-ith-owe-sook-uss

Period: Middle to Late Triassic

Main group: Reptilia

Length: Head to tail 2 meters (6⅓ feet) some estimates up to 4 meters (13 feet)

Diet: Medium-sized prey

Fossil sites: British Isles, other parts of Europe, South America

BEFORE THE DINOSAURS

BEFORE THE AGE OF DINOSAURS, AND OVERLAPPING
ITS BEGINNING, WERE THE SYNAPSIDS, SOMETIMES
CALLED "MAMMAL-LIKE REPTILES." EARLY TYPES
SUCH AS PELYCOSAURS WERE REPTILE-LIKE ANIMALS
WITH SCALY SKIN, COLD BLOOD AND SPRAWLING
LIMBS, AND SOME HAD TALL SAILS OF SKIN ON
THEIR BACKS. LATER TYPES LIKE CYNODONTS
WERE MUCH MORE MAMMAL-LIKE CREATURES
WITH HAIRY SKIN AND WARM BLOOD.

RIGHT Within 50 million years of freeing themselves from their
amphibian ancestry and the water, reptiles had evolved into
many different forms, from sharp-toothed, agile predators
to huge, hulking herbivores. Some of the former, such as
Euparkeria from the Early Triassic period, were standing tall
and running fast, and beginning to resemble the dinosaurs that
would appear later in this period.

DIMETRODON

ANIMAL FACTFILE

Dimetrodon

Meaning: Two-form teeth, two types of teeth

Pronunciation: Die-met-roe-don

Period: Early Permian

Main group: Synapsida (Pelycosauria)

Length: Head to tail up to 3.5 meters
(11½ feet)

Diet: Larger animals

Fossil sites: North America, Europe

One of the prehistoric animals most likely to be called a dinosaur, even though it was not, is *Dimetrodon*. It often appears in illustrations and reconstructions of the ancient world, sporting a large back "sail" and fearsomely long, sharp fangs. Yet *Dimetrodon* appeared, and died out before the dinosaurs, and in some modern classification systems it is not even regarded as a true reptile. Instead, it is placed in a group known as synapsids, which are defined by a certain opening in each side of the skull. Synapsids are also known informally and confusingly by yet another name: the "mammal-like reptiles." (See also the following pages of this chapter.) Within the synapsid group, *Dimetrodon* belonged to the pelycosaur subgroup, alongside its plant-eating cousin, and probable victim, *Edaphosaurus* (opposite).

Dimetrodon grew to 3.5 meters (11½ feet) in length and was one of the greatest land hunters of the Early Permian period, some 280 million years ago. It is a common find in the fossil-rich rocks of Texas and Oklahoma, as well as in some parts of Europe. It had a large head, a squat but long body, sprawling limbs at the sides, and a slim, tapering tail. Its teeth were varied in size and shape, which was unusual for reptile-like creatures of its time. They were smaller but sharp at the front of the jaw, for gripping; large and canine-like slightly farther back, for stabbing and tearing; and lower but more substantial at the rear of the jaws, for slicing and chewing. The "sail" or "fin" on *Dimetrodon*'s back was a thin layer of skin and flesh held up by spine-like extensions of the vertebrae (backbones), up to 1 meter (39 inches) tall.

RIGHT Paleoecological evidence from fossils preserved with *Dimetrodon,* of other animals and also plants, shows that it lived in a dry, scrubby landscape dotted with winding brooks and small pools but also subject to long droughts.

BELOW Many skeletons of *Dimetrodon* are virtually complete, especially those from the Permian rock formations in Texas known as the "Red Beds."

RIGHT The back sail or fin of *Edaphosaurus* was slightly more leaf- or shell-shaped than the crescent-like curve of *Dimetrodon's* (opposite). Also there were small cross-pieces of bone along the length of each stiff spine holding up the sail, which *Dimetrodon* lacked.

EDAPHOSAURUS

Like the flesh-eating *Dimetrodon* (opposite), *Edaphosaurus* was a member of the pelycosaur subgroup of early synapsids. Pelycosaurs appeared during the Late Carboniferous period. By the Early Permian, when *Edaphosaurus* and *Dimetrodon* lived, their fossils at certain sites – which were in scrubby uplands at the time – outnumber the fossils of all other backboned animals. Although pelycosaurs and other synapsids are sometimes called "mammal-like reptiles," *Edaphosaurus* was not very mammal-like and, despite its superficial resemblance to *Dimetrodon*, it was not a predator. It was probably a plant-eater, with peg-shaped teeth for gathering and chewing plant food. This partly mashed vegetation would be swallowed into the large, roomy guts in the tubby, short-legged body, where it could be fermented and digested to release its nutrients.

Like *Dimetrodon*, *Edaphosaurus* had a tall "fin" or "sail" on its back, held up by neural spines, long vertical extensions of the vertebrae (backbones). This sail- or fin-like arrangement has occurred in several different groups of prehistoric animals, including dinosaurs (see also page 266). The most common theory about the sail's function is that it helped with temperature regulation. The large area of the sail, when positioned at a right angle to the rising sun, would absorb warmth and pass it, via the blood flowing through it, into the animal's body. This would quickly raise the animal's body temperature to allow more and faster activity after the cool night. Alternatively, standing in the shade and at a right angle to a breeze would cool the body. In addition, the sail may have been brightly colored to aid in recognition, for example, by breeding partners.

ANIMAL FACTFILE
Edaphosaurus
Meaning: Pavement reptile
Pronunciation: Ed-aff-owe-sore-uss
Period: Early Permian
Main group: Synapsida (Pelycosauria)
Length: Up to 3 meters (10 feet)
Diet: Plants
Fossil sites: North America, Europe

MOSCHOPS

ANIMAL FACTFILE
Moschops

Meaning: Humor visage, funny face

Pronunciation: Moss-chops

Period: Late Permian

Main group: Synapsida (Therapsida)

Length: Head to tail up to 5 meters
(17 feet)

Diet: Plants

Fossil sites: Southern Africa

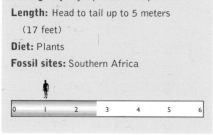

0	1	2	3	4	5	6

Moschops was a synapsid or "mammal-like reptile" (like the animals on the previous two pages, and those in the following pages of this chapter). Its fossils have been unearthed from the Karroo Beds (rock layers) of South Africa. It was a massive, heavily built beast, with a body about the size of an average rhinoceros and a short, slightly tapering tail. The rear limbs were smaller and directly under the body, while the front pair were powerful and sprawled at an angle, sideways and then downward. The general shape and posture of *Moschops* have led some to compare it to the sumo wrestlers of Japan.

Moschops had foreshortened jaws equipped with teeth shaped like chisels, which it used for cutting and chopping plants. Its most unusual feature was on its forehead and the top of its head, where the skull bone was greatly thickened. This suggests that *Moschops* had head-to-head battles, pushing or butting,

probably with others of its kind – perhaps to defeat rivals for partners at breeding time, or to establish a senior position in the group. (See also pachycephalosaur dinosaurs, page 304.)

Moschops belonged to the synapsid subgroup known as therapsids. These evolved during the Permian period and in many areas they took over from the previously more common rival subgroup of synapsids, the pelycosaurs, such as *Dimetrodon* and *Edaphosaurus*. Because of its thickened skull dome, *Moschops* is classified with the dinocephalian ("terrible-headed") therapsids, although it lacked the lumps, horns, bumps and spikes that grew on the heads of other types – some of which were even bigger.

ABOVE The heavily-muscled forequarters, squat posture and thickened forehead bone all suggest that *Moschops* engaged in pushing or head-butting contests, perhaps with rivals at breeding time.

LYSTROSAURUS

The creatures in the last portion of this chapter were all "mammal-like reptiles," although in newer classification schemes they are regarded as neither mammals nor reptiles, but as members of a distinct group, the synapsids. The earlier synapsids, such as *Dimetrodon* and the other pelycosaurs, were followed by the early therapsids, including *Moschops* (opposite). In the Early Permian period came another group of therapsids, the dicynodonts. *Lystrosaurus* and *Dicynodon* were two examples. *Lystrosaurus* was a later and fairly small type from the Early Triassic period. It was about the size of a pig but with stouter limbs, the front two being more splayed than the rear pair. Fossils of *Lystrosaurus* have been found over a huge range, including sites in eastern Europe, western Asia, China and India, southern Africa and Antarctica. This supports the view that these landmasses were joined together at the time.

The name dicynodont means "two dog teeth." Most types had two long teeth growing from near the front of the upper jaw, and usually pointing downward and being visible outside the mouth as tusks. The front of the upper jaw was also unusual, being shaped like a modern bird of prey's downwardly hooked beak. This feature was common in many plant-eating dinosaurs and also the reptiles known as the rhynchosaurs, which lived at the same time as the dicynodonts (see *Scaphonyx*, page 100). The dicynodonts were even more unusual in that most had very few teeth other than the tusks, or none at all. They cropped vegetation with their "beaks," and presumably mashed it up mainly in the guts. The possible uses of their tusks are discussed on the next page.

BELOW Long bodies and short tails, as shown by *Lystrosaurus,* were a feature of many herbivorous synapsids from the Late Permian and Early Triassic periods.

ANIMAL FACTFILE

Lystrosaurus

Meaning: Shovel reptile

Pronunciation: List-row-sore-uss

Period: Early Triassic

Main group: Synapsida (Dicynodontia)

Length: Head and body 1 meter (39 inches)

Diet: Plants

Fossil sites: Southern Africa, India, China, Russia, Antarctica

DICYNODON

This stocky plant-eater has given its name to the dicynodont group of synapsids (explained on the previous page). It was one of the earlier types, from the Late Permian period some 260–250 million years ago, and its fossils have been uncovered in Tanzania (East Africa) and also in South Africa. Like many other earlier dicynodonts, it was pig-sized, around 1 meter (39 inches) or slightly more in length, with a short tail, and was low-slung on short limbs. Later members of the group reached much greater sizes, up to 3 meters (9¹/₂ feet) long and perhaps 1 metric ton (1 ton) in weight – as big as a medium-sized hippopotamus today. There are other similarities to modern hippopotamuses too, in the wide, barrel-like body and stocky limbs. At one time, dicynodonts were regarded as semi-aquatic, living in swamps and lakes. However, other fossils found with their remains show that many kinds lived in fairly dry, scrubland-type landscapes.

Why did *Dicynodon* and its cousins have just two main tusk-like teeth? One suggestion is that they were used for digging, to reach ground-level or underground plant matter such as roots and runners.

Another idea is that they were used for defense against predators, since there were several types of larger meat-eaters at the time, including dry-land members of the crocodile family and other hunting reptiles. A third proposal is that the tusks were used for intimidating or jabbing rivals during the mating season, or, if not for actual battle, then in visual displays of strength and maturity.

The last dicynodonts lived at the end of the Triassic period. Like many other medium-sized plant-eaters, especially reptiles and reptile-like ones, they probably suffered from the rapid spread of the dinosaurs, including predation by the meat-eating types and competition for plant food by the herbivorous dinosaurs.

ANIMAL FACTFILE

Dicynodon

Meaning: Two dog-teeth

Pronunciation: Die-sigh-no-don

Period: Late Permian

Main group: Synapsida (Dicynodontia)

Length: Head and body 1.2 meters (4 feet)

Weight: 1 metric ton (1 ton)

Diet: Plants

Fossil sites: Africa

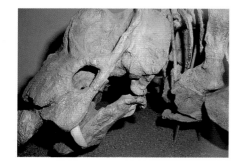

LEFT This fossil skull is of *Kannemeyeria*, a dicynodont very similar in overall shape to *Dicynodon*, but slightly later during the Early Triassic period, and larger – the size of a modern ox. The tusk is especially prominent.

BELOW Reconstruction of *Dicynodon* showing its squat posture, sprawling front limbs and tusk-like teeth.

LYCAENOPS

As time passed, the "mammal-like reptiles" shown over these pages gradually became less like reptiles and more like mammals, although they probably belonged to neither of these groups, being synapsids (see page 106). *Lycaenops* was a Late Permian type, and in its body posture and proportions it showed many changes from the usual reptile pattern. It probably stood tall on its four longish legs, which were positioned directly below the body as in dinosaurs and mammals, rather than splayed out to the sides as in most reptiles. *Lycaenops* also had a long, blunt snout with a high tip. This was partly to accommodate the roots of the canines – two long, fang-like teeth that grew from the upper jaw. These teeth are most familiar in mammal carnivores such as dogs and cats, and reached tremendous size in the saber-toothed cats, such as *Smilodon* (see page 427). The other teeth in the jaws of *Lycaenops* were smaller and more typical of reptilian flesh-eaters.

Remains of *Lycaenops* are known from the fossil-rich Late Permian rocks of South Africa, specifically the area known as the Karoo Basin, Great Karoo and Karoo Desert in the southwest of the country. The remains show that it was slim and lightly built, probably able to run faster and for longer distances than most of the other squat, heavily-built reptiles of its day. Perhaps it hunted in packs, like modern wolves, running down and slashing at big, slow herbivores. *Lycaenops* is placed in the subgroup called gorgonopsians within the larger therapsid group. Gorgonopsians may have evolved from the much more reptile-like pelycosaurs (shown on previous pages), such as *Dimetrodon*, but they became extinct towards the very end of the Permian period.

ABOVE *Lycaenops* sinks its canines (upper fangs) into a young dicynodont (see opposite) This synapsid had the build of a strong, persistent runner.

ANIMAL FACTFILE
Lycaenops
Meaning: Wolf face
Pronunciation: Lie-seen-ops
Period: Late Permian
Main group: Synapsida (Therapsida)
Length: Head and body up to 1 meter (39 inches)
Weight: 10–15 kilograms (22–33 pounds)
Diet: Prey animals, such as small reptiles
Fossil sites: South Africa, Asia

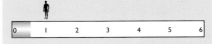

CYNOGNATHUS

ANIMAL FACTFILE

Cynognathus

Meaning: Dog jaw

Pronunciation: Sigh-nog-nay-thuss

Period: Early Triassic

Main group: Synapsida (Cynodontia)

Length: Head and body up to 1 meter
(39 inches)

Diet: Meat

Fossil sites: Africa, South America

Cynognathus, "dog jaw," was not a dog, although at a quick glance it might be mistaken for some strange kind of dog-like mammal. As it is usually reconstructed, it had a body covered with fur, ear flaps, crouching legs beneath its body and three types of teeth in its jaws, including an upper pair of long, sharp, dog-like canines. In fact, *Cynognathus* was a member of the subgroup known as the cynodonts, within the larger therapsid group, which was in turn part of the larger synapsid group. Synapsids are often known as "mammal-like reptiles," although they were neither mammal nor reptile. The cynodonts were the synapsids that resembled mammals the most. Indeed, they are regarded as the ancestors of the mammal group. (See also *Thrinaxodon*, opposite.)

Cynognathus was slightly smaller than a modern wolf, but much more heavily and powerfully built, with thicker limbs, a wider head and a more substantial, less pointed snout. Its jaws and teeth showed very mammal-like features. For example, the lower jaw was composed mostly of just one bone, the dentary,

while in most reptiles the dentary was just one of up to six or seven bones making up the lower jaw. Also, in most reptiles all the teeth in the jaws were much the same, but the teeth of *Cynognathus* and other cynodonts were of three types. There were small incisors at the front for nipping or cutting, then large spear-like canines for stabbing, and, behind them, in the cheek region, smaller teeth for slicing or shearing. The earbones were also mammal-like rather than reptile-like: fossils show signs of three ear bones (malleus, incus and stapes) in a row or sequence to conduct sounds, much like our own ears, while reptiles have just one longer bone, the columella. These tiny ear bones help to distinguish mammals from reptiles.

BELOW *Cynognathus* was perhaps the closest that the "mammal-like reptiles" came to truly mammalian predators such as wolves. Its teeth showed increasing specialization, with the typical carnivore's enlarged, sharp canine or "fang." This fossil is from the Karoo region of South Africa.

THRINAXODON

This small but well-equipped hunter was a cynodont or "dog-tooth" (as explained opposite). The synapsids, the main group to which it belonged, are sometimes called "mammal-like reptiles," but *Thrinaxodon* was very much toward the mammal end of the range, and only a few features separated it from the true mammals that would appear later in the Triassic period (see page 398). *Thrinaxodon* was about the size of a modern pet cat, but it had shorter, slightly more flexed or crouching legs – especially the front pair – and a short, tapered tail. Its build and slim body suggest that it may have lived like a stoat, in a burrow.

Thrinaxodon had three types of teeth, like *Cynognathus*, all suited to catching, impaling and slicing up animal prey like worms, grubs and small reptiles. Its skull shows tiny pits or holes toward the tip of the snout area. These are seen in many mammal skulls. They house the nerves that supply the roots of the whiskers, long, thick hairs that probably evolved after the basic covering of fur. It follows that *Thrinaxodon* and other cynodonts may well have been hairy or furry too. This suggests, in turn, that they could have been warm-blooded, with the fur for insulation. Inside the skull was a secondary bony palate, which separated the air passages between the nose and throat from the mouth chamber. This allowed breathing while eating – another mammalian feature. *Thrinaxodon*'s brain was relatively large compared to its body size. All of these traits, plus those described for *Cynognathus* opposite, made the cynodonts the most mammal-like of creatures, without actually being mammals.

ABOVE *Thrinaxodon* showed many mammal- rather than reptile-like features, such as a distinct heel bone on each foot, and a lower jaw made mostly of one bone rather than two or three.

ANIMAL FACTFILE
Thrinaxodon

Meaning: Three-pronged tooth, trident tooth

Pronunciation: Thrin-axe-owe-don

Period: Early Triassic

Main group: Synapsida (Cynodontia)

Length: 50 centimeters (19½ inches) including tail

Weight: 1–2 kilograms (2–4½ pounds)

Diet: Small animals

Fossil sites: Southern Africa, Antarctica

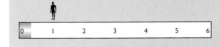

CHAPTER THREE

THE FIRST DINOSAURS

THE LATE TRIASSIC PERIOD SAW THE RISE OF REPTILES THAT WOULD
DOMINATE LIFE ON LAND FOR MORE THAN 160 MILLION YEARS – LONGER
THAN ANY OTHER GROUP OF CREATURES.

WHAT ARE DINOSAURS?

WHAT EXACTLY WAS A DINOSAUR? WAS IT A FIERCE CREATURE WITH GREEN SKIN, A TERRIBLE ROAR AND A MOUTH DRIPPING WITH BLOOD? PERHAPS, BUT NOTHING HAS BEEN FOUND AMONG THE FOSSILS TO SUPPORT THIS PICTURE. DINOSAURS ARE DEFINED FROM CERTAIN FEATURES OF THEIR FOSSILS, MAINLY BONES, TEETH, CLAWS AND HORNS. CERTAIN BONES OF THE SKULL AND SKELETON ARE IMPORTANT – THE UPPER SKULL, THE UPPER BONE IN THE LIMB (HUMERUS), THE FRONT DIGITS ("FINGERS"), THE HIPBONE (PELVIS), THE SHINBONE (TIBIA) AND THE ANKLEBONES (TARSALS).

DINOSAUR DETAILS

Some of these fossil features may seem small and insignificant. For example, the hipbone (pelvis) has a bowl-shaped socket called the acetabulum, into which fits the ball-shaped head (or upper end) of the thighbone (femur). This general structure of the hip joint is found in all vertebrates, but dinosaurs' hip joints are distinguished from those of other reptiles in three different ways. First, the pelvic socket had a ridge or rim that was thicker on the upper (higher) part than the lower. This acetabular ridge rested on the ball-shaped end of the thighbone. Second, the thighbone's head projected from its main length or shaft at a right angle. Third, the acetabulum socket was not a complete bowl of bone, but was "open," with a hole or window in the deepest part. Around ten other details of the skeleton, inconspicuous to the casual observer, add up to the suite of characteristics or traits that define a dinosaur, but the importance of finding a hipbone in a fossil cannot be underestimated.

STANDING TALL

The above details add up to a hip joint that, among reptiles, is unique to dinosaurs. On the animal's outside, it shows in the position of the leg relative to the main body. Dinosaurs had an "upright stance": when standing, the leg was directly below the main body, with the knee joint straight. This supported body weight efficiently, and in a naturally balanced way. In contrast, most other reptiles have had a "sprawling stance," as seen in today's lizards – the leg joins to the body at an angle, with its upper portion directed sideways and its lower part down. This structure needs more muscle power and is less energy efficient in movement. The upright stance may be one of the reasons why dinosaurs became so successful.

WHERE DINOSAURS BEGAN

Remains from South America, and especially Argentina, are among the earliest dinosaur fossils known to science. They date to almost 230 million years ago. As shown on the next few pages, most of these dinosaurs were from the theropod group – predators that habitually moved on their two larger rear limbs (bipedally), with smaller front "arms," and long, sharp teeth that they used to bite their prey. Likely ancestors for these types of dinosaurs are discussed in the previous chapter. The picture has been complicated by recent discoveries of fossils from different types of early dinosaurs, the prosauropods, in Madagascar. This may push the origins of the dinosaurs farther back, into the Middle Triassic. Almost as soon as the dinosaurs appeared, they began to spread and evolve into many shapes and sizes, with devastating effects on the creatures of the time.

PREVIOUS PAGE Three-toed dinosaur footprints, each larger than a dinner plate, are revealed in a curiously geometric mud-cracked slab of rock about 150 million years old, from Utah. These are footprints of a large theropod or meat-eating dinosaur, the group to which the huge and terrifying *Allosaurus* belonged.

LEFT Slight and slim, with alert and darting bird-like behavior, a small group of *Coelophysis* race through the dry upland terrain which is now New Mexico. This is one of the best-known early dinosaurs from 225 million years ago.

EORAPTOR

DINO FACTFILE

Eoraptor

Meaning: Dawn thief, dawn hunter

Pronunciation: Ee-owe-rap-tore

Period: Middle to Late Triassic

Main group: Theropoda

Length: 1 meter (39 inches)

Weight: 3–15 kilograms (7–21 pounds)

Diet: Small animals

Fossils: Argentina

Among the earliest dinosaur remains yet discovered, the fossils of *Eoraptor* have been dated to around 228 million years ago. They were unearthed in the Andean foothills of Argentina in 1991 by teams from the local area and the University of Chicago, and named two years later by Paul Sereno, of the university, and his colleagues. Layers of volcanic ash associated with the discovery allowed relatively accurate age assessment.

Eoraptor was a small theropod – a member of the meat-eating group of dinosaurs. In its proportions, it resembled many of the later predatory types, with a long slim head and neck, long and tapering tail, short forelimbs and long, powerful rear limbs for bipedal walking and running. However, the teeth at the front of the jaw were, unusually, leaf-shaped, rather than the sharp, blade-edged daggers or spear-like points typical of carnivorous dinosaurs.

Eoraptor can be viewed as a small, early, primitive theropod, exactly what might be expected as one of the first "twigs" on the predator branch of the dinosaurs' evolutionary tree. It had lightweight, hollow bones, similar to those of the slightly later and much better-known *Coelophysis*. *Eoraptor*, a slim, fast, agile predator, probably hunted various small creatures, including lizards and other little reptiles, and perhaps also large bugs and worms. It had five digits on each forelimb – an early feature, since the number of digits was reduced in later theropods to three or even two. *Eoraptor*'s digits had sharp claws for scrabbling in soil or grabbing victims. A less likely possibility is that *Eoraptor* scavenged on the dead and dying carcasses of larger reptiles, because its teeth were not designed for dealing with tough food. Rather they were small, sharp and back-curved, and so better suited to grabbing and cutting small prey.

RIGHT *Eoraptor* peers for any small creature that might make a meal. Its total length of about 1 meter (3 feet) is indicated by fossils, but weight estimates vary from 3 kilograms (6 pounds) to three times as much.

STAURIKOSAURUS

A much-debated discovery, *Staurikosaurus* is one of the few major fossil dinosaur finds from Brazil, where it was discovered in the far south near Santa Maria, and one of the most hotly debated of all dinosaur finds. In general features, this creature was a smallish theropod or meat-eater, larger than *Eoraptor* but not as bulky as *Herrerasaurus*, both dinosaurs from slightly earlier in the same period and found in neighboring Argentina. The remains of *Staurikosaurus* are relatively incomplete, but they allow estimates of its total length, snout to tail, at about 2 meters (6½ feet) or slightly more. It was a slim, quick predator, with long jaws armed with many small, pointed teeth. Its probable victims included varied small reptiles, and the young, and perhaps the eggs, of the larger reptiles that abounded at the time, such as the crocodile-like rauisuchians and the plant-eating rhynchosaurs.

Like its cousins, *Eoraptor* and *Herrerasaurus*, *Staurikosaurus* had made the advance to an almost fully upright posture. This important feature defines the group that included these dinosaurs and differs from the slightly sprawling posture shown by their ancestors (see page 116). It is the structure of the ball-and-socket hip joint that reveals this change. In a sprawling posture, with the thighbone at an angle to the bowl-like hip socket, the pressure pushes both upward and sideways, into the socket. The socket itself is strengthened to resist these stresses. In an upright posture, with the thighbone almost vertically below the socket, there is more weight-bearing pressure on the upper part of the bowl. *Staurikosaurus* shows an enlarged "lip" around the upper hip socket, to cope with this pressure. However the hipbone is one of only a few of its fossils discovered.

ABOVE Like many of the early meat-eating dinosaurs, *Staurikosaurus* had a slim and flexible neck, so that its long-jawed head could rapidly flick at, poke and peck food items.

DINO FACTFILE
Staurikosaurus

Meaning: Cross reptile (from the Southern Hemisphere constellation known as the Southern Cross)

Pronunciation: Store-ick-owe-sore-uss

Period: Late Triassic

Main group: Theropoda

Length: 2 meters (6½ feet)

Weight: 15 kilograms (33 pounds)

Diet: Small animals

Fossils: Southern Brazil

HERRERASAURUS

DINO FACTFILE

Herrerasaurus

Meaning: Herrera's reptile

Pronunciation: He-ray-raar-sore-uss

Period: Middle to Late Triassic

Main group: Theropoda

Length: 3 meters (10 feet)

Weight: 70 kilograms (154 pounds)

Diet: Small and medium-sized animals

Fossils: Argentina

One of the best-known early dinosaurs, *Herrerasaurus* was named after the Argentine farmer, Victorino Herrera, who was the first to notice a fossil skeleton of one of these creatures in the rocky outcrops of the Andean foothills near San Juan. In 1988 a team led by Paul Sereno of the University of Chicago excavated this well-preserved and almost complete specimen. Similar remains found in the same general area included bones from the back limbs, the hip and the tail. The possibility that *Herrerasaurus* was a very early type of dinosaur that predated the major division of the group into its two great subgroups, Saurischia and Ornithischia, has been proposed. Otherwise it may be that *Herrerasaurus* was a saurischian or "reptile-hipped" dinosaur, but had not yet evolved features that would place it in the main saurischian subgroup of meat-eaters – the theropods.

What is known, from reconstruction, is that *Herrerasaurus* was a medium-sized, powerfully built predator. It had many sharp, rear-curved teeth in its very long jaws. Its forelimbs were short and had five digits, but the fourth and fifth digits were greatly reduced and also clawless, more like stubby stumps. This dinosaur had strong hind limbs with short thighs, and very long feet and toes – the proportions of a rapid runner. Its tail was long and whippy, and helped *Herrerasaurus* to twist and turn at speed. The hunter ran with its body held horizontal and neck curved upward, so that its head could face forward. Other predators of around 228 million years ago in South America included the bigger and stronger but sprawling-postured, four-limbed, crocodile-like reptiles known as rauisuchians. *Herrerasaurus* and its cousins represent an evolutionary breakthrough among reptilian predators for the next 160 million years.

LEFT *Herrerasaurus* was about the same size as today's largest lizard, the powerful and muscular komodo dragon. However this very early predatory dinosaur could probably move far faster than its distant reptilian cousin of today.

COELOPHYSIS

Few early dinosaurs are as well known as *Coelophysis*. In the 1940s thousands of fossils were uncovered at a site known as Ghost Ranch in New Mexico. They were the jumbled, broken bones of hundreds of individual *Coelophysis* dinosaurs that had probably endured a mass death of some kind. Perhaps they all perished together in a flash flood, or perhaps they died in more scattered groups and then rushing waters washed their rotting remains into one small area. The fossils date from 220–225 million years ago.

Coelophysis was a predator, but very slim and lightly built. Its overall proportions, with long beak-like jaws, flexible stork-type neck, distinctively shaped pelvis (hipbone) joints, and hollow bones to save weight, are all features shared by early birds. The many small, sharp teeth are better suited to snapping up small creatures, like insects, with pecking movements of the long neck, than to tearing lumps of flesh from bigger prey. The sharp-clawed fingers could grab small items or scratch in earth for grubs and worms. *Coelophysis* may also have eaten fish, grabbing them with a forward jab of the head, in the manner of herons today. It was doubtless

a fast and agile mover, leaping and darting after prey, and also to escape from its enemies.

In 1998, a fossil skull of *Coelophysis* was taken into space in the space shuttle Endeavor. Transferred to the Russian space station Mir, it traveled more than 6 million kilometers (3.7 million miles) around the Earth. So it was that one of North America's earliest dinosaurs became the first "dino-astronaut."

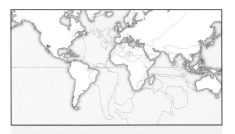

DINO FACTFILE
Coelophysis
Meaning: Hollow form, hollow shape
Pronunciation: See-low-fye-siss
Period: Late Triassic
Main group: Theropoda
Length: 3 meters (10 feet)
Weight: 35 kilograms (77 pounds)
Diet: Small animals
Fossils: Southwestern USA (New Mexico)

0	1	2	3	4	5	6

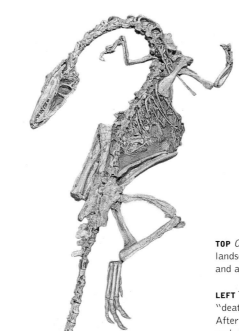

TOP *Coelophysis* snaps up a small reptile, in the dry landscape of the Late Triassic period. It was fast, light and agile, with hollow, bird-like, weight-saving bones.

LEFT This famous specimen of *Coelophysis* is in the "death curve" pose shown by many fossilized dinosaurs. After it perished, its body tissues stiffened and dried and shrank, and the neck and tail tendons shortened to bend the head and tail-tip over the back.

DINOSAURS BEGIN THEIR RULE

THE RISE OF THE DINOSAURS DURING THE TRIASSIC PERIOD HAD A HUGE EFFECT ON OTHER LAND REPTILES OF THAT TIME. THERE WERE HOWEVER ALSO TWO MYSTERIOUS "MINI-MASS-EXTINCTIONS" THAT SAW THE END OF SEVERAL REPTILE GROUPS, SUCH AS RHYNCHOSAURS, DICYNODONTS AND CYNODONTS. THIS LEFT RESOURCES SUCH AS FOOD, LIVING SPACE AND SHELTER READY TO BE EXPLOITED BY THE FIRST GROUPS OF DINOSAURS, MAINLY SMALLER MEAT-EATERS.

RIGHT Early dinosaurs including *Coelophysis,* along with gliding lizards and other reptiles, flee from a wildfire some 225 million years ago. At this time the animal landscape was changing rapidly with both predatory and plant-eating dinosaurs spreading fast.

SEGISAURUS

DINO FACTFILE

Segisaurus

Meaning: Segi reptile
  (after its discovery site)

Pronunciation: Say-ee-sore-uss

Period: Early Jurassic

Main group: Theropoda

Length: 1 meter (39 inches)

Weight: 5 kilograms (11 pounds)

Diet: Small animals

Fossils: USA (Arizona)

```
0     1     2     3     4     5     6
```

Segisaurus is not as well known as the similar *Coelophysis* (see page 121) because it did not leave plentiful fossil remains. The first specimen of what is now identified as *Segisaurus* was unearthed near Segi Canyon, Arizona, in an area known as Navajo Sandstone, in 1933 and described in 1936. It was incomplete, however, lacking a head with the all-important teeth. The fragmentary remains consisted of parts of the front and rear limbs, bits of the pelvis (hipbone) and a few ribs and vertebrae (backbones). From these parts, *Segisaurus* was reconstructed as a theropod (meat-eater), similar to but smaller than *Coelophysis*, and probably belonging to the theropod sub-group known as the ceratosaurs.

Segisaurus probably sprinted at speed on its long back legs and three-toed feet, holding its shorter forelimbs, with their sharp-clawed digits, near to its chest. The slender proportions of the fossil bones show that this dinosaur was lightly built, able to twist suddenly as it pursued prey, aided by flicking its tail sideways as a combined counterbalance and rudder to jerk the body in a new direction. Perhaps it snatched at large insects such as dragonflies or crickets, or small vertebrates such as frogs or lizards. The lack of teeth and jaw fossils means that proposals about the diet of *Segisaurus*, however, must come from comparisons with other, better-known relatives, especially *Coelophysis*.

RIGHT The head, jaws and teeth of "Segi reptile" are mainly conjectural, but this early dinosaur was certainly very light-framed and probably caught small creatures by a combination of alert senses and rapid reactions.

MELANOROSAURUS

Officially named in 1924 after its discovery site, for many years *Melanorosaurus* remained – along with *Plateosaurus* – one of the few large plant-eating dinosaurs known from the Late Triassic to Early Jurassic period. More recent discoveries, however, especially those in South America, such as *Riojasaurus*, have helped to increase our knowledge of how this major early group of big dinosaurs, the prosauropods, evolved and spread. In particular, the similarities between South African prosauropods, such as *Melanorosaurus*, and those from South America may be a consequence of the adjacent positions of these two continents during the Triassic.

Melanorosaurus was fairly typical of the prosauropod group, although perhaps larger than most. It had a small head, long neck and tail, bulky body and four very sturdy limbs, for plodding rather than walking. Its limb-bone fossils are well known and their thickness suggests weight-bearing adaptations, over the four broad five-toed feet, for a total body load of 1 metric ton (1 ton) or more. The rear limbs were longer, so the body sloped down from the hips to the shoulders. Estimates of the dinosaur's total length vary from 7 to 12 meters (23 to 40 feet). Like other prosauropods, *Melanorosaurus* probably craned its long neck to reach up into tree-sized plants, to crop the softer parts of the vegetation such as fern fronds, young conifer leaves, buds and shoots. Compared to *Plateosaurus*, it is less likely that *Melanorosaurus* could have raised its front legs off the ground, to support itself solely on its rear legs with the aid of its tail, as it reared to reach higher food sources.

DINO FACTFILE
Melanorosaurus

Meaning: Black Mountain reptile

Pronunciation: Mell-ann-ore-oh-sore-uss

Period: Late Triassic, Early Jurassic

Main group: Prosauropoda

Length: 10 meters (33 feet)

Weight: 1 metric ton (1 ton)

Diet: Plant matter, especially high-growing

Fossils: South Africa

LEFT *Melanorosaurus* may have possessed a longer, sharper claw on the first (innermost) digit of each foot, but the fossil evidence is not clear.

THECODONTOSAURUS

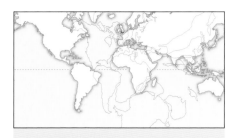

DINO FACTFILE

Thecodontosaurus

Meaning: Socket-toothed reptile

Pronunciation: Thee-coe-dont-owe-sore-uss

Period: Early Jurassic

Main group: Possibly Prosauropoda
(this classification is not accepted by
some authorities)

Length: 2.2 meters (7½ feet)

Weight: 10 kilograms (22 pounds)

Diet: Plants

Fossils: England, Wales

This dinosaur's name, referring to teeth set
in sockets in the jawbone, should not cause
confusion with the major group of reptiles
known as thecodonts, but now described as
archosauromorphs (see page 102). Such
similarity in names may seem irritating today,
but *Thecodontosaurus* received its official title
a long time ago, following the discovery of
fragmented fossils in rock fissures (cracks) near
Bristol in southwestern England. This was in
1843 – just after the name of the entire group,
Dinosauria, had been coined. In those days,
scientific views on prehistoric animals and
how they should be classified were far different
from modern systems.

Thecodontosaurus was a smallish plant-eating
dinosaur that stood and moved mainly on its
longer back legs. It could have held its shorter,
weaker front legs off the ground, except when
bounding along on all fours or perhaps when
leaning forward or bending down to feed on
surface-level vegetation. In this respect
Thecodontosaurus was similar to a much better-
known and more widespread prosauropod
cousin, *Anchisaurus*. There were five digits
on each "hand," the thumb being especially
large-clawed, and four digits on each foot.
The tail was long, the head and neck were
relatively small, and the teeth were small and
leaf-like, with serrated edges. Like *Anchisaurus*,
Thecodontosaurus is regarded by some experts
as a small, early type of prosauropod. It
represents a "dead end" in evolution, for
its group soon died out.

ABOVE Fossils associated with *Thecodontosaurus*
suggest that it lived in a dry, scrub-and-bush
habitat – a landscape common in the Late
Triassic and Early Jurassic, around 200 million
years ago.

RIOJASAURUS

First uncovered in the remote and windy Valley of the Moon, in the western Argentine province of La Rioja, fossils of this big plant-eater have since been found at other localities along the eastern foothills of the Argentine Andes. The first almost complete skeleton was excavated during the 1960s and named in 1969 by José Bonaparte, an eminent Argentine paleontologist. Another 20 or so specimens have since been located. *Riojasaurus* was one of the first dinosaurs to reach or even exceed 10 meters (33 feet) in length and 1 metric ton (1 ton) in bulk. It was a massive creature for its time, about 220 million years ago, and in many respects it foreshadowed the true giants, the sauropods, which became numerous and widespread during the Jurassic, the period that followed. But at the present time there is no evidence of a direct evolutionary link between *Riojasaurus* and the later sauropods.

The backbone of *Riojasaurus* was composed of large, sturdy vertebrae, both to carry its main body weight and to support its long neck and tail. The clawed feet on its elephant-sized legs were disproportionate, since those on the forelimbs were half the size of the rear pair. Perhaps the back legs took the main strain of the body weight, and *Riojasaurus* could even rear up on them, using its tail as a third support to avoid toppling backward. The teeth were small and leaf-shaped, suited to stripping and shredding foliage. This was swallowed without chewing, to be pulped in the massive stomach, perhaps with the aid of grinding stones, known as gastroliths ("stomach stones"), gulped down specially for this purpose.

DINO FACTFILE
Riojasaurus
Meaning: Rioja reptile
   (from its discovery site)
Pronunciation: Ree-oh-ha-sore-uss
Period: Late Triassic
Main group: Prosauropoda
Length: 10 meters (33 feet)
Weight: 1 metric ton (1 ton)
Diet: Plants
Fossils: Argentina

BELOW *Riojasaurus* was one of the first truly quadrupedal dinosaurs, that is, moving for most of the time on four legs. It could perhaps rear up for a short time on the rear limbs, but the size and sturdiness of the bones are adapted to support a considerable bulk.

RIGHT *Plateosaurus* is shown in its "kangaroo" posture, tilted up on its rear legs and counterbalanced and supported by its thick-based, heavy, muscular tail. In this position it could reach foliage at heights of almost 5 meters (16 feet) above the ground.

PLATEOSAURUS

DINO FACTFILE

Plateosaurus

Meaning: Flat reptile

Pronunciation: Plat-ee-owe-sore-uss

Period: Late Triassic

Main group: Prosauropoda

Length: 7–8 meters (23–26 feet)

Weight: Up to 1 metric ton (1 ton)

Diet: Plants

Fossils: France, Germany, Switzerland

Dozens of fossilized skeletons, from various locations in Europe, make this dinosaur one of the best known from the Late Triassic period, some 220 million years ago. It was also one of the largest land creatures of the time, probably approaching 1 metric ton (1 ton) in weight. Fossil finds include the original specimens from which the animal was named and described in 1837 – even before the dinosaurs themselves had received recognition as a group – along with further discoveries in the early 1910s, the early 1920s, and again in the early 1930s. The area surrounding the city of Trossingen, 100 kilometers (80 miles) southwest of Stuttgart, Germany, yielded some particularly well-preserved specimens.

Plateosaurus was a powerful prosauropod with the typical features of small head, long and flexible neck, tubby body, sturdy limbs and a tail that made up almost half of its total length. The rear legs were considerably larger than the front pair, and probably took most of the weight when walking. *Plateosaurus* is often pictured rearing up like a giant kangaroo, propped back on its tail, its head reaching out on its long neck for plants 5 meters (16 feet) or more above the ground. There was a large claw on each thumb, which may have worked as a hook for pulling branches to the mouth – or as a spike to jab into enemies. The 120 or so small teeth were leaf-shaped, with serrations around the edges, ideal for snipping or cropping softer leaves and fronds from the tall vegetation of Late Triassic times, which included conifers, tree-ferns and cycads. Bones from numerous individuals have been found piled together in fossilized heaps, which may indicate that the members of a herd all perished together, or that floodwaters washed scattered individuals into one site in a valley or on a riverbank. Newer fossil finds suggest that all of the fingers had long claws, like the thumb.

BELOW *Efraasia* and *Sellosaurus* have been variously regarded as two separate kinds or genera of dinosaurs, as species within the same genus, or as exactly the same species with the variation in fossil specimens representing different-aged individuals. Opinion now tends to two separate genera. This reconstruction reflects the body proportions of the *Efraasia* specimens.

SELLOSAURUS/EFRAASIA

In 1909, Eberhard Fraas discovered fossils of a plant-eating dinosaur about 2.4 meters (8 feet) long. It was similar in proportions to prosauropods such as *Plateosaurus*, which lived in the same region at around the same time. A scientific description of the remains proposed that they were a type of prosauropod. The name *Efraasia* was later bestowed in honor of the discoverer.

A year earlier, a similar prosauropod had been named *Sellosaurus* by another paleontologist, Friedrich Freiherr von Huene. (Von Huene was also to be the scientist behind the main accounts and descriptions of *Plateosaurus* itself, in the 1920s.) These remains eventually numbered mixed parts of about 20 skeletons, the largest nearing 7 meters (23 feet) in length. The general prosauropod similarities to *Plateosaurus* were confirmed by studying the fossils of both creatures in detail, and comparing the size and shape of the bones.

However, similarities between *Efraasia* and *Sellosaurus* gradually came to light, and it appeared that the former was likely a smaller version of the latter. The proportions were slightly different – for example, *Efraasia* had a shorter neck, compared to its overall length, than *Sellosaurus* did – but in dinosaurs as in living animals, the relative proportions of bodies change as they grow toward maturity. Further studies of the bones showed that *Efraasia* was perhaps a young *Sellosaurus*. Since the adult version had been named one year earlier, scientific convention determined that *Sellosaurus* became the official name. All specimens of *Efraasia* were for a time officially reclassified as *Sellosaurus*. Yet another recent study, however, shows the two are, after all, distinct dinosaurs. Fraas himself is also noted for studies of primate fossils from Egypt during the early 20th century.

DINO FACTFILE
Sellosaurus

Meaning: Saddle reptile

Pronunciation: Sell-owe-sore-uss

Period: Late Triassic

Main group: Prosauropoda

Length: 7 meters (23 feet)

Weight: 600 kilograms (1,325 pounds)

Diet: Plants

Fossils: Germany

FOOD FOR THE FIRST DINOSAURS

WHAT DID EARLY DINOSAURS EAT? THE SMALLER
CARNIVORES PROBABLY CAUGHT INVERTEBRATES
SUCH AS INSECTS AND WORMS, AND PERHAPS
LITTLE VERTEBRATES SUCH AS SMALLER REPTILES
OR THE OCCASIONAL EARLY MAMMAL. (THERE
WERE NO BIRDS AS YET.) THEY MAY HAVE
SCAVENGED ON LARGER CARCASSES TOO. THE
BIGGER HERBIVOROUS DINOSAURS CHOMPED ON
VARIED PLANTS, FROM LOW-GROWING MOSSES,
HORSETAILS AND FERNS, TO LARGER TREE-FERNS,
GINGKOES, CYCADS AND CONIFER TREES.
(FLOWERING PLANTS SUCH AS HERBS, GRASSES,
FLOWERS AND BROADLEAVED TREES WOULD NOT
EVOLVE UNTIL THE CRETACEOUS PERIOD.)

RIGHT Theropod dinosaurs of various sizes gather around the
carcass of an early type of plant-eating reptile, a rhynchosaur,
while others of its kind watch warily in the background.
Rhynchosaurs were a very successful group in terms of
numbers, but only for a relatively short time, in the mid-
to Late Triassic period.

MUSSAURUS

DINO FACTFILE

Mussaurus

Meaning: Mouse reptile

Pronunciation: Moo-sore-uss

Period: Late Triassic

Main group: Prosauropoda

Length: 3 meters (10 feet)

Weight: 150 kilograms (330 pounds)

Diet: Plants

Fossils: Argentina

0	I	2	3	4	5	6

Mussaurus was a dinosaur from the prosauropod group – a bulky, four-legged plant-eater, with a small head, long neck and long tail, and similar in overall appearance to other prosauropods. Why, then, did the Argentine paleontologists José Bonaparte and Martin Vince, who in 1979 named the 3-meter (10 feet), 150-kilogram (330-pound) beast, give it a name that means "mouse reptile"? *Mussaurus* was known only from the fossilized remains of babies, which are far from complete. A composite version from the fragments shows that they were, if not quite as small as real mice, then at least rat-sized – each around 20 centimeters (8 inches) in total length, with a long tail and a skull about the size of a human thumb. Some were hatchlings, just broken from their eggshells, when they perished; others were unhatched embryos, still in their shells when preserved.

The level of detail in these *Mussaurus* fossils, found in the 1970s in the Santa Cruz region of Argentina, is amazing. The jaws contain rows of teeth hardly larger than pinheads, and the ankle and foot bones are the size of rice grains. They are the smallest relatively complete dinosaur specimens of any type yet discovered.

More recently, fossils of adults have been positively identified, although they are mostly partial remains. The current estimate of the full-grown size, mentioned above, is based on these and the size ranges of other dinosaurs seen in the fossil record and the growth rates of today's reptiles. It is possible, however, that another dinosaur, *Coloradisaurus*, found in the same region and in the same rock layers, and dating from around 215 million years ago, could be the adult version. However, *Coloradisaurus* is, as yet, poorly known, as fossils of only the skull and jaws have been found.

BELOW An adult *Mussaurus* is usually reconstructed by applying typical prosauropod dinosaur growth rates and body proportions to the newly-hatched babies, which are the main fossil specimens known. However Argentinean fossils already described as *Plateosaurus* may actually be *Mussaurus* adults.

ANCHISAURUS

About the size of a large dog, *Anchisaurus* holds the honor of being the first dinosaur to be discovered from North America, specifically the Connecticut Valley, and to be officially described in the scientific literature on the basis of the fossils it left behind. That was in 1818, however, and the story has had several twists and turns since. For a time, the remains were thought to be from an ancient human being. By the 1850s, they were recognized as being a reptile, though not necessarily a dinosaur – the whole dinosaur group had received its official title and recognition only a few years earlier, in 1841. In 1885, Othniel Charles Marsh gave the name *Anchisaurus* to another set of fossils, this time from Massachusetts. In 1912, nearly a century after the remains were first described, they were finally identified as being *Anchisaurus*.

Anchisaurus lived about 195 million years ago. It had a typical prosauropod body, with a small head, and a long neck and tail. Its body and limbs were relatively slimmer, however, than those of bigger prosauropods, like *Plateosaurus* or *Massospondylus*. It probably moved slowly on all fours, in a loping manner, like a kangaroo of today, nosing for plants on the ground. Nevertheless, *Anchisaurus* could perhaps rear up onto its two larger back limbs to run at speed. Each front foot had five digits, with the first bearing a large, curved claw, possibly for defense. The rear foot had four digits, each with a large, nail-like claw. Like many prosauropods, *Anchisaurus* had small, leaf-like teeth with serrated edges, well suited to stripping plant matter such as leaves and fronds. Its habitat was a deep valley with many plant-fringed lakes.

DINO FACTFILE
Anchisaurus
Meaning: Near reptile, close reptile
Pronunciation: Ann-kee-sore-uss
Period: Early Jurassic
Main group: Prosauropoda
Length: 2.5 meters (8 feet)
Weight: 35 kilograms (77 pounds)
Diet: Plants
Fossils: USA (Connecticut Valley, Massachusetts), possibly South Africa

ABOVE *Anchisaurus* was one of the smaller prosauropods, also one of the most lightly built. It was probably able to trot or lope for considerable distances as it moved to new feeding areas of fresh plant growth.

THE TRIASSIC LANDSCAPE

THE TRIASSIC PERIOD, 250–203 MILLION YEARS AGO, WAS EVERYWHERE A TIME OF WARMTH. ALL OF EARTH'S CONTINENTS FORMED ONE GIANT LANDMASS, NOW CALLED PANGAEA. FERNS, CYCADS AND CONIFERS GREW ALONG COASTAL BELTS, BATHED IN MOIST WINDS, BUT VAST INLAND TRACTS OF THE DOUBLE-SUPERCONTINENT WERE SHRUB, SCRUB AND DESERT. INTO THIS WORLD CAME THE FIRST DINOSAURS.

RIGHT During the Late Triassic period, scattered pools and waterholes in the dry landscape would attract many animals (as they do today). In this reptilian scene a crocodile-like phytosaur rears from the water to confront a small group of *Coelophysis*-like theropod dinosaurs in the right foreground, with a shoulder-spiked plant-eating aetosaur and a large pareiasaur moving away in the background.

LEFT *Yunannosaurus* lived almost 200 million years ago, and shows features of both the prosauropod group and the later and larger group of sauropods. However chisel-shaped teeth which were once believed to belong to it, are now thought to come from another prosauropod that lived at the same time and place.

YUNNANOSAURUS

DINO FACTFILE
Yunnanosaurus
Meaning: Yunnan reptile (after its discovery site)

Pronunciation: You-nan-o-sore-uss

Period: Early Jurassic

Main group: Prosauropoda

Length: 7 meters (23 feet)

Weight: 600 kilograms (1,323 pounds)

Diet: Plants

Fossils: Southern China

This medium-sized prosauropod was first described and named in 1942, by Young Chung Chien, a famous Chinese paleontologist known in the West as C.C. Young. Fossil specimens of some 20 individuals have been located in Yunnan Province, southern China. In general body shape and proportions, *Yunnanosaurus* resembles other, mostly earlier prosauropods, such as *Plateosaurus*. Along with another similar prosauropod from the same area, *Lufengosaurus*, the discovery of *Yunnanosaurus* helped to demonstrate the almost worldwide distribution of the plant-eating prosauropod dinosaur group.

Like other prosauropods, *Yunnanosaurus* had a small head, though with a relatively short snout, a long neck, a bulging body, sturdy legs with the rear pair slightly longer and stronger, and a long, tapering tail. It probably spent most of its days plodding slowly among forests of conifers, cycads and tree-ferns, swinging its long neck so that its mouth could

rake in soft leaves, shoots and buds. It could reach down to the ground when on all fours, or perhaps rear up onto its back legs and stretch its neck for food more than 5 meters (16^1/$_2$ feet) above.

Yunnanosaurus has been the subject of great debate because of its supposed teeth, which numbered more than 60 and were slightly chisel- or spoon-shaped. In this respect, *Yunnanosaurus* was more similar to the sauropods – the later, more massive plant-eaters (see pages 218–255) – than to the prosauropods, which had mostly leaf-shaped teeth. It is because of these spoon-like teeth that some experts have suggested that *Yunnanosaurus* was an early sauropod, but some of the chisel-like teeth may come from another dinosaur. The province of Yunnan has yielded many fossils of dinosaurs and prehistoric animals, including apes such as *Lufengpithecus* and the early humans *Homo erectus*.

MASSOSPONDYLUS

In the same way that *Plateosaurus*, from the Late Triassic, is well known from dozens of preserved individuals found in Europe, so is *Massospondylus*, which is from the Early Jurassic, with dozens of preserved individuals in southern Africa. Discovery sites include places in South Africa, Lesotho and Matabeleland in western Zimbabwe. Remains of *Massospondylus*, or a very similar dinosaur, have also been uncovered in Arizona, possibly making it an exceptionally widespread dinosaur.

Massospondylus was relatively slim and lightly built for a prosauropod dinosaur. Its head, in particular, seems tiny – simply a mouth at the tip of the long neck, rather than the enlarged, bulging body part usually found at a dinosaur's front end. Also, its teeth are quite pointed, their edge serrations are prominent, and the whole jaw and skull structure seems too delicate for biting and pulling off tough, fibrous plant food. During the 1980s, these features led to protracted discussions among experts on the nature of

Massospondylus's diet. Did it rake or tear off, and swallow, plant matter whole, in the usual prosauropod manner? Or was it really a meat-eater? In some ways, the long, serrated teeth resemble those of carnivorous dinosaurs. Perhaps *Massospondylus* snapped up small prey, or scavenged by tearing soft, rotting meat from decaying carcasses. Then further comparisons showed that similar long, serrated teeth are found in some of today's plant-eating lizards. Also found with *Massospondylus* fossils were gastroliths – polished pebbles swallowed into the guts to help grind up tough plant food. Perhaps it was a typical prosauropod plant-eater, after all.

RIGHT The jaws and teeth of *Massospondylus* show a curious mixture of features, some indicating herbivory but others suggesting a diet of small prey items or even carcass-scavenging. Recent reviews of the evidence point more to plant-eating.

DINO FACTFILE
Massospondylus

Meaning: Massive vertebrae, big backbones

Pronunciation: Mass-owe-spon-die-luss

Period: Early Jurassic

Main group: Prosauropoda

Length: 5 meters (16½ feet)

Weight: 350 kilograms (772 pounds)

Diet: Plants

Fossils: Southeastern and southern Africa, possibly southern USA

0	1	2	3	4	5	6

LUFENGOSAURUS

It has been suggested often that *Lufengosaurus* and *Yunnanosaurus* are the same kind of dinosaur. They are similar in size and shape, at 6 or 7 meters (20 to 23 feet) in total length and half a metric ton (half a ton) or just above in weight. They are both prosauropod dinosaurs – small-headed with a long neck and tail, tubby torso and four-legged posture. They were named officially only one year apart, *Lufengosaurus* in 1941 and *Yunnanosaurus* in 1942, by the same eminent Chinese fossil expert, Young Chung Chien (known in the West as C.C. Young). Both, too, are very similar to another, earlier prosauropod from Europe, the very well-known *Plateosaurus*.

Nevertheless, details of the fossil bones from some 30-plus individuals show that *Lufengosaurus* was probably distinct from *Yunnanosaurus*. *Lufengosaurus* lived about 210–200 million years ago and its fossils were

recovered from the Early Jurassic rocks of the Lufeng Basin in central China's Yunan province. Its teeth were widely spaced and shaped more like leaves than the narrow spoons of *Yunnanosaurus*. For this reason, *Lufengosaurus* is sometimes included in the family of prosauropod dinosaurs known as the Plateosauridae, which contains *Plateosaurus* itself (and which also has leaf-shaped teeth). This is distinct from the family Yunnanosauridae, which contains the closest cousin of *Lufengosaurus* in geographical but not evolutionary terms, *Yunnanosaurus* (and which also has distinctive pointed teeth). Whatever the details of classification, *Lufengosaurus* probably plodded across the varied Triassic landscape, swinging its neck from side to side and also upward, even rearing on its hind legs to gain height, so that it could tear off soft pieces of plant matter, which it quickly swallowed.

DINO FACTFILE

Lufengosaurus

Meaning: Lu-feng reptile (from its discovery site)

Pronunciation: Lau-fung-owe-sore-uss

Period: Early Jurassic

Main group: Prosauropoda

Length: 6 meters (20 feet)

Weight: 500 kilograms (1,100 pounds)

Diet: Plants

Fossils: Southwestern China

| 0 | 1 | 2 | 3 | 4 | 5 | 6 |

RIGHT The difference between front and rear limbs is more marked in *Lufengosaurus* than in many other prosauropods, indicating that this dinosaur perhaps reared up habitually to reach higher-growing foliage.

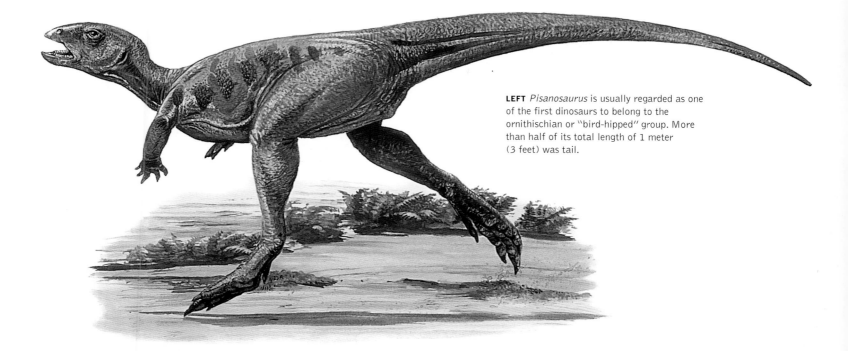

LEFT *Pisanosaurus* is usually regarded as one of the first dinosaurs to belong to the ornithischian or "bird-hipped" group. More than half of its total length of 1 meter (3 feet) was tail.

PISANOSAURUS

One of the most intriguing dinosaurs of the Late Triassic period, *Pisanosaurus* was a small plant-eater that was named in 1967, to honor Juan Pisano, an Argentine paleontologist. With few and fragmentary remains, however, experts have not been able to come to firm conclusions about its structure and lifestyle. The chief fossils are pieces of the neck, back, shoulder, hip, rear limb, front foot and, especially, parts of the jaws and teeth. Together the pieces show a small, slender, lightly built dinosaur with the same general proportions as little plant-eaters in the ornithopod group, such as *Lesothosaurus* and *Heterodontosaurus* (see page 272). The teeth of *Pisanosaurus* make it similar to these Early Jurassic dinosaurs too, and were quite different from those of other plant-eaters at the time, the much bigger Late Triassic prosauropods. *Pisanosaurus* had closely packed teeth that worked against each other to cut up plant

food, and abrade (get worn down) at the same time, therefore staying sharp and efficient. *Pisanosaurus* was probably a swift and agile mover, able to peck and snatch at plant matter, while darting away suddenly at the slightest hint of danger.

If this account is accurate – which is by no means agreed – *Pisanosaurus* holds an important place in dinosaur history as one of the first, or even the first, ornithischian. The whole group Dinosauria is divided into two great subgroups, Saurischia and Ornithischia, according to the pattern of the hipbone. All of the early dinosaurs shown on the preceding pages were meat-eating theropods or plant-eating prosauropods, and both of these types were saurischian. *Pisanosaurus* is therefore unique for its time as a very early ornithischian, a member of the major group that included the majority of plant-eating dinosaurs over the next 150 million years.

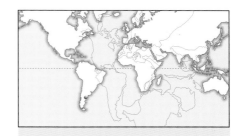

DINO FACTFILE
Pisanosaurus

Meaning: Pisano's lizard

Pronunciation: Peez-ahn-owe-sore-uss

Period: Late Triassic

Main group: Ornithischia

Length: 1 meter (39 inches)

Weight: 3 kilograms (6²/₃ pounds)

Diet: Plants

Fossils: Argentina

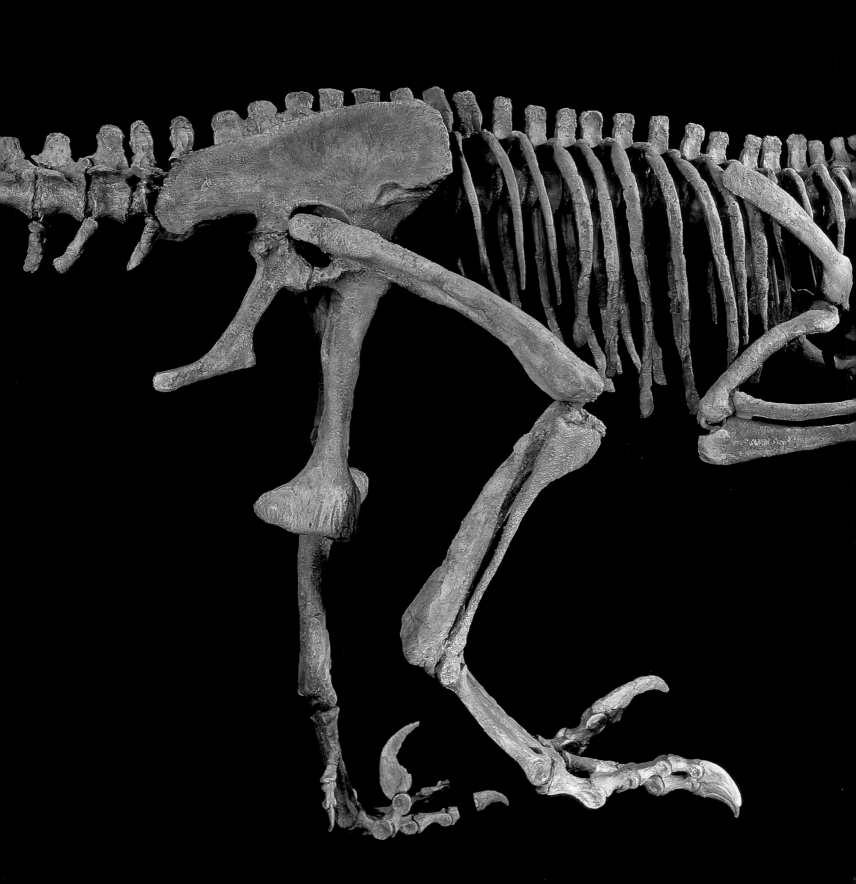

CHAPTER FOUR

THE SMALL MEAT-EATERS

TODAY WE HAVE WILDCATS, STOATS, MONGOOSES, FOXES AND SIMILAR
MAMMALIAN PREDATORS. IN THE MESOZOIC ERA, THEIR ROLES AS SMALLER
BUT STILL DEADLY KILLERS WERE TAKEN BY A VARIETY OF DINOSAURS – AND
SINCE ANIMALS WERE BIGGER THEN, SOME OF THESE MINOR MEAT-EATERS
WERE LARGER THAN TODAY'S TIGERS AND BEARS!

SMALLEST TO SMALL

IN GENERAL, SMALL PREDATORS HUNT SMALL (OR AT LEAST SIMILARLY SIZED) PREY. THE DINOSAURS DESCRIBED IN THIS CHAPTER WERE MOSTLY LESS THAN 3 METERS (10 FEET) IN TOTAL LENGTH AND WEIGHED LESS THAN 100 KILOGRAMS (220 POUNDS) – ABOUT AS HEAVY AS A LARGE ADULT MAN. THIS WAS SMALL FOR THE DINOSAUR AGE, WHEN SOME OF THE LARGER PREDATORS WERE 70 TIMES HEAVIER. ALL MEAT-EATING DINOSAURS, LARGE AND SMALL, ARE KNOWN AS THEROPODS, "BEAST-FEET." MANY OF THE SMALLER MEMBERS OF THIS GROUP WERE SLIM, HOWEVER, OR EVEN ALMOST DAINTY, WITH LIGHTLY BUILT SKELETONS. IN PARTICULAR, THEIR REAR FEET WERE THREE-TOED AND SOME BONES WERE HOLLOW – VERY LIKE MODERN BIRDS. SOME ARE KNOWN AS COELUROSAURIDS, AND WERE AMONG THE SMALLEST AND LIGHTEST OF ALL THE DINOSAURS. WHAT THEY LACKED IN STRENGTH AND POWER WAS COMPENSATED FOR WITH SPEED AND AGILITY, AS THEY TWISTED AND DARTED AMONG ROCKS AND UNDERGROWTH IN PURSUIT OF PREY.

SMALL TO MEDIUM

Slightly larger than these mini-hunters, and generally later in the Age of Dinosaurs, were the dromaeosaurs, medium-sized meat-eaters known informally as "raptors." They were part of a larger group of predators, maniraptorans. One of the best-studied raptors is *Deinonychus*, which was lithe and agile, and powerful enough to tackle prey larger than itself, perhaps the size of a modern pig. Clues in the fossil record suggest that the raptors lived together in groups and hunted in packs, cooperating by using their relatively large brains. In fact, relative to their bodies, their brains were bigger than those of any reptiles, living and extinct.

LIKELY PREY

What did these hunters devour? Their equivalents today often feast on myriad small rodents, like mice, voles or lemmings, and small birds like finches. These did not exist during the early dinosaur age, though – then mammals and birds were probably scarce. Instead, the smaller predatory dinosaurs pursued invertebrates, such as cockroaches and other insects, grubs, slugs, worms and spiders. There were also numerous types of small non-dinosaur reptiles, especially lizards and others resembling them, and their eggs and babies could have been eaten too. Cooperative pack hunting brought much bigger victims within range, such as large plant-eating dinosaurs, weighing a metric ton (1 ton) or more.

LIVING DESCENDANTS

Beginning in the 1960s, scientific studies of raptors such as *Deinonychus* helped to expose as false the myth that all dinosaurs were slow and stupid. Suggestions gained force that they were fast and clever, and even might have been warm-blooded. From the 1980s, fossil finds, especially in China, have thrown us another surprise – dinosaurs with feathers, like *Sinornithosaurus* and *Microraptor gui*, the latter with clear impressions of feathers on all four limbs. The front limbs of these types were not modified as wings – the muscles were not strong enough for true flight – so the fluffy, filamentous feathers may have been for insulation. Again, this implies warm blood, and a likely ancestry to birds.

PREVIOUS PAGE One of the biggest "small" meat-eating dinosaurs was *Utahraptor* – some half a ton of fast, agile, powerful hunter. It was as heavy as today's biggest land carnivores, the brown or grizzly bears. It had the massive curved claw on each second toe characteristic of the "raptor"-type dinosaurs known as dromaeosaurs.

LEFT Dinosaur "wolves" on the prowl: *Velociraptor* and similar dromaeosaurs are now reconstructed as fast, lithe, agile, probably intelligent, pack-hunting killers.

SALTOPUS

DINO FACTFILE

Saltopus

Meaning: Jumping foot, leaping foot

Pronunciation: Sall-toe-puss

Period: Late Triassic

Main group: Theropoda

Length: Less than 1 meter (39 inches)

Weight: 1–2 kilograms (2–5 pounds)

Diet: Small animals

Fossils: Scotland

0	1	2	3	4	5	6

If a fairly complete skeleton of this dinosaur had been found, it might be famous today as one of the smallest dinosaurs known from fossils. But remains are too broken and incomplete to form a reasonable picture of *Saltopus*, and how it might have survived in the Late Triassic period, some 225–220 million years ago. What are believed to be preserved bones of one individual were found in the Elgin region of Scotland, an area well known for fossils. *Saltopus* may have been a ceratosaur, a member of a group that included the slightly larger but still quite small *Coelophysis* as well as much bigger meat-eaters from the Jurassic period, including *Ceratosaurus* itself.

The remains of *Saltopus*, scarce though they are, suggest that it was a very slight, lightly built theropod – a predatory dinosaur that walked and ran mainly on its two longer rear legs. Its length and height overall were probably less, and its build much slimmer, than those of a modern cat. Its hip region shows that four of the five sacral vertebrae (backbones) were fused to the pelvis (hipbone), unlike those of other small predatory dinosaurs of the time, such as *Procompsognathus*, which had five fused or sacral vertebrae. However, *Saltopus* had five digits at the end of each forelimb, a relatively primitive feature, although the fourth and fifth digits were tiny. The general evolutionary trend of theropods losing digits continued through the Age of Dinosaurs, eventually leading to forelimbs with just two digits. *Saltopus* must have been quick and agile, able to dart after small prey like insects and baby reptiles.

RIGHT *Saltopus* is one of the smallest dinosaurs known, but its fossils are too incomplete to permit a confident reconstruction. It was probably only 25 centimeters (10 inches) tall when in its upright "standing" pose.

PROCOMPSOGNATHUS

In 1913, German paleontologist Eberhard Fraas gave fragmentary remains uncovered near Wittenberge (north of Berlin, Germany) the name *Procompsognathus*. It may suggest that this dinosaur was some kind of predecessor to the small and well-known *Compsognathus* ("pretty jaw" or "elegant jaw"). Despite the fossils of both dinosaurs being found in the same general region, and the two being similar in shape, an enormous gap of 70 million years separates them: *Procompsognathus* dates from the Late Triassic period, some 220 million years ago, and *Compsognathus* dates from about 155–150 million years ago (see page 148). The similarity in the name is, therefore, purely symbolic and does not indicate that *Procompsognathus* was a direct or even indirect ancestor of the better-known *Compsognathus*.

Procompsognathus was probably somewhat larger than its much later part-namesake. It was a lightweight, fast-running hunter of small prey like grubs, bugs and small vertebrates such as newly hatched reptiles. Its environment was dry, with sparse plant life forming scrubby bushland. The long rear legs attest to speed and agility, with only three of the four digits on each foot contacting the ground. The forelimbs were much shorter, but *Procompsognathus* had four strong digits on each of them, which it probably used for grabbing and perhaps tearing up victims. The head was long and narrow, with a pointed snout, and the jaws contained numerous small teeth, unsuited for heavy work such as gnawing carcasses. The tail was narrow and tapering, forming half the entire length of the creature. The structure of the caudal vertebrae (bones in the tail) suggests that the whole tail was relatively stiff, and could not be swished or whipped with flexibility like a length of rope.

DINO FACTFILE
Procompsognathus

Meaning: Before *Compsognathus* (see page 148)

Pronunciation: Pro-comp-son-ay-thuss

Period: Late Triassic

Main group: Theropoda

Length: 1.3 meters (4½ feet)

Weight: 2–3 kilograms (5–7 pounds)

Diet: Small animals

Fossils: Germany

| 0 | 1 | 2 | 3 | 4 | 5 | 6 |

RIGHT *Procompsognathus* was about the same weight as a pet cat of today, but much slimmer and more than twice a typical cat's nose-tail length. Its S-shaped neck allowed the head to dart in almost any direction.

COELURUS

This dinosaur's name – meaning "hollow form" in Latin – refers to its tube-like bones, which were thinly walled with chambers inside, saving weight while preserving much of their strength – a feature that other small theropod dinosaurs shared with today's birds. *Coelurus* has lent its name to several groupings of theropod dinosaurs; generally similar types of small predators have been referred to as "coelurosaurs," a convenient but loose term for a mixed bag. More precisely, though, the name Coelurosauria has been applied to small theropods surviving from Late Jurassic times through most of the Cretaceous period following. The family had a worldwide distribution, and it included such well-known forms as *Compsognathus* and *Ortitholestes*, as well as many more obscure types. But recent views have described the coelurosauria as a larger, more encompassing group that gave rise to several different subgroups, such as the huge tyrannosaurs, the ostrich-like ornithomimosaurs, and maniraptorans such as *Deinonychus*. (*Coelurosauravus* was a different type of reptile, a lizard-like glider, see page 98.)

Despite this fame, *Coelurus* itself is poorly known. It was used as the basis for grouping similar dinosaurs because it was one of the first of these general types to receive an official scientific name. In 1879, Othniel Charles Marsh, an eminent American dinosaur-hunter, coined the name *Coelurus* for remains 155–145 million years old found in Wyoming. A composite picture of *Coelurus* shows that it had a small, low head about 20 centimeters (8 inches) long, a flexible neck and a long, slim tail. The three large, strong, clawed digits on each forelimb must have had a powerful grasping grip. The femur (thighbone) measures some 55 centimeters (22 inches) in length, giving clues to the overall proportions of a light but strongly built theropod that moved on its rear legs. It probably fed on large insects, small vertebrates such as lizards or frogs and, perhaps, some of the small mammals of the time in the Late Jurassic forests and swamps of this American region.

DINO FACTFILE
Coelurus

Meaning: Hollow tail, hollow form

Pronunciation: Seel-yur-uss

Period: Late Jurassic

Main group: Theropoda

Length: 2 meters (6½ feet)

Weight: 15 kilograms (33 pounds)

Diet: Small and medium-sized animals

Fossils: USA (Wyoming)

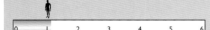

| 0 | 1 | 2 | 3 | 4 | 5 | 6 |

RIGHT The strong fingers and sharp claws on the forelimbs of *Coelurus* would have been useful tools for scrabbling after and grabbing small prey items like insects and worms.

LEFT The functions of the small bony crest or "horn" on the nose of *Ornitholestes* have been much debated. It seems too weak and insignificant for a weapon. Possibly it was a sign of sexual maturity or of sex itself, for example, possessed only by males.

ORNITHOLESTES

Ornitholestes was given its name – "bird robber" – because it was thought that it may have chased and eaten early types of birds, like *Archaeopteryx*. These lived at about the same time, 150 million years ago, but their fossil sites are separated by thousands of kilometers. Only one main specimen of *Ornitholestes* is known, an almost complete skeleton recovered in 1900 from the famous site of Bone Cabin Quarry near Como Bluff, Wyoming. The fossils were studied and named in 1903 by the legendary paleontologist Henry Fairfield Osborn, director of the American Museum of Natural History, with a follow-up report of further studies in 1916. Only a handful of very limited specimens, such as parts of a forelimb, are known from other individuals.

Ornitholestes is usually viewed as a coelurid, a cousin of *Coelurus* (see opposite). It was a lightweight, speedy theropod (predatory, or meat-eating dinosaur) that walked and ran on its slim but strong and long back legs. Its forelimbs were also long and powerful, with relatively massive "hands" with amazingly lengthy digits, comparable in size to the forearms. Each of the three digits had a sharply hooked claw, suggesting that *Ornitholestes* used them to catch and tear up its victims. The jaws could open wide to reveal small, sharp, well-spaced teeth, although only in the front half – the rear of each jaw was toothless. Two other features of *Ornitholestes* are also notable. Some reconstructions show a thin flange of bone on the snout, like a rounded nose crest, flattened from side to side which was perhaps a visual sign of maturity; and the tail of *Ornitholestes* was exceptionally long and whippy, forming more than half the total length of this dinosaur. The teeth were slightly unusual – those at the front of the mouth were almost conical in shape, while those farther back were more blade-like.

DINO FACTFILE
Ornitholestes

Meaning: Bird robber, bird thief

Pronunciation: Or-nith-owe-less-teez

Period: Late Jurassic

Main group: Theropoda

Length: 2.2 meters (7½ feet)

Weight: 15 kilograms (33 pounds)

Diet: Small and medium animals

Fossils: USA (Wyoming)

COMPSOGNATHUS

DINO FACTFILE

Compsognathus

Meaning: Pretty jaw, elegant mouth

Pronunciation: Comp-son-nay-thuss

Period: Late Jurassic

Main group: Theropoda

Length: 1.4 meters (4½ feet)

Weight: 3 kilograms (6½ pounds)

Diet: Small animals

Fossils: Germany, France

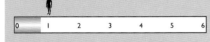

Among dinosaur afficionados, this tiny theropod has an enormous reputation as one of the smallest dinosaurs known from reasonably complete remains. There are two main fossil specimens. The smaller one, which has a total length of 70 centimeters (27½ inches), was perhaps a partly grown individual. It was excavated in the late 1850s in the Riedenberg area of Bavaria in southern Germany. The larger and probably full-grown individual was uncovered in 1972 from Var, near Nice, in southern France. It has an overall length of some 1.3 meters (4½ feet).

Compsognathus was not only small, it had an extremely light build, so it probably weighed just 2–3 kilograms (5–7 pounds). It was long thought that its hands had just two fingers, with slightly curved claws, and this is reflected in restorations and illustrations. However, new evidence shows the hands were probably three-fingered, with the first digit or thumb larger and thicker than the other two. Its head was long and low; the skull was mainly struts with spaces for flesh between them, rather than large plates of bone; and the relatively small jaws could be described as "elegant" (hence the dinosaur's name). The teeth were tiny and evenly spaced. The rear legs were also slim, with relatively short thighs and shins, but very long feet – the proportions of a rapid runner. Both the neck and tail were also long and their joints show they were flexible.

The overall impression of *Composognathus* is of a fast, lean, agile creature that could dart and twist at speed when chasing prey, dash into the undergrowth, or hide in narrow rock crevices to escape enemies such as bigger dinosaurs. There is evidence of diet in the German specimen: fossilized remains of a small lizard, *Bavarisaurus*, were found preserved within the body of *Compsognathus*.

BELOW The body of *Compsognathus* was about the same length and weight as a domestic cat today.

RIGHT The snout shape and proportions of the arms and legs are reasonably known from the few fossils of *Dromaeosaurus* discovered. The rest of the reconstruction relies on information borrowed from others in its group. Following its initial discovery, this dinosaur was thought to be a larger version of *Coelurus*.

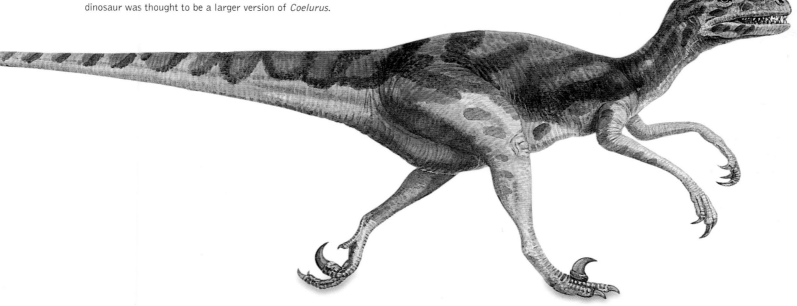

DROMAEOSAURUS

The dromaeosaurs, or "running reptiles," were named after this dinosaur, which was one of the first in the group to be described but is still one of the least understood. Barnum Brown, a respected fossil-finder of his time, dug up the first remains of *Dromaeosaurus* near Alberta's Red Deer River in 1914. Together with William Diller Matthew, Brown named this dinosaur in 1922, but on scanty evidence only – some skull and lower jaw parts, plus a few limb and foot bones. The situation changed drastically in the 1960s with the discovery of *Deinonychus* (see page 153) and subsequent discussions about intelligence, warm-bloodedness and, recently, whether the covering was feathers and not scales. By comparing the detailed fossils of *Deinonychus* with the less conclusive material for *Dromaeosaurus*, scientists were able to establish the *Dromaeosaurus* group as fast, powerful, predatory dinosaurs, but still under the original

name of dromaeosaurs. The more familiar or colloquial term for these dinosaurs is "raptors" (see next page), since the group also includes *Velociraptor*, *Utahraptor*, *Microraptor* and others.

Working backward from today's richer picture of the dromaeosaur group helps to fill some gaps in knowledge about *Dromaeosaurus* itself. It had a big head with large eyes, a tall and rounded snout, and powerful jaws bristling with fang-like teeth. The forelimbs were probably smaller than the rear limbs, but still powerful, and with sharply clawed digits. The rear limbs were also strong, suitable for running and leaping. The second digit of each foot bore the huge, curved "sickle claw" that is a major feature of the group. In overall size, *Dromaeosaurus* was comparable to *Velociraptor* (see page 154), being smaller than *Deinonychus* and especially *Utahraptor* (see page 152). It lived 75–72 million years ago.

DINO FACTFILE
Dromaeosaurus

Meaning: Running reptile, swift reptile

Pronunciation: Drom-ay-owe-sore-uss

Period: Late Cretaceous

Main group: Theropoda

Length: 1.7 meters (5½ feet)

Weight: 25 kilograms (55 pounds)

Diet: Animals, carrion

Fossils: Midwestern USA, Canada (Alberta)

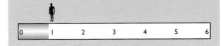

| 0 | 1 | 2 | 3 | 4 | 5 | 6 |

Were dinosaurs warm-blooded?

Since the 1960s, opinions have strengthened that some dinosaurs — especially raptors like *Deinonychus* — were probably warm-blooded. Fossils showing the inner details of their preserved bones reveal that the micro-cellular structure was more similar to the bones of mammals than of modern cold-blooded reptiles. Being warm-blooded would allow faster movement and more stamina in cool conditions.

RIGHT A lone dromaeosaur or raptor, *Deinonychus*, stalks a small herd of larger, plant-eating *Tenontosaurus*. It may be waiting for one of the younger herbivores to wander from its herd, or perhaps it will attack in the cool of the evening, when the movements of *Tenontosaurus* slow down — but the warm-blooded predator is just as quick and agile.

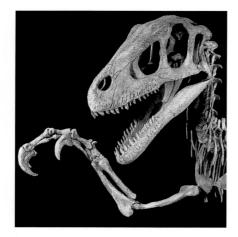

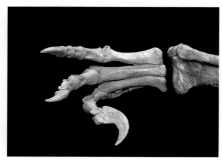

TOP The ferocious teeth and claws of *Utahraptor*.

ABOVE The second toe had very flexible joints to allow the "sickle" claw its fast-slashing motion.

RIGHT *Utahraptor* stood taller than an adult human, and in overall length and weight it rivaled today's biggest reptile, the saltwater crocodile.

DINO FACTFILE
Utahraptor
Meaning: Utah thief, Utah hunter
 (from its discovery site)
Pronunciation: You-taw-rap-tore
Period: Early Cretaceous
Main group: Theropoda
Length: 5–6 meters (16–20 feet)
Weight: 500 kilograms (1,100 pounds)
Diet: Larger animals
Fossils: USA (Utah)

UTAHRAPTOR

This hunter is one of the most recently discovered and largest of the dromaeosaurs, or "raptors." It shot to fame in the early 1990s as a result of fact following fiction. The clever, co-operative dinosaurs of the 1993 movie *Jurassic Park* are based on smaller dromaeosaurs, such as *Velociraptor* and *Deinonychus*, but to make them a match for human adversaries they were enlarged to slightly more than the height of an adult person and to several meters (yards) in length. During production of the movie, in 1991, fossil remains of just such a raptor were uncovered in eastern Utah, giving a factual basis for *Jurassic Park*'s fearsome monsters.

Several further part-specimens of *Utahraptor* have been identified in the past few years at various North American sites. Combined with knowledge from other raptors, *Utahraptor* is reconstructed as a powerful predator, fairly light and fast for its overall length and height, with rows of sharp, curved fangs, each around the size of a human thumb, in its jaws. It was twice the length of *Deinonychus* (see opposite) and weighed perhaps ten times more. Like other dromaeosaurs, it possessed a huge "sickle claw" on the second digit of each hind foot, which could be flicked around in a slashing arc.

At more than 20 centimeters (8 inches) long, this claw was longer than most human hands. Presumably *Utahraptor* kicked and sliced at big prey to gash them open. Its fossils date to the Early and mid-Cretaceous period – 120–110 million years ago – making it one of the earliest known dromaeosaurs. It was probably a hunter of weaker plant-eating dinosaurs, such as sauropods or ornithopods, able to tackle prey larger than itself. This dinosaur also throws new light on how the raptor group may have evolved. The main fossils come from rocks known as the Cedar Mountain Formation in central Utah, and the name was given in 1993 by James Kirkland, Robert Gaston and Donald Burge.

DEINONYCHUS

In 1964, John Ostrom, Grant Meyer and a team of excavators were exploring a new fossil site in southern Montana. Over the next few years, they recovered many specimens, but most exciting were the remains of a medium-sized theropod (predatory, or meat-eating dinosaur). Several good skeletons from 115–110 million years ago rendered a detailed reconstruction of this hunter, *Deinonychus*, with its powerful yet agile physique, wide and gaping jaws armed with saw-edged fangs, large strong "hands" for a vice-like grip, and straight, stiff tail . The vicious extra-large "terrible claw" that gives this dinosaur its name was on the second digit of each foot, and could be flicked around in a slicing motion like a knife. Further remains were uncovered in Wyoming, and the study of these remarkable finds continued for several years.

In 1969, John Ostrom's reports on *Deinonychus* caused a sensation. Suddenly,

it appeared that not all dinosaurs were cold-blooded, slow and stupid! Several lines of evidence suggested that *Deinonychus* and its kin were fast movers, with great leaping ability, quick reactions and relatively big brains. It even was suggested that they were capable of learned, intelligent behavior, and perhaps, were warm-blooded, too. Although debate continues, on the issues of intelligence and warm-bloodedness in particular, the perception of dinosaurs among the general public, and certain scientists, was revolutionized forever. One interpretation of *Deinonychus* fossils *in situ* (as they were found) suggests that raptors coordinated their attacks on larger prey. The site includes the remains of a potential victim, a one metric ton ornithopod dinosaur named *Tenontosaurus*. Did the hunters gather to leap upon and slash open the plant-eater, as a pack of wolves today might surround a deer, or a pride of lionesses bring down a wildebeest?

DINO FACTFILE
Deinonychus
Meaning: Terrible claw
Pronunciation: Die-non-ee-kuss
Period: Mid-Cretaceous
Main group: Theropoda
Length: 3 meters (10 feet)
Weight: 60 kilograms (130 pounds)
Diet: Animals
Fossils: USA (Montana, Wyoming)

RIGHT *Deinonychus* weighed about as much as a typical adult human, but stood slightly shorter, probably around 1.5 meters (5 feet) to head height. Its tail was stiffened rather than flexible and whip-like.

VELOCIRAPTOR

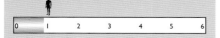

DINO FACTFILE

Velociraptor

Meaning: Speedy thief, fast hunter

Pronunciation: Vell-oss-ee-rap-tore

Period: Late Cretaceous

Main group: Theropoda

Length: 1.7 meters (5½ feet)

Weight: 20–30 kilograms (45–65 pounds)

Diet: Small animals

Fossils: China, Mongolia

This small, well-muscled predator has been known since 1924. It was during a series of major fossil-finding expeditions organized by the American Museum of Natural History that remains were first recovered, from the Byan Dzak (Shabarakh Usu) region of Mongolia. *Velociraptor*'s place within the theropod group remained unclear until the discovery of *Deinonychus* and its links with *Dromaeosaurus* in the 1960s. It then became clear that *Velociraptor*, with the characteristic scythe-like claw on the second digit of each foot, was one of the raptors. It probably displayed the same behavior, hunting for prey that it grabbed with its powerful clawed "hands," then kicked with its rear feet, and finally slashed open with its sickle-like claw.

Like other dromaeosaurs, *Velociraptor* had a tail stiffened by bony, overlapping, rod-like tendons, meaning that the tail could be flexed at the base only. While not particularly useful as a weapon, the tail may have been important as a counterbalance, swinging to one side as the dinosaur twisted its head and body rapidly to the other side. Another older suggestion is that the tail was a prop-like support, allowing *Velociraptor* to lean back onto it, kangaroo-style, as it struck out with its rear feet.

One amazing group of fossils found in 1971 in the Mongolian region of Toogreeg, is of a *Velociraptor*, apparently in a fight to the death in the dry scrub some 80 million years ago, with a pig-sized horned dinosaur called *Protoceratops*. The carnivore *Velociraptor* seems to be biting its opponent's snout and kicking at its throat, while the herbivore *Protoceratops*, in defense of itself or perhaps its egg-filled nest, has *Velociraptor*'s forelimb in its powerful parrot-like beak. The two, locked in mortal combat, were wiped out by a collapsed sand dune or sandstorm that has preserved them almost perfectly.

TROODON

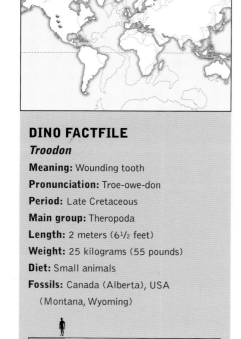

DINO FACTFILE

Troodon

Meaning: Wounding tooth

Pronunciation: Troe-owe-don

Period: Late Cretaceous

Main group: Theropoda

Length: 2 meters (6½ feet)

Weight: 25 kilograms (55 pounds)

Diet: Small animals

Fossils: Canada (Alberta), USA
(Montana, Wyoming)

If, as many scientists argue, the ratio of an animal's brain size to its body size is an indication of what could be called intelligence, then *Troodon* was, perhaps, one of the cleverest among the dinosaurs. This 2-meter (6½-foot) long predator from 70 million years ago would stand chest-high to a human being. The fossils found in Alberta, Canada, and two US states (Montana, Wyoming) indicate that it had the slim build of a fast runner, in many ways more like a bird than a reptile, with a long, low head, and large eyes that looked to the front for distance-judging stereoscopic vision. It is possible (as discussed on later pages) that *Troodon* was warm-blooded and covered in downy or fiber-like feathers. The large, curved claw on the second digit of its foot, ready to be flicked around in an arch, was typical of the raptor-like dromaeosaur group. Its strong forelimbs were suited to reaching out and grabbing, hence the name given to the larger group to which *Troodon* belongs: maniraptora, "seizing hands."

Information on this dinosaur remained confusing for some 130 years after it was given its name (which means "wounding tooth") in 1856. The name was bestowed on the scarcest of evidence: a single, narrow, triangular, saw-edged tooth. Fossils discovered since that time show that there were, in fact, about 120 such teeth in the jaws. In the 1980s, teeth similar to these were linked by revised studies to bones of other small meat-eating dinosaurs, like *Stenonychosaurus*. In the reshuffling of classification that followed, the earliest given name took precedence. *Troodon* emerged as a rapid, dashing predator of small vertebrates like lizards, frogs and, perhaps, small birds and rat-sized mammals. Its fossils were found in Alberta, as well as Montana and Wyoming, where they have been found associated with eggs and other dinosaurs such as *Orodromeus* (see page 278).

LEFT *Velociraptor* was slim but well muscled. It kept the scythe claw on the second toe of each foot tilted up and back, clear of the ground, as it walked.

BELOW A preserved *Velociraptor* skull from the Djadochta Formation rock layers of Mongolia, dated to about 70 million years ago. Its total length is 31 centimeters (12½ inches).

THE PACK-HUNTERS

One quarry site has yielded remains of four *Deinonychus*, near fossils of a *Tenontosaurus* (a cousin of *Iguanodon*). It is tempting to reconstruct a "pack attack," as the agile, powerful carnivores leapt from all sides to slash-kick the plant-eater, which weighed one metric ton (1 ton). However, this implies a degree of planning and coordination among the raptors, a type of behavior far beyond the reptiles of today.

RIGHT About 110 million years ago in what is now Montana, USA, three *Deinonychus* move in for the kill as *Tenontosaurus* struggles to save itself. The dromaeosaurs are able to leap powerfully onto the victim's back or kick from the sides with the huge, curved, slashing claw on the second toe of each foot.

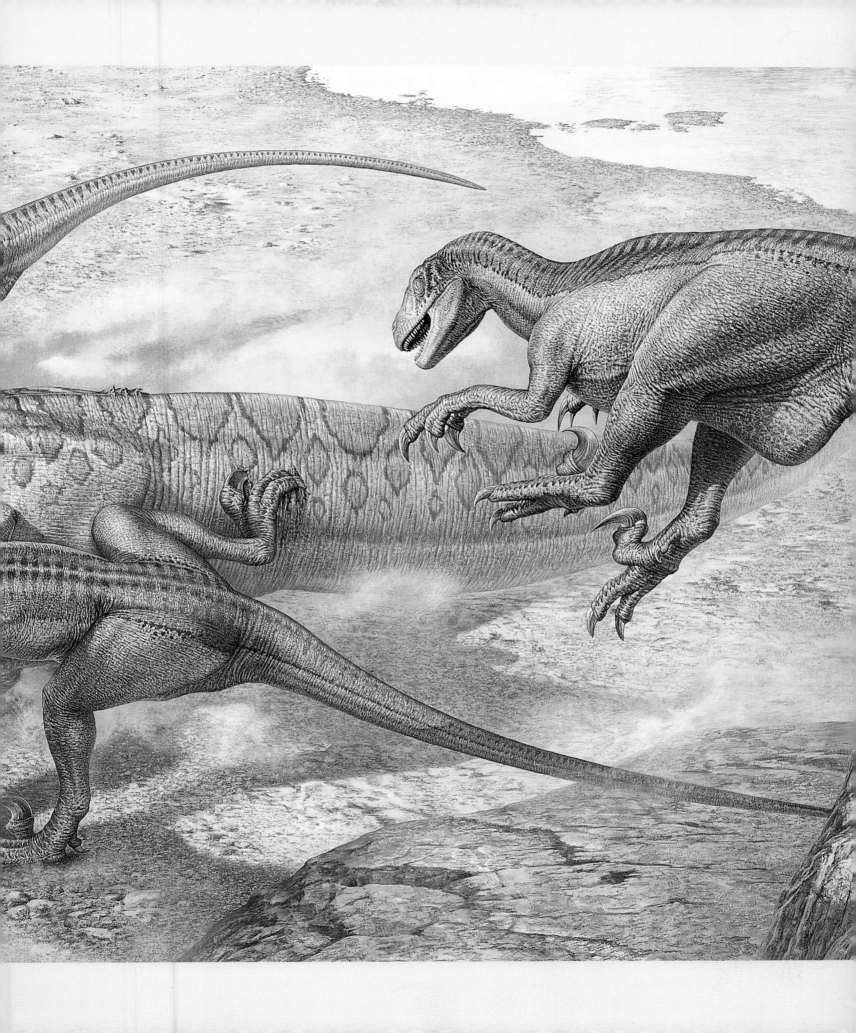

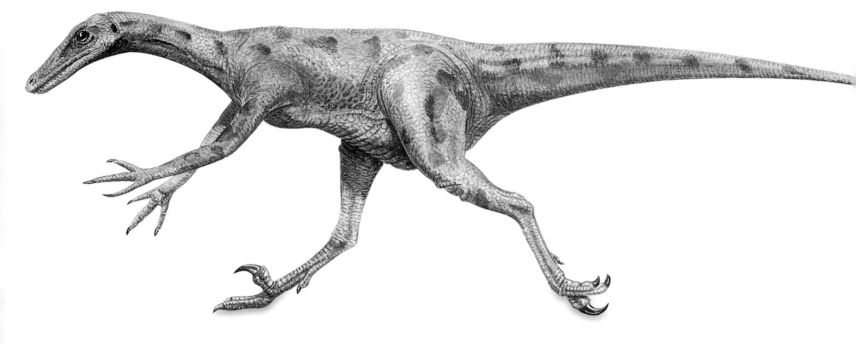

SAURORNITHOIDES

DINO FACTFILE

Saurornithoides

Meaning: Bird-like reptile

Pronunciation: Saw-roar-ni-thoy-deez

Period: Late Cretaceous

Main group: Theropoda

Length: 2 meters (6½ feet) some remains
  suggest 3.5 meters (11½ feet)

Weight: 30 kilograms (65 pounds)

Diet: Small animals

Fossils: Mongolia

In many ways, *Saurornithoides* was an Asian version of *Troodon* (see page 154). Its fossils came to light in 1923, during the legendary and incredibly productive Central Asiatic Expedition organized by the American Museum of Natural History. Remains included parts of a skull, backbone, hips, and pieces of leg and foot bones. They were found in the Byan Dzak (Shabarakh Usu) region of the Gobi Desert, a few kilometers from those of its cousin, *Velociraptor*, and many other Late Cretaceous creatures. The fossils are dated at about 85–77 million years old. Henry Fairfield Osborn, then the director of the museum, named *Saurornithoides* in 1924 after its bird-like skeleton and body proportions.

At the time of its discovery, it was even suggested that *Saurornithoides* was not a reptile at all, but an early toothed bird. Since then, however, there have been several further discoveries of similar fossils in Mongolia, plus comparisons with dinosaurs such as *Troodon*

and *Velociraptor*. *Saurornithoides* fits the typical picture of a fleet-footed hunter, running rapidly on its long, slender rear legs, and probably using its strong forelimbs, with their sharp-clawed digits, to grasp prey. Like *Troodon*, its eyes were relatively huge compared to those of most dinosaurs. This led to suggestions that *Saurornithoides* was crepuscular, meaning that it hunted in the twilight of dusk and dawn, when many other predators were unable to see clearly in the gloom. If *Saurornithoides* was warm-blooded, this might have given it an added edge, as cold-blooded reptiles – both potential victims and competing predators – became cooler and so less active in the early and late hours of the day.

ABOVE Slim and speedy, "bird-like reptile" was identified as a bird when its fossils were first studied. Its teeth were small but sharp like tiny blades, and serrated-edged but only on the posterior (rear-facing) edge.

"ORNITHODESMUS"

The tale of how fossil-hunters and paleontologists have viewed the small collection of *Ornithodesmus* fossils has taken many twists and turns. The first known remains came from the Isle of Wight, off the coast of southern England and which has sometimes been given the nickname "Dinosaur Island" because of its wealth of remains. *Ornithodesmus* was identified first not as a dinosaur, but as a pterosaur or winged reptile, and named in 1887 by Harry Grovier Seely, who wrote an early account popularizing pterosaurs, *Dragons of the Air*. It was Seely who devised the method of dividing the entire dinosaur group into saurichians (lizard-hipped) and ornithischians (bird-hipped) based on pelvis structure. The main specimen of the species *Ornithodesmus cluniculus*, uncovered at Brook Bay and dated at 127–120 million years old, was the sacrum (the central part of the hip girdle), formed from six sacral vertebrae fused together. Seely inferred a connection to flying and chose a name meaning "bird ligament" or "bird link."

Later, more fossils were found and in 1913 these were identified as being from *Ornithodesmus latidens*, another species in the same genus. In 1993, further studies reported that the original specimen was not a pterosaur, but a small theropod dinosaur, and *Ornithodesmus* was grounded. Since then the "dinosaur" *Ornithodesmus* has been compared variously to troodontids, such as *Troodon*; to dromaeosaurs, such as *Deinonychus*; and even to other dinosaur predators, such as the coelurids. The evidence is limited and there continue to be many disagreements. In the meantime, other fossils once included with *Ornithodesmus* as a dinosaur have been regrouped back again as a pterosaur. Some have been reclassified as *Istiodactylus*, a tail-less or pterodactyl-like pterosaur with a 5-meter (16-foot) wingspan. Currently the situation is under review with pterosaur experts retaining *Ornithodesmus* for the flying reptile while the dinosaur fossils removed from that collection are informally known as "Ornithodesmus."

DINO FACTFILE
"Ornithodesmus"

Meaning: Bird ligament, bird strap, bird link

Pronunciation: Orr-nith-owe-des-muss

Period: Early Cretaceous

Main group: Theropoda/Petrosauria

Length: 1.7 meters (5½ feet)

Weight: 15 kilograms (33 pounds)

Diet: Small animals

Fossils: England

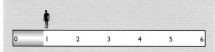

RIGHT The pterosaur (winged reptile) *Ornithodesmus,* shown on the upper right, was originally reconstructed using some fossil bones that are now believed to come from a dinosaur. This is informally called "*Ornithodesmus*" and provisionally reconstructed as shown to the right.

OVIRAPTOR

DINO FACTFILE
Oviraptor
Meaning: Egg thief, egg hunter
Pronunciation: Owe-vee-rap-tore
Period: Late Cretaceous
Main group: Theropoda
Length: 2 meters (6½ feet)
Weight: 30 kilograms (65 pounds)
Diet: Unclear
Fossils: Mongolia, possibly China

This dinosaur was given its name, meaning "egg thief," because one set of its fossils was found associated with remains of dinosaur eggs. George Olsen made the find in 1923, during one of the expeditions to Asia organized by the American Museum of Natural History. Experts concluded that this *Oviraptor* perished while raiding the nest of another dinosaur, and the strange head and jaws of this dinosaur support such an idea. The skull was tall, with deep jaws shaped like the pointed beak of a bird like a parrot. The jaws lacked teeth but were suited to exerting great pressure along their edges to crack hard objects, like nuts – or eggs. Also interesting was the tall, thin, curved crest on the snout, which varied between the two species of *Oviraptor*: one, *Oviraptor philoceratops*, had a snout crest shaped like a parallelogram (a skewed or distorted rectangle); the other, *Oviraptor mongoliensis*, had a taller, more rounded crest (see also *Ingenia*, opposite). The rest of *Oviraptor*'s body was fairly typical of many small theropods – long, slim, rear legs for running, and large forelimbs, each ending in three elongated, powerful digits

tipped with sharp claws. The neck and tail, however, were less lengthy than in many comparable theropods.

The situation became clearer in the 1990s with further discoveries of *Oviraptor* fossils, in Mongolia and China, again associated with egg remains. But the evidence this time was more of a dinosaur tending its own nest, rather than stealing from the nests of others. In one find, the preserved skeleton of a tiny *Oviraptor* embryo was lying in fragments of shell. In another, it appeared that an *Oviraptor*-type adult had died while extending its forelimbs over 22 eggs in the nest, perhaps as protection against a rainstorm or a predator. However, there are disputes over whether these newer finds represent *Oviraptor* or another similar genus (see also *Protoceratops*, page 355).

RIGHT The head crest of *Oviraptor philoceratops* is shown clearly in this illustration. *Oviraptors* are sometimes pictured with a body partially covered by fine downy feathers rather than scaly skin.

BELOW It can no longer hatch, being solid rock, but the fossilized *Oviraptor* egg shows how these dinosaurs bred more than 70 million years ago, in what is now Mongolia.

INGENIA

This dinosaur is usually called an oviraptorid, meaning that it has many similarities with, and may be a close cousin of, *Oviraptor* (opposite). *Ingenia* was perhaps slightly smaller, nearer 1.5 meters (5 feet) in total length. Most of its known bodily features are reminiscent of *Oviraptor*, and it lived at about the same time, around 80 million years ago, and in the same region, now Mongolia. It received its official name in 1981. Like *Oviraptor*, *Ingenia*'s diet remains something of a mystery. It may have been an omnivore, pecking at and cracking open all kinds of food, including bugs, eggs, hard-cased animals like shellfish or snails, other small animals and even roots and seeds. Or it may have scavenged meat and bone from carcasses, as vultures and condors do today, or pecked at vegetation. The beak-like jawbone was probably covered with a horny layer or sheath, as in birds today, maybe providing an even more sharply edged and hook-shaped eating tool.

Oviraptor is the better-known theropod. Certain fossil skulls with deep, toothless, parrot-like, beaked jaws similar to an *Oviraptor*'s, but with very small snout crests or no crest at all, were once identified as young *Oviraptor*. The reasoning was that features such as crests and horns, in prehistoric creatures as in today's animals, would be relatively very small in juveniles and grow faster as the individual matured. However, other details of these skulls led to some of them being assigned to the newer genus *Ingenia*. In recent years renewed studies of the fossils of *Ingenia*, coupled with new knowledge about how beaks work in living birds, favors the plant-eating view.

BELOW The powerful hooked beak of *Ingenia* could have tackled many kinds of hard foods, from nuts and seeds, to the stringy gristle and marrow-filled bones of small mammals. One suggestion is that *Ingenia* hunted in shallow water for crustacean animals such as freshwater shrimps and crayfish. Another is an herbivorous diet of tough plant parts like roots and wood-cased, sappy stems.

ANIMAL FACTFILE
Ingenia

Meaning: From the area of its discovery, Ingeni-Khobur Depression in Mongolia

Pronunciation: In-gen-ee-a

Period: Late Cretaceous

Main group: Theropoda

Length: 1.5-2 meters (5–6¹/₂ feet)

Weight: 25 kilograms (55 pounds)

Diet: Uncertain

Fossils: Mongolia

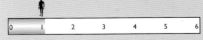

SAURORNITHOLESTES

DINO FACTFILE

Saurornitholestes

Meaning: Bird-thief reptile, avian
    robber reptile

Pronunciation: Saw-roar-nith-owe-less-teez

Period: Late Cretaceous

Main group: Theropoda

Length: 1.8–2 meters (6–6½ feet)

Weight: 5–20 kilograms (11–45 pounds)

Diet: Small animals

Fossils: Canada (Alberta)

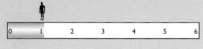

The fast-moving, meat-eating *Saurornitholestes* was a member of the dromaeosaur or "raptor" group that lived in North America during the last phase of the Cretaceous Period, its fossils dated to 75–73 million years ago. This was a time when the great predatory dinosaurs, such as the fearsome *Albertosaurus* and the even mightier *Tyrannosaurus*, roamed what is now North America. *Saurornitholestes* was hundreds of times smaller than these giants, and would have stood only waist-high to an adult human being. Nevertheless, it was just as deadly to its victims, which were probably small vertebrates like lizards, snakes or frogs, and perhaps birds, as well as mammals about the size of rats, that are known to have been present in the region around this time.

Saurornitholestes bore some similarities to *Velociraptor* (see page 154), and has been viewed as its North American counterpart. Hans-Dieter Sues named *Saurornitholestes* in 1978, more than 50 years later than *Velociraptor* was named. The main fossils recovered include parts of the skull, some teeth, and parts of forelimb bones. It is a reasonable assumption that *Saurornitholestes* was bipedal, moving only on its long, strong but slender, rear limbs. Its total length approached 2 meters (6½ feet). Estimates of its build and weight vary, due to the incompleteness of its remains, from five kilograms (11 pounds) to four times that much. Another, earlier suggestion was that *Saurornitholestes* was more like *Troodon* (see page 154), with powerful grasping hands, and perhaps a large brain capable of learning and relatively intelligent behavior. Further studies showed greater similarities with *Velociraptor* than with *Troodon*.

LEFT A fine action-posed skeleton of *Saurornitholestes* from the Royal Tyrrell Museum in Alberta, Canada, near the region of its discovery.

CHIROSTENOTES

This powerfully built theropod dinosaur was long a mystery, known only from fossilized bones discovered in Alberta's Red Deer River region, and named by American fossil expert Charles Gilmore in 1924. The find included bones from its forelimbs, each of which had three extremely elongated, clawed digits, the middle one being even longer than the other two. For many years, there was very little further information on these strangely proportioned remains of *Chirostenotes*. There were attempts to link them to some teeth and part of a lower jaw, found some miles away in the same rock layers, and dating back almost to the end of the Cretaceous period. These would fill out the picture and assign *Chirostenotes* to the dromaeosaur group, along with *Deinonychus* and *Velociraptor*. Other experts suspected that *Chirostenotes* might have been more closely related to another group, the ornithomimosaurs or ostrich-dinosaurs (see page 208).

In 1932 Charles Sternberg named another group of fossils *Macrophalangia* ("big toes"). They were noted as being very similar to, and have since been reclassified as, *Chirostenotes*. Also, parts of other skeletons have become involved, including one that

had lain largely unprepared in a museum, still in rock as dug from the ground, for 60 years. These "new" fossils provided parts of the skull, pieces from most sections of the long spinal column (backbone), and parts of the hip region. One current view is that *Chirostenotes* may have been more similar to *Oviraptor*, with a bird-like head, a beak like a parrot's, sturdy rear limbs and powerful forelimbs. The mystery has yet to be conclusively solved.

DINO FACTFILE
Chirostenotes

Meaning: Slim hands, slender fingers

Pronunciation: Kye-row-sten-owe-teez

Period: Late Cretaceous

Main group: Theropoda

Length: 2 meters (6½ feet)

Weight: 35 kilograms (65 pounds)

Diet: Possibly small animals

Fossils: Canada (Alberta)

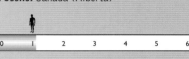

LEFT This composite reconstruction of *Chirostenotes* follows the modern view that it was an oviraptosaurid, with a deep, hooked, beak-like mouth and tall, thin skull crest. There have been several other possibilities over the years, including the suggestion that *Ingenia* was a type of dromaeosaur or "raptor" like *Deinonychus*.

AVIMIMUS

DINO FACTFILE

Avimimus

Meaning: Bird mimic, bird pretender

Pronunciation: Aye-vee-mim-uss

Period: Late Cretaceous

Main group: Theropoda

Length: 1.6 meters (5½ feet)

Weight: 10–15 kilograms (22–33 pounds)

Diet: Small animals, perhaps seeds and plants

Fossils: Mongolia, China

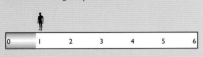

The idea that some dinosaurs had body coverings of feathers, not scales, has made a huge impact in the past few years. An earlier suggestion that this might have been the case came in 1981, when Sergei Mikhailovich Kurzanov, a Russian dinosaur expert, described and named *Avimimus*. He based his description on fossils found in the Omnogov region of Mongolia during the extensive expeditions mounted in the Gobi and surrounding areas in the 1970s jointly by Soviet and Mongolian investigators.

Kurzanov identified several close similarities between *Avimimus* and birds, including the toothless beak; long skull; slim and flexible neck; muscle scars on the humerus (upper forelimb bone); arm joints that allowed the forelimb to fold like a wing (see page 143); a deep, compact body; and fused bones in the upper foot. One piece of evidence Kurzanov highlighted was a ridge running along the ulna, one of the bones of the forelimb. Unknown in other theropods, this ridge happened to be in the same position where a modern bird's equivalent bone would have a row of tiny knobs, like pimples. They are called papillae and are small mounds where the muscles that move (tilt and twist) the feathers are anchored to the bone. Kurzanov's conclusion was that *Avimimus* had feathers, at least along this part of the forelimb. No imprints, however, or signs of feathers were found among the fossilized remains. *Avimimus* thus blazed a trail, of sorts, for the notion of feathered dinosaurs. From the mid 1990s, discoveries of feathered dinosaurs came thick and fast, and the concept is now generally accepted.

Avimimus probably ran at speed in the open countryside of the region, about 83 million years ago, snapping up small animals with its powerful beak. It remains something of a puzzle, and the evidence for its feathers is still conjectural. But even with feathers, the forelimbs are too small and weak for powered, sustained flight, so perhaps the feathers performed another function. They may have helped to insulate the warm-blooded body, or worked as some kind of trap for flying prey such as dragonflies.

RIGHT This is one of the "naked" reconstructions of *Avimimus*, leaving aside the suggestion that the forelimbs had feathers. The evidence for feathers was slim and received with huge doubt in the 1980s, but from the 1990s many feathered dinosaur remains have been found.

ABOVE *Sinosauropteryx* probably grabbed smaller creatures like mammals and lizards as prey. Its feathery covering resembled the fine, hairy "down" which baby birds possess to keep their bodies warm.

SINOSAUROPTERYX

The rural Chinese province of Liaoning, north of Beijing, has yielded some of the most exciting dinosaur finds since about 1994. One is *Sinosauropteryx*, which in some respects is a fairly standard *Compsognathus*-like theropod dinosaur from about 120 million years ago. It was small and lightly built, with long rear limbs for walking and running, short forelimbs, and a long tail, which helped to balance the body when *Sinosauropteryx* was sprinting. But there was a surprise. The very finely grained rocks in which the remains were found had allowed detailed preservation, including impressions that looked like feathers. These were not the fully formed, wide-vaned feathers that modern birds use for flight and outer body covering, but smaller, downier or hair-like "plumes," each about ½ centimeter (¼ inch) long. The fossils showed these feather traces mainly on the animal's neck and shoulders, and also along the back and parts of the tail.

The first discovered specimen of *Sinosauropteryx* was probably a juvenile, about 55 centimeters (22 inches) in total length, half of this being the tail. Chinese fossil experts Ji Qiang and Ji Shu-An described and named it in 1996. Soon after, paleontologists uncovered another larger and probably fully-grown specimen. It too had impressions of feathers. What looked like the remains of a small mammal, with jaws and teeth and other parts, were preserved with it, and are probably evidence of the dinosaur's diet.

The role of the feathers has been much discussed (see following page). They might have been for insulation, to retain body heat, which would imply that *Sinosauropteryx* was warm-blooded – a view gaining new acceptance. They may have been brightly colored, perhaps to attract a mate at breeding time, or dull in color, to blend in with the surroundings for camouflage.

DINO FACTFILE

Sinosauropteryx

Meaning: China's winged or feathered reptile

Pronunciation: Sye-no-saw-op-tur-icks

Period: Late Jurassic Period

Main group: Theropoda

Length: 1 meter (39 inches)

Weight: 3 kilograms (6½ pounds)

Diet: Small animals

Fossils: China

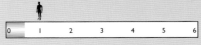

From the Ground to the Air?

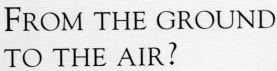

Many experts propose that types of meat-eating dinosaurs, probably of the Maniraptoran ("grasping hands") group, gave rise to the birds. Their key characteristic was a small, crescent-shaped bone in the wrist, that enabled the wrist to twist and swivel swiftly – the same system used by modern birds to flap and fold their wings. Troodon was a later member of the Maniraptoran group, when birds were already established. It had a large brain and big eyes, and was a swift hunter of smaller victims.

RIGHT A discovery from China announced in 2003 is a species of the genus *Microraptor* known as *Microraptor gui*. Dating from the Early Cretaceous period, this had feathers not only on the front limbs and tail, like several other small meat-eaters, but on the rear legs too. It seems that the forelimb muscles were too small for true flight, but the dinosaur may have been able to glide for short distances. The feather impressions show up clearly on several specimens.

RIGHT The fanned, vaned feathers of *Caudipteryx* were located on the forelimbs and tail. Their size and detailed shape, coupled with the size and muscular power of the forelimbs, show that this dinosaur was not capable of flight. The function(s) of the feathers remain a mystery.

CAUDIPTERYX

DINO FACTFILE

Caudipteryx

Meaning: Tail wing, tail feather

Pronunciation: Cawd-ip-tur-icks

Period: Early Cretaceous

Main group: Theropoda

Length: 80 centimeters (31 inches)

Weight: 5 kilograms (11 pounds)

Diet: Varied, perhaps animals and plants

Fossils: China

0	1	2	3	4	5	6

This creature has been the subject of great discussion since the description of its fossils, from Liaoning Province in China, in 1998. It has been identified variously as a very unusual offshoot of the main group of small theropods, or as a flightless descendant of as-yet-unknown dinosaurs, or even a descendent of birds that evolved from flying to flightless. *Caudipteryx* lived slightly later than *Archaeopteryx*, the earliest fully flying bird, so it could not have been an ancestor to that group. Likely it was a member of a group of dinosaurs that left no descendants, whether among reptiles or among birds.

The mix of features in this animal is certainly confusing. Some of its skeleton is similar in structure and proportions to a generalized small predatory dinosaur. But the tail is extremely short, and the forelimbs are too, although *Caudipteryx* had three long, clawed digits on each, just as did many other dinosaurs. The head is long and the mouth has a curved beak, like *Oviraptor* (see page 160). There are teeth at the front of the upper jaw, but they are sharp and stick out slightly, almost like a fringe. The legs are long and slim for fast movement, and some of their bones and joints are again reminiscent of *Oviraptor*, while other parts are said to be more like a typical (modern) bird's legs.

Perhaps the weirdest feature is the feathers. On the forelimbs and tail these have vanes and quills, generally like a bird's flight feathers. Those at the end of the tail are up to 20 centimeters (8 inches) long and spread out in a fan shape. Yet the feathers were not shaped in detail like true flight feathers, and the size and power of the forelimbs show that *Caudipteryx* was not capable of flying. The main body seems to have been covered in fluff or fibrous downy feathers, like *Sinosauropteryx* (see page 165).

THERIZINOSAURUS

In the late 1940s, a joint Soviet–Mongolian fossil-hunting expedition to the Gobi Desert yielded some amazing bony claws of huge size. They were thought to come from a dinosaur or similar large beast, and this otherwise unknown animal was named *Therizinosaurus* – "scythe reptile" – in 1954. More claws turned up in Central Asia during the 1950s and 1960s, as well as parts of a forelimb skeleton and a few fragments of hind limb. Then, finds in China led experts to conclude that the bones belonged to a group of similar dinosaurs, which became known collectively as therizinosaurs and which include the 1993 find, *Alaxasaurus*, and *Beipiaosaurus*, found in 1996. These later finds helped to fill in parts of the picture – and the results are truly astonishing. *Therizinosaurus* was an enormous theropod dinosaur, meaning that it fits in with the group of meat-eaters, yet it may have lived more like a giraffe or a gorilla, consuming only plants.

Therizinosaurus dates to 75–70 million years ago and was one of the later representatives of its group. The three digits on the forelimb each had a massive claw, slightly curved and flattened, and tapered to a sharp point. But the first digit bore the largest claw – more than 60 centimeters (23 inches) in length – and the whole forelimb was 2.5 meters (8 feet) long. The neck was immense, the head small with a beaked mouth, the body deep, the hips wide, and the rear limbs sturdy, with broad, short feet each ending in four digits. *Therizinosaurus* may have been huge, more than 10 meters (33 feet) in length or height, and covered in downy feathers.

As a group, the therizinosaurs may have been cousins of *Oviraptor* (see page 160). Their behavior is hotly debated. Perhaps they craned their long necks to peck and grab at fruit and other vegetation in trees. The claws may have been used as rakes to gather food, as defensive weapons, or as signs of social status and sexual maturity (like a walrus's tusks), or to rip open termite and ant nests, in the manner of the great-clawed giant anteater today. Other "scythe reptiles" included *Segnosaurus*, *Nanshiungosaurus*, *Erlikosaurus* and *Enigmosaurus*. The evidence for a feathery covering is mainly from fossils of *Beipiaosaurus*.

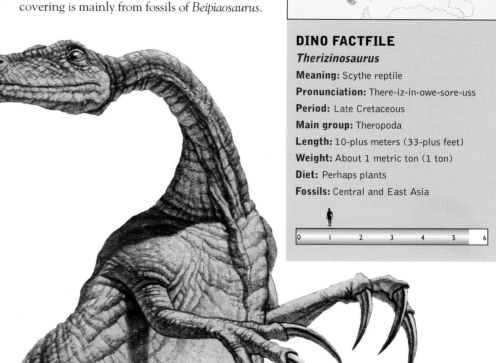

DINO FACTFILE
Therizinosaurus
Meaning: Scythe reptile
Pronunciation: There-iz-in-owe-sore-uss
Period: Late Cretaceous
Main group: Theropoda
Length: 10-plus meters (33-plus feet)
Weight: About 1 metric ton (1 ton)
Diet: Perhaps plants
Fossils: Central and East Asia

0	1	2	3	4	5	6

LEFT One of the strangest of all dinosaurs, *Therizinosaurus* is sometimes reconstructed with a scaly covering, as here, and sometimes with feathers. The largest of the "scythe" claws were each as long as a human arm and hand.

BIRDS AS DINOSAURS

AT ONE TIME, WE CONSIDERED ANY CREATURE WITH FEATHERS TO BE A BIRD. RECENT FINDS OF FEATHERED DINOSAURS HAVE CAUSED A MAJOR RETHINK, HOWEVER. PERHAPS FEATHERS EVOLVED INITIALLY AS INSULATION OR AS A "NET" TO CATCH SMALL PREY, OR FOR CAMOUFLAGE. FLIGHT DEVELOPED SUBSEQUENTLY AS TREE-CLIMBERS CONTROLLED DOWNWARD SWOOPS OR AS FAST RUNNERS FLAPPED FORELIMBS TO JUMP UP WHEN CHASING PREY OR ESCAPING PREDATORS. TO CONFUSE MATTERS MORE, MODERN CLASSIFICATION DOES NOT REGARD BIRDS AS A MAJOR GROUP – EQUIVALENT TO REPTILES OR MAMMALS – BUT AS SUBGROUP OF DINOSAURIA. IN EFFECT, THEREFORE, BIRDS ARE LIVING, WARM-BLOODED, FEATHERED DINOSAURS.

RIGHT One of the world's most famous and valuable fossils shows *Archaeopteryx* beautifully preserved in the typical sprawled-out "death pose," where neck tendons tighten after death and pull the head up and over the back. The long, bony tail projects upper left, and the wing feather impressions fan out upper right and lower center.

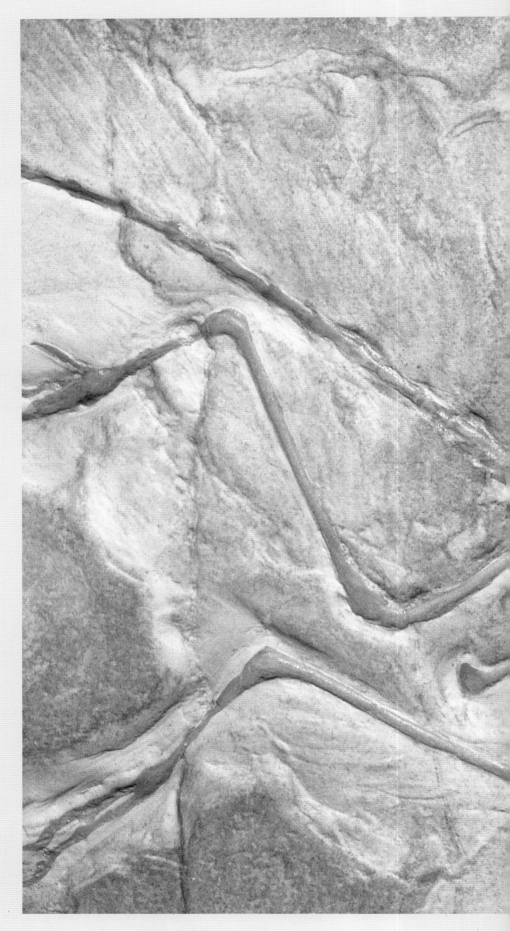

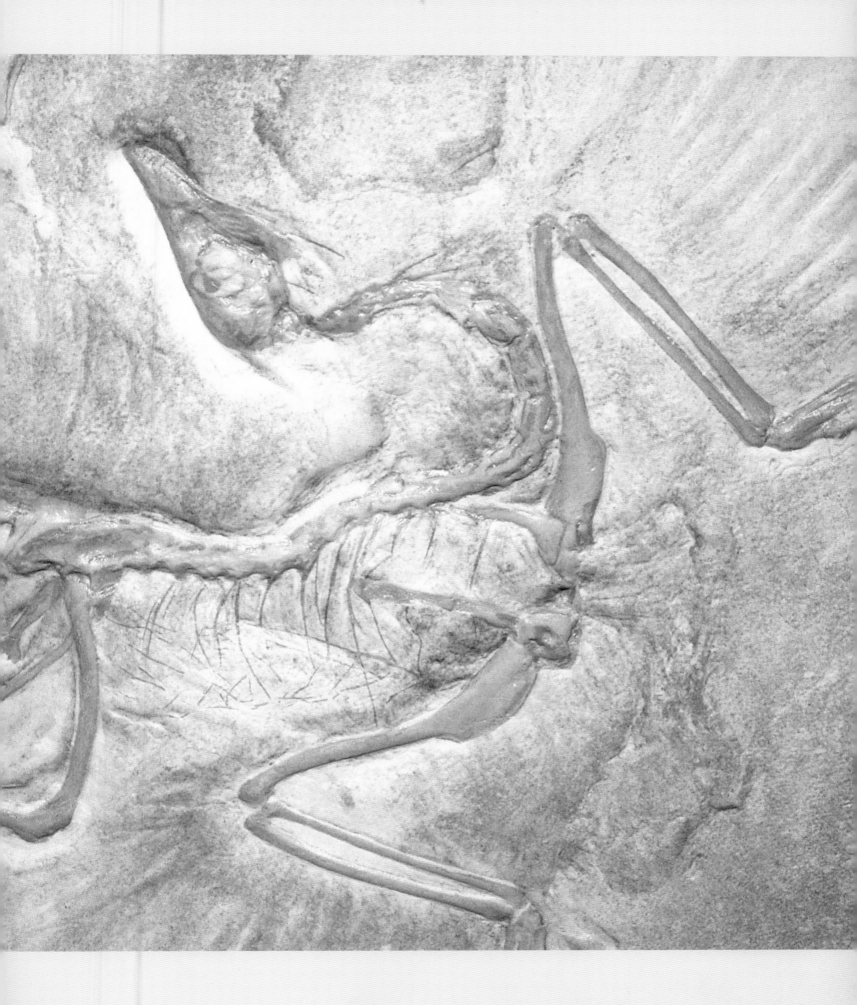

ARCHAEOPTERYX

BIRD FACTFILE

Archaeopteryx

Meaning: Ancient wing

Pronunciation: Ark-ee-op-tur-icks

Period: Late Jurassic

Main group: Aves (Birds)

Length: Beak to tail 60 centimeters
(24 inches)

Wingspan: 70 centimeters (28 inches)

Diet: Insects and other small animals

Fossils: Germany

0	1	2	3	4	5	6

Almost every year, prehistory records are broken as yet bigger, earlier or stranger creatures are discovered and described. The time may come when *Archaeopteryx* loses its perch, but for now it remains the earliest known representative of the birds – a group whose definition becomes more blurred with every year (see page 166). *Archaeopteryx* is known from seven fossils, one being just a feather, and another being a spectacular and beautiful specimen showing the whole creature with outstretched wings, feathers, skull, body, legs and tail in glorious detail. It was preserved in very finely grained limestone in the Solnhofen region of Bavaria in southern Germany. *Archaeopteryx* was given its name, meaning "ancient wing," by Hermann von Meyer, a German paleontologist, in 1861.

For a long time, two other partial specimens of *Archaeopteryx* were long identified as small meat-eating or theropod dinosaurs, similar to *Compsognathus*, which lived around the same time and has been found in the same region. They were reassigned to *Archaeopteryx* in the

1950s and 1970s. This emphasized the similarity between certain theropods, especially the dinosaurs called raptors, and the bird group, as described on page 143. *Archaeopteryx* was a patchwork of features reptilian and avian. The latter included its beak-like mouth, forelimbs modified as wings, long feathers, and feet suited to perching, with a reversed hallux (rear-facing big toe). On the reptilian side, it had teeth in its jaws, claws on its three wing fingers, and a long tail of vertebral bones. Its feathers were not fluffy down but were fully adapted for flight, each with a central shaft and asymmetric vane, as in birds today. *Archaeopteryx* could probably fly, but not with the grace, agility or endurance of modern birds, as it ran, flapped and snapped at insects and similar small creatures.

BELOW *Archaeopteryx* flaps in preparation for take-off, as another of its kind glides past in the background. The feathers of this first known bird are fully designed for flight, and no earlier evidence has been found of part-evolved versions – although there are many later specimens with a variety of feather designs.

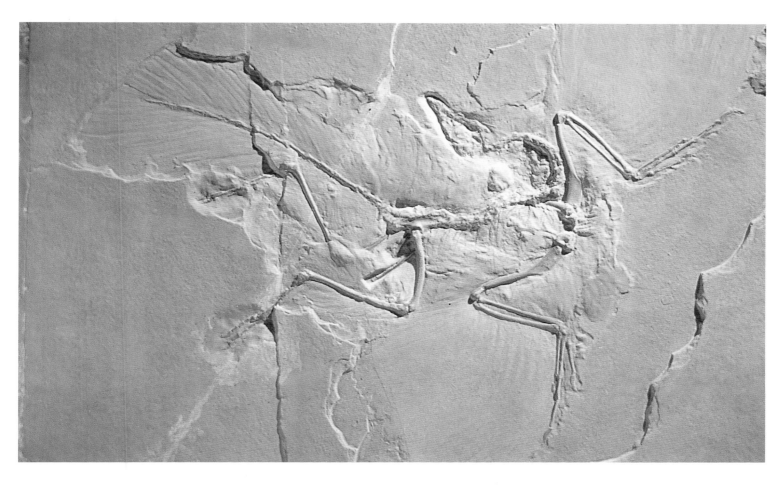

CONFUCIUSORNIS

Named in honor of Confucius, the philosopher and teacher whose ideas have been dominant in China for two thousand years, this magpie-sized bird lived during the Early Cretaceous period, over 120 million years ago. There are some similarities between *Confuciusornis* and the much earlier *Archaeopteryx* (opposite). *Confuciusornis* retained reptilian skeletal features, such as clawed fingers and the detailed structure of its wrists and hips, but it had also developed avian (bird-like) features. It had no teeth in the horn-covered beak, but it did have sturdy clavicle bones (colloquially known in modern birds as the "wishbones") in the shoulders. Its tail was not a row of 20-plus vertebral bones, as in *Archaeopteryx*, but a short lump of fused-together bones, like the feature known in modern birds as the pygostyle (or "parson's nose").

Based on numerous and varied fossils from Liaoning (see page 176), it seems that *Confuciusornis* lived in colonies, was an able flier, and was adept at perching in trees.

Although it lacked tailbones, it did have a tail. Feather impressions show that some individuals had very elongated tail feathers, shaped like long-stemmed paddles, while others lacked these and had rear ends covered in "normal" body feathers as in most modern birds. It is difficult to imagine a practical physical use for the long trailing tail feathers, whether for finding food or for avoiding enemies, so it is tempting, instead, to assume that the feathers were for visual display. In today's bird species, it is almost always the male that has extravagant plumage, which it uses to attract a female at breeding time. Perhaps the two types of *Confuciusornis* specimens represent males and females.

ABOVE *Confuciusornis* fossils resemble those of *Archaeopteryx* (one example is shown above, see also page 170) but are not so complete or detailed. The long bony tail of the latter was not present, replaced by a small lump of bone as in modern birds.

BIRD FACTFILE
Confuciusornis

Meaning: Confucius bird

Pronunciation: Kon-foo-see-orn-iss

Period: Early Cretaceous

Main group: Aves (Birds)

Length: Beak to tail 35 centimeters (13½ inches)

Wingspan: About 70 centimeters (27½ inches)

Diet: Plants

Fossils: China

0		1	2	3	4	5	6

ALTERED EGGS

MOST REPTILES TODAY LAY EGGS. (SOME SNAKES AND A FEW OTHERS GIVE BIRTH TO WELL-FORMED YOUNG.) DINOSAURS LAID EGGS TOO, AS AMPLY DEMONSTRATED BY FOSSILS OF NESTS CONTAINING EGGSHELLS AND BABY DINOSAURS, AND EVEN DINOSAUR EMBRYOS, DELICATELY PRESERVED, UNHATCHED WITHIN THEIR SHELLS. PRESUMABLY THE BIRDS CONTINUED THIS METHOD OF REPRODUCTION. HOWEVER MOST BIRD EGGS TODAY HAVE HARD, BRITTLE SHELLS, WHILE MOST REPTILE EGGS HAVE MORE FLEXIBLE SHELLS, WITH A SLIGHTLY PAPERY OR LEATHERY TEXTURE. WHEN THIS SHIFT IN EGGSHELL STRUCTURE TOOK PLACE IS NOT CLEAR, BUT WITH NUMEROUS DINOSAURS ROAMING THE LAND DURING THE MESOZOIC ERA, EGGS OF ALL KINDS MUST HAVE BEEN A STAPLE FOOD FOR MANY OF THE SMALL MEAT-EATERS.

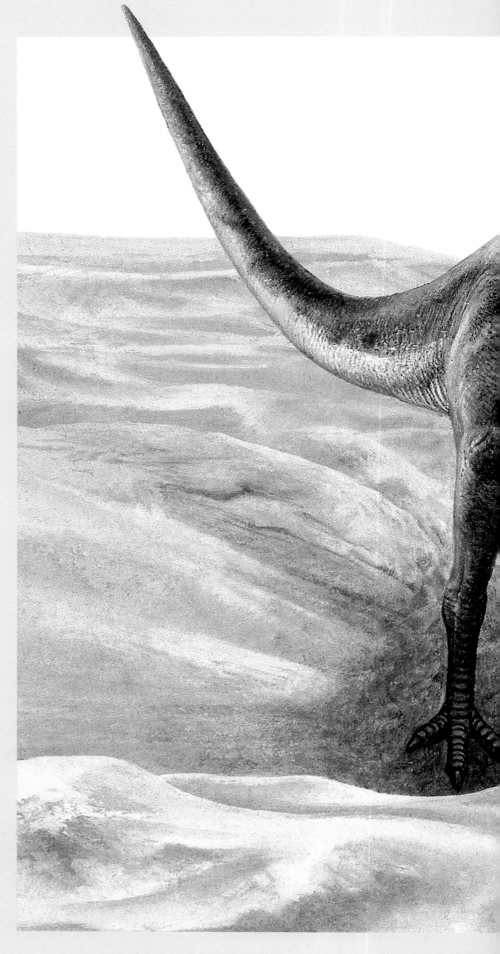

RIGHT An *Ornitholestes*-type theropod indulges in egg-stealing, while keeping senses tuned for signs of a returning parent. Eggs were not only nutrient-packed snacks, they also provided valuable fluids in dry habitats. Most modern reptiles lay their eggs and then leave, spending no time on guard duty or caring for the young. However females in one group of reptiles do help their offspring from the shells and protect them for a time. These are the dinosaurs' closest living reptilian relatives – the crocodiles.

LIAONINGORNIS AND PROTARCHAEOPTERYX

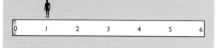

Since the 1990s, the province of Liaoning, in northeastern China, has been one of the "hot spots" for the discovery of fossils from the Age of Dinosaurs. They include *Confuciusornis* (see previous page), *Liaoningornis* and *Protarchaeopteryx*. At one site it seems that a disaster – probably a volcanic eruption – killed almost everything in the area, providing a "snapshot in time." At first, some experts dated the fossils as Late Jurassic, perhaps 150 million years old. Others, however, have estimated that they come from the Early Cretaceous period, 130–120 million years ago. In any case, the discoveries have caused intense debate. In particular, the fossils of both *Liaoningornis* and *Protarchaeopteryx* are difficult to interpret, and challenge many established ideas about reptiles and birds (see page 170).

Liaoningornis was an early bird much the same size as a modern sparrow. It had a very

deep keel – the flange on the sternum (breastbone) that anchors the main wing-flapping flight muscles. This feature and other details suggest that *Liaoningornis* was more like modern birds, and did not belong in the more ancient groups that include *Archaeopteryx* and *Confuciusornis*. If so, *Liaoningornis* may be the earliest truly "modern" bird. At first *Protarchaeopteryx* was also regarded as a bird and, as its name suggests, it had features that seemed to indicate that it was some kind of predecessor of *Archaeopteryx* (see page 172). It lived much later than *Archaeopteryx*, however, and it was probably not a bird, but a dinosaur. This theropod (meat-eater) was unable to fly but possessed feathers on its arms, most of its body, and fanned out from its short tail. Perhaps they were for insulation of the warm-blooded body and/or for visual display during courtship (see page 168).

BIRD FACTFILE
Liaoningornis

Meaning: Liaoning bird
  (from its discovery region)

Pronunciation: Lee-ah-hoh-nin-orn-iss

Period: Early Cretaceous

Main group: Aves (Birds)

Length: Beak to tail 15–18 centimeters
  (6–7 inches)

Diet: Likely omnivorous

Fossils: China

```
0    1    2    3    4    5    6
```

BIRD FACTFILE
Protarchaeopteryx

Meaning: Before *Archaeopteryx*

Pronunciation: Prote-ark-ee-op-tur-icks

Period: Early Cretaceous

Main group: Theropoda

Length: 70 centimeters (28 inches)

Diet: Probably small prey or omnivorous

Fossils: China

```
0    1    2    3    4    5    6
```

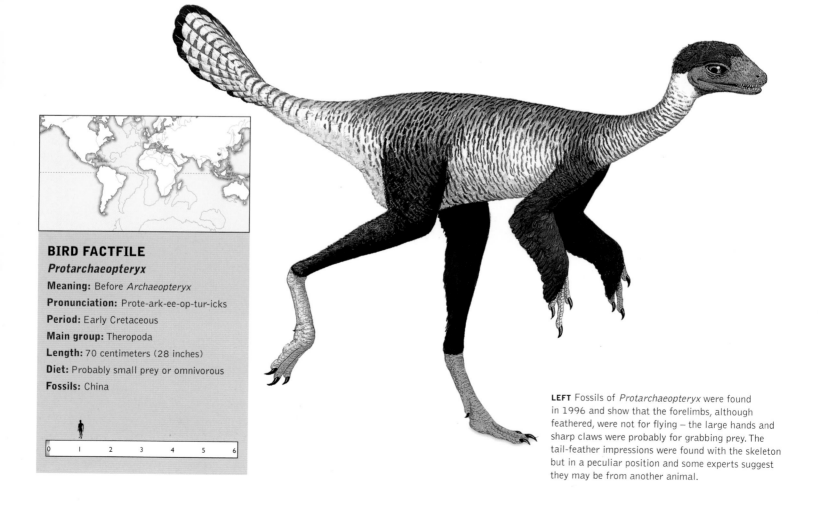

LEFT Fossils of *Protarchaeopteryx* were found in 1996 and show that the forelimbs, although feathered, were not for flying – the large hands and sharp claws were probably for grabbing prey. The tail-feather impressions were found with the skeleton but in a peculiar position and some experts suggest they may be from another animal.

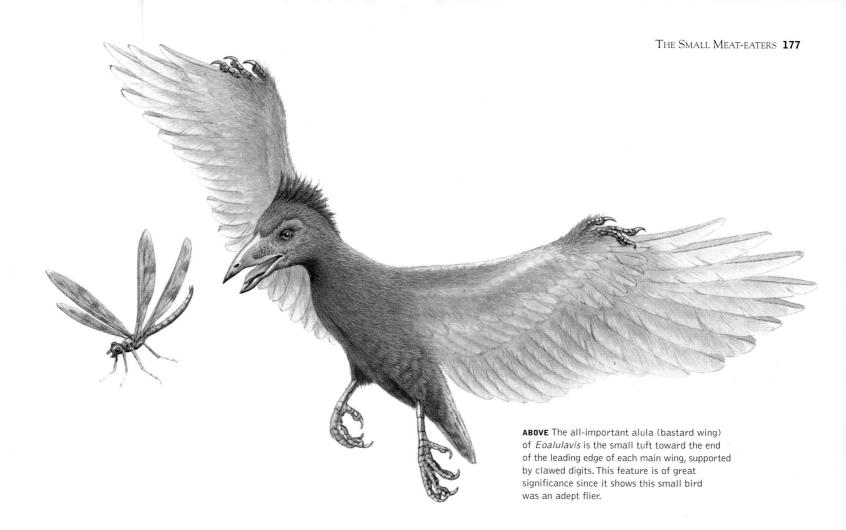

ABOVE The all-important alula (bastard wing) of *Eoalulavis* is the small tuft toward the end of the leading edge of each main wing, supported by clawed digits. This feature is of great significance since it shows this small bird was an adept flier.

EOALULAVIS

This very small bird, similar in size to today's sparrow, was described in 1996 from fossils found in Spain. It is noted for being the earliest known type of bird to possess an alula, a feather or small feather group on the front or leading edge of the wing, positioned in the "thumb" region where the main leading edge angles back, as the bony skeletal part gives way to the large wingtip feathers. The alula is sometimes known as the "bastard wing" and is supported by the thumb (first digit) bone. The alula helps to adjust the airflow over the wing, especially at low speeds, giving much greater control of flight. (Airplanes extend flaps at the leading and also the trailing edges of their wing at low speeds, such as when landing, for the same effect.) All birds today retain the alula.

The fossil site of *Eoalulavis* consisted of a "pocket" of limestone rocks called Las Hoyas near Cuenca in Central Spain. Most of the remains found there date to around 115 million years ago and include dinosaurs, fish, amphibians, insects and crustaceans, which all lived in and around a lake.

Eoalulavis seems to have been on a side-branch of the main evolutionary groups that led to modern birds. Like *Iberomesornis* (page 178), it belongs to a subgroup known as the enantiornithes, or "opposite birds," meaning they had an arrangement of bones in the shoulder and chest, including the scapula (shoulder blade) and coracoid (wishbone), oriented in a pattern which mirrors that of modern birds. *Eoalulavis* probably lived much like a modern sparrow, in the Early Cretaceous period, hopping and flapping, and pecking at a variety of foods. Its large breast-bone had a broad area for anchoring the pectoral muscles, which pull the wings down strongly on their power stroke, showing that this little bird was a strong and able flier. The enantiornithes are believed to have become extinct around 70 million years ago.

BIRD FACTFILE
Eoalulavis

Meaning: Dawn little wing bird

Pronunciation: Ee-owe-all-you-lav-iss

Period: Early Cretaceous

Main group: Aves (Birds)

Length: 15 centimeters (6 inches)

Weight: About 50 grams
   (2 ounces)

Diet: Omnivore

Fossils: Spain

0	1	2	3	4	5	6

IBEROMESORNIS

BIRD FACTFILE

Iberomesornis

Meaning: Iberian intermediate or middle bird

Pronunciation: Eye-bur-oh-mez-or-niss

Period: Early Cretaceous

Main group: Aves (Birds)

Length: Beak to tail 15 centimeters (6 inches)

Diet: Small animals such as insects, grubs

Fossils: Spain

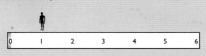

One of the smaller birds from the dinosaur age, *Iberomesornis* was hardly the size of a sparrow or robin today, at 15 centimeters (6 inches) from tip of beak to end of tail. It was named in 1992 by José Luis Sanz and José Bonaparte after the fossil region of Spain, on the Iberian Peninsula of southwestern Europe, where it was found. Exactly where *Iberomesornis* fits in the scheme of bird evolution is debatable, since many early groups of birds seem to have been "dead ends," with no modern survivors.

One bird group is named the ornithothoraces, and their characteristic feature was the alula, a small tuft of feathers at the front or leading edge of the wing, which greatly aided low-speed flight and aerial agility – see *Eoalulavis* (page 177) for a fuller explanation. The alula is prominent in many modern aerobatic birds rather than high-soarers.

A subgroup of the ornithothoraces was the enantiornithes, which includes *Iberomesornis* and *Eoalulavis*. These were Cretaceous birds that showed some evolutionary change, especially during the early and middle part of that period, but which then seem to have died out. They differed from modern birds in the structure of their shoulder and chest regions, where the strut-like coracoid bone and the scapula or shoulder blade are positioned the other way around or opposite to modern birds – enantiornithes means "opposite birds." There are also differences from modern birds in the orientation of the bones that make up the hip. Most of the enantiornithes were toothless, but *Iberomesornis* had tiny, spiky teeth in its small bill. It was probably a reasonable flier and may have eaten small creatures like worms, grubs or bugs.

ABOVE *Iberomesornis* could flap and flutter among the branches with reasonable ease as it searched for small creatures such as insects, which it grabbed in its spike-toothed beak.

HESPERORNIS

One of the largest birds known to have lived during the dinosaur age was *Hesperornis*. It was given its name, which means "western bird," by Othniel Charles Marsh in 1872, after its fossil sites near the Smoky Hill River in Kansas. This makes it one of the earliest birds to receive a scientific name. *Hesperornis* dates from near the end of dinosaur times, the Late Cretaceous period. It stood at least 1 meter (39 inches) tall, and some estimates go as high as a modern adult human, at 1.8 meters (6 feet). It may seem odd that after millions of years developing flight in birds generally, *Hesperornis* had lost this ability, although its remains – which include almost all parts of the skull and skeleton in various specimens – show that it was descended from flying ancestors.

Hesperornis was a swimmer rather than a flier or runner. Its strong legs and large feet were set far back on the body, giving it an upright waddling stance on land, like the birds called divers or loons today. This structure is excellent for swimming, as the webbed feet provide pushing power at the rear of the body for maximum propulsive efficiency. The keel or flange of the sternum (breastbone), which anchors powerful wing-flapping muscles in flying birds, had almost disappeared in *Hesperornis*. So had the wing bones – the very small, almost stub-like wings may have been used for steering as *Hesperornis* swam. The neck was long and strong, and so were the skull and jaws, which were equipped with tiny teeth suited to gripping wriggling prey. *Hesperornis* may have swum along the shores of the shallow seas that covered Late Cretaceous Kansas, using its flexible neck and powerful bill to grab a variety of sea creatures.

BIRD FACTFILE
Hesperornis
Meaning: Western bird
Pronunciation: Hess-purr-orn-iss
Period: Late Cretaceous
Main group: Aves (Birds)
Standing height: 1.8 meters (6 feet)
Diet: Fish, water animals
Fossils: USA (Kansas)

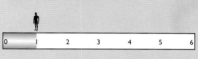

BELOW *Hesperornis* probably had a lifestyle similar to those of modern penguins, swimming rapidly underwater after fish and other small sea creatures. In size it was at least as tall as the largest type of penguin, the emperor. However penguins swim by flapping their wings, but *Hesperornis* used its large webbed feet.

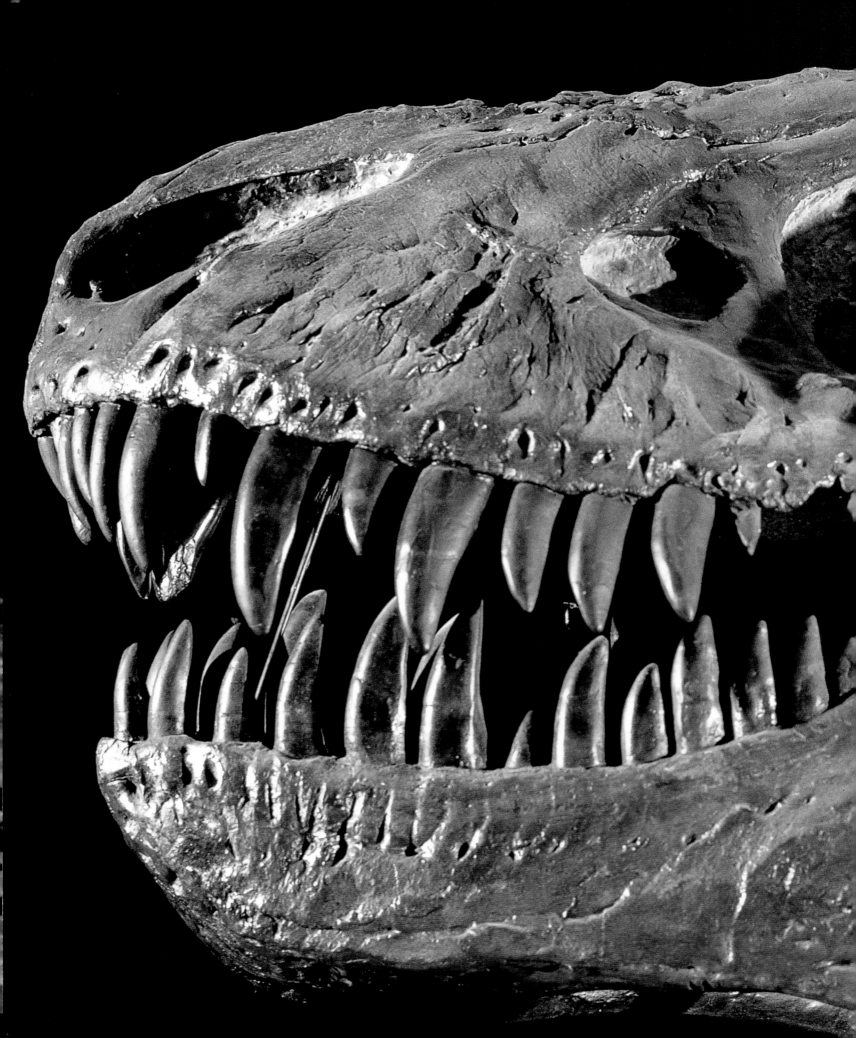

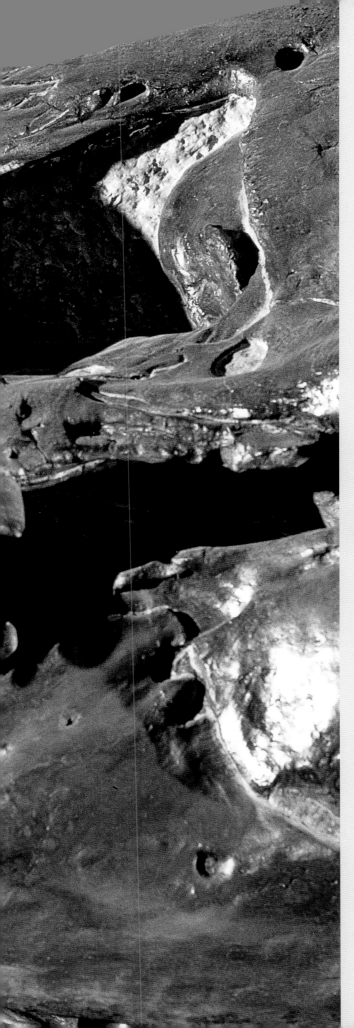

THE GREAT PREDATORS

THE MOST MASSIVE MEAT-EATERS TO STALK THE EARTH, SUCH AS
ALLOSAURUS, *TYRANNOSAURUS*, AND *GIGANOTOSAURUS*, CAN STILL
BE FRIGHTENING MORE THAN 65 MILLION YEARS AFTER THEIR DEMISE.

THE BIGGEST MEAT-EATERS

THE THEROPOD GROUP INCLUDES ALL PREDATORY DINOSAURS, LARGE AND SMALL. AMONG THE SUBGROUPS WERE SEVERAL THAT BOASTED THE LARGEST LAND HUNTERS THE WORLD HAS EVER SEEN. IT IS WORTH NOTING, HOWEVER, THAT EVEN MORE GIGANTIC PREDATORS, SUCH AS THE PLIOSAUR LIOPLEURODON, EXISTED IN THE PREHISTORIC SEAS, AND THAT THERE ARE SIMILARLY VAST HUNTERS ROAMING THE OCEANS TODAY – THE SPERM WHALES – WHICH WOULD OUTWEIGH THE GREATEST PREDATORY DINOSAURS SEVERAL TIMES OVER.

HOW BIG WAS BIG?

The big theropod dinosaurs were several times larger than the record-holding land hunters of today, such as the grizzly bear or the Siberian tiger, which weigh less than 1 metric ton (1 ton) each. The well-known *Tyrannosaurus* of North America weighed more than 5 metric tons (5 tons), while *Giganotosaurus*, whose fossils were discovered much more recently in South America, was another metric ton or two heavier. Recently excavated fossils, also from South America, hint at even greater sizes.

GROUPS OF GREAT HUNTERS

The big meat-eaters came from several dinosaur subgroups. One was the ceratosaurs, such as *Dilophosaurus* and *Carnotaurus*, and *Ceratosaurus* itself. The name ceratosaur means "horned reptile," but not all ceratosaurs had horns, and plenty of other non-ceratosaurs did. These predators were successful mainly in the Jurassic period, but faded thereafter in the northern continents. The tetanurans, or "stiff tails," such as *Eustreptospondylus*, *Megalosaurus*, *Spinosaurus* and *Allosaurus* took their place. Later in the Age of Dinosaurs came even bigger tetanurans, such as *Giganotosaurus* and, at the very end, *Tyrannosaurus* (see pages 187 and 202).

HUNTERS OR SCAVENGERS?

Much of the debate today concerns whether these great beasts were primarily hunters or scavengers. If they were scavengers, they might have followed the great herds of huge plant-eating dinosaurs, to feast on any easy victim – the dead or dying, old or young, sick or injured. If they were hunters, did they ambush or pursue their prey? Did they stalk and then lie in wait to charge at a surprised victim, or doggedly chase the victim until it tired and slowed down? The evidence from fossilized footprints shows that dinosaurs like *Tyrannosaurus* could run as well as walk. But it is not clear whether they pounded along slowly and deliberately, or sprinted at higher speed. Estimates of their top speed range from less than 20 to more than 50 kilometers (10 to 30-plus miles) per hour. The teeth and skulls of many big meat-eaters certainly seem very strongly built, able to withstand the stresses caused by a struggling prey, while their necks, too, were powerful structures, capable of jerking and twisting their heads as, perhaps, they wrenched off great chunks of flesh.

OPPORTUNISTIC APPETITES

Perhaps, in life, the great predatory dinosaurs did not have to decide among ambush, pursuit or scavenging. Like hyenas, jackals and wolves today, they may have simply taken advantage of any opportunity that came their way. Recent discoveries of *Tyrannosaurus* fossils suggest that they lived as families or larger groups. The prospect of a ravenous pack of these flesh-eaters, some ambushing, some pursuing, others, perhaps the young, scavenging, is truly awesome.

PREVIOUS PAGE Each tooth of *Tyrannosaurus* was 15 centimeters (6 inches) long, back-curved and serrated-edged. The uneven nature of the teeth was due to the pattern of renewal – when a particular tooth was broken or lost, a new one grew in its place, so the jaws always had a mixture of teeth in different stages of growth. This pattern is seen in living reptiles such as crocodiles. There was no "whole set" replacement as there is in mammals such as ourselves.

LEFT A hungry *Ceratosaurus* approaches a towering *Brachiosaurus*, as their confrontation disturbs a flock of *Rhamphorhynchus* pterosaurs, in this Late Jurassic scene (approximately 150 million years ago).

DASPLETOSAURUS

DINO FACTFILE

Daspletosaurus

Meaning: Frightful reptile, frightful flesh-eater reptile

Pronunciation: Dass-pleet-owe-sore-uss

Period: Late Cretaceous

Main group: Theropoda

Length: 9–10 meters (30–33 feet)

Weight: 3 metric tons (3 tons)

Diet: Large prey, carcasses

Fossils: Canada (Alberta)

Charles M. Sternberg first excavated remains of this big, powerful and strongly built predator in 1921, in the Steveville area of the Red Deer River, Alberta, Canada. They were first identified as *Gorgosaurus*, a *Tyrannosaurus*-like dinosaur that had been discovered and named in 1914. In 1970, however, Dale Russell, an American paleontologist and dinosaur expert, reported on a lengthy study of these types of dinosaurs in western Canada, and as a result specimens of *Gorgosaurus* with a lighter build were reclassified as *Albertosaurus*. Others, with sturdier or more robust body frames, were newly named *Daspletosaurus*. At various times since, however, *Daspletosaurus* has been proposed alternatively as a heavier male form of one of the species from the genus *Albertosaurus*, and as a smaller ancestor of the slightly later, and larger, *Tyrannosaurus* itself.

Opinions are still divided and await more fossil evidence.

The fearsome *Daspletosaurus* lived about 75–72 million years ago. Fossils of other animals and plants found with the dinosaur remains suggest that it lived in a marshy or swampy habitat. It had several notable features. Its teeth were among the longest of any dinosaur's, with the crown (the exposed part above the gum) measuring 20 centimeters (8 inches) or more. Like two rows of large, rear-curved daggers set into the strong jaws of a massive head, they suggest a very powerful hunter that could tackle the toughest of prey, including hadrosaurs and perhaps *Triceratops*. Its forelimbs are small, but relatively larger than in almost any other tyrannosaur. There were also little "horns," one slightly above and just in front of each eye, as in several other large theropods.

RIGHT *Daspletosaurus* had jaws which were slightly shorter (front to rear) and taller (top to bottom) than most *Tyrannosaurus*-like meat-eaters. Also its teeth were huge, but well spaced and fewer in number than in its cousins.

ACROCANTHOSAURUS

Some fossil specimens of this large predatory dinosaur that were uncovered in Oklahoma, chiefly in Atoka County, possess over half of their skeletal material. In addition to the usual theropod features of powerful back legs, long thick-based tail, and great head with long, sharp teeth, one of the immediately noticeable features is the backbone. The individual vertebral bones from the neck to the base of the tail have tall, upward (or dorsal) projections, known as neural spines, which at their longest project over 40 centimeters (16 inches). These may have formed the internal support for a long ridge or flap of fleshy skin, similar to that of the "sail-backed" *Spinosaurus* (see page 199), but shorter, along the animal's back. The function of such a flap or ridge has been widely debated, but is often considered to be temperature control.

Other features of *Acrocanthosaurus* skeletons, and the dating of the remains at about 114–106 million years ago, place this

formidable hunter as a probable cousin of the late Jurassic *Allosaurus* rather than the later meat-eaters, the tyrannosaurs. In particular, *Acrocanthosaurus*'s arms were relatively long and each ended in three powerful digits tipped with "sickle claws." These seem suited to grabbing and tearing. The 68–70 teeth were long and sharp, with serrated edges, but relatively thin, and were set into a skull some 1.4 meters (4$\frac{1}{2}$ feet) in length.

Acrocanthosaurus was named in 1950, and fossils have been located in Oklahoma, Texas and Utah. Several trackways (sets of fossilized footprints) have also been attributed to this formidable carnivore.

ABOVE *Acrocanthosaurus* is noted for the ridge along its back, although whether it was thick and fleshy, or thinner and more membrane-like, is not clear.

DINO FACTFILE
Acrocanthosaurus

Meaning: Top-spined reptile, high-spiked reptile

Pronunciation: Ak-row-can-thoe-sore-uss

Period: Early Cretaceous

Main group: Theropoda

Length: Up to 12 meters (39 feet)

Weight: 2.5 metric tons (2$\frac{1}{2}$ tons)

Diet: Large animals

Fossils: USA (Oklahoma, Texas, Utah)

ALLOSAURUS

DINO FACTFILE

Allosaurus

Meaning: Other reptile, different reptile

Pronunciation: Al-owe-sore-uss

Period: Late Jurassic

Main group: Theropoda

Length: 11–12 meters (36–39 feet)

Weight: 1.5–2 metric tons (1½–2 tons)

Diet: Medium-sized and large animals

Fossils: USA (Utah, Colorado), Portugal, Australia, Africa

Among the world's most famous animals – even though it has been extinct for 140 million years – *Allosaurus* was one of the biggest and most terrifying predators ever to walk the earth. As North America's preeminent Jurassic hunter, it reached a size not seen again in the region until the tyrannosaurs appeared over 50 million years later. Some 12 meters (39 feet) long, and weighing perhaps 2 metric tons (2 tons) or more, *Allosaurus* had an enormous (yet proportionately lightweight) skull, with jaws that gaped hugely to reveal some 50 sharp teeth, each reaching 10 centimeters (4 inches) long. Its neck was sturdy, rather than lengthy, its forelimbs were short but powerful, each with three digits tipped by 25-centimeter (10-inch) claws, and each of its feet placed the three main toes on the ground with a shorter fourth one held higher and facing to the rear, which is actually the first or big toe.

Allosaurus is known from hundreds of specimens found in various locations, chiefly in midwestern North America. Othniel Charles Marsh named this great predator in 1877, mainly from Colorado fossils. In 1927, an amazing find at the Cleveland–Lloyd Dinosaur Quarry in Utah yielded dozens of individuals in close proximity. This raised the idea that *Allosaurus* hunted in packs, or at least lived in groups. A single *Allosaurus* would be capable of bringing down herbivores of perhaps 1 metric ton (1 ton) in weight, such as the widespread *Iguanodon*-like *Camptosaurus* (see page 263). A group of *Allosaurus* might even prey on the gigantic plant-eaters of the time, like *Diplodocus* and *Brachiosaurus* – one fossil bone of a plant-eating *Apatosaurus* has *Allosaurus*-like tooth marks. Remains of very similar theropods have also been unearthed in southeastern Africa and southeastern Australia.

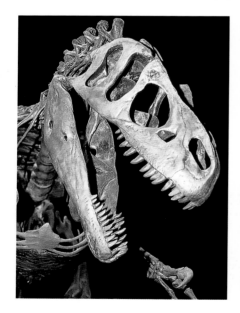

ABOVE A victim's view of the teeth of *Allosaurus*, showing the weight-saving gaps in the massive skull.

RIGHT *Allosaurus* stalks through a Jurassic forest, listening intently and sniffing the air as it peers for prey.

LEFT *Giganotosaurus* lived in the "land of the giants," now Argentina, where this largest of meat-eaters tackled the biggest of plant-eaters such as *Argentinosaurus*. However new finds of partial fossils suggest even greater meat-eaters.

GIGANOTOSAURUS

"The king is dead: long live the king!" For almost 90 years, *Tyrannosaurus rex* reigned in the existing fossil record as the largest land predator the world had seen. But in 1994, Ruben Carolini, a car mechanic and part-time fossil enthusiast, was hunting in Patagonia, a region of southern Argentina, and came upon what proved to be a two-thirds complete skeleton of an even greater predator. A team from the increasingly well-known Carmen Funes Museum in Neuquén, Argentina, led by Rodolfo Coria with his colleague Leonardo Salgado, excavated the fossils. They were named in 1995. (See also *Carcharodontosaurus*, page 206.)

Giganotosaurus was a meter or two (3 to 6 feet) bigger and a ton or two heavier than *Tyrannosaurus*. Length estimates vary from 13 to 15-plus meters (43 to 49-plus feet). Dated at 100–90 million years old, *Giganotosaurus* was separated by a continent and 25 million years from its "king of the dinosaurs" rival, *Tyrannosaurus*. *Giganotosaurus* had a brain that was smaller than that of *Tyrannosaurus*, but its skull was bigger, at 1.8 meters (6 feet) – it alone was as long as a tall adult human being. The teeth were shaped not so much like daggers as like arrowheads, serrated along their edges, and over 20 centimeters (8 inches) long. The small forelimbs had three clawed digits, and the massive back legs each carried a few tons' weight as *Giganotosaurus* pounded along in search of food. Few additional specimens of this monster have been found, but in time, new discoveries may allow more speculation as to its behavior and probable prey. It may have eaten herbivorous dinosaurs, which are known to have been plentiful in the region, since fossils from over 20 species, including one of the biggest of all sauropods, *Argentinosaurus*, were found there and dated from roughly the same time.

DINO FACTFILE

Giganotosaurus

Meaning: Giant southern reptile

Pronunciation: Jee-gah-noe-toe-sore-uss

Period: Mid-Cretaceous

Main group: Theropoda

Length: 14 meters (46 feet)

Weight: 8 metric tons (8½ tons)

Diet: Large animals

Fossils: Argentina

| 0 | 1 | 2 | 3 | 4 | 5 | 6 | 7 | 8 |

FEARSOME FAMILIES

MOST OF THE LARGEST LAND PREDATORS OF
TODAY, LIKE BEARS AND TIGERS, FOLLOW A
MAINLY SOLITARY LIFESTYLE. FAR FEWER LIVE IN
FAMILY GROUPS – LIONS AND WOLVES BEING
EXAMPLES. HUGE MEAT-EATING DINOSAURS WERE
ONCE ALL CONSIDERED SOLITARY STALKERS.
MOST, LIKE *ALLOSAURUS* AND *DASPLETOSAURUS*,
PROBABLY WERE. BUT RECENT FINDS OF SEVERAL
DIFFERENT-AGED SPECIMENS OF *TYRANNOSAURUS*
AT THE SAME SITE, MAY POINT TO A SOCIAL OR
FAMILY WAY OF LIFE.

RIGHT A terrified *Triceratops* attempts to ward off two adult
Tyrannosaurus. However if the meat-eaters were able to
mount a co-ordinated attack, one could approach from the
side, thereby avoiding the sharp horns and bony neck cover.
Recent fossil finds suggest that *Tyrannosaurus* may have lived
in groups, not only adults together but also juveniles
accompanying them.

BARYONYX

DINO FACTFILE

Baryonyx

Meaning: Heavy claw

Pronunciation: Bare-ee-on-icks

Period: Early Cretaceous

Main group: Theropoda

Length: 9.5 meters (31 feet)

Weight: 2 metric tons (2 tons)

Diet: Animals, perhaps fish

Fossils: England

The fossils of the creature now named "heavy claw" caused many surprises when they were excavated from a clay pit in Surrey, a county in southern England. Not least was the initial surprise of William Walker, plumber and amateur fossil sleuth, who chanced upon an enormous claw in 1983. Named in 1987 by Angela Milner and Alan Charig, British paleontologists based at London's Natural History Museum, *Baryonyx* was revealed as an unusual theropod, probably a cousin of *Spinosaurus* (see page 199). In some respects it was a "dino-croc" from 125–120 million years ago, with several parallels with members of an entirely different and still surviving reptile group, the crocodilians. There are also similarities between *Baryonyx* and a newer dinosaur find, *Suchomimus* (see page 207).

The massive claw that gives *Baryonyx* its name is more than 30 centimeters (12 inches) along its outer curve, and belonged on its "thumb." The other two digits on each of its forelimbs had proportionately normal-sized, less curved claws. Other striking features that marked out *Baryonyx* were its neck, skull, teeth and tail. Instead of the typical S shape, the neck was almost straight. The skull had a very long, low profile, with a flattened snout, quite unlike the tall skulls of big carnivores like *Tyrannosaurus* and *Allosaurus*. The teeth were very numerous, with two-thirds of the total of over 90 in the lower jaw, and larger ones in the upper jaw. The tail was narrow-based, very long, gradually tapered, and fairly stiff. Preserved fish scales of *Lepidotes*, and various fish and dinosaur bones, some possibly from a young *Iguanodon*, were found with the remains.

BELOW Most reconstructions place *Baryonyx* in a marshy or waterside habitat, grabbing fish in its long, crocodile-like jaws.

Yangchuanosaurus

In 1978, Chinese paleontologist Dong Zhiming and his colleagues named *Yangchuanosaurus* after its discovery region, which is in China's southeastern Sichuan (Szechuan) Province. It is a sizable theropod, approaching 10 meters (33 feet) in length, and the original skeleton forms an impressive display in the Natural History Museum of Beijing. *Yangchuanosaurus* has been linked to *Eustreptospondylus* (page 192). It seems to have been more of a typical allosaur, however, living at around the same time as *Allosaurus* itself, some 150–140 million years ago. It was slightly smaller all around than was its North American cousin.

Yangchuanosaurus had the typical large theropod physical characteristics: huge head; wide-gaping mouth; long, sharp teeth with serrated edges; powerful but fairly short neck; deep body; small forelimbs, perhaps for holding or gripping; very strong legs for walking and wounding prey with a kick, and a long, thickly based, symmetrically tapering tail that formed

about half of the creature's total length. There were three digits, each armed with a claw, on each of its four limbs. The skull was more than 1 meter (39 inches) in length, and had eye-snout ridges and a small lump of bone on the nose.

Like *Allosaurus*, a lone *Yangchuanosaurus* probably stalked the young of large dinosaurs, or it might have hunted in groups to overcome the full-grown adults. Another possibility is that this meat-eater searched for carrion. Unfortunately, the limited number of *Yangchuanosaurus* finds, compared to the many known specimens of *Allosaurus*, allow few speculations about its patterns of behavior.

ABOVE *Yangchuanosaurus* is often regarded as an East Asian version of the North American *Allosaurus*. After death, as its carcass dried, the tendons along the top of the neck and tail would dry out and shrink, curling the head and tail tip over the back.

DINO FACTFILE
Yangchuanosaurus

Meaning: Yang-ch'un reptile (after its discovery site)

Pronunciation: Yan-hoo-an-owe-sore-uss

Period: Late Jurassic

Main group: Theropoda

Length: 9 meters (30 feet)

Weight: 2 metric tons (2 tons)

Diet: Animals

Fossils: Southeastern China

EUSTREPTOSPONDYLUS

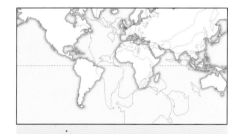

DINO FACTFILE

Eustreptospondylus

Meaning: Well or sharply curved vertebrae, true reversed backbone

Pronunciation: You-strep-toe-spon-die-luss

Period: Mid- to Late Jurassic

Main group: Theropoda

Length: 7-8 meters (23–26 feet)

Weight: 230 kilograms (510 pounds)

Diet: Animals

Fossils: England

A medium-to-large predator with a speedy-looking appearance, *Eustreptospondylus* fossils were studied in 1841, the same year that the group Dinosauria itself received its official name, and by the same comparative anatomist, Richard Owen. Its original name, however, was not *Eustreptospondylus* at all, but *Megalosaurus*, a term that was already in general use for a variety of large reptilian carnivores. More than a century later, in 1964, Alick Walker, a British fossil expert, reviewed the two sets of "*Megalosaurus*" fossils and showed that one partly grown, well-preserved but incomplete specimen from near Wolvercote in Oxfordshire, England, deserved its own identity. Suggestions for calling it *Streptospondylus* were made, but the name was already suggested for another fossil reptile. So it was called *Eustreptospondylus*, in reference to the curved surfaces of the vertebral bones in its backbone. The classification of Eustreptospondylus is uncertain. It has some similarities with the great North

American theropod of about the same time period, *Allosaurus*, but also with *Spinosaurus*.

Eustreptospondylus lived some 170 million years ago and was long, lean and probably mean. The large head, with weight-saving gaps in the skull bones, bore a huge mouth. The teeth were long and sharp, with serrated edges, yet they were not especially large. The small forelimbs each had three digits, and the powerful back legs had sturdy bones and big bird-like feet, with three digits on the ground and one above it in the rear. The tail was fairly narrow at the base and tapered slowly to form almost half of the animal's total length. Its prey may have included armored plant-eaters like *Sarcolestes* and sauropods like *Cetiosaurus*.

ABOVE *Eustreptospondylus*, like many large meat-eating dinosaurs, was originally confused with *Megalosaurus*. It is now considered to be an early or primitive member of the spinosaur group, which has come to prominence since about 1990 with the discovery of several new members, including *Suchomimus* (see page 207).

CARNOTAURUS

Carnotaurus was a large Cretaceous theropod or predatory dinosaur with many unusual features. José Bonaparte, an eminent Argentine expert on dinosaurs, named it in 1985 from almost complete skeletal remains excavated in the fossil-rich region of Chubut, Argentina. Studies showed that *Carnotaurus* was a cousin of *Abelisaurus*, also named by Bonaparte and colleagues in 1985. The abelisaurids were a group of primitive theropods that nonetheless had a long history through the Cretaceous period. The prey of *Carnotaurus* may have been young or old or sick herbivores, like the sauropod *Chubutisaurus*, known from fossils from about the same time and place. However the peculiar jaw proportions make views on diet very varied.

Carnotaurus had a small conical projection, like a short cow's horn, above each eye. The eyes themselves were relatively small but – unusually among dinosaurs – they looked partly forward rather than largely sideways, giving

Carnotaurus stereoscopic, or binocular, vision for accurate assessment of distance. The snout was short and deep, giving the face a bull-nosed appearance, with powerful jaw muscles. The lower jaw, however, was strangely shallow and not very sturdy, and the teeth were smaller and weaker than would be expected in such a large head. The forelimbs were almost laughably tiny, even smaller than those of *Tyrannosaurus* (see page 202). The tail was lengthy and tapered very gradually. Accompanying the remains, which are dated at 100–95 million years old, were skin impressions showing a rough hide with rows of low, lumpy scales along the sides and back, and also rounded, disc-like scales.

ABOVE The strange "wing"-like brow horns, and the slim or shallow lower jaw compared to the tall or deep upper skull, mark out *Carnotaurus* as an unusual large theropod from the abelisaurid group.

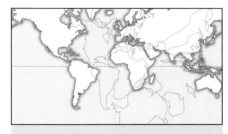

DINO FACTFILE
Carnotaurus

Meaning: Carnivorous bull, meat-eating bull

Pronunciation: Kar-noe-tore-uss

Period: Mid-Cretaceous

Main group: Theropoda

Length: 7.5 meters (24½ feet)

Weight: 1 metric ton (1 ton)

Diet: Animals

Fossils: Argentina

RUNNING SPEEDS

CLUES TO VARIOUS DINOSAURS' TOP SPEEDS COME
FROM MANY SOURCES, ESPECIALLY THE SIZE AND
PROPORTIONS OF THE LIMB BONES, THE PATCHES
ON THE FOSSILS SHOWING WHERE MUSCLES WERE
ATTACHED, AND PRESERVED TRACKWAYS GIVING
THE LENGTH OF STRIDE BETWEEN INDIVIDUAL
FOOTPRINTS. IT IS POSSIBLE THAT SOME OSTRICH
DINOSAURS OUTPACED MODERN OSTRICHES, WITH
SPRINT SPEEDS IN EXCESS OF 80 KILOMETERS
(50 MILES) PER HOUR.

RIGHT Megaraptors running in pursuit of prey. The largest
"raptor-like dinosaur" find to date took place in Patagonia,
Argentina. The 33-centimeter (13-inch) slashing toe-claw can
be clearly seen.

DILOPHOSAURUS

DINO FACTFILE

Dilophosaurus

Meaning: Two-ridged reptile, double-crested reptile

Pronunciation: Die-loaf-owe-sore-uss

Period: Early Jurassic

Main group: Theropoda

Length: 6 meters (20 feet)

Weight: 400 kilograms (880 pounds)

Diet: Animals

Fossils: USA (Arizona), possibly China

0	1	2	3	4	5	6	7	8

This medium-to-large carnivore is one of the few of its general type that is well known from plentiful remains. The fossils date to as far back as the Early Jurassic period, almost 200 million years ago, making it one of the earliest big predatory dinosaurs. It is included in the ceratosaur group (see opposite). Fossils have been found in Arizona and, possibly, in the Yunnan region of China. Among the American specimens are three individuals preserved together – they may have been a hunting pack. American paleontologist Sam Welles named this dinosaur, but it took two attempts. The three Arizona specimens were excavated in 1942, after a member of the Navajo nation, Jesse Williams, guided experts to their remains. Later, Welles studied them, and in 1954 he described them as a new species of *Megalosaurus*. Then, in 1964, further discoveries of fossils of these crested types of dinosaur,

some by Welles himself, led him to distinguish the creatures from *Megalosaurus*. In 1970 he created the new name *Dilophosaurus*.

At 6 meters (19½ feet) long, *Dilophosaurus* was relatively slim and probably weighed less than half a metric ton (½ ton). The name refers to the two prominent crests on the head. Each is a curved bony ridge, like one-third of a dinner plate and barely as thick, projecting at an angle above the eye. These crests were so thin and fragile that they were probably for visual and symbolic, rather than physical, use, perhaps as a sign of gender and/or maturity. Trackways (fossilized sets of footprints) assigned to *Dilophosaurus* show just its claws making impressions, and with a stride of some 2 meters (6½ feet). A version of *Dilophosaurus* is seen in the movie *Jurassic Park*, but, unlike the cinematic monster, the real thing probably did not spit poison or have a neck frill.

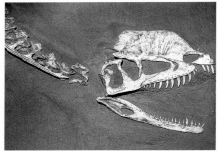

ABOVE Fossilized skull of *Dilophosaurus* showing a side view of the crest to indicate its height.

RIGHT *Dilophosaurus* confronts a rival – perhaps males competing for females during the breeding season.

CERATOSAURUS

Allosaurus was the greatest predator in Late Jurassic North America, but *Ceratosaurus* was its lesser rival. Named for the thin, jutting horn on its nose – and also showing a ridge-like crest above each eye – this theropod was a meter or two (3½ to 6½ feet) smaller all-around than *Allosaurus*. Yet it was still a formidable hunter, with a weight approaching 1 metric ton (1 ton) – heavier than any bear, big cat or other terrestrial carnivore of today.

The great American fossil-hunter Othniel Charles Marsh named *Ceratosaurus* in 1884. Marsh was struck by the tall upper and lower spine-like extensions of the caudal vertebrae (tailbones). He compared this tail shape to that of a crocodile and suggested that *Ceratosaurus* might have been a fine swimmer in swamps of 150 million years ago.

Established so early in the scientific history of dinosaurs, *Ceratosaurus*'s name was given to one of the major subgroups of the theropods (bipedal predators) – the Ceratosauria – which groups together over 20 species. This is the earlier counterpart of another great theropod group, the Tetanurae, and includes *Coelophysis* and *Dilophosaurus* (see opposite). Despite some primitive features in the hips and other parts, including four digits on each forelimb rather than three and then two as in later theropods, *Ceratosaurus* must have been an able predator. It sported huge fang-like teeth and powerful rear limbs for fast running. Fossils of individuals have been found with more plentiful remains of several *Allosaurus*, suggesting that the former was a lone hunter while the latter roamed in packs. *Ceratosaurus* fossils have also been identified in Portugal and possibly in East Africa too.

ABOVE The curious nose horn of *Ceratosaurus* has stimulated great discussion but no clear consensus on its use. It was probably too small and weak to be a weapon, and so may have been a sign of maturity and readiness to breed, or possessed by one sex only. (Compare this reconstruction with that shown on page 182.)

DINO FACTFILE
Ceratosaurus
Meaning: Horned reptile

Pronunciation: Se-rat-owe-sore-uss

Period: Late Jurassic

Main group: Theropoda

Length: 6 meters (20 feet)

Weight: 700–850 kilograms
(1540–1875 pounds)

Diet: Animals

Fossils: USA (Colorado, Utah, Wyoming),
Portugal, possibly Africa

MEGALOSAURUS

DINO FACTFILE
Megalosaurus
Meaning: Great reptile
Pronunciation: Meg-ah-low-sore-uss
Period: Mid-Jurassic
Main group: Theropoda
Length: 9 meters (30 feet)
Weight: 1 metric ton (1 ton)
Diet: Larger animals
Fossils: England

Megalosaurus – "great reptile" – holds an honored but confusing position among all the creatures that eventually became known as dinosaurs. It was the first to receive an official scientific name, from William Buckland in 1824. And when the Dinosauria were recognized as a distinct group of reptiles, in 1841, *Megalosaurus* was a founding member. For another half a century and more, almost any large reptile of this general type that seemed like a fang-toothed carnivore, and was not distinctive enough to be called something else, became *Megalosaurus*. But gradually, detailed studies and comparisons have lifted much of the confusion surrounding this creature. Various specimens once labeled *Megalosaurus* were reclassified and renamed as other theropods, including several mentioned on these pages.

Today, *Megalosaurus* is classified as a large Middle Jurassic predator, an early tetanuran or "stiff-tail" in the theropod group (see page 183). It is known widely, because of its place in the history of paleontology and the dinosaur group, but poorly, because the fossils still attributed to it after decades of discussion are scarce and fragmentary. The original pieces of jawbone examined by Buckland show long older teeth, with new replacement teeth just pushing up from the bone, and interdentary plates separating the teeth. The early specimens also included sections of backbone, and parts of the hip and rear leg bones. They were found in quarries near Stonesfield in Oxfordshire, England. Other remains of *Megalosaurus* had been known since the 1670s. The main fossil in this respect was the lower rounded or knuckle-shaped end of the thighbone, possibly from *Megalosaurus*. It was reported in 1673 and illustrated by Robert Plot in 1676. The illustration still exists, but the original fossil can no longer be traced.

SPINOSAURUS

One of the most unusual of the large predatory dinosaurs, *Spinosaurus* was distinguished by a huge sail-like structure on its back. This was probably an enormous flap of skin held up by long, strap-like extensions, known as neural spines, jutting from the vertebrae (backbones). *Spinosaurus* was also one of the largest of the predatory dinosaurs, rivaling even *Tyrannosaurus* in length, although it was more lightweight in build. Its fossils were first discovered near an oasis in Egypt in 1912, and were described and named three years later by Ernst Stromer von Reichenbach, a German paleontologist. The limited remains were taken to Munich, in Germany, for safe-keeping in a museum, but were destroyed during a bombing raid in World War II. Since then, speculations about the size, structure and behavior of *Spinosaurus* have been based on documentation of these first specimens, along with more recent finds from Morocco.

The function of the extraordinary "sail," which rose almost 2 meters (6½ feet) above the backbone at its highest point, may have been control of body temperature and/or visual display (see page 107). During the mid- to Late Cretaceous period, 100–90 million years ago, there appears to have been an evolutionary trend in this region for such sails. The plant-eating, *Iguanodon*-like *Ouranosaurus* (see page 266), and perhaps also the sauropod *Rebbachisaurus* possessed them too. From the limited evidence of *Spinosaurus* remains, it is conjectured it may have had a long, low snout, similar to that of *Baryonyx* and *Suchomimus*, and was perhaps also suited to catching fish. The teeth are slim, sharp and with few serrations, but fewer in number than *Baryonyx* had, so it has been suggested that this massive beast, with its slender and less muscular body proportions, scavenged soft meat from rotting carcasses.

DINO FACTFILE
Spinosaurus
Meaning: Spiny reptile, thorn reptile
Pronunciation: Spin-owe-sore-uss
Period: Mid- and Late Cretaceous
Main group: Theropoda
Length: 12–14 meters (40–46 feet)
Weight: 3 metric tons (3 tons)
Diet: Animals
Fossils: Egypt, Morocco

RIGHT *Spinosaurus* has been used as the main specimen to establish a growing family of newly discovered, big meat-eating dinosaurs, all with characteristically long, low, crocodile-like snouts and teeth. However it is the only type with such a relatively big "sail" on its back.

THE SAILBACKS

LARGE BACK STRUCTURES SHAPED LIKE SAILS,
FLAPS OR FINS HAVE APPEARED SEVERAL TIMES
INDEPENDENTLY WITHIN THE DINOSAUR GROUP,
AND IN OTHER LAND VERTEBRATE GROUPS TOO,
SUCH AS PELYCOSAURS LIKE *DIMETRODON*. THE
"SAIL" SEEMS DESIGNED TO MAXIMIZE SURFACE
AREA WHILE CONTAINING A MINIMAL VOLUME
OF FLESH AND OTHER TISSUE. THE FAVORED
EXPLANATION IS THERMOREGULATION. THE
"SAIL" FUNCTIONED AS A REVERSIBLE HEAT-
EXCHANGER. IT SOAKED UP WARMTH FROM THE
ENVIRONMENT WHEN THE ANIMAL'S BODY WAS
COLDER THAN ITS SURROUNDINGS, AND THEN
RADIATED EXCESS WARMTH FROM THE BODY
TO PREVENT OVERHEATING IN EXTREMELY
HOT CONDITIONS.

RIGHT *Spinosaurus* splashes through the shallows in pursuit
of prey. This is one of the most intriguing of dinosaurs, due to
its tremendous size and unusual jaw shape, also the fact that
most of its fossils have been lost to science (see previous page),
and of course its fin-like back sail.

TYRANNOSAURUS

DINO FACTFILE

Tyrannosaurus

Meaning: Tyrant reptile

Pronunciation: Tie-ran-owe-sore-uss

Period: Late Cretaceous

Main group: Theropoda

Length: 12 meters (40 feet)

Weight: 6 metric tons (6 tons)

Diet: Large animals

Fossils: Western North America

One of the most famous nonhuman animals ever known on the planet, the "tyrant reptile" has had entire books, far larger than this one, written about it. No longer considered the largest of all land predators, *Tyrannosaurus* is nevertheless famous thanks to its numerous well-studied fossils. It was one of the last of all the dinosaurs to disappear. In 1990, an almost complete, and partly mummified specimen – a huge female nicknamed "Sue" after its discoverer, Susan Hendrickson – was located in South Dakota. "Sue" and other *Tyrannosaurus* individuals preserved at nearby sites have provided much valuable new evidence about this giant carnivore, and "Sue" is now displayed in the Field Museum in Chicago. Various aspects of the senses, lifestyle, hunting methods, diet and behavior patterns of *Tyrannosaurus* are discussed throughout this chapter, including the notion that it hunted in groups or packs.

Tyrannosaurus had an enormous head, with a skull 1.4 meters (4½ feet) long, but gaps or "windows" in the bones helped to reduce the weight of the head. It had over 50 teeth, which were huge and sharp, with serrated edges, some over 20 centimeters (8 inches) long, and also wide-based, which suggests they could cope with great forces. The vast mouth gaped wide enough to swallow a modern adult human. The neck was also thick and sturdy, again suggesting massive forces at work when *Tyrannosaurus* bit and tore off chunks of its prey. The forelimbs, often dismissed as tiny and useless, were nevertheless quite muscular, and the two digits at the end of each of them had sharp claws. *Tyrannosaurus* bore its elephant-like weight on three digits on each bird-like foot, with only the heavily clawed tips touching the ground.

LEFT Older reconstructions of *Tyrannosaurus* show it adopting a semi-upright posture, rather like a kangaroo. The heavy tetanuran ("stiff") tail was probably held out horizontally to the rear, to counterbalance the head and body over the massive, muscular thighs. This allowed speedy running.

ABOVE The massive skull of *Tyrannosaurus* had the jaw joint in the rearmost position, allowing a vast gape. This fine specimen is displayed at South Dakota's Black Hills Institute of Geological Research.

BELOW *Tarbosaurus,* shown here hunting a young ornithopod dinosaur, is included as a species within the genus *Tyrannosaurus* in many new schemes. Another very similar Asian genus is *Alectrosaurus.*

TARBOSAURUS (TYRANNOSAURUS BATAAR)

For many years, *Tarbosaurus* was regarded as the slightly smaller, east Asian counterpart and contemporary of *Tyrannosaurus* (opposite). Its existence was established from fossils uncovered in the Nemegt Basin of Mongolia's Gobi Desert, where remains of about seven individuals were found during a Soviet expedition. In 1955, Evgenii Aleksandrovich Male'ev described and named them *Tarbosaurus bataar,* a species of a new genus, *Tarbosaurus.*

From the outset, however, there was the view that this dinosaur was so similar to *Tyrannosaurus* that it should be called *Tyrannosaurus.* There were suggestions that if the *Tarbosaurus* fossils had been found in a region of North America, rather than Asia, then indeed they would have been designated *Tyrannosaurus,* although not the best-known species of that genus, *Tyrannosaurus rex.* Over recent years, these views have continued to bring pressure. Today, many experts regard the name *Tarbosaurus* invalid. The creature

they represent has been reclassified as a member of the genus *Tyrannosaurus,* and as one of two distinct species, *Tyrannosaurus bataar* or the slightly smaller *Tyrannosaurus efremovi.*

Tarbosaurus/Tyrannosaurus had all the power and weaponry of a big theropod – a huge mouth, long sharp teeth, powerful jaws, large eyes and nose for sensing prey, tiny forelimbs, massive back legs and a long, thick, counterbalancing tail. It can be distinguished from *Tyrannosaurus* by its overall size and some of the detail in the skull bones. A new discovery in Thailand has suggested that the tyrannosaur group may have been present in Asia long before it appeared in North America. This type of tyrannosaur is called *Siamotyrannus,* the former name of Thailand being Siam. Its fossils date to the Early Cretaceous period, some 120 million years ago. Perhaps the pattern of spread in this group, which has been assumed by some to be North America to Asia, was the reverse.

DINO FACTFILE
Tyrannosaurus (Tarbosaurus) bataar
Meaning: Alarming reptile
Pronunciation: Tar-bow-sore-uss (see also *Tyrannosaurus,* opposite)
Period: Late Cretaceous
Main group: Theropoda
Length: 10 meters (33 feet)
Weight: 4 metric tons (4 tons)
Diet: Large animals
Fossils: Mongolia

ALIORAMUS

DINO FACTFILE

Alioramus

Meaning: Different branch

Pronunciation: Al-ee-owe-ray-muss

Period: Late Cretaceous

Main group: Theropoda

Length: 6 meters (20 feet)

Weight: 1 metric ton (1 ton)

Diet: Animals

Fossils: Mongolia

Known largely from just a partial skull and partial foot bones, this medium-sized predator is regarded as an unusual cousin of the last major group of dinosaur meat-eaters, the tyrannosaurs. It lived at the end of the dinosaur age, 70–65 million years ago. It was named in 1976, from fossils found in Mongolia by Sergei Mikhailovich Kurzanov, a Soviet expert on fossils who has also attracted attention with his studies and opinions on the much smaller and possibly feathered theropod, *Avimimus* (see page 164).

While the lack of fossils of leg or body bone makes it difficult to determine actual size, it is thought that *Alioramus* was far smaller than its great tyrannosaur cousins, but still a huge and powerful hunter, much larger than most land carnivores of today. Some experts conjecture that it probably reached 6 meters (20 feet) in total length and about 1 metric ton (1 ton) in weight. Its fossil foot bones show

that it was lighter and probably faster than the bigger theropods. Some expert estimates for its running speed are in excess of 40 kilometers (25 miles) per hour. The body structure and proportions were fairly typical of tyrannosaurs, with tiny arms, long and strong rear legs and a long, stiff tail.

The head, however, was more unusual. The head shape is known from the partial skull, which was long and shallow with a lengthened snout rather than tall and with a shorter snout, as in most tyrannosaurs. Also, there were bony projections, including four small bump-like "horns" in a row along the center of the nose, and another pair higher up, one near each eye. *Alioramus* may not have been the dominant predator of its world. It probably shared its time and place, the Late Cretaceous of East Asia, with the much larger species of tyrannosaur formerly known as *Tarbosaurus*.

LEFT *Alioramus* is distinguished from most other tyrannosaurs by its long shallow snout, small bony projections on the nose and above the eyes, and its relatively small size compared to its huge cousins.

LEFT *Albertosaurus* is shown here in the upright "kangaroo" posture, which it may have adopted for scanning the scene from the highest possible viewpoint.

BELOW The result of an attack—a skeletal reconstruction in a museum showing *Albertosaurus* about to feed on its victim, the horned dinosaur *Centrosaurus*.

ALBERTOSAURUS

A similar but smaller cousin of *Tyrannosaurus*, *Albertosaurus* roamed what is now northwestern America during the Late Cretaceous period, near the end of the dinosaur age but before its great cousin. *Albertosaurus* had all the typical features of a larger meat-eating dinosaur: long, sharp teeth in strong jaws; a large, deep-snouted head; thick neck and deep chest; small and apparently useless forelimbs with two clawed digits each; very powerful rear legs with three long, clawed digits on each foot; and a long, thick-based, tapering tail. The teeth numbered about 16 in the lower jaw and slightly more, 18 or 19, in the upper. As in most other big hunting dinosaurs, the teeth had wavy or serrated edges, useful for sawing and slicing though flesh in the manner of a steak knife.

At one site, about nine *Albertosaurus* individuals of different ages were preserved together, suggesting that they may have lived in a group.

Albertosaurus was named by Henry Fairfield Osborn, then head of the American Natural History Museum, in 1905, the year that the Canadian province it is named after was formed. But the fossils, including two partial skulls, were discovered earlier than that, in about 1884 and 1890–91, in the Red Deer River region of what was to become Alberta. They had already been named *Laelaps* and then *Dryptosaurus* before Osborn reclassified them. In 1913, a well-preserved skeleton of a similar creature was found, and named *Gorgosaurus*. In 1970, Dale Russell reviewed the situation and concluded that the specimens known as *Gorgosaurus* were really juveniles of *Albertosaurus* or a smaller species. Recently, in another swing of the pendulum, the name *Gorgosaurus* has resurfaced again as applicable to the earlier species of *Albertosaurus*, *Albertosaurus libratus*. This leaves the main species as before, *Albertosaurus sarcophagus*.

DINO FACTFILE
Albertosaurus
Meaning: Alberta reptile
Pronunciation: Al-bert-owe-sore-uss
Period: Late Cretaceous
Main group: Theropoda
Length: 9 meters (30 feet)
Weight: 2.5 metric tons (2½ tons)
Diet: Animals
Fossils: Western North America

CARCHARODONTOSAURUS

DINO FACTFILE

Carcharodontosaurus

Meaning: Shark tooth reptile

Pronunciation: Kar-kar-owe-don-toe-sore-uss

Period: Mid-Cretaceous

Main group: Theropoda

Length: 14–15 meters (46–49 feet)

Weight: 7–8 metric tons (7–8 tons)

Diet: Large animals

Fossils: Sahara (Africa)

Part of this dinosaur's name will be familiar to people who know about sharks, since the scientific name of the great white shark is *Carcharodon carcharias*. This "shark-tooth reptile" vies with *Giganotosaurus* as the largest meat-eater ever to prowl on land. *Carcharodontosaurus* has undergone a spectacular renaissance as the result of studies of fossils found in North Africa in 1996 by Paul Sereno and his colleagues from the University of Chicago (see also *Suchomimus*, opposite). The fossils represent a theropod maybe 14 meters (46 feet) long and over 7 metric tons (7 tons) in weight, outsizing *Tyrannosaurus*. Yet *Carcharodontosaurus* has a long history despite recent fame. It was originally named by Ernst Stromer von Reichenbach in 1931, from a partial skull and other remains found in the Sahara in 1927. Like many other fossils of large meat-eating theropods, these at first had been attributed to *Megalosaurus*. Unfortunately, these earlier finds were lost during World War II (see

Spinosaurus, page 199). Sereno's 1996 find revived the dinosaur's reputation and rewrote the record books. New fossil finds in South America since 2000, although scarce and fragmentary, have suggested that there could have been even bigger meat-eaters and so the situation may change again.

Carcharodontosaurus in Africa was similar in some ways to *Giganotosaurus* of South America. Both are classified as mid-Cretaceous "remnants" of the theropod group that included *Allosaurus* and had enjoyed most success earlier in the Late Jurassic period. Links are seen in parts such as the three digits on each forelimb, contrasting with the two digits of later giant theropods like *Tyrannosaurus*. *Carcharodontosaurus* was heavily built, with very sturdy bones, and its skull was as long as many human beings today are tall – 1.6 meters (5 feet). The teeth are truly fearsome, tapering triangles some 20 centimeters (8 inches) long with serrated edges, far larger and stronger than the teeth of any shark.

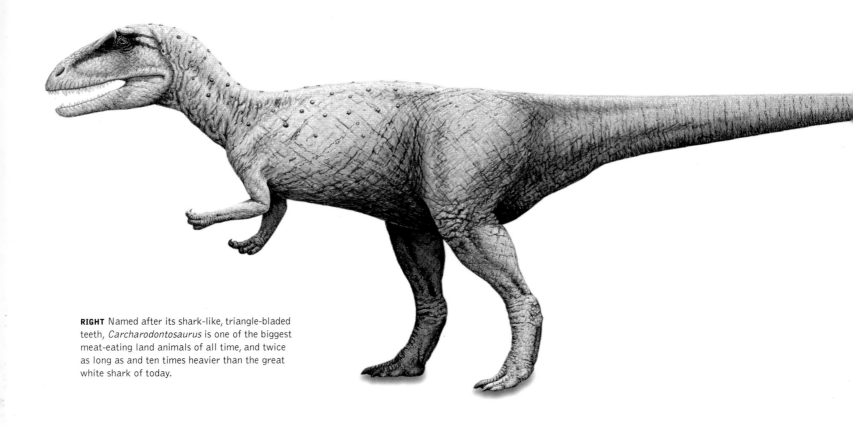

RIGHT Named after its shark-like, triangle-bladed teeth, *Carcharodontosaurus* is one of the biggest meat-eating land animals of all time, and twice as long as and ten times heavier than the great white shark of today.

SUCHOMIMUS

After discovering a new specimen of *Carcharodontosaurus* (opposite), Chicago-based paleontologist Paul Sereno and his team scored another success in 1997, with the discovery in the Sahara, around Tenere, in Niger, of fossils that represented about two-thirds of the skeleton of a huge meat-eater. This was named *Suchomimus*, "crocodile mimic," after the shape of its head. But unlike most great theropods (meat-eaters), *Suchomimus* had a very long, low snout and narrow jaws studded with some 100 teeth, not very sharp and curving slightly backward. The tip of the snout was enlarged and carried a "rosette" of longer teeth. The animal is reminiscent of crocodilians that eat mainly fish, such as the living gharial, a type of large crocodile with a very long, slim snout, from the region of India. *Suchomimus* also had tall extensions of its vertebrae which may have held up some kind of low flap, ridge or sail of skin, as seen in much more exaggerated form

in *Spinosaurus* (see page 199). The overall impression is of a massive and powerful creature that ate fish and meat 100 million years ago, when the Sahara was a lush, swampy habitat. *Suchomimus* has been placed in the spinosaur group of predators.

Apart from the back ridge, *Suchomimus* was very similar to *Baryonyx* (see page 190), which also had strong forelimbs and a huge sickle-curved claw on its "thumb." And, as with *Baryonyx*, the claw was the first fossil part to be noticed by paleontologists. *Suchomimus* was considerably larger than *Baryonyx*, but the latter might almost have been a juvenile of the former. Detailed study shows that the specimen of *Suchomimus* was itself not fully grown when it died.

RIGHT The long, low snout of *Suchomimus* is similar to that of *Baryonyx* and several kinds of modern crocodiles. It is suited to swishing sideways fast through the water and grabbing slippery, wriggling prey such as fish.

DINO FACTFILE
Suchomimus

Meaning: Crocodile mimic
Pronunciation: Soo-koe-mim-uss
Period: Early and mid-Cretaceous
Main group: Theropoda
Length: 11 meters (36 feet)
Weight: 2 metric tons (2 tons)
Diet: Animals, perhaps fish
Fossils: Sahara (Niger)

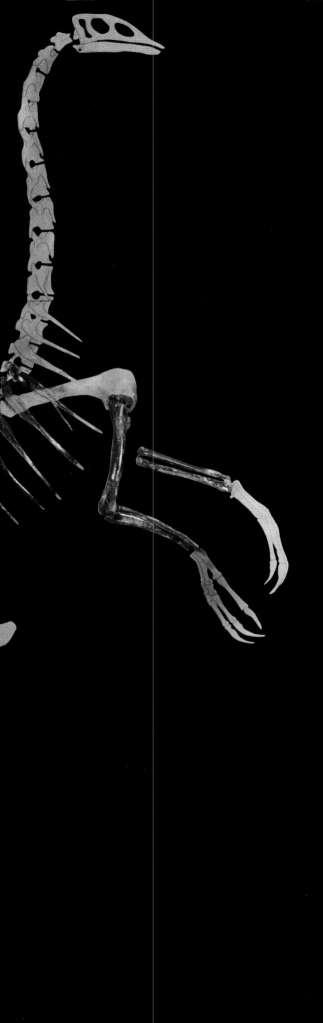

CHAPTER SIX

OSTRICH DINOSAURS

Among the strangest groups of dinosaurs were the ornithomimosaurs. Most had no teeth at all, and pecked at food with beaks.

LIKE A BIRD'S BEAK

SEVERAL KINDS OF DINOSAURS HAD BEAK-LIKE FRONTS TO THEIR MOUTHS, INCLUDING LARGE-SIZED PLANT-EATERS LIKE *TRICERATOPS* AND *STEGOSAURUS*. BUT AMONG THE MEAT-EATERS, ONLY THE ORNITHOMIMOSAURS EVOLVED THIS FEATURE. THEIR NAME, WHICH MEANS "BIRD MIMIC REPTILES," REFERS PARTLY TO THE PRESENCE OF A BEAK. IN FOSSILIZED REMAINS, THIS CONSISTS OF BONES FORMING THE UPPER AND LOWER JAWS, WHICH ARE LONG AND LOW, LIKE A PAIR OF NEEDLE-NOSE PLIERS. TEETH WERE ENTIRELY ABSENT IN MOST TYPES (BUT SEE BELOW). IN LIFE, THE JAWBONES WOULD HAVE BEEN COVERED WITH HORN SHEATHS, AS IN MODERN BIRDS. THE HORN GREW SLOWLY AND REPAIRED ITSELF, PROTECTING THE BONE WITHIN. IT MIGHT ALSO HAVE FORMED SHARP EDGES OR RIDGES ALONG THE JAWS, SO THAT THEY COULD BE USED TO CUT RATHER THAN SIMPLY SQUASH FOOD.

MORE LIKE AN OSTRICH

The beaks of birds vary hugely in size and shape. Among those of living birds, the beaks most like those of ornithomimosaurs belong to ostriches. Indeed, not only the beak, but the head, neck and rear limbs of an ornithomimosaur all resembled those of a modern ostrich. One of the best-known ornithomimosaurs is named *Struthiomimus*, meaning "ostrich mimic," and the whole group is often called the ostrich dinosaurs. It is important not to be misled by this. The similarities between ostrich dinosaurs and ostriches are accidents of evolution, not signs of any close relationship, and there are important differences between them and the bird after which they are named; after all, they were prehistoric reptiles, not modern birds. An ostrich's forelimbs are wing-like, while ostrich dinosaurs had sizably long arms that dangled below the body and were tipped with sharply clawed digits that could scratch, dig and grab. Finally, no modern bird has the long series of tailbones possessed by dinosaurs. While today's ostrich body is covered with feathers, there is, so far, no good fossil evidence either way as to whether ostrich-dinosaurs had scales, like most other reptiles, or feathers, like some dinosaurs and all birds.

BEHAVIOR PATTERNS

In spite of the differences, the similarities suggest that ostrich dinosaurs lived in ways similar to ostriches today. They probably strode across the landscape, their large eyes held well above the ground by the long legs and neck, scanning for food and enemies. If danger appeared, an ostrich dinosaur would use its chief method of survival – it would run. The bones of their limbs, and reconstructions of their muscles, indicate that ornithomimosaurs were probably the fleetest of all dinosaurs. Some could equal or even exceed the speed of a modern ostrich, which has been measured at around 80 kilometers (50 miles) per hour. If an ornithomimosaur detected food, it might peck it up using its long neck and head. Alternatively, its front limbs could grab small prey, such as lizards and baby dinosaurs. Ostriches today are master omnivores. They eat almost anything, including leaves, stems, shoots, buds, eggs, insects, grubs and other small animals. Ostrich dinosaurs may well have done the same.

EVOLUTION

Ostrich dinosaurs were one of the last groups of dinosaurs to appear. Most lived toward the end of the Cretaceous period, and most of their fossils have been found on northern land masses – North America, Europe and East Asia. One of the earlier types was *Pelecanimimus*, from Europe. It still had teeth – more than 60 at the front of the upper jaw, and 140 below them in the lower jaw, but all of them tiny. This shows how ostrich dinosaurs gradually lost the normal dinosaur teeth as their beaks took over. The group seems to have been evolving still and spreading when the great extinction brought them to an abrupt end (see pages 407–409).

PREVIOUS PAGE The typical ornithomimosaur features of inadequate-looking head, gangly front limbs, long and powerful rear limbs, and lengthy tail are all apparent in this reconstructed skeleton.

LEFT The Australian ostrich dinosaur *Timimus* settles to hibernate under a log, as small ornithopod dinosaurs, including *Leaellynasaura*, make their way through the fern-draped mid-Cretaceous forest, in a scene lit by the vast, high-altitude, curtain-like shimmering of the Southern Lights (*Aurora Australis*).

ORNITHOMIMUS

DINO FACTFILE
Ornithomimus

Meaning: Bird mimic, avian pretender
Pronunciation: Or-nith-owe-mim-uss
Period: Late Cretaceous
Main group: Theropoda
Length: 4–6 meters (13–20 feet)
Weight: 130–160 kilograms
  (290–350 pounds)
Diet: Probably omnivorous
Fossils: Western USA, possibly Mongolia

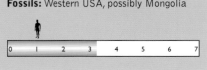

The scientific history of ostrich dinosaurs began with a "big bang" in 1890, when Othniel Charles Marsh, eminent paleontologist and prolific namer of dinosaurs, named three species of this genus from fossils unearthed a year or two earlier by George Cannon in Denver, Colorado, and by John Bell Hatcher in Montana. Marsh suspected that these creatures were bird-like reptiles and probably ornithopods, from the same main group of dinosaurs as the much larger *Iguanodon*. Two more species followed in 1892, but by then Marsh had realized that these dinosaurs were probably theropods, that is, bipedal predators. After more finds and some confusion with the related *Struthiomimus*, *Ornithomimus* assumed its place as the founding member of a newly classified group, the ornithomimosaurs ("bird mimic reptiles"), or ostrich dinosaurs.

Ornithomimus had all the features that are typical of the group: slim build; hollow bones; long low skull; toothless beak; big eyes and brain; strong front limbs with three clawed and grasping fingers; extremely long, slender rear legs powered by strong hip muscles; very long metatarsals (foot bones); three big digits on each foot on the ground; and a long, thin tail with up to 40 caudal vertebrae (backbones). It was one of the larger members of the group, at 5 meters (16^1/$_2$ feet) or more in total length, slightly larger than *Struthiomimus*, although estimates vary from less than 4 to more than 6 meters (13 to 20 feet). Its fossils have been provisionally identified in Mongolia, as well as on the North American continent. Like most ostrich dinosaurs, it was probably an omnivore, pecking and snapping at almost any kind of food, from juicy worms to tough seeds.

ABOVE *Ornithomimus* would have stood taller than an adult human, at well over 2 meters (6½ feet) when in this erect posture. For sprinting the head and neck were probably lowered, and the tail raised, so that both were horizontal and level with the body, forming one long, arrow-like shape.

DROMICEIOMIMUS

Today's second largest bird, after the ostrich, is the emu of Australia (*Dromaius novae-hollandiae*), which can be as tall as a large adult human. Since *Struthiomimus* had been named after the ostrich, it seemed logical to give the name of *Dromiceiomimus* to one of the next bird-like dinosaurs to be studied. It was coined by Dale Russell in 1972 for fossils found in Late Cretaceous rocks in Alberta, Canada. The fossils previously, in the 1920s, had been attributed to two species, *Struthiomimus brevitertius* and *Struthiomimus samueli*. In fact, *Struthiomimus brevitertius*, (established in 1928 by William Parks from a specimen from the Red Deer River near Steveville), included the first well-preserved skull known from any ostrich dinosaur.

The skull of *Dromiceiomimus* shows huge eye sockets, which have led to the view that this Late Cretaceous omnivore fed in the twilight of dusk and dawn. Much of its skeleton is similar to that of other ostrich dinosaurs, but its torso is even more condensed and compact, its forelimbs are elongated, and its pelvic (hip) bones are also distinctive. In the proportions of its legs, its shinbones (tibia and fibula) were around one-fifth longer than its thighbone (femur), the latter having an average length of 47 centimeters (18$\frac{1}{2}$ inches). This is greater than the already high shin–thigh ratio found in most ostrich dinosaurs, suggesting that *Dromiceiomimus* was an even faster sprinter than its cousins, maybe exceeding 60 kilometers (38 miles) per hour.

DINO FACTFILE
Dromiceiomimus

Meaning: Emu mimic

Pronunciation: Drom-ee-say-owe-mim-uss

Period: Late Cretaceous

Main group: Theropoda

Length: 3.5 meters (11 feet)

Weight: 120 kilograms (265 pounds)

Diet: Omnivore

Fossils: Canada (Alberta)

LEFT Perhaps one of the fastest of all dinosaurs, *Dromiceiomimus* also had very long forelimbs for an ostrich dinosaur. It could stoop down to scrabble with its front claws in soil and sand for food such as bugs and worms, and peck at these by darting out its head on the very flexible neck.

GALLIMIMUS

DINO FACTFILE

Gallimimus

Meaning: Chicken mimic, rooster pretender

Pronunciation: Gal-ee-mim-uss

Period: Late Cretaceous

Main group: Theropoda

Length: 6 meters (20 feet)

Weight: 400 kilograms (880 pounds)

Diet: Omnivore

Fossils: Mongolia

In the late 1960s and early 1970s, Polish-Mongolian fossil-finding expeditions to the Gobi desert collected many amazing discoveries. One was the "chicken mimic" *Gallimimus*, with two almost complete skeletons, another missing only its skull, and another skull with various smaller pieces, at the site of Altan Ula, Mongolia. Far from being the size and shape of a hen, this ostrich dinosaur was the largest of the well-known types in its group, at some 6 meters (20 feet) in total length. It dated from 75–70 million years ago. Based on these Gobi remains, Mongolian paleontologist Rinchen Barsbold with Polish colleagues Halszka Osmólska and Ewa Roniewicz named *Gallimimus* in 1972.

Gallimimus was big and long in almost every respect except for its head. Its main torso was relatively elongated compared to those of its relatives – other ostrich dinosaurs

– as were its gangly front limbs, each bearing three digits tipped with small claws. On a long and flexible S-shaped neck, the strikingly small head had a long, toothless beak that seemed suited to any kind of food, animal or vegetable. The front of the lower beak was shaped like a scoop, and there were comb-like flanges inside the mouth, perhaps used for shoveling soil and sifting out food items from mud. Big eyes stared out sideways from their sockets, one on either side of the skull, keeping a watch all around for enemies and other dangers. Rearing up straight, *Gallimimus* could crane its neck to raise its head more than 4 meters (13 feet) above the ground. On the move, its body and neck tilted forward to become more horizontal, balanced over the powerful hips by the long, stiffened tail, placing the head around 2 meters (6½ feet) above the ground.

RIGHT The front feet of *Gallimimus* are less hand-like, for grasping, and more spade-like, suited for digging and shoveling. But the huge size of this ostrich dinosaur makes it unlikely that it could survive on a diet of tiny prey items like grubs or worms.

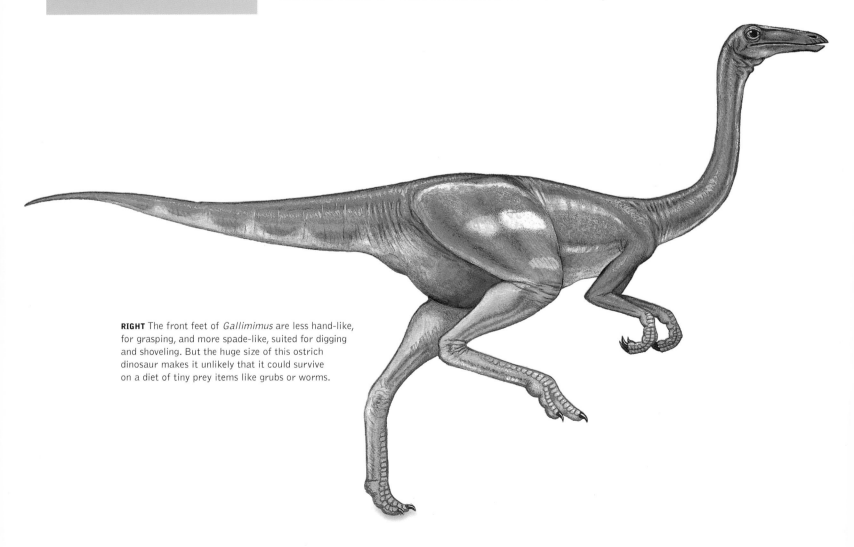

STRUTHIOMIMUS

Standing about as tall as an adult human, *Struthiomimus* was the first ostrich dinosaur to be described from fairly complete remains. Most of a skull and skeleton from Alberta, Canada, were studied and named in 1916–17 by Henry Fairfield Osborn, then curator of the American Museum of Natural History. He noted the great similarity in the reptile's size, shape and proportions to today's flightless birds, such as the ostrich, and so called the new find "ostrich mimic." The whole ostrich dinosaur group was founded on his proposals, and *Struthiomimus* is still one of the best known of its North American members. Further possible finds of *Struthiomimus* remains have been found as far east as New Jersey.

Struthiomimus dates from around 75–73 million years ago. Its long, low skull and toothless beak, 25 centimeters (10 inches) in length and constructed from almost wafer-thin bony plates and struts, are extremely similar in shape and size to the skull of the

modern ostrich. As in other members of the ornithomimosaur group, the bones of the upper and lower jaws would have been covered with horny sheaths to form the beak or bill as seen on the outside. The proportions of the rear legs are also amazingly similar to those of ostriches, with bulging muscles around the thigh, leaving the long shin, even longer foot (metatarsal bones), and three clawed digits on the feet extremely light. *Struthiomimus* could probably swing its long legs back and forth with maximum speed and efficiency when running. It probably used its sharp claws to scrape for grubs in soil, gather food such as berries, or perhaps grab and tear up small prey like lizards, while using its beak to peck at anything edible.

ABOVE Like most ostrich dinosaurs, *Struthiomimus* had very thin skull bones, which were probably linked by flexible joints in life. This meant the jaws could twist or "warp" slightly, making the upper and lower beak tilt for lopsided pecking or snapping.

DINO FACTFILE
Struthiomimus
Meaning: Ostrich mimic
Pronunciation: Strew-thee-owe-mim-uss
Period: Late Cretaceous
Main group: Theropoda
Length: 3.5–4 meters (11–13½ feet)
Weight: 140 kilograms (310 pounds)
Diet: Omnivore
Fossils: Canada (Alberta), USA (possibly New Jersey)

DEINOCHEIRUS

DINO FACTFILE

Deinocheirus

Meaning: Terrible hand, horrible fingers

Pronunciation: Day-noe-kye-russ

Period: Late Cretaceous

Main group: Theropoda

Length: Estimated 8–12 meters
 (26–40 feet)

Weight: Estimated 4–7 metric tons
 (4–7 tons)

Diet: Presumably animals, carrion

Fossils: Mongolia

One of the most puzzling, exciting and potentially awe-inspiring fossil finds is a pair of forelimbs from Late Cretaceous rocks in the eastern area of the Nemegt Basin, which is part of the Gobi Desert in southern Mongolia. Even the day of their discovery in 1965, during the joint Mongolian–Polish expeditions of the 1960s and 1970s, was notable – in a place where droughts last years, it was raining. The specimens included bones from the front limbs, some claws and a few associated bits of ribs and backbones. No other parts of the creature have been found. In 1970, Halszka Osmólska and Ewa Roniewicz, Polish members of the expedition, named the find *Deinocheirus*, meaning "terrible hand."

The forelimbs broadly follow the ostrich dinosaur pattern, with all three digits around the same length, although the overall proportions of the limbs are relatively slender. The great shock was their size. Each forelimb was around 2.4 meters (8 feet) long, each digit alone was bigger than a human arm, and the hook-shaped claws are among the largest of any dinosaur, measuring more than 25 centimeters (10 inches) in length. It is tempting to speculate that these massive front limbs belonged to a great ostrich dinosaur. Scaled up in proportion from others in the group, the whole creature could have been 12 meters (40 feet) long and weighed more than 7 metric tons (7 tons) – the size of *Tyrannosaurus* but with the addition of huge forelimbs. Informed description of *Deinocheirus* must wait, however, until further remains of this mysterious monster are unearthed.

RIGHT Known mainly from isolated forelimb bones and claws, this reconstruction of *Deinocheirus* – like any other – is extremely speculative. The enormous size of the fossils means that the dinosaur could easily have been as long as *Tyrannosaurus* and able to reach as high into the trees as the modern giraffe.

ELAPHROSAURUS

Elaphrosaurus appears to combine features of the general theropod (meat-eating) group known as the coelurosaurs, which thrived from the Early Jurassic period, with features of the ostrich dinosaurs, which form a more specialized subgroup within the coelurosauria (see page 146). So *Elaphrosaurus* has been proposed as an ancestor of the ostrich-dinosaur group, or an animal similar to this ancestor. On the other hand, it may be a more primitive type, linked to *Coelophysis* or even *Ceratosaurus*. A major problem is that the main skeleton of *Elaphrosaurus* is known only from a specimen found in East Africa, which lacked a skull – and so the usual distinguishing features of skull bones, jaws and teeth, which provide so much information, are missing. The rock layers of the region that contained the skeleton also harbor many small teeth, which could have fitted into the jaws of *Elaphrosaurus* if they were toothed.

The shape and proportions of *Elaphrosaurus* were certainly both coelurosaur-like and ostrich-like, with long slim rear legs; slender forelimbs with three digits each; a lightweight body; long, stiff tail; and long, flexible neck. The single fossil specimen came from quarries at Tendaguru in what was then German East Africa (later Tanganyika, now the larger portion of Tanzania). The site also yielded many other notable finds, not least *Brachiosaurus*, *Kentrosaurus* and *Dicraeosaurus*, during a four-year expedition begun in 1908 and led by Werner Janensch, the German paleontologist who named *Elaphrosaurus* in 1920. The most recent studies of *Elaphrosaurus* suggest transferring it to the ceratosaur group.

ABOVE *Elaphrosaurus* has long puzzled experts as to its basic grouping. Recent reviews tend to place it in the ceratosaur group, as a long, slim predator, likely with teeth in its jaws, rather than in the beaked ornithomimosaur (ostrich dinosaur) group.

DINO FACTFILE
Elaphrosaurus

Meaning: Light lizard

Pronunciation: El-aff-row-sore-uss

Period: Late Jurassic

Main group: Theropoda

Length: 3-5 meters (10–16 feet)

Weight: 100-150 kilograms (220–330 pounds)

Diet: Uncertain

Fossils: East Africa, possibly USA (Wyoming)

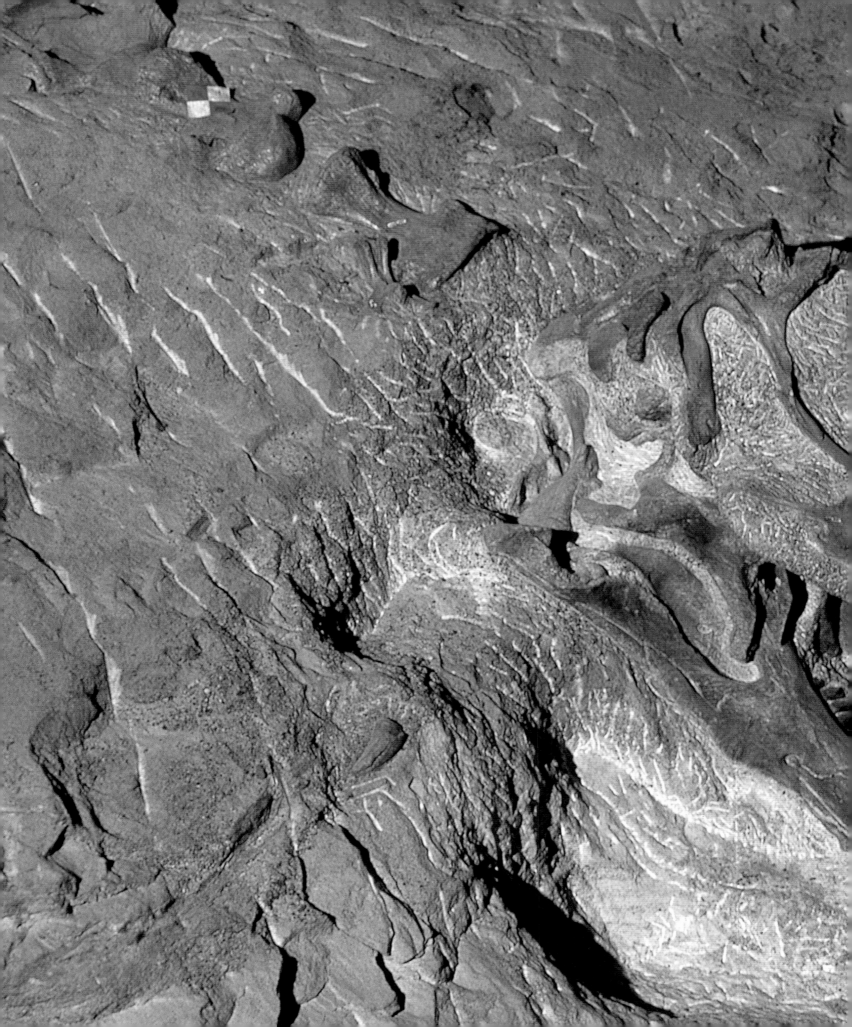

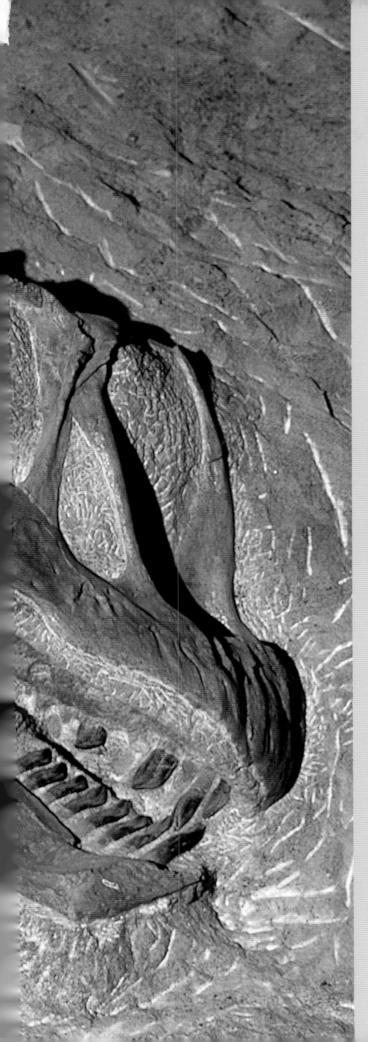

CHAPTER SEVEN

THE
GIANTS

BIG, BIGGER, BIGGEST — IT SEEMS THAT EVERY FEW YEARS A NEW RECORD-HOLDER IS DISCOVERED AMONG THE MOST MASSIVE ANIMALS EVER TO SHAKE THE EARTH WITH THEIR STEPS.

BREAKING RECORDS

THE RIVALRY BETWEEN MAMMALS AND DINOSAURS FOR THE TITLE OF LARGEST ANIMAL EVER TO HAVE LIVED IS MUCH CLOSER THAN IT SEEMED TO BE SEVERAL YEARS AGO. NEW FINDS OF FOSSILS FROM GIANT DINOSAURS OF THE SAUROPOD GROUP, SUCH AS *ARGENTINOSAURUS*, MEAN THAT THESE REPTILES RIVAL TODAY'S GREAT WHALES, SUCH AS THE BLUE WHALE, FOR THE TOP SPOT. THERE WERE SEVERAL MAIN GROUPS OF SAUROPODS THROUGH THE AGE OF DINOSAURS, AND EACH HAD ITS GIANT MEMBERS. THE DIPLODOCIDS WERE EXCEPTIONALLY LONG AND THRIVED DURING THE LATE JURASSIC PERIOD, ESPECIALLY IN NORTH AMERICA. CAMARASAURUS AND ITS COUSINS VARIED GREATLY, FROM BIG TO ENORMOUS, AND ALSO LIVED AT THIS TIME, IN NORTH AMERICA AS WELL AS IN EUROPE AND ASIA. THE BRACHIOSAURIDS HAD ESPECIALLY LONG FRONT LEGS, AND THEY ALSO ENJOYED SUCCESS IN THE LATE JURASSIC PERIOD IN NORTH AMERICA, EUROPE AND AFRICA. DURING THE CRETACEOUS PERIOD THAT FOLLOWED, THE TITANOSAURIDS APPEARED ON ALMOST ALL CONTINENTS AND BECAME PARTICULARLY PROMINENT IN SOUTH AMERICA.

ADVANTAGES OF BEING BIG

Why did sauropod dinosaurs grow so huge, reaching more than 10 times the weight of today's largest land animals, the elephants? There are several advantages to increased body size. One is enhanced self-defense. Larger dinosaurs had more weight and power with which to defend themselves against predators. They could wield their long tails like massive whips, or swing their long necks like huge blackjacks, or turn and lean on an enemy to squash its life away. Most predators, even the biggest meat-eating dinosaurs, were less than one-fifth of the weight of the greatest sauropods.

STAYING WARMER LONGER

Another advantage might have been in body temperature regulation. One of the main factors that affects heat loss from a warm object to cooler surroundings is the ratio between the object's surface area and its volume. The greater the surface area compared to the volume, the greater the rate of heat loss. Bigger objects have much less surface area relative to volume than do smaller objects, so heat loss is reduced as size increases. This might have been important for the sauropods if they were "cold-blooded," or, more accurately, ectothermic – gaining body heat from their surroundings. After absorbing the sun's warmth by day, a huge dinosaur would retain much of the heat in the core of its body, for use through the cool night. A warmer dinosaur could remain active and alert as it searched for food or fought enemies.

PROBLEMS OF SIZE

But being very big has its problems. The amount of bone needed to support more weight rises at a rate higher than the actual increase in weight. More powerful muscles are needed to move the bulk, again at a greatly increasing rate. Food requirements become gargantuan, posing difficulties in gathering such a large mass of plant matter with a relatively small head, to keep the vast guts supplied. Also, the environment could have been put under strain as plants were consumed in quantities such that they disappeared, especially if these giant sauropods lived in herds – and much of the fossil evidence suggests that they did. Sauropods had their greatest success in the Late Jurassic, when the warm, moist climate encouraged rapid plant growth. Even so, whole areas would have been stripped bare of suitable vegetation, meaning that the herd had to move on.

PREVIOUS PAGE This skull of *Camarasaurus* is from the Dinosaur National Monument site in Utah. The sauropod had a tall skull with three large openings on each side – the huge nostril at the front then the orbit or eye socket; and the infraorbital fenestra, a gap allowing the jaw muscles to bulge, to the lower rear.

LEFT Sauropods on the move would have been an awesome sight, as they scanned the area for suitable plant growth as new browsing. Many examples of their fossilized footprints show these vast dinosaurs moved in close-knit groups.

BAROSAURUS

DINO FACTFILE

Barosaurus

Meaning: Heavy reptile

Pronunciation: Bar-oh-sore-uss

Period: Late Jurassic

Main group: Sauropoda

Length: 27 meters (89 feet)

Weight: 30 metric tons (30 tons)

Diet: Plants

Fossils: Western USA, Tanzania

Barosaurus is one of the many sauropods discovered in North America during the "Wild West Dinosaur Hunts" of the late nineteenth century. Othniel Charles Marsh named it in 1890. The name is also applied to specimens once called *Tornieria*. Starting in 1922, three fairly complete *Barosaurus* skeletons were dug out of Carnegie Quarry, Utah, by a team led by Earl Douglass of the Carnegie Museum. Earlier, he had excavated *Apatosaurus* from the same site and had been involved in the setting up of the Dinosaur National Monument there in 1915. More *Barosaurus* remains were uncovered in South Dakota and, more recently, pieces of skull, limbs and other fragments of a specimen from Tanzania in East Africa have also been assigned to *Barosaurus*.

Barosaurus was a large but fairly typical *Diplodocus*-type sauropod of the Late Jurassic period, around 150 million years ago. In fact, in many respects *Barosaurus* was very similar to *Diplodocus* itself (see opposite), but with slight differences: much longer backbones or vertebrae,

a shorter tail, and a much longer neck. Although its cervical vertebrae (neckbones) numbered 15 in total, just as in *Diplodocus*, some of them were more than 1 meter (39 inches) long. The scoops and hollows in their structure mean that the neck as a whole was relatively light. Probably more than four-fifths of this plant-eater's total length of perhaps 27 meters (89 feet) was neck and tail. Presumably it had a small head, although no specimen of its skull has been recovered. The American Museum of Natural History in New York shows a "mother" *Barosaurus* skeleton rearing on its hind legs to an enormous height, to protect her offspring from a small allosaur. Her head would be level with the fifth story of a building.

ABOVE The skull of *Barosaurus* is not known from fossil remains and so is reconstructed in the manner of cousins such as *Diplodocus*. This sauropod had such a compact body that in proportion to its total length, it was more "neck and tail" than almost any other dinosaur.

DIPLODOCUS

Dinosaurs known from partial remains recently discovered may have been longer than *Diplodocus* (see pages 222, 224), but this Late Jurassic leviathan is still just about the longest dinosaur known from fairly complete specimens, and it still has one of the longest tails known – 13 meters (43 feet). Sam Williston found partial remains near Canyon City, Colorado, in 1877 and the next year Othniel Charles Marsh gave them their name. Twenty-two years later, a much more complete specimen was recovered from Albany County, Wyoming. The name means "double beam" and is said to refer to the caudal vertebrae (tailbones), of which there were more than 70. In the middle section of the tail, each vertebra had a downward projection that carried a front and rear extension or skid on the base, facing forward and back, like an upside-down T with a very short upright.

Toward the rear section, the vertebrae become simpler in form, so that at the whip-like tail tip they are simple rods.

Diplodocus has lent its name to a whole group of sauropods with similar skulls. The forehead is low and slopes down to a somewhat blunted snout, and the peg-like teeth are around the front of the upper and lower jaws, working like a comb or rake to gather foliage. One recent study, however, indicates that dinosaurs of this type could not lift their heads very high. The nostrils are high on the forehead, almost between the eyes. As in most sauropods, each of the four feet had five digits, but only the first bore a proper claw. Despite the great length of *Diplodocus*, its slim legs and body suggest that it was relatively lightweight, possibly about 10–15 metric tons (10–15 tons). Recent finds of skin impressions that are probably from *Diplodocus* show a row of spines along the back.

DINO FACTFILE
Diplodocus
Meaning: Double-beamed
Pronunciation: Dip-lod-ick-uss
Period: Late Jurassic
Main group: Sauropoda
Length: 27 meters (89 feet)
Weight: 10–15 metric tons (10–15 tons)
Diet: Plants
Fossils: USA (Colorado, Wyoming)

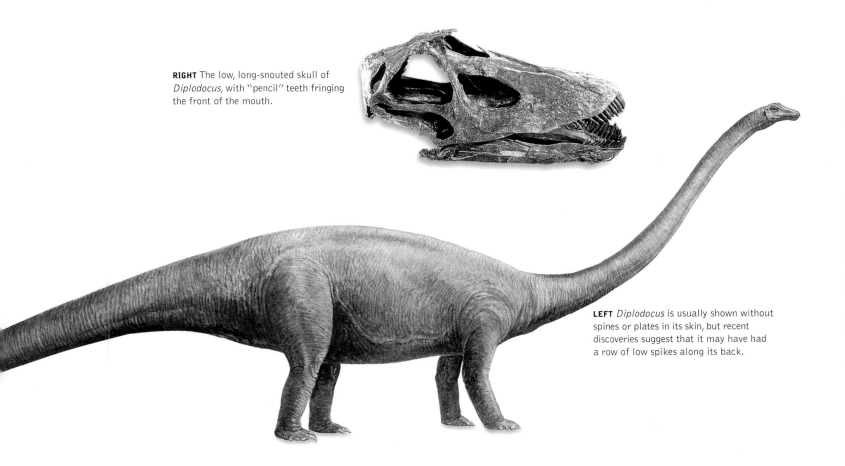

RIGHT The low, long-snouted skull of *Diplodocus*, with "pencil" teeth fringing the front of the mouth.

LEFT *Diplodocus* is usually shown without spines or plates in its skin, but recent discoveries suggest that it may have had a row of low spikes along its back.

SUPERSAURUS

DINO FACTFILE

Supersaurus

Meaning: Super reptile

Pronunciation: Soo-pur-sore-uss

Period: Late Jurassic

Main group: Sauropoda

Length: Estimated 30–40 meters
(98-131 feet)

Weight: Estimated 30–50 metric tons
(30–50 tons)

Diet: Plants

Fossils: USA (Colorado)

Supersaurus was a *Diplodocus*-type sauropod in North America in the Late Jurassic period. James Jensen first excavated its fossils in western Colorado in 1972, but it was not named until 1985. Enough of the skeleton has been recovered to show that this was a truly massive beast, probably over 30 meters (98 feet) long but possibly almost 40 meters (131 feet), and as much as 50 metric tons in weight. The shoulder blades alone are far larger than an adult human, at 2.4 meters (8 feet) in length. The ribs measure 3 meters (10 feet), and some of the individual neckbones (caudal vertebrae) are 1.4 meters (4½ feet) long. Unfortunately, the remains are scattered and are nowhere as complete as for other giants, such as *Brachiosaurus*, so the true dimensions of *Supersaurus* remain a matter for speculation.

Supersaurus probably lived like other sauropods, swinging its long neck for hours at a time to gather vast amounts of plant food, which it swallowed without chewing, to fuel its massive bulk. If it could stretch its head upward, it might have been able to eat leaves 15 meters (49 feet) off the ground. This dinosaur is placed in the family Diplodocidae, which is characterized by a long, whip-like tail, and teeth shaped like pegs or pencils. Its cousins included *Amargasaurus*, *Apatosaurus*, *Barosaurus* and the similarly enormous *Seismosaurus*. James Jensen has proposed another giant, *Ultrasauros* (with an "o"), but this is now regarded by many sauropod experts as a misnomer for a chance finding in Colorado of mixed fossils of *Supersaurus* and *Brachiosaurus* (see page 232).

BELOW One of many giant sauropods known from relatively few outsized fossils, *Supersaurus* is a contender for longest (although not heaviest) dinosaur. It was probably a member of the diplodocid family.

BELOW The very limited fossils of *Dicraeosaurus* show a curious mix of features from several sauropod groups, including the diplodocids and cetiosaurids. In particular it had few neck and tail bones compared to most sauropods – perhaps only 12 in the neck, making its body look relatively long.

DICRAEOSAURUS

Fossils of this Late Jurassic sauropod, which could be called medium-sized for its group, even though it was far longer than any land animal today, were excavated by German-organized expeditions in 1908–12 to Tendaguru, then in the colony of German East Africa (later Tanganyika and now part of Tanzania). The fossils represent many parts of the skeleton, including a fine skull specimen.

Tendaguru yielded many other now well-known remains, including *Brachiosaurus* and *Kentrosaurus* (the "spiky reptile"), an African cousin of *Stegosaurus*. The fossils were studied by Werner Janensch, curator of the Natural History Museum of Berlin, and named by him in 1914 (see also page 245).

Dicraeosaurus has been included variously in the family Diplodocidae or in its own group, Dicraeosauridae. It shows similarities to the South American sauropod *Amargasaurus* (see page 230).

The "two forks" in the name *Dicraeosaurus* refer to the neural spines or upward extensions of the various vertebrae (backbones), which branch or fork into two. These probably held up a ridge of fleshy skin, or a thinner, low, sail-like structure, which could have had various functions, such as temperature regulation and / or visual display (possible functions for these kinds of sails are discussed on page 107).

The skull shows typical diplodocid features: the eyes are set high up on the top; the nostrils are also set high up, almost between the eyes; the snout is long, low and horse-like; and the teeth are fine and almost pencil-shaped, set in two curved clusters around the fronts of both jaws.

Dicraeosaurus's tail, with its forked, skid-like chevrons beneath some of the vertebrae, was not as long and whippy as the tail of its sauropod relative *Diplodocus*.

DINO FACTFILE
Dicraeosaurus

Meaning: Two-forked reptile

Pronunciation: Die-kree-owe-sore-uss

Period: Late Jurassic

Main group: Sauropoda

Length: 13–20 meters (43–66 feet)

Weight: 10 metric tons (11 tons)

Diet: Plants

Fossils: Tanzania

| 0 • | 5 | 10 | 15 | 20 | 25 | 30 |

SEISMOSAURUS

DINO FACTFILE

Seismosaurus

Meaning: Earthquake reptile

Pronunciation: Size-mow-sore-uss

Period: Late Jurassic

Main group: Sauropoda

Length: Estimated 35–52 meters (115–170 feet)

Weight: Estimated 30–50 metric tons (30–50 tons)

Diet: Plants

Fossils: USA (New Mexico)

The 1990s saw scientific reports of many newly discovered giant dinosaurs. One was *Seismosaurus*, so named because it presumably shook the ground like an earthquake as it moved, perhaps at a trot or even a gallop. The Late Jurassic remains were located in New Mexico and named in 1991 by David Gillette. They included parts of the vertebrae forming the spinal column (backbone), some ribs, pieces of the pelvis (hipbone), and other pieces. The vertebrae are some of the longest ever found, at 1.8 meters (6 feet) each – the same as the height of an adult human. Many smooth, rounded pebbles or gastroliths (stomach stones) were found with the fossils. The dinosaur swallowed these to help it grind up its food (which it gulped without chewing) in its muscular gut.

Similarities have led to suggestions that *Seismosaurus* is actually an outsized form, or species, of the genus *Diplodocus* (see page 223),

rather than a separate genus. Features of the vertebrae, including their skid-like chevrons underneath, and other preserved bones identify *Seismosaurus* as a *Diplodocus*-type sauropod from the same time, about 155–144 million years ago. Indeed, *Seismosaurus* and other finds made in the 1990s have helped to displace *Diplodocus* from its position as the longest-ever dinosaur and land animal. Working from the sparse remains, estimates of the overall length of *Seismosaurus* are as high as 52 meters (170 feet) – almost twice that of *Diplodocus*'s 27 meters (89 feet)– but other calculations suggest a length of 40 or perhaps 35 meters (131 or 115 feet). Weight estimates are similarly varied, from 30 up to 80 metric tons (30–80 tons), although *Seismosaurus*, being a slim, lightweight diplodocid, probably did not have the great bulk of the *Brachiosaurus*-type sauropods.

BELOW *Seismosaurus* is one of the longest of all dinosaurs, and indeed, of all animals that every lived. However estimates of its length vary greatly due to the limited extent of its fossils, from 30 to more than 50 meters (98–164 feet). The blue whale of today reaches a maximum of about 30 meters (98 feet).

LEFT Like most of the huge sauropods, *Apatosaurus* must have spent most of its time gathering vegetation. Its pencil- or peg-like teeth continually pulled and raked in plant matter, which was swallowed directly into the huge stomach.

APATOSAURUS (BRONTOSAURUS)

Brontosaurus is one of the best known of all dinosaurs, yet in scientific terms its name does not exist. It did exist once, at least the name, in 1879, when Othniel Charles Marsh described two massive sauropod skeletons from Como Bluff, Wyoming, and coined the famous name, which means "thunder lizard." Two years earlier, Marsh had described another huge sauropod from remains found by Arthur Lakes in rocks near Morrison, Colorado, and named them *Apatosaurus*. Also included in this early batch of sauropods was *Atlantosaurus*, yet another name coined by Marsh, this one for specimens that he had already described as *Titanosaurus*. But he was to find that the name *Atlantosaurus* was already in use, so that it had to be hurriedly changed. Another sauropod, *Camarasaurus*, was also mixed up in the general confusion. Gradually, however, it became clear that *Apatosaurus*, *Brontosaurus* and *Atlantosaurus* were one and the same – and the first name, being the earliest in the

scientific literature, took precedence. So the title *Brontosaurus* was removed from official lists of valid dinosaur names. Nevertheless, *Brontosaurus* has lived large in the public imagination ever since.

Apatosaurus was a close cousin of *Diplodocus*, from the same Late Jurassic period and in the same area of the North American southwest. But it was shorter and sturdier, however, and probably more than twice as heavy. Around a dozen preserved skeletons have been excavated and studied over many years, yet the shape of its skull was not clear until 1975, when Jack MacIntosh and David Berman sorted out some more of the confusion. A new fossil find of a skull showed that *Apatosaurus* did not possess a long, rounded head like that of *Camarasaurus*, as reconstructions had shown up to that time. Instead, it had a low, short-snouted head with nostrils high up almost between the eyes, and weak, peg-shaped teeth. In all these features it resembled *Diplodocus*.

DINO FACTFILE
Apatosaurus
Meaning: Deceptive reptile
Pronunciation: Ap-at-owe-sore-uss
Period: Late Jurassic
Main group: Sauropoda
Length: 21–23 meters (69–75½ feet)
Weight: 25–35 metric tons (25–35 tons)
Diet: Plants
Fossils: Southwestern USA, Mexico
(Baja California)

| 0 • | 5 | 10 | 15 | 20 | 25 | 30 |

LIKE A HERD OF ELEPHANTS – BUT BIGGER

THERE IS AMPLE EVIDENCE THAT VARIOUS
SAUROPODS LIVED IN GROUPS OR HERDS. MANY
FOSSIL SITES YIELD SEVERAL SPECIMENS IN ONE
SMALL AREA. THESE ARE OFTEN OF MIXED AGES,
FROM JUVENILES TO ADULTS. EXAMPLES OF
PRESERVED FOOTPRINTS SHOW GROUPS ON THE
MOVE, WITH SMALLER TRACKS IN THE MIDDLE AND
LARGER ONES TO THE SIDE. WERE THE ADULTS
FLANKING THEIR YOUNG FOR PROTECTION?

RIGHT Late Jurassic *Brachiosaurus*-type sauropods gather
at their traditional breeding ground in this proposed scenario.
In the background a female and male sway and twine necks
during their courtship ritual. The female to the left prepares
to lay her eggs in a scrape in the ground. The clutch of eggs
in the foreground will soon be covered by sand, by the female's
great foot, and will then incubate in the dry warmth.

AMARGASAURUS

DINO FACTFILE

Amargasaurus

Meaning: La Amarga reptile

Pronunciation: Ah-mar-gah-sore-uss

Period: Early Cretaceous

Main group: Sauropoda

Length: 10 meters (33 feet)

Weight: 5–7 metric tons (5–7 tons)

Diet: Plants

Fossils: Argentina

"La Amarga reptile" is named for the valley in Argentina where fossils of this sauropod were found. Like many Argentine dinosaur remains, they are dated to the Cretaceous period, in this case about 130–125 million years ago. They include a fairly complete skeleton, lacking only the front end of the skull and the tail. They were named in 1991 by Leonardo Salgado and José Bonaparte. The general proportions of *Amargasaurus* are typically sauropodian, with a small head, long neck and, probably, long tail, a bulky, rounded body and four pillar-like legs. But with a total of just 10 meters (33 feet) it is one of the smaller members of the sauropod group, similar in length to a reticulated python, the longest reptile alive today. Its neck was proportionally long, its front legs were shorter than the rear pair, and its feet bore the typical five digits, with the first (the "big toe") clawed, as in most sauropods.

Amargasaurus was probably a member of the *Diplodocus* family of sauropods. It is notable for the row of double spines along much of its vertebral column – neck, back and tail. The role of these spines has been widely discussed. They occur in certain other groups of dinosaurs, including huge theropods (meat-eaters) such as *Spinosaurus*; the plant-eating *Iguanodon*-like *Ouranosaurus*; fellow sauropod *Dicraeosaurus*; and some non-dinosaur prehistoric reptiles, such as *Dimetrodon* (see page 106). The usual explanation is that they held up a fleshy or skin-like flap or "sail" – or, in the case of *Amargasaurus*, two of them. The flaps may have been for body temperature regulation, visual display, or, perhaps in the case of *Amargasaurus*, intimidation of, and protection from, the massive and powerful predatory dinosaurs that roamed South America during the Cretaceous period.

RIGHT The extent of the back spines of *Amargasaurus* is debated, with some views that they were on the neck and body only, and others that they extended mainly along the neck. The spines may have been separate structures or coated with a long flap of thin skin, like a sail or fin.

QUAESITOSAURUS / NEMEGTOSAURUS

Fossilized skulls are relatively rare among the sauropods. After all, skulls are among the smallest parts of a sauropod body and consist more of strips and struts of bone than of great slabs or girders. It is perhaps ironic then that these two sauropods, *Quaesitosaurus* and *Nemegtosaurus*, are named solely from remains of skulls. Both were found in the Gobi Desert in Mongolia, both date from the Late Cretaceous period, and both have been compared to the *Diplodocus*-based family of sauropods, and possibly to *Dicraeosaurus* (see page 225). Extrapolating from existing remains, using typical diplodocid proportions, yields an overall length for each of these dinosaurs of around 12–13 meters (39–43 feet), but this is highly speculative. With further finds of other body parts, including perhaps more skulls, both may turn out to be the same type of dinosaur.

Quaesitosaurus (a name variously misspelled as *Qaesitosaurus*, *Questosaurus*, even *Questiosaurus*) was discovered by a Soviet–Mongolian expedition in 1971 and named

in 1983. The skull shows that this dinosaur probably had good hearing, since there is a large opening and a chamber in its ear region that would have allowed sounds to resonate there. The overall skull shape is low and broad, with insubstantial, peg-like teeth that appear capable of raking in only soft food, perhaps water plants.

The skull of *Nemegtosaurus* was found during the Polish–Mongolian expeditions of the late 1960s and early 1970s and named in the year that *Quaesitosaurus* was found, 1971. Its name evokes the Nemegt Basin or Valley, a famous fossil site in the Gobi Desert that has yielded the remains of many well-known dinosaurs, although similar fossils have also been found in China. The skull is more complete than that of *Quaesitosaurus*, and also long and low, but not quite as broad across the snout. It has similar peg-like teeth at the front of the jaws only, not in the cheek region like *Quaesitosaurus*.

DINO FACTFILE
Quaesitosaurus / Nemegtosaurus

Meaning: Unusual or abnormal reptile / Nemegt reptile

Pronunciation: Kye-sit-owe-sore-uss / Nem-egg-toe-sore-uss

Period: Late Cretaceous

Main group: Sauropoda

Length: Estimated 12–13 meters (39–43 feet)

Weight: Estimated 5–10 metric tons (5–10 tons)

Diet: Plants

Fossils: Mongolia, perhaps China

| 0 · | 5 | 10 | 15 | 20 | 25 | 30 |

LEFT *Quaesitosaurus* is nearly all guesswork – only parts of its fossil skull have been found. This has a long, horse-like muzzle shape, with weak teeth that must have pulled in fairly soft vegetation.

BRACHIOSAURUS

DINO FACTFILE
Brachiosaurus
Meaning: Arm reptile

Pronunciation: Brack-ee-owe-sore-uss

Period: Late Jurassic to Early Cretaceous

Main group: Sauropoda

Length: 25 meters (82 feet)

Weight: 50 metric tons (some estimates 80 metric tons) (50–80 tons)

Diet: Plants

Fossils: Western North America, southwestern Europe, North and East Africa

| 0 • | 5 | 10 | 15 | 20 | 25 | 30 |

Monstrous by any standards, *Brachiosaurus* remains the biggest dinosaur well known from complete remains. It has also given its name to a family of sauropods, the Brachiosauridae, that includes many other giants, such as *Sauroposeidon* and *Bothriospondylus*. One of the group's key features is reflected in the meaning of its name, "arm reptile" – the front limbs were much longer than the rear pair, while other families of sauropods, based on *Diplodocus* or *Titanosaurus*, had rear legs longer than the front ones. Great forelimbs gave brachiosaurids a sloping profile from neck down to shoulders, down the back to the hips, and on down the tail, which

was relatively short. There are also key features in the brachiosaurid skull. It had a high forehead with nostrils set right on top above the eyes, a kink that angled from the forehead into the low snout, and large spoon- or chisel-shaped teeth, 26 around the front of each jaw.

American paleontologist and fossil hunter Elmer Riggs collected the first specimens of *Brachiosaurus* in 1900 in western Colorado's Grand River Valley. He coined the name in 1903. Expeditions to Tendaguru, then in German East Africa (later Tanganyika, now Tanzania) in 1908 yielded a spectacular skeleton that helped to fill in many details of this great beast. In addition to being one of the biggest dinosaurs, *Brachiosaurus* was also very widespread. Further finds have been made, not only in various parts of the United States, but also in Portugal and possibly in Algeria. Many aspects of its feeding methods and other behavior patterns are discussed on other pages in this chapter.

RIGHT *Brachiosaurus* is usually shown rearing up to reach the tallest vegetation, some 13–14 meters (42–46 feet) above the ground. This is more than twice the height of today's tallest animal, the giraffe. Whether the heart of *Brachiosaurus* was powerful enough to pump blood to such a great height is much debated.

SAUROPOSEIDON

Brachiosaurus long held the record as the tallest dinosaur, based on its ability to extend its great neck upward rather than forward (see opposite). A recent challenger for the title of "giraffe of the dinosaurs" is *Sauroposeidon*. At full neck stretch on its elongated front limbs, *Brachiosaurus* probably stood around 13–14 meters (43–46 feet) tall, more than twice as tall as today's giraffe. *Sauroposeidon* in the same pose has been estimated at 16 or 18 meters (52$\frac{1}{2}$–59 feet). In a modern setting, *Brachiosaurus* could look into a window on the fifth story of a building, but *Sauroposeidon* could perhaps peer into the sixth floor.

A great deal of what is said about *Sauroposeidon*, however, including its overall length and weight, is little more than informed guesswork. Few parts of the huge beast have been identified, mainly neck vertebrae, some nearly 1.5 meters (5 feet) in length, and associated ribs. They were first noticed in 1994 by Bobby Cross, an amateur fossil-spotter who was out walking and exercising the bloodhounds that he was training for prison

and police work in Otaka County, Oklahoma. Huge fossil footprints near Glen Rose, Texas, have also been attributed to *Sauroposeidon*, which was named in 1999 by American paleontologists Matt Wedel and Richard Cifelli.

In Greek myth, Poseidon was the god of the sea and also of earthquakes; *Sauroposeidon* had a periscope-like neck and probably made the earth tremble as it walked. The great plant-eater lived some 110 million years ago, considerably later than other long-necked types, although *Brachiosaurus* itself may have survived to around the same time. As far as the fossils show, these were among the last of the great longnecks to survive in North America. However sauropods from other families continued for millions of years elsewhere.

ABOVE Recent reports of the fossil evidence suggest that *Sauroposeidon* and cousins such as *Brachiosaurus* (opposite) may not have been able to raise their heads to full height. Instead the head was swung around more horizontally on its lengthy neck in a great arc, to cover the maximum feeding area while saving the energy of moving the dinosaur's massive bulk.

DINO FACTFILE
Sauroposeidon

Meaning: Poseidon [earthquake or sea god] reptile

Pronunciation: Sore-owe-pos-eye-don

Period: Early Cretaceous

Main group: Sauropoda

Length: Estimated 25–30 meters (82–89 feet)

Weight: Estimated 50, perhaps even 80, metric tons (50–80 tons)

Diet: Plants

Fossils: USA (Oklahoma, Texas)

| 0 | 5 | 10 | 15 | 20 | 25 | 30 |

ULTRASAUROS (ULTRASAURUS)

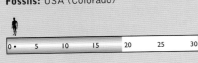

DINO FACTFILE

Ultrasauros

Meaning: Ultra reptile, beyond reptile

Pronunciation: Ull-trah-sore-oss

Period: Late Jurassic

Main group: Sauropoda

Length: Estimated 25–35 meters
(82–115 feet)

Weight: Estimated 30–100 metric tons
(30–100 tons)

Diet: Plants

Fossils: USA (Colorado)

This dinosaur may or may not have existed. It has a checkered history of discovery, identification and naming. Many now view the fossils on which its identity is based as a mixture of specimens from two other giant sauropods, *Brachiosaurus* and *Supersaurus*. Events began with the 1979 discovery of some huge dinosaur remains in the well-known fossil-rich rocks called the Morrison Formation, in western Colorado. James Jensen, a paleontologist who had excavated *Supersaurus* fossils there in the early 1970s, studied the specimens, chiefly a scapula (shoulder blade), some vertebrae (backbones) and part of the pelvis (hipbone or hip girdle), and in 1985 he named this giant *Ultrasaurus*.

But the name "*Ultrasaurus*" had already been given to another, smaller *Brachiosaurus*-like sauropod, from the Cretaceous period.

Its fossils had been found in the 1970s, far away from Colorado in South Korea. That find was named *Ultrasaurus* in 1983 by Haang Mook Kim, but, being established from very partial remains, its identity was also dubious. Even so, the confusion could not be allowed to worsen, so in 1991 the American *Ultrasaurus* was renamed by changing one letter, to *Ultrasauros* (species *Ultrasauros macintoshi*). Estimates of its size varied greatly because the remains were so incomplete. The most common maximum estimates were of a length around 30 meters (99 feet) and a weight up to 80 metric tons (80 tons), although one scientist argued for a breathtaking 130 metric tons (130 tons). Any debate will prove to be in vain if it turns out that the shoulder blade is in fact from *Brachiosaurus* and that the vertebrae came from another dinosaur, such as *Supersaurus*.

RIGHT *Ultrasauros* is one of several truly gigantic sauropods named on the basis of slim evidence. Its fossils may turn out to be from two similar dinosaurs, *Brachiosaurus* and perhaps *Supersaurus*.

LEFT *Haplocanthosaurus* was a member of the long-surviving and widespread sauropod group called cetiosaurids or "whale reptiles."

HAPLOCANTHOSAURUS

"Single spine reptile" was one of the first cetiosaur-like sauropods to be discovered in North America, and its scientific history is mixed up with that of England's "whale reptile" (see page 253). In 1901, John Bell Hatcher, an industrious American paleontologist, discovered *Haplocanthosaurus* remains, in fact, parts of the skeletons of two individuals, in Colorado. The site near Canyon City had already yielded numerous sauropod and other remains, such as *Diplodocus* and *Camarasaurus*, many of them described and named by Othniel Charles Marsh or his great rival, Edward Drinker Cope. Hatcher described *Haplocanthosaurus* in 1903, naming it after the neural spines or upward exensions on its vertebrae (backbones). From details of the vertebrae, *Haplocanthosaurus* might be a smaller cousin of *Brachiosaurus*; and it was also decided that the *Haplocanthosaurus* genus included dinosaurs previously called *Haplocanthus*.

In the meantime, English fossil experts had been following the study of *Haplocanthosaurus* with great interest. A number of reports noted the growing list of similarities between it and *Cetiosaurus* (see page 253), which had already been named for over 60 years and known as a dinosaur for more than 30. By making detailed comparisons between the two dinosaurs, the fossil experts saw that the two were different enough to have their own genera, thus helping to confirm the place of *Cetiosaurus* and establish *Haplocanthosaurus* both as members of the same group – medium-sized to large, fairly early sauropods, family Cetiosauridae. The 15 or so members of this family had blunter heads and shorter necks than the later sauropods, and based on a survey of all the members of this group they lived all over the world. They existed from Early Jurassic times through to the mid-Cretaceous period.

DINO FACTFILE
Haplocanthosaurus

Meaning: Single-spine [spike] lizard

Pronunciation: Hap-low-kan-thoe-sore-uss

Period: Late Jurassic

Main group: Sauropoda

Length: 21–22 meters (69–72 feet)

Weight: Estimated 20 metric tons (20 tons)

Diet: Plants

Fossils: USA (Colorado, Wyoming)

| 0 • | 5 | 10 | 15 | 20 | 25 | 30 |

MAMENCHISAURUS

ANIMAL FACTFILE

Mamenchisaurus

Meaning: Mamenxi (Mamen) reptile

Pronunciation: Ma-men-chee-sore-uss

Period: Late Jurassic

Main group: Sauropoda

Length: 22–25 meters (72–82 feet)

Weight: 12–15 metric tons (12–15 tons)

Diet: Plants

Fossils: China

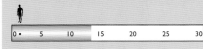

Often said to have been the dinosaur with the longest neck of them all, *Mamenchisaurus* certainly had an amazingly elongated neck, 14 or even 15 meters (46 or 49 feet) in length, comprised of perhaps 19 cervical vertebrae (neckbones), more than are known in any other dinosaur. *Sauroposeidon* (see page 233) however, came to challenge *Mamenchisaurus* for the record.

Mamenchisaurus was given its name in 1954 by Young Chung Chien, a prominent Chinese paleontologist known in the West as C.C. Young. It was named after its discovery site, Mamen Brook or Ferry, in the Chinese province of Sichuan (Szechwan). Its remains have also been unearthed in Gansu and Xinjiang provinces. The head and skull are known only from partial fragments, most found in the 1980s, so, following the scientific conventions, *Mamenchisaurus* is reconstructed with a head

adapted from similar sauropods, such as *Euhelopus*. *Mamenchisaurus* lived about 160–155 million years ago, and in much of its anatomy it resembles the sauropods in general, and *Euhelopus* (see opposite) in particular. Why should it have had an ultra-long neck? The details of the vertebrae show that the neck was relatively light for its size, and the junction of neck and shoulder bones suggests that the neck angled upward at this point. *Mamenchisaurus* may have craned its head to reach foliage 10 meters (33 feet) or more above the ground. Another suggestion is that low-growing plants were its main food and *Mamenchisaurus* would swing its head in a vast arc to gather them as it stood in one place, then repeated the swing after it had plodded forward. The older idea that sauropods lived in swamps and floated their necks around on the surface, to chomp water plants, is now largely discounted.

RIGHT The neck of *Mamenchisaurus* was almost half of the creature's total length. This sauropod remains one of the largest Asian dinosaurs discovered to date, its fossils coming from near Chongqing City in Sichuan Province, China.

EUHELOPUS

Two East Asian sauropods, *Euhelopus* and *Omeisaurus*, have a complex history. Occasionally, they were regarded as within the same family, but recent arguments suggest that they are different enough to belong to separate sauropod families.

Euhelopus fossils come from China's Shandong province and, named in 1929, they were the first Chinese sauropod to be scientifically described. The remains had originally been called *Helopus*. The fossils suggest a long-necked, long-tailed herbivore of medium size, 12–15 meters (39–49 feet) in length, with similarities to the *Camarasaurus*-based family (see page 247). All four limbs were of approximately equal length, and the dinosaur had a boxy skull, strong spoon-shaped teeth and large nostrils on the top of its head. But the neck of *Euhelopus* was relatively longer than that of *Camarasaurus*, at about 5 meters (16 feet), forming almost half of the total length of the animal. It also

contained more cervical vertebrae, up to 19 compared to the 12 in *Camarasaurus*.

Omeisaurus was also Late Jurassic, and was up to 20 meters (65½ feet) long. It was named to honor its discovery area, Emei Mountain, by Young Chung Chien (called C.C. Young in the West) in 1939. It was formerly allied to the *Cetiosaurus*-based sauropod family, and had a relatively short tail. Fossils of many individuals were located in Sichuan (Szechwan) province in China, suggesting that an entire herd had perished and been preserved together.

Another view is that both *Euhelopus* and *Omeisaurus* are related to the well-known and extremely long-necked *Mamenchisaurus*, and belong in a family based on these, the Euhelopodidae. Unfortunately, yet another Late Jurassic Chinese sauropod, *Zigongosaurus*, complicates the current picture further. At present the family Euhelopodidae is thought to take precedence over the Mamenchisauridae.

DINO FACTFILE
Euhelopus
Meaning: Good marsh foot

Pronunciation: You-hel-owe-puss

Period: Late Jurassic

Main group: Sauropoda

Length: 10–15 meters (33–49 feet)

Weight: 10–25 metric tons (10–25 tons)

Diet: Plants

Fossils: China

| 0 • | 5 | 10 | 15 | 20 | 25 | 30 |

LEFT Most of the front part of the skeleton, including the skull, has been found for *Euhelopus*. It had a fairly short, blunt snout and spoon-shaped teeth common to the camarasaurid family of dinosaurs.

VULCANODON

DINO FACTFILE

Vulcanodon

Meaning: Vulcan tooth

Pronunciation: Vul-can-owe-don

Period: Early Jurassic

Main group: Sauropoda

Length: 6.5 meters (21½ feet)

Weight: 500–800 kilograms (1100–1760 pounds)

Diet: Plants

Fossils: Africa (Zimbabwe)

| 0 • | 5 | 10 | 15 | 20 | 25 | 30 |

Vulcanodon is one of the smaller, earlier members of the sauropod group. It has interesting features as reconstructed from its partial, headless remains and correlated with similar types, such as *Barapasaurus*. It lived in the Early Jurassic period, about 210–200 million years ago, and has been estimated at 6 or 7 meters (20–23 feet) in length. The fossil site of Mashonaland North, in Zimbabwe, gives clues to the early evolution and spread of the sauropod group. There is also a possibility that preserved footprints in Lesotho were made by this dinosaur. At one time, the trackways were attributed to the sauropod "*Deuterosauropodopus*," but this name, established solely from these prints, is no longer used. The tracks show four nail-ended digits, with a larger claw on the first (the "big toe"). *Vulcanodon* was named after the Roman god of fire, Vulcan, because dinosaur teeth in the region were found in rocks formed from

a volcanic eruption. It is unlikely, however, that the teeth belonged to *Vulcanodon* itself. The remains from Zimbabwe (then Rhodesia) were studied and named by Mike Raath in 1972, and a revised report was produced by another paleontologist, Mike Cooper, in 1984. The evidence from both reports and the discussion they generated was that the *Vulcanodon* was a small-headed, long-necked, long-tailed, barrel-bodied, elephant-legged herbivore of the general sauropod type. Parts of the hipbones show features reminiscent of the prosauropods, the major group of large plant-eaters such as *Plateosaurus* that preceded the sauropods in many parts of the world (see page 128). In contrast, however, the front legs seem quite long in relation to the body and rear limbs, giving a more quadrupedal stance.

RIGHT *Vulcanodon* lived at the time of the prosauropod dinosaurs, some 200 million years ago, and shows some skeletal features in common with this group. However the majority of the fossils suggest it was an early, smallish type of sauropod.

BELOW The immense size of the sauropod *Jobaria* is shown by comparison with a theropod (meat-eating) dinosaur, which in this reconstruction would be standing slightly taller than an adult human, and is trying to raid the sauropod's nest of eggs.

JOBARIA

Teams led by Paul Sereno, a paleontologist based at the University of Chicago, had many successes when seeking dinosaurs in North Africa during the 1990s. A towering example was *Jobaria*, a huge sauropod from the Early Cretaceous period, about 135 million years ago. Its fossils were noticed near Agadez, a desert town in central Niger. Most of the excavations took place in 1997, with workers toiling in temperatures of nearly 50°C (112°F). The rewards were tremendous, however, with one adult specimen almost 95 percent complete, plus much of a juvenile skeleton, and a "graveyard" with assorted bones from other adults and youngsters, indicating that a mixed-age herd had perished together (see page 228). One of the ribs from a juvenile seems to have tooth marks on it, which could have been made by a large predator, the theropod *Afrovenator*, whose fossils have been found in the same country, Niger.

Jobaria was named in 1999 in honor of Jobar, a creature important in the myths of the Tuareg people of north Africa and especially in Niger. The completeness of the main specimen allowed experts to deduce that this was a "survivor sauropod." It did not belong to one of the main sauropod families, such as the diplodocids or brachiosaurids, but was a leftover or remnant from earlier times, as several features indicate. Its neck is relatively short, with 12 vertebrae (some later sauropods had 18 or 19). The vertebrae all along the spinal column lack the complex projections, scoops and air-filled cavities also shown by many other later sauropods, and they show less sign of specialization, such as the rods that form the whiplike tail-tip of *Diplodocus. Jobaria* probably stripped vegetation with its spoon-shaped teeth – 135 million years ago the Sahara was a lush mosaic of woods, forests, rivers and lakes, with crocodiles lurking in the pools.

DINO FACTFILE

Jobaria

Meaning: Of (for) Jobar

Pronunciation: Joe-bar-ee-ah

Period: Early Cretaceous

Main group: Sauropoda

Length: 21 meters (69 feet)

Weight: 18–20 metric tons (18–20 tons)

Diet: Plants

Fossils: Africa (Niger)

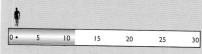

| 0 • | 5 | 10 | 15 | 20 | 25 | 30 |

BIGGEST BABIES FROM BIGGEST EGGS

MANY KINDS OF DINOSAUR EGGS HAVE BEEN PRESERVED AS FOSSILS, INCLUDING THOSE OF THE GIANT SAUROPODS. THEY WERE OFTEN LAID IN GROUPS OR NESTS, ALTHOUGH EVIDENCE FOR PARENTAL CARE OF THE EGGS OR HATCHLINGS IS LACKING. THE EGGS WERE ABOUT THE SIZE OF ELONGATED SOCCER BALLS AND THE YOUNG THAT HATCHED WOULD HAVE MEASURED UP TO ONE METER (39 INCHES) FROM HEAD TO TAIL-TIP.

RIGHT Among the giant sauropod dinosaurs, fossil eggs have been found in South America and Africa which could have been laid by titanosaurids. Calculations based on modern reptile growth rates suggest the hatchlings would take 50-plus years, and possibly more than 80 years, to reach adult size.

CHUBUTISAURUS

ANIMAL FACTFILE

Chubutisaurus

Meaning: Chubut reptile (from the
   discovery province)

Pronunciation: Hoo-boot-ee-sore-uss

Period: Mid-Cretaceous

Main group: Sauropoda

Length: 24 meters (78½ feet)

Weight: 20–25 metric tons (20–25 tons)

Diet: Plants

Fossils: Argentina

0 •	5	10	15	20	25	30

The province of Chubut, toward the south of Argentina, has produced many exciting fossils over the years and continues to be a focus for paleontologists. *Chubutisaurus*, named after the province, has been linked to the *Brachiosaurus* type of massive plant-eating dinosaurs. Another opinion, however, places it among the family called titanosaurids. Many of these great herbivores lived in the southern land masses during the Cretaceous period – indeed, they were some of the last sauropods to survive before the great extinction of all dinosaurs and many other types of reptiles, 65 million years ago. The family was established using *Titanosaurus* as its "founder member" in 1885 by Richard Lydekker, a British paleontologist. It has seen a revival in recent years with the

discovery of newer members such as *Saltasaurus*, *Janenschia* and *Argentinosaurus*. There have also been finds of possible predators in these southern regions from the Cretaceous, including *Carnotaurus* from the same site, and the mighty *Giganotosaurus* (see page 187).

Chubutisaurus was named in 1974, based on two partial specimens dated at about 110–95 million years old. Using information from related species to fill in details, it probably had a humped back and body armor consisting of bony plates or lumps in the skin, like the later *Saltasaurus*. In common with other sauropods, it likely raked in leafy food with its small teeth, swallowing it whole to be ground up in the muscular gut with gastroliths (stomach stones) swallowed for the purpose.

BELOW *Chubutisaurus* is known from various vertebrae (backbones) including those in the tail, parts of limb bones from the front and rear legs, front foot bones and also parts of the hip.

ARGENTINOSAURUS

As amazing new finds of dinosaur fossils continue around the world, the record books need constant updating. South America has come to the fore in recent years, with some of the earliest dinosaurs, such as *Eoraptor*; the largest predators, including *Giganotosaurus*; and possibly the largest dinosaur of them all – perhaps the greatest creature ever to walk the Earth – *Argentinosaurus*. This monster was named in 1993 for its country of discovery by two Argentine paleontologists, José Bonaparte and Rodolfo Coría. Two years later, Coría, from Carmen Funes Museum in Neuquén, named a possible predator of *Argentinosaurus*, the massive *Giganotosaurus* (see page 187).

Argentinosaurus was certainly huge, but its fossilized remains are nowhere near as complete or numerous as for rivals like *Brachiosaurus*. They consist mainly of sections of the spinal column (backbone), including the sacrum that forms part of the hipbones, as well as some ribs and the tibia (shinbone) of the rear limb. The general features and proportions suggest that *Argentinosaurus* was a titanosaurid, a member of a family of sauropods that survived through the Cretaceous period on the southern continents. Estimates of its size are as high as 40 meters (131 feet) in length and 100 metric tons (100 tons) in weight. Changing a few assumptions, however, can reduce these dimensions by one-fifth. The behavior patterns of *Argentinosaurus* were probably much the same as for other sauropods, with most hours of the day spent gathering leafy food into its tiny mouth, plodding from one feeding area to the next, and using its vast bulk as its main means of self-defense.

DINO FACTFILE
Argentinosaurus

Meaning: Argentina reptile

Pronunciation: Are-jen-teen-owe-sore-uss

Period: Mid-Cretaceous

Main group: Sauropoda

Length: 35–40 meters (115–131 feet)

Weight: 75–100 metric tons (75–100 tons)

Diet: Plants

Fossils: Argentina

LEFT The first fossils of *Argentinosaurus* were located in 1987 near a road in the vicinity of Plaza Huincul, in Neuquén Province, north-central Argentina. Some of the partial limb bones were mistaken for preserved tree trunks. The skull was found by a local prospector, Daniel Eseisa.

SALTASAURUS

DINO FACTFILE

Saltasaurus

Meaning: Salta reptile
  (from its discovery region)

Pronunciation: Sall-tah-sore-us

Period: Mid- and Late Cretaceous

Main group: Sauropoda

Length: 12 meters (39 feet)

Weight: 10 metric tons (10 tons)

Diet: Plants

Fossils: Argentina, Uruguay

0 •	5	10	15	20	25	30

The "reptile from Salta" caused a variety of surprises when it was first discovered and described, in 1980. A report announced that this medium- to long-necked South American plant-eater had armor-like lumps and studs in its skin. It was only the second case of a sauropod being credited with this type of protection, which was formerly known from only a few other major dinosaur groups, mainly the ankylosaurs. For many years, however, the evidence had literally been staring local fossil-hunters in the face. Fossilized lumps, studs and plates had been found with the remains of sauropods, but the armor had been assumed to come not from them but from the usual armored suspects, ankylosaurs. Using fossil impressions of the skin, José Bonaparte and Jaime Powell, who named and described *Saltasaurus*, demonstrated that the protection belonged to a sauropod after all.

Saltasaurus was a type of titanosaurid, a member of a sauropod family that survived on the southern continents through the Cretaceous period. Its remains are dated to 80–75 million years ago, making it one of the later sauropods from anywhere in the world. Up to 20 individuals are known from fossil specimens, perhaps representing two or three species within the genus, but are incomplete. *Saltasaurus* was small compared to many sauropods, at only 12 meters (39 feet) long. It had a low, stocky build with a thick neck and well-muscled tail. The "armor plating" consisted of small rounded ossicles, about the size of peas up to marbles. It is likely that thousands of them protected most of the dinosaur's body. Spaced out among them along the back and sides were larger, low knobs, or scutes, about the size of a human palm, which may have had spikes on them.

BELOW Following a claim in 1896 that a Madagascan sauropod dinosaur had body "armor," which was soon dismissed, the next evidence for this feature did not surface until the report on *Saltasaurus* in 1980.

JANENSCHIA

Rupert Wild named *Janenschia* in 1991 after the German paleontologist, Werner Janensch, curator of the Natural History Museum in Berlin during the early part of the 20th century. With Edwin Hennig, Janensch had organized expeditions in 1908–12 to the Tendaguru Hills of Mtwara in what was then German East Africa (later Tanganyika, now the larger part of Tanzania). These expeditions uncovered a wealth of Jurassic fossils, including *Brachiosaurus, Dicraeosaurus, Kentrosaurus* and many others.

Only a limited assortment of fossils of these sauropods have been found – parts of two front legs and a front foot, three rear legs and some vertebrae from backs and tails. The rear feet seem to have had claws on the digits. Most sauropods had a claw on the first digit (or "big toe") of each foot, front and rear, and perhaps structures resembling nails or hooves on the other digits. Many older

reconstructions, however, show the first three digits with claws and, at least in some cases, this seems to have been the case on the rear feet of, for example, *Saltasaurus*. There are also possible *Janenschia* specimens from farther south, in Zimbabwe. They are enough to show that it was one of the larger dinosaurs, more than 20 meters (65½ feet) in length, and lived about 155–150 million years ago. It is usually included in the sauropod family Titanosauridae, a mainly Cretaceous southern-continent grouping that included later types from South America. Indeed, *Janenschia*, dating from the Late Jurassic, is one of the earliest of the titanosaurids.

BELOW *Janenschia* was at first dubbed *Gigantosaurus* because of its size, and then *Tornieria*, with the official name *Janenschia* being agreed in 1991. It was one of the earliest titanosaurs, suggesting this group may have arisen in Africa, although most of the later specimens from the Cretaceous period are South American.

DINO FACTFILE
Janenschia

Meaning: Of (for) Janensch

Pronunciation: Yan-en-schee-ah

Period: Late Jurassic

Main group: Sauropoda

Length: 24 meters (78½ feet)

Weight: 25–30 metric tons (25–30 tons)

Diet: Plants

Fossils: East and Southeast Africa

0 •	5	10	15	20	25	30

LEFT After many years of obscurity, the titanosaurs are becoming better known due to exciting new finds, mainly in Argentina. Here *Titanosaurus* is depicted with bony studs of armor, like its cousin *Saltasaurus*.

TITANOSAURUS

DINO FACTFILE
Titanosaurus

Meaning: Titanic (huge) reptile

Pronunciation: Tie-tan-owe-sore-uss

Period: Late Cretaceous

Main group: Sauropoda

Length: 12–18 meters (39–59 feet)

Weight: 5–10 metric tons (5–10 tons)

Diet: Plants

Fossils: India

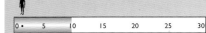

| 0 • | 5 | 10 | 15 | 20 | 25 | 30 |

"Titanic reptile" is one of a select group of dinosaurs that is both well known, and yet not well known. Its remains were studied and named as long ago as the 1870s and established a whole dinosaur family, Titanosauridae. Subsequent finds of sauropod fossils were compared with this and other families of giant long-necked, long-tailed, plant-eating dinosaurs, and thereby slotted into place in the lists of classifications. However, the original fossils, from which *Titanosaurus* was named by Richard Lydekker, a British paleontologist, in 1877, and the family in 1885, were a sparse and mixed set from India. Later remains came from Europe, and from South America too. As with the meat-eating dromaeosaurids and the duck-billed hadrosaurids, the family now contains members known much more thoroughly from much more complete fossils than the original member on which the family was based.

The titanosaurid family includes more than 20 genera of sauropods, mainly from Late Jurassic to Late Cretaceous times, and mainly from the southern land masses. They have various features in common. Examples are *Saltasaurus*, *Chubutisaurus*, *Neuquensaurus* and the truly mammoth *Argentinosaurus* of South America; and possibly *Janenschia* of Africa. *Titanosaurus* itself was thought to have the usual sauropod body, with a total length of up to 18 meters (59 feet). In 1996, Ruben Martinez excavated the first good specimen of a titanosaurid skull. It has a low, longish snout, narrow, well-spaced teeth, and nostrils high on the forehead in front of the eyes. The original *Titanosaurus* fossils included only a few caudal vertebrae (tail backbones) and a slender femur (thighbone). Remains of similar dinosaurs known as *Antarctosaurus* and *Jainosaurus* are sometimes regarded as *Titanosaurus*.

CAMARASAURUS

Probably the best known of all North American sauropods, from its plentiful fossil remains, *Camarasaurus* has given valuable insight into the herding and breeding patterns of these huge dinosaurs (see page 228). It once also gave its name to a whole family of long-necked giants, the Camarasauridae. Its four limbs were of roughly equal length, in contrast to *Brachiosaurus*'s longer forelegs, or *Diplodocus*, with its longer hindlegs, so that its back was almost parallel to the ground. Its build was thick-set and compact for a sauropod, with a big body, and a neck and tail that were relatively short for sauropods.

The name *Camarasaurus*, meaning "chambered reptile," is derived from the hollows found in its large vertebrae. These helped to save weight. The skull was short and relatively short-muzzled, with powerful jaws and sturdy, spoon-like, deep-rooted teeth that extended backward almost into the cheeks, unlike the front-only teeth of some sauropod families.

Camarasaurus could probably crop in tougher vegetation than its contemporaries in the Late Jurassic forests of what are now the states of Colorado, Wyoming and Utah.

The history of *Camarasaurus* fossils and naming are mixed up with the histories of several other large Late Jurassic sauropods from the region, including *Diplodocus* and *Apatosaurus* (see page 227). It was named in 1877 by Edward Drinker Cope from the evidence of some vertebrae (backbones) found earlier that year near Canyon City, Colorado. Other remains – which had been given names such as *Uintasaurus*, *Morosaurus*, *Caulodon*, or species of *Apatosaurus* – were reassigned as *Camarasaurus* in 1958 by Theodore White. One of the key finds, in the early 1920s, was of a very complete and well-preserved specimen of a young *Camarasaurus* at the National Dinosaur Monument in Utah. A much newer find, made in Colorado and currently dubbed *Cathetosaurus*, is probably *Camarasaurus*.

DINO FACTFILE
Camarasaurus

Meaning: Chambered reptile

Pronunciation: Cam-are-ah-sore-uss

Period: Late Jurassic

Main group: Sauropoda

Length: 18 meters (59 feet)

Weight: 15–20 metric tons (15–20 tons)

Diet: Plants

Fossils: USA (Colorado, Utah, Wyoming, New Mexico) and possibly Portugal

| 0 • | 5 | 10 | 15 | 20 | 25 | 30 |

RIGHT For a sauropod, *Camarasaurus* was relatively short-necked and short-tailed.

OPISTHOCOELICAUDIA

DINO FACTFILE

Opisthocoelicaudia

Meaning: Tail backbone with cupped rear, posterior tail cavity, hollow-backed tailbone (and many other versions)

Pronunciation: Owe-piss-thoe-seel-ee-cawd-ee-ah

Period: Late Cretaceous

Main group: Sauropoda

Length: 10–12 meters (33–39½ feet)

Weight: 15–20 metric tons (15–20 tons)

Diet: Plants

Fossils: Mongolia

Noted for one of the longest and most complex names of any dinosaur, *Opisthocoelicaudia* was a medium-sized sauropod that had several similarities to *Camarasaurus*. It lived some 60–70 million years later, however, during the Late Cretaceous period, and on another continent entirely, Asia. Its fossils were recovered in 1965 by one of a series of Polish–Mongolian expeditions to the Gobi Desert in Mongolia. They were the largest bones to be dug out of the Nemegt Basin there, but they lack the skull and most of the neck. The specimen and some associated fragments were described and named in 1977 by Magdalena Borsuk-Bialynicka, a Polish paleontologist.

Opisthocoelicaudia was probably 10–12 meters (33–39½ feet) long and sturdily built so that its body weight may have equaled that of *Diplodocus*, which was twice as long but far slimmer. In its general structure and behavior, *Opisthocoelicaudia* was most similar to titanosaurids. The complex name refers to the caudal vertebrae (tailbones). The forward-facing surfaces of some of these were domed, or convex, each nestling into the scooped or concave rearward-facing surface of the vertebra in front. This contrasts with the joints between the tailbones in most other sauropods, where both of these surfaces are much flatter. The entire backbone also shows other interesting features, such as well-developed pleurocoels (hollowed-out cavities or openings in the sides), and roughened areas for the attachment of strong muscles and ligaments.

RIGHT Fossils of plants and animals found with those of *Opisthocoelicaudia* suggest that it lived in open lowland forests, and probably consumed 70-80 kilograms (154–176 pounds), the weight of a well-built adult human, of vegetation each day.

SHUNOSAURUS

This long-necked, medium-sized plant-eater from the Middle Jurassic was often grouped with *Camarasaurus* in an early family of the main sauropod group. Another and perhaps complementary view is that it was part of a sauropod family that diverged and gave rise to several of the later groups. *Shunosaurus* is well known from more than 20 varied but essentially similar and relatively complete skeletons, about five with skulls – unusual among sauropod remains. It was named in 1983 after one of its fossil sites in the Shuozhou (Shuo-xian) area of central China, by three productive paleontologists, Dong Zhiming, Zhou Shiwu and Zhang Yihong.

Shunosaurus was similar in overall size, shape, and behavior to *Camarasaurus*. Compared to later sauropods, *Shunosaurus* was more heavily built and had a relatively shorter neck and tail, with fewer vertebrae (backbones) along the spinal column – 12 in the neck, 13 in the main back, four fused

together to form the sacrum (part of the hip girdle) and 44 in the tail. The most notable feature was the tail "club." As this was not noticed from the first specimens reconstructed, it is missing in earlier restorations. The lobed club was formed from enlarged tail-tip vertebrae and probably had two (or two pairs) of spikes or spines. The overall shape resembles a scaled-down version of the hammer-like tail of an ankylosaurid armored dinosaur, such as *Euoplocephalus* (see page 333). To date, *Shunosaurus* is the only sauropod with such a feature, presumably used in self-defense.

ABOVE *Shunosaurus* had spoon- or ladle-shaped teeth to crop low-growing leaves and stems. Like many of the larger prosauropods, its estimated lifespan was 100-plus years. Its name "Shuo reptile" is derived from Shu, an ancient name for China's Sichuan region.

DINO FACTFILE
Shunosaurus

Meaning: Shuo reptile
  (from its discovery site)

Pronunciation: Shoo-noe-sore-uss

Period: Middle Jurassic

Main group: Sauropoda

Length: 10–11 meters (33–36 feet)

Weight: 5–10 metric tons (5–10 tons)

Diet: Plants

Fossils: China

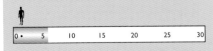

HIGH-LEVEL BROWSERS

SAUROPODS DID NOT HAVE THE TEETH,
OR THE TIME, TO CHEW THEIR PLANT FOOD
THOROUGHLY, IN ORDER TO CRUSH IT AND
RELEASE ITS NUTRIENTS DURING DIGESTION.
THE TINY HEADS OF THESE GIANT DINOSAURS
WERE LITTLE MORE THAN FOOD-GATHERING
TOOLS, STRIPPING AND RAKING IN ALL KINDS
OF VEGETATION, WHICH WAS SWALLOWED WHOLE.
MANY SAUROPODS ALSO SWALLOWED PEBBLES.
THE GASTROLITHS – "STOMACH-STONES" OR
"GIZZARD-STONES" – WORKED LIKE A GRINDING
MILL WITHIN THE GUT, TO SQUASH AND
PULVERIZE SWALLOWED PLANTS. THE PEBBLES
WERE MOSTLY FIST-SIZED AND BECAME ROUNDED
AND POLISHED IN THE PROCESS. THEY ARE OFTEN
FOUND ASSOCIATED WITH SAUROPOD REMAINS.

RIGHT A large brachiosaur-type sauropod could easily reach
more than 10 meters (33 feet) into a tree, to crop the upper
layers of vegetation. During the Jurassic period, when most of
these giants lived, the main tall plants were tree ferns, ginkgoes
(maidenhair trees), conifers related to today's pines, Chilean
pines or monkey puzzles, and redwoods or sequoias.

"HYPSELOSAURUS" AND AMPELOSAURUS

"*Hypselosaurus*" was for many years regarded as a smallish dinosaur – for a sauropod. Its total length has been estimated at 8–12 meters (26–39½ feet), and its weight at 5–10 metric tons (5–10 tons). "High ridge reptile" was found in Europe, in France and Spain. It was named early in the scientific history of dinosaurs, in 1869, by Philippe Matheron, who also named the smallish *Iguanodon*-like ornithopod dinosaur, *Rhabdodon*, in the same year. Matheron found some fossil eggs in 1859, which in 1877 were declared by Paul Gervais to be from a dinosaur – although no one took much notice. This remains the earliest report of dinosaur eggs.

However, the mixed preserved bones of "*Hypselosaurus*" are no longer regarded as a safe basis for establishing a dinosaur genus, so the name "*Hypselosaurus*" is now regarded as invalid.

There is an excellent replacement in *Ampelosaurus*, which is as "new" as

"*Hypselosaurus*" is "old." Its fossils are about 72 million years old and were found in 2002 at Campagne-sur-Aude, near Espéraza in the southwest of France near the Pyrenees. The specimen is nicknamed "Eva" after its discoverer, geology student Eva Morvan, and is the most complete dinosaur skeleton ever found in France. In life this individual was probably about 12 meters (39½ feet) long and 10 metric tons (10 tons) in weight, but it was thought to be a relative youngster at the time of death, since similar bones found in the area are almost twice the size and probably from adults. The fascinating find also includes lumps of body armor.

DINO FACTFILE

Ampelosaurus

Meaning: Vineyard reptile

Pronunciation: Am-pell-owe-sore-uss

Period: Late Cretaceous

Main group: Sauropoda

Length: 12 meters (26–39½ feet)

Weight: 5–10 metric tons (5–10 tons)

Diet: Plants

Fossils: Europe (France, Spain)

| 0 • | 5 | 10 | 15 | 20 | 25 | 30 |

RIGHT The fossils of *Hypselosaurus* are no longer regarded as representing one kind of dinosaur, but an ill-defined mixture of types. However the newer discovery of *Ampelosaurus* would be similar in its overall sauropod-like shape, although larger.

BELOW *Cetiosaurus* was the first sauropod to be described for science, but not as a dinosaur. At the time, almost two centuries ago, its remains were thought to be those of a whale. It was not recognized as a dinosaur until 1869, when it found temporary fame as the largest land-living animal discovered to that time.

CETIOSAURUS

Today it may seem difficult to confuse a dinosaur with a whale, but, in the early years of scientific fossil-hunting, matters were very different. The remains of *Cetiosaurus* were first collected in the 1830s, possibly 1809, and later studied by Richard Owen and also William Buckland, the English geologist and naturalist of *Megalosaurus* fame, at Oxford in the 1830s. Buckland's French colleague and rival, Georges Cuvier, then the preeminent authority on fossils and living animals, saw some likeness to whales, especially in size and in associated remains of sea creatures (see page 397). Then British paleontologist Richard Owen discerned similarities to the skeletons of reptiles. In 1841, the year he coined the term Dinosauria for the whole dinosaur group, Owen also named *Cetiosaurus* ("whale reptile"). At this stage, *Cetiosaurus* was still viewed as a non-dinosaur. Only in 1869, after the discovery of a reasonably complete skeleton in Oxfordshire, England,

did Thomas Henry Huxley, close colleague of Charles Darwin and champion of the then-new theory of evolution, finally conclude that *Cetiosaurus* was a dinosaur.

Cetiosaurus was an early sauropod from the Middle Jurassic period, about 18 meters (59 feet) long and over 20 metric tons (20 tons) in weight. The individual vertebrae (backbones) each had a very large central part, called the vertebral body, with small, flange-like extensions where the spinal muscles were attached. This contrasted greatly to the slim, scooped, large-extensioned vertebrae of later sauropods.

The rear legs were massive and thick-set, and considerably taller than the front limbs, to carry the great body weight. The front limbs of other early sauropods, such as *Patagosaurus*, *Shunosaurus* or *Barapasaurus*, are shorter and weaker in comparison. Cetiosaur fossils have been found in many parts of England.

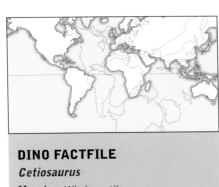

DINO FACTFILE
Cetiosaurus
Meaning: Whale reptile
(Cetaceans = whales and dolphins)
Pronunciation: Set-ee-owe-sore-uss
Period: Middle Jurassic
Main group: Sauropoda
Length: 16–18 meters (52½–59 feet)
Weight: 15–20 metric tons (15–20 tons)
Diet: Plants
Fossils: England

RHOETOSAURUS

DINO FACTFILE

Rhoetosaurus

Meaning: Rhoetus reptile, Trojan lizard

Pronunciation: Reet-owe-sore-uss

Period: Middle Jurassic

Main group: Sauropoda

Length: 15–18 meters (49–59 feet)

Weight: 10–20 metric tons (10–20 tons)

Diet: Plants

Fossils: Australia (Queensland)

0 •   5   10   15   20   25   30

Rhoetosaurus is one of a very limited number of sauropod dinosaurs – perhaps just two or three – known from remains found in Australia. Its presence there during the Middle Jurassic period, some 180–175 million years ago, suggests that sauropods had reached the continent from other land masses, had then evolved and perhaps died out there. Apart from *Rhoetosaurus*, the only other serious Australian sauropod candidate is *Austrosaurus*, from the early Cretaceous.

The remains of *Rhoetosaurus* were excavated from Durham Downs, near Roma in central Queensland, northeastern Australia, in 1924, and named the year after by Heber Longman after Rhoetus, a giant from Greek mythology. Further finds, in 1975, yielded a mix of parts that now include caudal vertebrae (tailbones), parts of a rear leg and an almost complete foot, pieces of the hip, ribs and backbones from the chest region (thoracic vertebrae), and neck (cervical vertebrae).

Rhoetosaurus was similar in overall appearance and proportions to other sauropods of its time, such as *Shunosaurus* (see page 249) or the larger *Cetiosaurus* of Europe. It had a long neck and tail, but not as extended as the Late Jurassic sauropods. The body was bulky, held up on strong, elephant-like legs that could bear considerable weight. The head was quite roomy, almost box-like. The robust tailbones show that the whole tail tapered rapidly and was well muscled, which may suggest that *Rhoetosaurus* possessed a tail "club," like that of *Shunosaurus*, to swing at enemies, although no fossils of this part have been located.

RIGHT The fossils of *Rhoetosaurus* are far from complete, but many experts view it as a close relative of the Chinese sauropod *Shunosaurus*. The notion that it had a tail club, like *Shunosaurus*, is much more contentious and without direct fossil evidence.

BARAPASAURUS

Fossils of dinosaurs from the Indian subcontinent are relatively rare, and *Barapasaurus* is one of the very few sauropods known from there. In 1961, over 300 fossils of *Barapasaurus* were discovered in the Godavari Valley of south central India, between Nagpur and Hyderabad, making up the partial skeletons of six individuals. There were no skulls or feet, however, both of which help with classification. "Big limb reptile" was named in 1975.

Barapasaurus was one of the first known sauropods, living in the Early Jurassic period, probably between 200 and 185 million years ago. It bears several of the early features of the group, such as vertebrae (backbones) with very few weight-saving scoops or hollows.

In this respect, it is similar to other early sauropods such as *Cetiosaurus*, and has been placed in that dinosaur's family, Cetiosauridae. Other features, however, make it similar to *Vulcanodon*, another very early sauropod from the same period, but in Africa, not Asia (see page 238). With an overall length of 20 meters (66 feet), *Barapasaurus* already had the greatly elongated neck and tail of the sauropod group, and was probably just as slow and plodding, feeding for many hours each day, stripping vegetation for swallowing and grinding in the muscular gut with gastroliths (stomach stones), swallowed and then retained in the gizzard, or stomach, for this purpose. *Barapasaurus* is currently placed in the family Vulcanodontidae.

DINO FACTFILE

Barapasaurus

Meaning: Big-leg reptile, heavy-limb reptile

Pronunciation: Bah-rarr-pah-sore-uss

Period: Early Jurassic

Main group: Sauropoda

Length: 18–20 meters (59–66 feet)

Weight: 15–25 metric tons (15–25 tons)

Diet: Plants

Fossils: India

| 0 • | 5 | 10 | 15 | 20 | 25 | 30 |

BELOW Weight estimates for *Barapasaurus* range from 15 to 50 metric tons (15–50 tons), depending mainly on the muscle bulk given to the limbs and main body. The thighbone alone was as tall as an adult human.

Chapter Eight

Bird-foot Dinosaurs

The ornithopods were perhaps not the most spectacular of dinosaurs, but they were certainly among the most numerous and successful of all dinosaur groups.

"BIRD FEET"

MOST ORNITHOPOD ("BIRD-FOOT") DINOSAURS HAD THREE FORWARD-POINTING DIGITS ON EACH OF THEIR REAR FEET. THESE "TOES" WERE SLIGHTLY SPLAYED AND TIPPED WITH CURVED CLAWS, WHICH WERE NEVER VERY SHARP. MANY KINDS ALSO HAD A FOURTH DIGIT, WHICH WAS MUCH SMALLER AND HELD OFF THE GROUND, FACING TO THE REAR. THIS STRUCTURE HAS MANY SIMILARITIES TO THE FEET OF NUMEROUS BIRDS TODAY, BUT SO DID THE FEET OF MANY OTHER DINOSAURS. ORNITHOPODS WERE NAMED AS A GROUP BEFORE THIS MORE WIDE-RANGING SIMILARITY HAD BECOME APPARENT.

ONE GROUP OR MORE?

The ornithopods include a wide variety of dinosaurs, from some that were almost as small as a modern pet cat to others that were larger than a modern elephant. They were all plant-eaters and all belonged to the great ornithischian ("bird-hipped") group, one of the two major dinosaur groups. But, other similarities among the ornithischians are less well-defined. Several types, like *Heterodontosaurus* and *Hypsilophodon*, had specialized teeth not seen in other ornithopods. They seem to have had little defense other than to run – they were probably very fast moving and agile. They were common in certain habitats, especially drier scrublands, and in some regions, particularly Europe and southern Africa. In newer classification schemes some of the smaller, earlier kinds like *Lesothosaurus* are often included in other groups, leaving those such as *Hypsilophodon*, *Camptosaurus*, *Iguanodon* and its cousins, and the hadrosaurs or duckbills (see next chapter) as "true" ornithopods.

BIGGEST AND BEST

The largest non-hadrosaur ornithopods, and the best known from fossils, are *Iguanodon* and its cousins. Indeed, they are among the most studied of all dinosaurs. Hundreds and hundreds of preserved ornithopod specimens have been found, not only of bones and teeth but also stomach contents; their droppings, known as coprolites; patches of skin and scales; footprints; and eggs. The iguanodontids appeared in the Jurassic period, perhaps alongside *Dryosaurus* (see page 280). In the period that followed, the Cretaceous, they increased in size and enjoyed enormous success on almost every continent around the world, along with *Camptosaurus*, *Iguanodon* itself, *Altirhinus* and *Muttaburrasaurus*.

WHY DID *IGUANODON* AND ITS RELATIVES SUCCEED?

The precise reasons for the success of the iguanodontids are not clear. They may include: the rows of teeth in their powerful jaws, which formed a very efficient chewing mechanism; the beak-like fronts to their mouths, suited for tearing vegetation fronds off their stalks; their adaptable front limbs, which could be used for walking or grasping or fighting (with their "thumb" claws); and their large size, which served as defense against predators. *Iguanodon* could feed at any level from the ground to 7 or 8 meters (23 or 26 feet) above it. The Cretaceous period was a time of rapidly evolving vegetation, as flowering plants – flowers, bushes, herbs and blossom trees – appeared and spread fast, so perhaps the iguanodontids were suited to this new type of food source. On the behavioral side, these dinosaurs also show patterns of herd-dwelling and migration (see pages 261). But they could not sustain their success, and as the Cretaceous period continued they became less common, possibly giving rise to their great competitors and fellow ornithopods, the "duckbilled" hadrosaurs.

PREVIOUS PAGE Snowy conditions mean a modern reptile would be too cold to move. But small Australian ornithopods like *Leaellynasaura* may have been warm-blooded, and here are trekking to their regular hibernaculum, or winter sleeping quarters. The discovery of the fossils of these *Hypsilophodon*-like dinosaurs, and the environment in which they lived, has changed many ideas about "slow, stupid, cold-blooded" dinosaurs.

LEFT This scene shows two possible modes of movement for *Iguanodon*. The youngster is walking bipedally, head held high to peer around. The adult is quadrupedal, loping or trotting on all fours. In reality this ornithopod probably used both methods, and perhaps others – even galloping like a giant horse.

ALTIRHINUS

DINO FACTFILE

Altirhinus

Meaning: High snout, tall nose

Pronunciation: All-tee-ryne-uss

Period: Early and mid-Cretaceous

Main group: Ornithopoda

Length: 7–8 meters (23–26 feet)

Weight: 4 metric tons (4 tons)

Diet: Plants

Fossils: Mongolia

Altirhinus was originally identified as representing a small Asian species of the main genus *Iguanodon*. Its remains were called *Iguanodon orientalis*, previously named (also from some other, very scant remains) by Anatoly Konstantinovich Rozhdestvensky in 1952, but it was also called *Iguanodon mongoliensis* or *Iguanodon bernissartensis*. In 1998, however, English paleontologist David Norman, a renowned authority on iguanodontids, reported detailed studies on the remains of this plant-eater. He concluded that it was different enough from the various species of *Iguanodon* to deserve a separate genus, and proposed to call the genus *Altirhinus* and the species *Altirhinus kurzanovi*. The main distinguishing feature, as the new name meaning "high snout" indicates, is the shape of the snout – the nasal bones are much more curved or arched than in the genus of *Iguanodon*, forming a bulbous bulge between the beak-like front of the mouth and the eyes. Another factor in the name change was that Mongolia, where the remains of *Altirhinus* were found, is a vast distance from Europe, where most *Iguanodon* fossils were discovered.

The remains of *Altirhinus* include one reasonably complete skull, jaw parts and a second skull, plus varied associated bones of skeletons, probably representing a total of five individuals, two of them juveniles. They were recovered from Khuren Dukh, in the Dornogov region of southern Mongolia. Apart from the bulging nose, *Altirhinus* is a fairly typical iguanodontid (see page 259). It is thought to have had a large spike on each of the first digits ("thumbs") of its forefoot, and its back legs were longer than its front legs, although it was still able to walk on all fours.

RIGHT *Altirhinus* lived about 120-100 million years ago. When in the all-fours position as shown here, sniffing and peering for low-growing plant food, it would have stood about two meters (6½ feet) tall at the hips.

LEFT The extensive distribution of *Iguanodon* continues to expand, with the recent discovery of partial remains in Mongolia that could represent this dinosaur. It is already known from more than a dozen major sites in Europe, and possibly North America.

IGUANODON

Iguanodon – "iguana tooth" – holds a very special place in the early scientific history of dinosaurs. It was named on the basis of some large teeth acquired from the Cuckfield area of Sussex, in southern England, by Gideon Mantell, a family doctor and part-time fossil enthusiast, or perhaps by his wife, Mary Ann. After consulting experts of the time, including William Buckland and Georges Cuvier, Mantell noted the likeness of the teeth to those of the modern lizard, the iguana, although the fossils were much larger. In 1825, he proposed that they came from a long-extinct type of plant-eating lizard, which he named *Iguanodon*. Thus, *Iguanodon* became only the second dinosaur, after *Megalosaurus*, in 1824, to receive a scientific name. This was well before the dinosaurs themselves received their group name, Dinosauria, from Richard Owen, in 1841. Then, in 1878, workers in a coal mine in Bernissart in southwest Belgium discovered the buried and jumbled fossils of more than 30 almost complete *Iguanodon* skeletons. This

and plentiful later finds around Europe have made *Iguanodon* one of the best known and most studied of all dinosaurs.

Iguanodon was a 10-meter-long (33-feet), 5-meter-tall, (16½-feet), 5-metric-ton (5-ton) plant-eater that was probably able to walk on its rear legs, or stoop down to move on all fours. The front of the mouth was toothless and shaped like a beak, while the cheek regions contained tall, ridged teeth that it used for chewing and grinding. The forepaw was unusually specialized, with a grasping fifth digit (or "little finger") and three strong middle digits with hoof-like claws perhaps joined as a pad. A stout, pointed spike on the first digit (or "thumb"), stuck out at a right angle and was presumably used as a weapon of self-defense. Fossils of *Iguanodon* often occur in groups, indicating that it lived in herds, and there are also many trackways (sets of preserved footprints). Overall, *Iguanodon* gives much useful information about dinosaur life in Europe in the Early and mid-Cretaceous period.

DINO FACTFILE
Iguanodon
Meaning: Iguana tooth
Pronunciation: Ig-wan-oh-don
Period: Early to mid-Cretaceous
Main group: Ornithopoda
Length: 10 meters (33 feet)
Weight: 4–5 metric tons (4–5 tons)
Diet: Plants
Fossils: Europe (England, Belgium, Germany, Spain and elsewhere), possibly North America

Muttaburrasaurus

DINO FACTFILE

Muttaburrasaurus

Meaning: Muttaburra reptile

Pronunciation: Mutt-ah-burr-ah-sore-uss

Period: Mid-Cretaceous

Main group: Ornithopoda

Length: 7 meters (23 feet)

Weight: 3 metric tons (3 tons)

Diet: Plants

Fossils: Australia

Like *Altirhinus* (see page 260), *Muttaburrasaurus* had a bulge on its snout, from the nostrils up toward the eyes. Apart from this feature, it was typically iguanodontid and resembled *Camptosaurus* in particular. Using its horn-covered toothless "beak," it cropped plant material from the ground, bushes and low trees and cut up the material with its shear-like cheek teeth before swallowing it. Like *Iguanodon* and other members of the family, *Muttaburrasaurus* probably moved bipedally, on its back legs only, with its body leaning forward, held almost horizontal and balanced over the hips by the powerful, thick-based tail. The neck was arched in a right angle, forward and then up, so that the head could look to the front as it moved. But, it is also possible that this ornithopod used its sizable forelimbs to lope along on all fours, perhaps reaching a speedy gallop of more than 30 kilometers (20 miles) per hour. When feeding, *Muttaburrasaurus* might have stooped down and rested on its forelimbs to reach ground plants, or reared up on its back legs to crane its neck high, or even to pull branches and foliage toward its mouth with its front paws, which each had five digits.

Muttaburrasaurus is named after a town close to its discovery site, near the Thompson River in central Queensland, Australia. Rancher Douglas Langdon found the fossil in 1963 and when Alan Bartholomai and Ralph Molinar named the genus in 1981 they called it *Muttaburrasaurus langdoni*. In 1987, another fossil skull, this one crushed and distorted, was found farther north in Queensland, near Richmond. Teeth from Lightning Ridge, Australia, may also belong to this plant-eater.

LEFT Fossils of *Muttaburrasaurus* are now known from several sites in central and northern Queensland. During its time, 100 million years ago, the region supported varied plant life such as cycads, conifers and ferns, which would have provided plentiful food for this herbivore.

RIGHT The varied and relatively common fossils of *Camptosaurus* were originally classified as about eight species within this genus, as well as other genera such as *Brachyrhophus, Cumnoria* and *Symphyrhophus*. This dinosaur may have been one of the first with fleshy cheek pouches to retain food while chewing – a feature that most modern reptiles lack.

CAMPTOSAURUS

There seems to have been a trend among the *Iguanodon*-like dinosaurs for their size to increase through time. *Dryosaurus*, in the Late Jurassic period, was small and light, although it may have been more like *Hypsilophodon* in build (see page 273). *Camptosaurus* was larger and heavier, and *Iguanodon* itself was bigger and weightier still.

Like its cousins, *Camptosaurus* could probably walk on its two hind legs, with its body held horizontally in front and balanced over the hips by using the horizontal tail behind, or it could drop down onto all fours. Preserved trackways show this quadrupedal mode of locomotion. Its forelimbs and hands, however, were not as strong or as well developed as those of *Iguanodon*. Also, the digits were probably not joined together in a pad or "mitten," as those of *Iguanodon* appear to have been. The rear feet had four digits, but the first digit (the "big toe") was actually

very small and held above the ground toward the ankle and bore no weight.

Camptosaurus is well known from many fossils, which show its growth from a youngster, about 1.2 meters (4 feet) long, to juvenile and then to adult. It was also widespread, with remains from various sites in North America, and from England, Portugal and other parts of Europe. It was named in 1885 by Othniel Charles Marsh, famous as a dinosaur-hunter, from specimens uncovered in 1879 by Earl Douglass and others in Wyoming and Utah.

It was also earlier in 1879 that fossils of *Cumnoria*, a very similar ornithopod, were found far away from North America at Cumnor in Oxfordshire, England. Its remains have since been reclassified as *Camptosaurus*. So, too, have those of *Symphyrophus* ("fused roof") and *Camptonotus* ("flexible back"), another creature originally named by Marsh in 1879, and other ornithopods of this size range.

DINO FACTFILE
Camptosaurus
Meaning: Bent reptile, flexible reptile
Pronunciation: Kamp-toe-sore-uss
Period: Late Jurassic to Early Cretaceous
Main group: Ornithopoda
Length: 5–7 meters (16½–23 feet)
Weight: 1–2 metric tons (1–2 tons)
Diet: Plants
Fossils: North America, Europe

ORNITHOPODS ON THE MOVE

Various strands of fossil evidence, including trackways, or footprints, the size and strength of the limbs compared to the body, and collections of many individuals preserved together as a herd, suggest that ornithopod dinosaurs such as *Iguanodon* migrated. Alternatively, perhaps they wandered at random in search of any new areas with fresh plant food, rather than following regular, well-worn seasonal trails.

RIGHT *Camptosaurus*-like ornithopods pause for a rest and food, before setting off again on their wanderings. Various feeding postures are shown, taking advantage of low ground plants and also leaves and fronds high up. After a few hours, with all the easy picking consumed, the herd will move on.

RIGHT *Ouranosaurus* lived about 110 million years ago. It shows several features in common with the hadrosaurs (duckbilled dinosaurs). It may have resembled the ancestors of this later offshoot from the main iguanodontid dinosaur group (but see also *Probactrosaurus,* opposite).

DINO FACTFILE

Ouranosaurus

Meaning: Brave reptile, brave monitor lizard

Pronunciation: Oo-ran-owe-sore-uss

Period: Early and mid-Cretaceous

Main group: Ornithopoda

Length: 7 meters (23 feet)

Weight: 3–4 metric tons (3–4 tons)

Diet: Plants

Fossils: Africa (Niger)

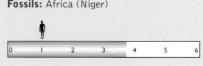

OURANOSAURUS

The remains of two specimens of *Ouranosaurus* were found in 1966 lying in the sands of the Sahara in northeastern Niger. Ten years later, Philippe Taquet, a French paleontologist, named the remains. While similar in many respects to its close cousin *Iguanodon* (see page 261), and a member of the same family, the Iguanodontidae, *Ouranosaurus* displays several notable exceptions to the family pattern. Most obvious is the tall flap or sail along its back. This is reconstructed from the long, strap-like extensions of the vertebrae (backbones), called neural spines, that ran from the shoulders to near the end of the tail. Many possible uses of such a structure have been suggested. One involves thermoregulation, or control of body temperature, which might also apply to other "sailbacks," such as the great predatory dinosaur *Spinosaurus* or the non-dinosaur meat-eater *Dimetrodon* (explained on page 106). Another idea is that the sail was brightly colored and served to advertise

Ouranosaurus to potential mates at breeding time, much as many male birds now display their brightly colored plumage to females during courtship.

Ouranosaurus was slightly smaller than *Iguanodon,* at about 7 meters (23 feet). Its limbs were similar to those of other iguanodontids, with two larger, powerful rear legs to carry most of the weight, but it also had substantial forelimbs for ambling on all fours in a stooped or head-down posture. *Ouranosaurus* had a low bump or ridge on its forehead, just in front of the eyes. The snout was long and low, with a widened, toothless "beak" at the front, like a duck's bill, or the "beaks" of the hadrosaurs (duckbilled dinosaurs, see page 282). In the Early to mid-Cretaceous period the habitat where *Ouranosaurus* lived, which is now sandy desert, would have been a mosaic of rivers, swamps and drier land, as shown by fossils of semi-aquatic crocodiles such as *Sarcosuchus* (see page 387).

PROBACTROSAURUS

The position of this dinosaur in the scheme of evolution, and therefore in today's scientific classification, has been vehemently debated. *Bactrosaurus* ("club-spined reptile") was a dinosaur in the duckbill or hadrosaur group. This is often regarded as a "sister" group to the *Iguanodon*-like plant-eaters, known as the family Iguanodontidae (and is the subject of the next chapter). *Bactrosaurus* itself was about 6 meters (20 feet) long and weighed up to 2 metric tons (2 tons). It was a member of the lambeosaur subgroup of hadrosaurs (see page 298) and lived during the mid- and Late Cretaceous periods. Its fossils were found in Mongolia and China, and named in 1933.

Probactrosaurus certainly lived before *Bactrosaurus*, during the Early and mid-Cretaceous periods. But this dinosaur is usually regarded as a member of the *Iguanodon* family, not a hadrosaur. In fact, it shows many similarities to *Iguanodon* itself. Anatoly Rozhdestvensky named *Probactrosaurus* in

1966, and fossils attributed to it have been found in various areas, including the Dashuigou Formation rocks of China's Gobi Desert, and also in Mongolian parts of the same region. The overall remains include much of a skeleton, also a fragmentary skull, and pieces of the rear of a skull and other bits of other skeletons. Despite *Probactrosaurus* being an iguanodontid, it might show some features in common with the hadrosaurs. It has been suggested that, if it was not a direct ancestor of hadrosaurs, then it was at least the type of dinosaur that could have given rise to this later group. Its name, however, remains misleading: There is no evidence that it was the direct ancestor of *Bactrosaurus*. Also, the Bactria region (best known for the Bactrian camel) once flanked the river known to ancient Europe as the Oxus, now generally called the Amu Darya, which runs through northern Afghanistan, Turkmenistan, Uzbekistan and Tajikistan – a long way from Mongolia and China.

DINO FACTFILE
Probactrosaurus
Meaning: Before Bactria reptile
Pronunciation: Pro-back-troe-sore-uss
Period: Mid- to Late Cretaceous
Main group: Ornithopoda
Length: 5–6 meters (16½–20 feet)
Weight: 1–1.5 metric tons (1–1½ tons)
Diet: Plants
Fossils: China, Mongolia

LEFT *Probactrosaurus* lived about 115 million years ago. Its teeth, in particular, were intermediate in structure and arrangement between the iguanodontids and the hadrosaurs. Its back, hips and tail were stiffened by long, crisscrossing, bone-hardened tendons which reduced their flexibility, so the tail especially was straight and rigid.

DRINKER

The odd name of this dinosaur does not imply that it was an especially thirsty reptile. The name honors Edward Drinker Cope, an American fossil-hunter and paleontologist whose "Wild West Dinosaur Wars" with his great rival Othniel Charles Marsh led to the discovery of many dinosaur fossils that are world famous today. (Marsh is similarly remembered – see *Othnielia* later in this chapter, page 279.) The name *Drinker* was bestowed in 1990 by Robert Bakker, one of the paleontologists who have challenged the view of dinosaurs as slouching, cold-blooded sluggards (see page 153).

The dinosaur *Drinker* was a small ornithopod, a plant-eater only around 2 meters (6½ feet) in total length. It lived during the Late Jurassic period, 155–144 million years ago. Remains of possibly three individuals, an adult, a sub-adult and a youngster, were found in Wyoming. The fossils from the larger individual include pieces of caudal vertebrae (tailbones) that suggest the tail was flexible, as well as a digit from the rear limb and a tooth. Those pieces from smaller individuals include more teeth, parts of the jaws, the central or main "bodies" of the backbones, and sections of both front and rear limbs, including a humerus (forearm), a femur (thigh) and foot bones.

Associated fossils include lungfish teeth and remains of marsh vegetation, suggesting that these small herbivores lived, or at least died, in or near a swamp. There are basic similarities between *Drinker* and a very well-known small ornithopod, *Hypsilophodon* (see page 273), and *Drinker* has been placed in the family Hypsilophodontidae.

DINO FACTFILE
Drinker

Meaning: Drinker (in honor of Edward Drinker Cope)

Pronunciation: Drink-er

Period: Late Jurassic

Main group: Ornithopoda

Length: 2 meters (6½ feet)

Weight: 10–25 kilograms (27–55 pounds)

Diet: Plants

Fossils: USA (Wyoming)

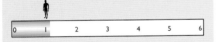

0	1	2	3	4	5	6

RIGHT *Drinker* is reconstructed with very large, splayed, long-toed feet. These may have helped to spread its weight in soft marshy ground or when walking among water vegetation, in the same way that birds called lilytrotters or jacanas move today.

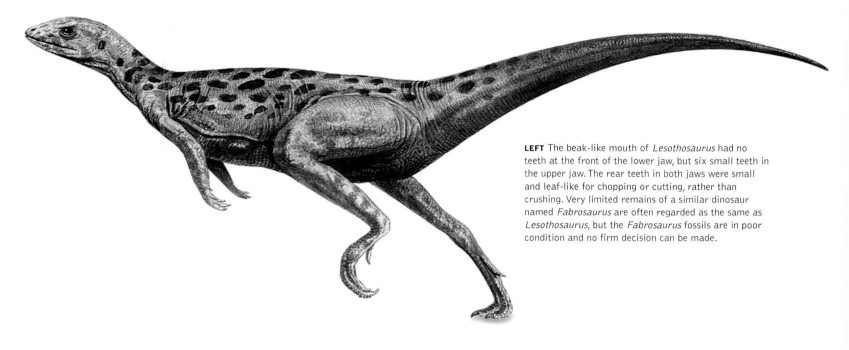

LEFT The beak-like mouth of *Lesothosaurus* had no teeth at the front of the lower jaw, but six small teeth in the upper jaw. The rear teeth in both jaws were small and leaf-like for chopping or cutting, rather than crushing. Very limited remains of a similar dinosaur named *Fabrosaurus* are often regarded as the same as *Lesothosaurus*, but the *Fabrosaurus* fossils are in poor condition and no firm decision can be made.

LESOTHOSAURUS (FABROSAURUS)

Lesothosaurus was a member of the great dinosaur group Ornithischia, the "bird hips," to which many other plant-eaters also belonged. Within that group, it was once regarded as a very early type of ornithopod, one of the first members of the same family as later, larger types, such as *Iguanodon* (see page 261), the hadrosaurs (duckbill dinosaurs) and perhaps the tiny *Hypsilophodon* (see page 273). It is now thought, however, that *Lesothosaurus*, which lived around 208–200 million years ago, came too early to be an ornithopod, and is better described as a "pre-ornithopod," in a group of its own with no close cousins.

Lesothosaurus was tiny, hardly larger than a modern cat. It had a light build; very small front legs, each with five digits; an elongated torso; the long, slim rear legs of a fast runner; and a long, stiff, gradually tapering tail. The thighs were powerful and well muscled, the shins elongated, and the feet very long too, with three weight-bearing digits and a smaller first digit like a "dew claw." The head was long and low, with big eyes, a horny, toothless, beak-like front to the lower jaw, and small, leaf-like teeth for shredding rather than grinding plant food. *Lesothosaurus* was discovered near Mafeteng in Lesotho, in southern Africa, and was named in 1978 by Peter Galton. The situation of these fossils and similar ones of *Abriciosaurus* have led to suggestions that these tiny dinosaurs died during a hibernation-like sleep, perhaps to escape the hot, dry season.

A very similar dinosaur, which was named *Fabrosaurus* in 1964 (with just a piece of jawbone found by Leonard Ginsburg), is seen by some authorities as the same type as *Lesothosaurus*.

Recently studied fossils from Venezuela have also been provisionally identified as *Lesothosaurus*. Africa and South America were joined at the time this dinosaur lived, the Early Jurassic period.

DINO FACTFILE
Lesothosaurus (= Fabrosaurus?)

Meaning: Lesotho reptile
Pronunciation: Le-soe-toe-sore-uss
Period: Late Triassic to Early Jurassic
Main group: Ornithopoda
Length: 1 meter (39 inches)
Weight: 2–3 kilograms (5–8 pounds)
Diet: Plants
Fossils: Africa (Lesotho)

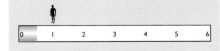

| 0 | 1 | 2 | 3 | 4 | 5 | 6 |

DEFEND OR ESCAPE

ORNITHOPOD DINOSAURS, ESPECIALLY
SMALLER ONES SUCH AS *LESOTHOSAURUS* AND
HYPSILOPHODON, DO NOT SEEM TO HAVE POSSESSED
MUCH IN THE WAY OF SELF-DEFENSE: THEY HAD
LITTLE OR NO ARMOR PLATING, SHARP HORNS OR
POWERFULLY KICKING FEET. THE LONG THUMB
SPIKE SEEMS TO HAVE BEEN THEIR ONLY WEAPON.
PERHAPS THEIR SURVIVAL RESULTED MORE FROM
KEEN SENSES, DETECTING DANGER READILY, AND
SPEEDY AGILITY, FOR PROMPT ESCAPE.

RIGHT Two extremes in the size range of the hypsilophodontids
were *Hypsilophodon* itself, vulnerable but small and quick,
and *Tenontosaurus,* which weighed perhaps 50 times more
and could use its bulk against predators.

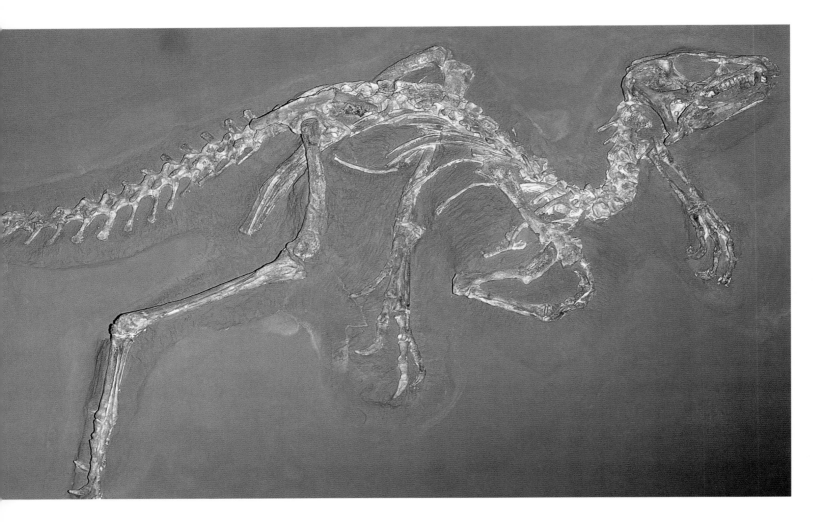

HETERODONTOSAURUS

DINO FACTFILE
Heterodontosaurus

Meaning: Different-teeth reptile

Pronunciation: Het-er-owe-don-toe-sore-uss

Period: Early Jurassic

Main group: Ornithopoda

Length: 1.2–1.3 meters (4–4½ feet)

Weight: 10–20 kilograms (22–44 pounds)

Diet: Plants

Fossils: Southern Africa

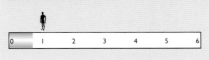

The long teeth that we call tusks in some animals can appear to signify fierce meat-eaters, yet various herbivores have them today. *Heterodontosaurus*, one of the herbivorous dinosaurs, had them too, which is why Alfred Crompton and Alan Charig christened this dinosaur "different-teeth reptile" in 1962. It was one of the smallest of all dinosaurs, about the size of a small modern dog, with a lightweight build and long rear legs for fast running. Its head was quite tall and short-snouted, with big eyes. The front legs were small and strong, with the first three digits suited to curling and grasping. The tail was long and probably whipped from side to side as *Heterodontosaurus* ran – which it would have done often in the scrubby, dry habitat of southern Africa's hazardous Early Jurassic world some 210–200 million years ago.

Apart from the two upper tusks fitting into grooves in the opposing jaw, *Heterodontosaurus* also had two other main types of teeth. At the front of the upper jaw were small incisors, which it probably used for nipping off plant food against the toothless lower front of the jaw. Behind the tusks were tall, ridged cheek teeth used to crush food. This dentition was a great departure from that of other dinosaurs, and even other reptiles. In most reptiles, living and extinct, there is mainly just one type of tooth in the mouth. They may be of different sizes, since they fall out when old and worn and are replaced by new ones which grow larger but retain the same shape. Why other reptiles did not evolve "heterodont" (mixed-tooth) dentition, and why mammals did, is a question that remains.

ABOVE A fine, almost complete specimen of *Heterodontosaurus* showing one forelimb bent under the neck and a rear leg folded up near the hip.

HYPSILOPHODON

A casual, uninformed glance could find little difference between *Hypsilophodon* and another very small plant-eating dinosaur, *Heterodontosaurus* (opposite). But the two were separated by more than 80 million years, a whole continent, and many differences in internal features. Thomas Henry Huxley, the noted biologist and vociferous supporter of Charles Darwin's theory of evolution, named *Hypsilophodon* in 1869. The first of its fossils were recovered from England's "Dinosaur Island," the Isle of Wight, in 1849. They were examined by Gideon Mantell and Richard Owen, and at first were believed to be the young of *Iguanodon*. Then more discoveries by William Fox convinced Huxley that they were adults of a previously unknown kind of dinosaur. Huxley suggested that they might have lived in trees, like modern tree-kangaroos (an idea since disproved). There are now numerous fossil skeletons, some in excellent preservation and mingled together, perhaps from a herd that met a common fate such as drowning in a flood.

Hypsilophodon was named for its 30 or so long cheek teeth, which had grooves and ridges for efficient shredding and chewing of plant matter like leaves and stems. When the jaws were closed and the teeth came together, the teeth in the upper jaw slid down against the outside of the teeth in the lower jaw with a diagonal shearing and rubbing action. This kept both sets of teeth sharp. The shape of the jaw suggests that *Hypsilophodon* may have had cheeks – an uncommon feature among reptiles – which kept food in the mouth while chewing. The skull was long but with a short snout only around 12–14 centimeters (4 1/2–5 inches) long, in profile almost half the size of a human hand. Each forefoot had five digits, and each rear foot four, with three bearing the weight. It is possible that one or two rows of low bony plates set flat into the skin ran along the animal's back.

DINO FACTFILE
Hypsilophodon

Meaning: High-crested tooth, tall-ridge tooth

Pronunciation: Hip-sill-owe-foe-don

Period: Early Cretaceous

Main group: Ornithopoda

Length: 1.5–2.3 meters (5–7 1/2 feet)

Weight: 20–40 kilograms (44–88 pounds)

Diet: Plants

Fossils: England, Spain, possibly USA (South Dakota)

| 0 | 1 | 2 | 3 | 4 | 5 | 6 |

RIGHT "Hypsy" was a small, lightweight plant-eater. It could have led a life similar to small gazelles and antelopes today, with herds munching on plant matter but senses alert and ready to detect danger for a speedy getaway.

THESCELOSAURUS

Fossils of this medium-sized ornithopod, which lived in North America in the Late Cretaceous period, were first studied and named in 1913 by Charles Gilmore. They had been found 22 years earlier, but were considered unremarkable and left in a crate at the Smithsonian Institution in Washington, D.C. – hence the species name *Thescelosaurus neglectus* ("neglected"). More remains have since been recovered from various sites, both in the U.S. (Wyoming, Montana, South Dakota and Colorado) and in Canada (Alberta and Saskatchewan). They show a well-built herbivore with a small head, short front limbs, stout body, long and powerful rear legs, and a long, tapering tail. *Thescelosaurus* was once regarded as a member of the hypsilophodont family of ornithopods, but some recent studies have linked it with the family Iguanodontidae, or suggested that it is distinctive enough to form its own family, Thescelosauridae.

One of the most remarkable finds in the history of dinosaurs, if confirmed, was a *Thescelosaurus* skeleton unearthed near Buffalo, South Dakota, in 1993 and dated to 66 million years old. It includes what has been identified as the animal's heart – an incredibly rare find, since soft tissues of the body such as muscles and hearts are almost never preserved. This individual was nicknamed "Willo," after the wife of the rancher who owned the property.

The heart has been examined by CT (computerized tomography) scanning and is described as four-chambered. This suggests that the dinosaur was warm-blooded, since birds and mammals have this type of heart but modern, cold-blooded reptiles do not. However other experts have proposed that this object is not a heart at all, but simply a natural lump of rock of the type called an ironstone concretion, formed by chance within the preserved dinosaur's body cavity.

DINO FACTFILE
Thescelosaurus

Meaning: Marvelous reptile, wonderful reptile

Pronunciation: Thess-kell-owe-sore-uss

Period: Late Cretaceous

Main group: Ornithopoda

Length: 3.5–4 meters (11½–13 feet)

Weight: 300 kilograms (660 pounds)

Diet: Plants

Fossils: Western North America

0	1	2	3	4	5	6

LEFT *Thescelosaurus* is known from a variety of fossils including one almost complete specimen "Willo," about eight partial skeletons and varied isolated bones and teeth. Most controversial is the "fossil heart" of "Willo," which may be this soft-tissue organ turned to stone, or a natural rock formation. "Willo" also shows preserved cartilaginous parts such as sections of the ribs, which are very unusual.

LEAELLYNASAURA

The finding of a fossil skull at "Dinosaur Cove," on the coastal Otway Range near Melbourne in southern Australia, has opened up a huge new area of debate about dinosaur habitats and behavior. *Leaellynasaura* was named in 1989 for the daughter of its discoverers, Patricia Vickers-Rich and Thomas Rich. It was a small, lightly-built ornithopod of the hypsilophodon family, about 2 meters (6½ feet) in length, with a beak-like front to the mouth and chewing cheek teeth. It has been dated as 110–105 million years old. Many other exciting discoveries have been made at Dinosaur Cove (see page 15).

Remarkable features of this dinosaur, which mark it out within its family, are its relatively large brain and huge eyes. Why should they have been so large? One suggestion is that *Leaellynasaura* lived deep in gloomy forests, and so would have needed big eyes for sharp vision in the permanent twilight. Linked to

this is the position of the continent of Australia at the time. It was farther south than today, forming part of a slowly splitting southern supercontinent which was well within the Antarctic Circle. The climate there was nowhere near as extreme as in Antarctica today, but it was still probably very seasonal, and there would have been a long period of winter darkness, offset by permanent daylight in summer.

Perhaps *Leaellynasaura*'s big eyes were an adaptation to the long, dark winters. This dinosaur could have been the "dormouse" of its group. It may even have hibernated, or become torpid, when temperatures fell to around freezing point.

ABOVE *Leaellynasaura* was a small herbivore with a beak-like front to the mouth for cropping vegetation such as ferns, cycads, and possibly a new type of food — the flowering plants (flowers and herbs) which were spreading around the world at the time.

DINO FACTFILE
Leaellynasaura
Meaning: Leaellyn's reptile
Pronunciation: Lee-ell-in-owe-sore-ah
Period: Mid-Cretaceous
Main group: Ornithopoda
Length: 2–3 meters (6½–10 feet)
Weight: 10 kilograms (22 pounds)
Diet: Plants
Fossils: Australia (Victoria)

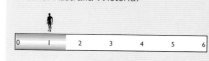

0	1	2	3	4	5	6

Dinosaurs in ice and snow?

During the mid-Cretaceous period, the climate in Australia was probably cold enough for snow, with long dark winters. Smaller ornithopods such as *Leaellynasaura* might have hidden away through this season. Great debate centers on whether these plant-eaters were cold-blooded and so became too cool to move as a consequence of environmental temperature — a condition known as torpor — or were normally warm-blooded but dropped their body temperature to save energy, as some mammals do today when they hibernate.

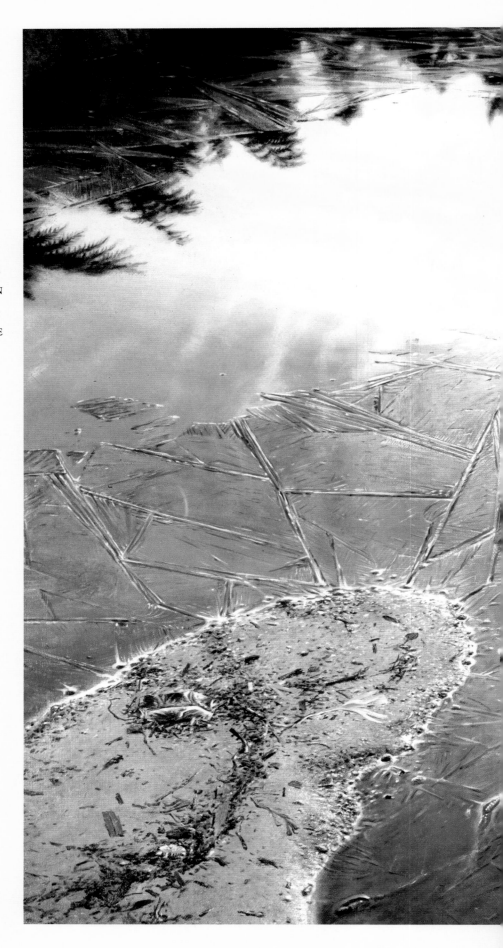

RIGHT About 110 million years ago, in what is now southern Australia, a smallish ornithopod *Leaellynasaurus* is overcome by cold while out in the open, and freezes to death on the icy riverbank. The rest of its clan (group) have reached the shelter of the deep forest, where they are preparing to hibernate in thick undergrowth.

ORODROMEUS

DINO FACTFILE

Orodromeus

Meaning: Mountain runner

Pronunciation: Orrow-drom-ee-uss

Period: Late Cretaceous

Main group: Ornithopoda

Length: 2 meters (6½ feet)

Weight: 10 kilograms (22 pounds)

Diet: Plants

Fossils: USA (Montana)

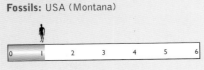

The fossils of this "mountain runner" were found in a hilly region in Montana. *Orodromeus* was a small, lightweight and undoubtedly speedy mover. It was a type of hypsilophodontid, less than 3 meters (10 feet) in length, with the typical family features: a mouth with a beak-shaped front, lacking front teeth in the lower jaw but with upper and lower, self-sharpening cheek teeth; large eyes; a short neck, sturdy body, small forelimbs and long and muscular hind limbs for fast running; and a very long, gradually tapering tail.

John Horner and David Weishampel named *Orodromeus* in 1988. One *Orodromeus* specimen has an almost complete skull, with parts of the skeleton but not the tail, and is on display at the Museum of the Rockies in Bozeman, Montana. Other fossils show how *Orodromeus* grew in size and changed proportions with age.

More famous than *Orodromeus*, however, are its fossil site and the other dinosaurs found there. Indeed, the region near Bynum, Montana, has been dubbed "Egg Mountain" due to the discovery of dinosaur eggs and nests, especially of the hadrosaur ("duckbill" dinosaur) *Maiasaura*. Remains of the small but big-eyed and big-brained meat-eater *Troodon* have also been identified, along with clutches of eggs. The eggs were attributed to *Orodromeus* but a more recent view is that they were laid, in pairs, by *Troodon* (see page 154). Some have been analyzed and found to contain tiny fossilized embryos.

ABOVE *Orodromeus* nibbles at low vegetation, in this scene from 75 million years ago. Some reconstructions show this dinosaur tending its nest of eggs or perhaps babies. But the fossil eggs are now thought to have belonged to the small meat-eating dinosaur *Troodon*.

OTHNIELIA

Othniel Charles Marsh (1831–1899), aided by teams of field workers and laboratory assistants, named up to 500 kinds of prehistoric animals and groups of animals. This prolific output was due in part to his great rivalry with Edward Drinker Cope. The latter is remembered in the name of the small ornithopod *Drinker* (see page 268). Marsh has an even smaller ornithopod, placed like *Drinker* in the hypsilophodontid family, named in his honor. *Othnielia* was named by Peter Galton, a British paleontologist based in the USA, in 1977, from fossils found in Colorado and Utah. Ironically, a jawbone named by Marsh himself in 1877 as *Nanosaurus* may be from the same creature.

Othnielia was one of the smallest dinosaurs of any group, less than 1.5 meters (5 feet) long.

Its fossils are from the Late Jurassic period, around 156–144 million years ago. It had a small head with large eyes, a beak-like snout for nipping off plant food and chisel-like cheek teeth that rubbed and abraded against each other, getting sharpened as they chopped and crushed. Like other hypsilophodontids, *Othnielia* may have had fleshy cheek pouches to retain food, although cheeks are not a common feature of reptiles. The smaller forelimbs had five digits each, and the very long rear limbs each had four. The proportions of the limbs, with long thighs and even more elongated shins and foot bones, indicate a very fast runner. The stiff tail was probably swished to the side when *Othnielia* was moving at speed, to help the body make quick turns.

DINO FACTFILE
Othnielia

Meaning: For Othniel (Othniel Charles Marsh)

Pronunciation: Oth-nigh-eel-ee-ah

Period: Late Jurassic

Main group: Ornithopoda

Length: 1.1–1.4 meters (3²/₃–4 feet)

Weight: 20–25 kilograms (44–55 pounds)

Diet: Plants

Fossils: USA (Colorado, Utah)

| 0 | 1 | 2 | 3 | 4 | 5 | 6 |

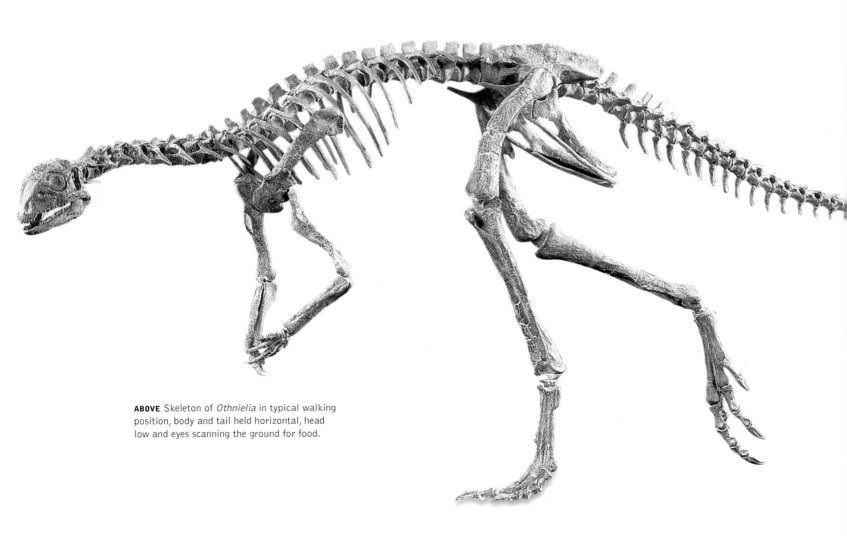

ABOVE Skeleton of *Othnielia* in typical walking position, body and tail held horizontal, head low and eyes scanning the ground for food.

DRYOSAURUS

"Oak tree reptile" was named in 1894 by Othniel Charles Marsh. Its fossils have been found at numerous sites in western North America, including Colorado, Wyoming, and Utah, suggesting that it was fairly widespread. It has been included in the family Hypsilophodontidae but being Late Jurassic, it is an early example of this group, and it is also larger – with an overall length of over 3 meters (10 feet) – than many other, later members of the group, such as *Hypsilophodon* itself (see page 273). Other views gaining more acceptance are that it represents a separate family of its own, Dryosauridae, which is in turn closely related to the family Iguanodontidae, which gradually evolved into larger sizes during the Cretaceous period.

Dryosaurus was a fast mover on its long back legs, each with three digits (in contrast to *Hypsilophodon*, which had four digits on each of its back feet). The mouth had a horny beak at the front for pecking and nipping off food items, and long, sharp cheek teeth for thorough chewing. Other features include the smaller front legs, with five digits each, and the very long, stiff tail, which tapered gradually. Like other ornithopod herbivores, it must have used speed and agility as its main defense against predators, such as the great *Allosaurus*.

Fossils of a dinosaur very similar in size and structure to *Dryosaurus* were found in Tanzania in East Africa. At first, they were given the name *Dysalotosaurus* ("lost wood reptile"), but further studies have led to this creature being named *Dryosaurus*.

DINO FACTFILE

Dryosaurus

Meaning: Oak tree reptile, tree reptile

Pronunciation: Dry-owe-sore-uss

Period: Late Jurassic

Main group: Ornithopoda

Length: 3–3.5 meters (10–11½ feet)

Weight: 50–80 kilograms (110–176 pounds)

Diet: Plants

Fossils: USA (Colorado, Wyoming, Utah), Tanzania

0	1	2	3	4	5	6

ABOVE *Dryosaurus* fossils include a fairly complete adult skeleton, parts of a very young individual, various teeth and isolated bones. Along with *Valdosaurus,* it is usually placed in its own family, Dryosauridae, with the iguanodontids as closest relatives.

TENONTOSAURUS

Most members of the ornithopod family Hypsilophodontidae were at the smaller end of the range of dinosaur sizes. *Hypsilophodon* itself was around 2 meters (6½ feet) in length, and others were almost half this size. *Tenontosaurus*, however, was three times longer and many times heavier, perhaps weighing up to 1 metric ton (1 ton). The fossils of *Tenontosaurus* come from several places in the United States, including Montana, Utah, Oklahoma, and perhaps Texas. The dinosaur was named by John Ostrom in 1970.

Tenontosaurus has been regarded as an "aberrant" hypsilophodontid from the Early Cretaceous, placed in this family due to various skeletal features. In particular, the skull and teeth of *Tenontosaurus* resemble those of *Hypsilophodon* (see page 273), although its much greater size and heavier build would mean that its forelimbs were larger and sturdier, in proportion to its body, approaching the size of the rear limbs. But it

has also been considered a cousin of *Iguanodon*, due to other similarities in the teeth and in the bones of the forelimbs and hip. Yet another opinion is that it is more closely related to *Dryosaurus* (see opposite).

Reconstructions often show *Tenontosaurus* on all fours, cropping vegetation from ground plants and low shrubs, rather than walking on its hind legs with body horizontal, like *Iguanodon*, or rearing up to reach leaves higher in trees. Similar reconstructions may show *Tenontosaurus* trying to feed but being interrupted by a "pack attack" from the theropod dinosaur *Deinonychus*. At one fossil site the remains of probably three *Deinonychus* were found near those of an adult *Tenontosaurus*, leading to speculation about group behavior in the predator (see page 156).

DINO FACTFILE

Tenontosaurus

Meaning: Sinew reptile

Pronunciation: Ten-on-toe-sore-uss

Period: Early Cretaceous

Main group: Ornithopoda

Length: Up to 7.5 meters (24 feet)

Weight: Up to 1 metric ton (1 ton)

Diet: Plants

Fossils: USA (see text)

LEFT Specimens of *Tenontosaurus* range in length from less than two meters (6½ feet) to more than seven (23 feet). It has a complex combination of features that link it with various ornithopod groups, such as those of *Hypsilophodon*, *Iguanodon* and *Dryosaurus*.

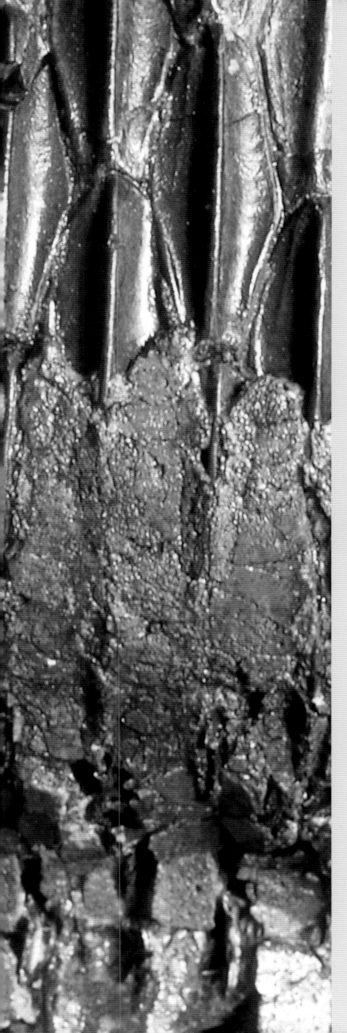

CHAPTER NINE

THE DUCKBILLS

HADROSAURS WERE AMONG THE LAST MAJOR DINOSAUR GROUPS TO EVOLVE, AND HAD MANY NEW FEATURES. THEY MAY HAVE BEEN THE NOISIEST AND MOST COLORFUL OF ALL REPTILES.

LATE STARTERS

HADROSAURS PROBABLY ORIGINATED LESS THAN 100 MILLION YEARS AGO, FROM ANCESTORS SIMILAR TO *IGUANODON*. THEIR HEYDAY WAS THE LATE CRETACEOUS PERIOD, FROM 80 TO 65 MILLION YEARS AGO. MOST HADROSAUR FOSSILS ARE FROM NORTH AMERICA, BUT THERE HAVE ALSO BEEN FINDS IN EAST ASIA AND ON OTHER CONTINENTS, WITH THE POSSIBLE EXCEPTIONS OF AFRICA AND AUSTRALIA. THE GROUP RAPIDLY EVOLVED INTO MANY LARGE AND VARIED FORMS, SOME MORE THAN 12 METERS (39 FEET) LONG AND 5 METRIC TONS (5 TONS) IN WEIGHT. SEVERAL DISTINCTIVE FEATURES SET HADROSAURS APART FROM OTHER PLANT-EATERS OF THE TIME, NOT LEAST THEIR BEAKS, TEETH, HEAD CRESTS AND BREEDING BEHAVIOR.

BEAKS

Hadrosaurs are usually known as "duckbills" because of the shape of the front of the mouth, which was generally wide, flat and toothless, like the bill or beak of a waterbird such as a duck or goose. At one time, the duckbill shape seemed to be evidence that hadrosaurs dwelled in water, as were the tall ridges along the upper and lower tail, which suggest a finned or crocodile-like tail shape. The hadrosaurs would have lashed their tall tails to swim, while pecking and dabbling at water plants. But, with few other body parts appearing to be adapted to an aquatic existence, this idea has been largely discounted. Even so, with their powerful and bulky build hadrosaurs would have had no problem wading through an occasional swamp or fording a river. Their limbs allowed them to walk on all fours or on just the two rear legs.

TEETH

Hadrosaurs's only teeth were in the cheek region, toward the rear of the jaw. They were arranged in small column-like groups of three to five adjacent teeth. These groups were closely packed into large "batteries" of 50 or more, and the batteries were arranged along the upper and lower jaws, but with their working surfaces at opposing angles. As the teeth came together, they rubbed and scraped diagonally past each other, like sets of rasps or files, so that the enamel ridges on the teeth shredded even the stringiest, most fibrous plant foods. Some hadrosaurs had more than a thousand teeth at any time, and these were replaced regularly, like all dinosaur teeth. Some preserved hadrosaurs have been found with fossilized pine needles and twigs in the stomach region, showing that these dinosaurs could tackle the toughest vegetation.

CRESTS

A few hadrosaurs had unremarkable, low and typically reptilian heads, but many had crests of bone projecting from the top of their skulls. In some, the crests were long and rod-like, while others had lower, rounded crests. An early theory was that these crests were breathing devices, since at first they were thought to be open to the air at the top, for use as snorkels when the dinosaur was almost submerged in water. This tied in with the theories of aquatic behavior mentioned above. However, more fossil finds and further studies showed that the crests were not open at the top: the chambers within them formed part of the animal's breathing passages, linked to the nose. A more widely accepted suggestion is that the crests somehow functioned as vibrators or resonators to produce sounds, in the way that an elephant trumpets through its trunk. In addition, the crests may have been brightly colored, perhaps to attract the attention of mates for breeding.

PREVIOUS PAGE Massed ranks of sharp-ridged cheek teeth from one of the largest duckbilled dinosaurs, *Edmontosaurus*. There were hundreds in the mouth, forming one of the most powerful chewing mechanisms known in the animal kingdom.

LEFT Various types of hadrosaurs gather around a source of plentiful food, a lowland lake. In the foreground are two *Parasaurolophus*, with their tall, tubular, hollow head crests of bone. The scene may have been noisy too as each of these kinds of dinosaurs produced its own characteristic calls, such as honks, bellows, blares and grunts.

PROTOHADROS

DINO FACTFILE

Protohadros

Meaning: Beginning hadrosaur [duckbilled dinosaur], early bulky reptile

Pronunciation: Proe-toe-had-ross

Period: Mid-Cretaceous

Main group: Ornithopoda

Length: 4.5–6 meters (14½–19½ feet)

Weight: Estimated 1 metric ton (1 ton)

Diet: Plants

Fossils: USA (Texas)

Gary Byrd, a part-time paleontologist, discovered fossils of this duckbill in 1994 at Flower Mound, Denton County, north-central Texas. The creature was described and named in 1998 by Jason Head of the Dedman College of Humanities and Sciences in Texas. It lived about 95 million years ago, much earlier than most other hadrosaurs, making it one of the oldest known duckbills and an often-quoted candidate for the ancestry of the group (see also *Bactrosaurus*, page 292). Before the discovery of *Protohadros*, the ancestry of the hadrosaurs, which probably developed from *Iguanodon*-like predecessors, was thought to lie in Asia. This new find has moved the focus of attention to North America, though there are still disputes about which was the first hadrosaur.

With the remains of *Protohadros* including just a partial skull and possibly pieces of ribs and foot bones, so much of a reconstruction of this dinosaur is speculative. *Protohadros* reached 6 meters (19½ feet) in length and had many duckbill features. It probably had a large, deep set of jaws, with the typical toothless "beak" at the front of the mouth, and, in its cheeks, extensive rows or "batteries" of chewing teeth with which it crushed tough vegetation. As with later members of the group, its rear legs were probably longer than the front pair, and it could move on all fours, especially when feeding from ground plants and low shrubs, or walk and run on its hind limbs only. There were nails or "hooves," rather than claws, on its large and powerful feet. During the mid-Cretaceous period, the region where *Protohadros* lived was a low-lying mix of woods and marshes, and the climate was warm and humid, providing plenty of vegetation.

RIGHT The fossils of *Protohadros* from Texas are certainly some of the oldest found to date for a hadrosaur. Also their structure and features show them to be primitive, that is, from an early stage in the evolution of the group. This dinosaur had the wide beak-like mouth and plentiful grinding cheek teeth of later duckbills.

BELOW The description of *Hadrosaurus* fossils about a century and a half ago, by Joseph Leidy, helped to found the hadrosaur, or duckbill, dinosaur group. The Haddonfield site where the fossils were excavated, just before the American Civil War, has been marked with a commemorative stone and a small park.

HADROSAURUS

Hadrosaurus – "bulky reptile" – is one of several dinosaurs famous for its name rather than its remains. Like *Dromaeosaurus* among the meat-eating "raptors," its name has established a whole group of dinosaurs: the hadrosaurs or "duckbills." But *Hadrosaurus* is poorly known itself, from scarce and fragmentary fossils. This is because the remains of *Hadrosaurus* were found early in the scientific study of dinosaurs. In fact, *Hadrosaurus* was one of the first North American dinosaurs to receive a scientific description and name. Its fossils were first noticed in 1838, at a marl pit on the farm of John Hopkins, near Haddonfield, New Jersey, but were left there, unexamined. It was 20 years before their significance was recognized, by William Parker Foulke, a friend of Hopkins who was on vacation in the area. *Hadrosaurus* remains were quickly recovered, described and named in 1858 by Joseph Leidy who

noted similarities to, yet differences from, *Iguanodon*, another ornithopod among the earliest dinosaurs to be described, though in this case in Europe. The skeleton of *Hadrosaurus* was the first of any dinosaur's to be reconstructed and displayed in North America, at the Philadelphia Academy of Science in 1868.

At the time, the remains of *Hadrosaurus* included parts of a jaw, some teeth, vertebrae (backbones) and pieces of the limbs, all probably from one individual. Although very fragmentary, these remains were more complete than any known fossils of *Iguanodon* at that time. Leidy's description of *Hadrosaurus* further helped to establish dinosaurs as a distinctive group, as proposed by Richard Owen in 1841, with many reptilian yet also curiously bird-like features. *Hadrosaurus* probably grew to 10 meters (33 feet) in length and a couple of metric tons in weight.

DINO FACTFILE
Hadrosaurus

Meaning: Bulky reptile, big reptile

Pronunciation: Had-roe-sore-uss

Period: Late Cretaceous

Main group: Ornithopoda

Length: 7–10 meters (23–33 feet)

Weight: 2–3 metric tons (2–3 tons)

Diet: Plants

Fossils: USA (New Jersey)

BELOW *Maiasaura* adults make their way to their traditional breeding site for the nesting season. The fossilized remains of the nests, each 2 meters (6 feet) across, suggest that the same area was used year after year. The newly hatched young had shorter snouts and larger eyes relative to their overall size, compared to the adults – a common feature of younger animals.

MAIASAURA

DINO FACTFILE

Maiasaura

Meaning: Good mother reptile

Pronunciation: My-yah-sore-ah

Period: Late Cretaceous

Main group: Ornithopoda

Length: 9 meters (29½ feet)

Weight: 3–4 metric tons (3–4 tons)

Diet: Plants

Fossils: USA (Montana), Canada

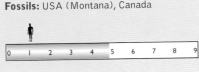

The long-established public image of dinosaurs as slow, stupid, robot-like automatons was jolted in the 1960s by work on the meat-eating *Deinonychus*, and further in the late 1970s by studies of the "duckbill" *Maiasaura*. This 9-meter (29½-foot) plant-eater was named in 1979 by John ("Jack") Horner and Robert Makela, from fossils found by Marion Brandvold and her family near Bozeman, Montana. One of the hadrosaurs, *Maiasaura*, had a long head, in profile not unlike a horse's, with a ridge near each eye. The front of the mouth was typically "duckbilled," wide and toothless, but the cheeks were filled with rows of crushing teeth that self-sharpened their ridges as they chewed. *Maiasaura* lived during the Late Cretaceous period, about 78–73 million years ago. Today, many of its best fossils are displayed at the Museum of the Rockies in Bozeman, Montana.

Thousands of these fossils were found in Montana, at the location near Bynum nicknamed "Egg Mountain." The remains included not only adults but juveniles, nests, eggs and just-hatched babies. An overall picture emerges of many *Maiasaura* nesting as a colony, as some birds do today. These massive breeding herds were possibly many thousands strong. The dinosaurs not only made nests for their eggs, but probably also guarded or brooded them, and possibly protected and brought food for the hatchlings (see page 300). At the same location fossils of the much smaller, lighter ornithopod, *Orodromeus*, were also found as well as fossils of the predators *Bambiraptor* and the small, lithe, agile, big-brained, big-eyed meat-eater *Troodon*. It has been proposed by some scientists that some of these dinosaurs were also breeding at the time of the catastrophe, when volcanic ash preserved these huge quantities of remains.

EDMONTOSAURUS

Fossils of *Edmontosaurus*, one of the biggest and most powerful of the duckbilled dinosaurs, have been found in numerous states of the American west, as well as in the western provinces of Canada. The southernmost finds are probably those in Colorado, while those farthest north are in Alaska. This immensely wide distribution has led to the theory that *Edmontosaurus* herds migrated with the seasons, much as caribou do today. At some sites, especially those in Alberta, there are fossils of many *Edmontosaurus* individuals close together, suggesting that they lived in herds. Lawrence Lambe named this duckbill in 1917.

Edmontosaurus was a bulky hadrosaur with strong jaws, which were typically toothless and expanded at the front to form a duck-like beak, but filled with batteries of sharply ridged teeth in the cheeks. One partly mummified specimen reveals pine needles, twigs and seeds lying in what would have been the gut region. Another has fossil impressions of the leathery skin, showing larger bumps among many smaller, pebbly scales. *Edmontosaurus* had only four digits on its front feet: these may have been embedded in a mitten-like fleshy pad. Its tail was "deep," that is, high from top to bottom, rather than wide. The shape of the upper skull and the texture of its surface suggest that *Edmontosaurus* may have had loose skin flaps on its nose, which it could have inflated like a balloon, perhaps as a colorful visual display while courting or impressing rivals, and/or to make honking or bellowing sounds. One well-preserved and almost complete *Edmontosaurus* skeleton has been used as a basis to estimate muscle power, leg motion, stride length and other aspects of movement. It's estimated that hadrosaurs such as *Edmontosaurus* could sprint briefly at perhaps 50 kilometers (about 30 miles) per hour, and trot or lope at half that speed for great distances. This design for movement lends weight to the various migration theories for hadrosaurs and ornithopods in general.

DINO FACTFILE
Edmontosaurus

Meaning: Edmonton reptile (for the capital city of Alberta)

Pronunciation: Ed-mon-toe-sore-uss

Period: Late Cretaceous

Main group: Ornithopoda

Length: 13 meters (42½ feet)

Weight: 3–5 metric tons (3–5 tons)

Diet: Plants

Fossils: USA (Montana, North and South Dakota, Wyoming, Alaska, Colorado), Canada (Alberta and Saskatchewan)

BELOW A rare specimen of fossil dino-skin shows *Edmontosaurus*'s pebble-like scales.

LEFT *Edmontosaurus* was far larger than an elephant today and, although bulky, had long limbs for sustained walking or trotting.

SHANTUNGOSAURUS

DINO FACTFILE

Shantungosaurus

Meaning: Shandong lizard

Pronunciation: Shahn-dung-owe-sore-uss

Period: Late Cretaceous

Main group: Ornithopoda

Length: 12–15 meters (39–49 feet)

Weight: 5 metric tons (5 tons)

Diet: Plants

Fossils: China

Hadrosaurs are best known from North America and Asia. *Shantungosaurus* is an Asian example, and possibly the largest known type of the whole duckbill group, at up to 15 meters (49 feet) in length, and weighing more than 5 metric tons (5 tons). This is reflected in its species name, *Shantungosaurus giganteus*, given in 1973. The genus name is taken from the discovery site in Shandong (or Shantung) province, in the far east of central China. *Shantungosaurus* lived about 80–75 million years ago; many other hadrosaurs came after its time.

Remains of at least five individuals are known, consisting of pieces of skulls and other parts of the skeleton, and one of them can be pieced together as fairly complete. A combined reconstruction, filled in with features of other hadrosaurs, shows a dinosaur similar in many ways to *Edmontosaurus* (see previous page).

The tail is extremely long – perhaps half the dinosaur's overall length. It shows the tall, narrow structure that led many paleontologists to suggest that hadrosaurs spent much of their time in water and swam by swishing their tails from side to side, like crocodiles. But in many hadrosaurs bony, rod-like tendons overlapping the tailbones lengthwise suggest that the tails were probably stiff rather than flexible. They could have been used, perhaps, as side-swipe weapons against the massive meat-eaters such as *Tyrannosaurus* or *Tarbosaurus*, that roamed the region during the same period. The head is low and broad or wide, presumably like *Edmontosaurus*, with rows or "batteries" of chewing cheek teeth in the left and right halves of the upper and lower jaws. In each battery there were more than 50 individual teeth, in smaller and closely packed groups of about three to five (see page 285).

BELOW *Shantungosaurus* was one of the largest hadrosaurs, and so one of the biggest members of the whole ornithopod dinosaur group. Its fossils come from rocks of the Shanyang Formation near Shaanxi, in China's Shandong region.

ANATOTITAN

The finding and naming of this dinosaur has caused confusion and controversy. In 1882, Edward Drinker Cope's fossil collectors J. L. Wortman and R. S. Hill excavated a fairly complete and fairly well-preserved skeleton from South Dakota's Black Hills, with the skull and lower jaw indicating a long, low head and wide bill-like front to the mouth. Some dubbed this a "duckbill" and so the commonly used name of the group began with Cope's specimen. It was officially titled *Anatosaurus* in 1942, by Richard Swan Lull and colleagues, from various fossils, including a part-mummified specimen recovered by Charles H. and Charles M. Sternberg (father and son) in 1908. Over the year, more finds were added to and taken away from the *Anatosaurus* catalog but disagreements persisted about whether this was a truly independent genus or a mishmash of other, similar creatures. By 1990 the situation

was clarified after a survey of the fossil evidence. Ralph Chapman and Michael Brett-Surman reclassified some of the *Anatosaurus* fossils as a newer genus, *Anatotitan*, meaning "giant duck," while others were attributed to *Edmontosaurus*, as probably part-grown individuals.

Anatotitan was of fairly "standard" hadrosaur size, at some 10 meters (33 feet) in length. It probably survived to the end of the dinosaur age, around 65 million years ago. Overall, it was similar to *Edmontosaurus* (see page 289), but lighter, slimmer and longer-limbed. Its mouth had a wide toothless bill at the front and rows of crushing teeth in the cheek regions. The digits of the forelimbs were thought to be wrapped in fleshy pads, often called "mittens" or "webs." These formed part of the evidence from the 1908 find used to support the picture of amphibious or semiaquatic behavior patterns among the hadrosaurs.

DINO FACTFILE
Anatotitan
Meaning: Giant or titanic duck [reptile]
Pronunciation: Ann-at-owe-tie-tann
Period: Late Cretaceous
Main group: Ornithopoda
Length: 10 meters (33 feet)
Weight: 3–4 metric tons (3–4 tons)
Diet: Plants
Fossils: USA (South Dakota)

BELOW Controversy continues over whether *Anatotitan* was a distinct type of duck-billed dinosaur or a species within the genus *Edmontosaurus*. Its long, powerful back legs each had three hoof-like toes on the foot.

BACTROSAURUS

DINO FACTFILE

Bactrosaurus

Meaning: Club-spined reptile

Pronunciation: Back-troe-sore-uss

Period: mid–Late Cretaceous

Main group: Ornithopoda

Length: 6 meters (19¹/₂ feet)

Weight: 1.5 metric tons (1¹/₂ tons)

Diet: Plants

Fossils: Asia (Uzbekistan, Mongolia, China)

0 1 2 3 4 5 6 7 8 9

The name *Bactrosaurus* (sometimes misquoted as *Bactrasaurus*) means "club-spined reptile." It is derived from the thick, spine-like extensions projecting upward from the backbones (vertebrae), seen in many hadrosaurs. These "spines" may have held up a ridge of muscle, flesh and skin along the animal's back and tail. They seem too short and substantial to have supported a thin, low, skin-like "sail," as in certain other dinosaurs, such as the ornithopod *Ouranosaurus* (see page 266).

The name of this dinosaur is sometimes said to derive from Bactria, an ancient region in Central Asia that is now divided among Afghanistan, Tajikistan and their neighbors. This is a misinterpretation, however, and its fossils were in any·case found far to the northeast and east of ancient Bactria – in what is now Uzbekistan, Mongolia and China. *Bactrosaurus* was named by Charles Whitney Gilmore, an American paleontologist who studied and described many dinosaurs in both North America and Asia, including the Gobi, as well as fossil lizards and other prehistoric reptiles. *Bactrosaurus* was an early type of hadrosaur, dated to around 95 million years ago (see also *Protohadros*, page 286). It was also fairly small for a duckbill, at about 6 meters (19¹/₂ feet) in length. Fragments and parts of about six individuals are known. Teeth once viewed as belonging to a species from another dinosaur genus, *Cionodon*, may belong to *Bactrosaurus*. The genus *Cionodon* was named in 1874 by Edward Drinker Cope; the species *Cionodon kysylkumensis*, which is now regarded as *Bactrosaurus kysylkumensis*, was named in 1931 by A.N. Riabinin.

BELOW Some fossils of *Bactrosaurus* were found near Erenhot City, Mongolia. The spine- or rod-like upward projections along its backbone may have supported a fleshy ridge of tissue. The function of such a ridge is unclear, since its surface area seems too limited to help with body temperature regulation, as in dinosaurs such as *Ouranosaurus*.

ABOVE *Prosaurolophus* was one of the first flat-crested hadrosaurs. Its low crest consisted of small knobs above the eyes and a short, rearward-pointing spike.

PROSAUROLOPHUS

Barnum Brown, an energetic and always well-dressed fossil-hunter, was assistant curator of the American Museum of Natural History in the early twentieth century. In 1912, he described and named the duckbill *Saurolophus* (see page 296). Four years later, he followed with its possible predecessor, *Prosaurolophus*, from fossils excavated in Alberta. The remains were found in rocks about 75 million years old. *Prosaurolophus* was a medium-sized hadrosaur and had a low, flat head without the elaborate head crest seen in certain other members of the duckbill group. Fossils of up to 25 individuals are now known, including more than seven skulls, with some from Montana as well as Alberta.

Prosaurolophus probably grew to about 8 meters (26½ feet) in length. It has some similarities to the larger *Edmontosaurus*, including the front-of-mouth structure after which the duckbills are named – the widened, flattened, toothless "beak." Behind this, in the cheek region, were rows of dozens of sloping chewing teeth which sheared against those in the opposing jaw to grind up tough vegetation and also maintain sharpness. The rest of the body was fairly typical of the hadrosaurs, with larger rear limbs and three substantial walking digits on each foot, but also strong front limbs with "hands" adapted for bearing weight. *Prosaurolophus* could walk bipedally, on the two rear legs, or lope and gallop on all fours – as confirmed by many examples of their trackways (sets of fossilized footprints). In 1992, John "Jack" Horner named one species *Prosaurolophus blackfeetensis* after the Native American people known as the Blackfeet, whose traditional homeland is Montana. Another species is *Prosaurolophus maximus*. This was the original specimen named by Brown in 1916. Other species have been proposed but not confirmed.

DINO FACTFILE
Prosaurolophus

Meaning: Before Saurolophus
Pronunciation: Proe-saw-oh-loaf-uss
Period: Late Cretaceous
Main group: Ornithopoda
Length: 8 meters (26½ feet)
Weight: 2 metric tons (2 tons)
Diet: Plants
Fossils: Canada (Alberta), USA (Montana)

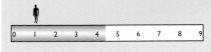

0　1　2　3　4　5　6　7　8　9

THE NOISIEST DINOSAURS

MANY HADROSAURS OF THE LATE CRETACEOUS IN NORTH AMERICA WERE SIMILAR IN OVERALL SIZE AND BODY PROPORTIONS. PERHAPS THEIR BODILY COLORS AND PATTERNS, AND THE SHAPES OF THE HEAD CRESTS IN SOME TYPES, WERE USED AS COLORFUL RESONATORS TO MAKE LOUD HONKS, TRUMPETS, BLARES AND OTHER CALLS. THE DIFFERENT SOUNDS WOULD ENABLE DUCKBILLS TO SOUND THE ALARM AT APPROACHING DANGER, SUCH AS A PREDATOR OR FOREST FIRE, AND TO FIND OTHERS OF THEIR OWN KIND WHEN HERDING AND COURTING.

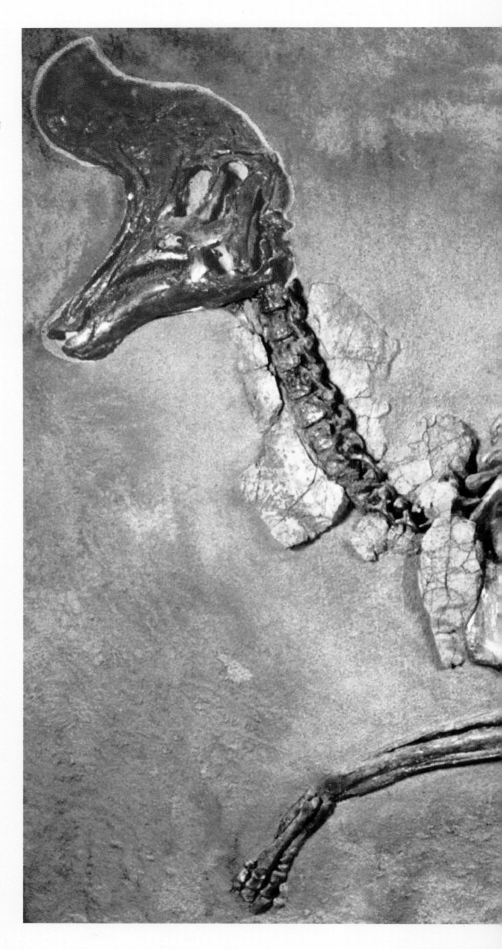

RIGHT A wonderfully preserved fossil of a *Lambeosaurus* from the Royal Tyrrell Museum at Drumheller, Alberta, Canada. It shows clearly the head crest which is thought to have been used as a resonator for making loud calls.

SAUROLOPHUS

DINO FACTFILE

Saurolophus

Meaning: Ridged reptile, crested reptile

Pronunciation: Sore-owe-loaf-uss

Period: Late Cretaceous

Main group: Ornithopoda

Length: 9–10 meters (29½–33 feet)

Weight: 2 metric tons (2 tons)

Diet: Plants

Fossils: USA, Canada, Mongolia

Barnum Brown of the American Museum of Natural History named *Saurolophus* in 1912 (see *Prosaurolophus* on page 293). Meaning "crested" or "ridged" reptile, the name refers to the bony feature on the top of its head. Many hadrosaurs had these adornments or crests, and their functions have been widely discussed: were they for visual display, signs of sexual or breeding maturity or social signals to others of its kind? The ridge or crest of *Saurolophus* ran up the forehead and between the eyes, and projected upward and to the rear. Fossils of this hadrosaur have been located in both Canada and the USA, and in Mongolia. The upward projection or "prong" seems more prominent in the Asian specimens, at around 13 centimeters (5 inches). The crest may have supported a flap of skin over the snout, which could have been inflated to produce noises and make a visual display. The flatness of the skull on either side of the snout has been cited as evidence for this view. Another idea is that the topmost "prong" was a strut or support to hold up a flap of skin, which could have been colored or patterned. (See also *Parasaurolophus*, opposite.)

The rest of *Saurolophus* is relatively standard for medium-sized hadrosaurs, with an overall length of about 10 meters (33 feet). There is a wide, flat, beak-like front to the mouth, which is slightly upturned on the upper tip, and there are rows of hundreds of teeth in the cheek regions of the upper and lower jaws, for thorough pulverizing of food. The front limbs were long and sturdy, and the rear limbs even more so, for walking on back legs only or on all fours. The hip and tail region of the vertebral column (backbone), as in most hadrosaurs, was stiffened by bony rods and unsuited for flexing or whipping from side to side. *Saurolophus* lived around 70 million years ago.

RIGHT This reconstruction of *Saurolophus* shows the loose "bag" of stretchy skin on the nose, which could have been inflated like a balloon and resonated to produce a honking call, as in some seals today.

PARASAUROLOPHUS

Parasaurolophus was a sizable and powerful duckbilled dinosaur from the Late Cretaceous period. In most respects, its main body, limbs and tail were fairly typical. The immediately distinctive feature is the enormous bony head crest, bigger than that of any other hadrosaur, sloping up and back from the forehead, in the fashion of a long tube. The crest was up to 1 meter (39 inches) long and was also hollow. The subgroup of hadrosaurs that possessed hollow head crests are known as lambeosaurids or lambeosaurines, as distinct from the hadrosaurids/-ines. William Parks named *Parasaurolophus* in 1922, from a fairly complete specimen found in Alberta.

The hollow spaces inside the head crest were not isolated air chambers. They were tubes, connected to the dinosaur's breathing airways. From each of the left and right nostrils or nasal openings, which opened toward the tip of the snout, an air tube ran up and back,

just under the surface of the forehead, and then continued up and back through the front or upper part of the crest. The left and right air tubes then U-turned at the topmost of the crest, which had no air openings to the outside. The tubes continued downward along the lower or underside part of the crest, and back into the upper rear region of the main head, where air could continue its route down into the throat and lungs. *Parasaurolophus* could breathe through this complex airway route, and, perhaps, make the whole crest structure vibrate or resonate like a trumpet or trombone, to create deep or low-pitched noises. (This topic is further discussed on page 294.)

ABOVE In this reconstruction a narrow flap of skin is shown attached between the lower surface of the crest and the neck. Tilting the head down would extend the flap, perhaps revealing colored patterns.

DINO FACTFILE
Parasaurolophus
Meaning: Beside crested /ridged reptile
Pronunciation: Parah-sore-owe-loaf-uss
Period: Late Cretaceous
Main group: Ornithopoda
Length: 12 meters (39 feet)
Weight: 3 metric tons (3 tons)
Diet: Plants
Fossils: USA, Canada

LAMBEOSAURUS

DINO FACTFILE

Lambeosaurus

Meaning: Lambe's reptile

Pronunciation: Lam-bee-oh-sore-uss

Period: Late Cretaceous

Main group: Ornithopoda

Length: Up to 15 meters (49 feet)

Weight: 5–6 metric tons (5–6 tons)

Diet: Plants

Fossils: USA, Canada, Mexico

0 1 2 3 4 5 6 7 8 9

Lambeosaurus rivals *Shantungosaurus* as the largest known member of the hadrosaur group, at 15 meters (49 feet) in length and 5 metric tons (5 tons) in weight. It has given its name to the lambeosaurid or lambeosaurine subgroup of hadrosaurs – those with hollow head crests. In this case, the crest projects at a right angle from the forehead, almost between the eyes. It is somewhat angular or rectangular, and is often called "hatchet-shaped." As in other lambeosaurids, the crest is hollow. The air tube from each nostril passes from the nose, along the upper muzzle, and then up and inside the crest. Here, shelf-like flanges of bone project into the air passage. The airways from the left and right nostrils merge inside the lower rear of the crest, and the main airway then runs downward through the throat to the lungs. There is also a spur or spike of bone, at a right angle to the main crest, pointing up and rearward from the top of the head, just between the eyes, as in *Saurolophus*. This part of the crest is solid, not hollow.

William Parks, who had also named *Parasaurolophus* the previous year, named *Lambeosaurus* in 1923. The name honors Lawrence Lambe, an eminent Canadian paleontologist who had described and named many dinosaurs during the 1910s, including the large hadrosaur *Edmontosaurus*. Sites of *Lambeosaurus* fossils stretch from Alberta in Canada, through Montana, to Baja California (Mexico) in the far southwest of North America. There are also specimens of its fossilized skin showing small, pebble-like scales embedded in the leathery hide.

ABOVE *Lambeosaurus* was the weight of a large elephant, but probably able to stride along at moderate human running speed for several hours.

CORYTHOSAURUS

Corythosaurus was a member of the lambeosaurid or lambeosaurine subgroup of hadrosaurs – those with bony, hollow head crests. It was first described and named in 1914 by Barnum Brown, following the discovery of Late Cretaceous fossils in Alberta, Canada. The name refers to the tall, curved head crest, which in profile is similar to the shape of helmets worn by soldiers in ancient times, including those from Corinth in Greece. Since 1914, more remains have been discovered, including those from Montana. These were also studied and named as *Corythosaurus*, but have been differentiated into species, such as *Corythosaurus casuarius*, *Corythosaurus excavatus* and *Corythosaurus intermedius*. Distinctions were made based on the detailed shape of the head crest, and its size, area and curvature in relation to the rest of the skull and the whole animal.

In 1975, Peter Dodson, an anatomist at the University of Pennsylvania, produced a wide-ranging report on lambeosaurid dinosaurs, detailing the comparative measurements, especially of their head crests, and drawing comparisons with the size range and sexual differences in certain animals of today. As a result, it was suggested that up to seven former species of *Corythosaurus*, known from 20-plus skulls, were probably members of just one species. The variation in head crests could be explained by the differential growth of various parts of the skeleton with age, where some body regions develop faster than others, and also sexual dimorphism (differences between males and females). It may be that adult males had the largest crests, followed by those of adult females, while juveniles had much smaller crests in relation to body size. The dinosaur formerly known as *Tetragonosaurus* is now included with *Corythosaurus*.

DINO FACTFILE

Corythosaurus

Meaning: Helmet reptile

Pronunciation: Ko-rih-thoe-sore-uss

Period: Late Cretaceous

Main group: Ornithopoda

Length: 10 meters (33 feet)

Weight: 3–4 metric tons (3–4 tons)

Diet: Plants

Fossils: USA (Montana), Canada (Alberta)

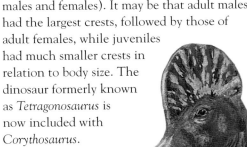

ABOVE The narrow, semicircular head crest of *Corythosaurus* was linked into the breathing passages and probably used to produce sounds as well as for visual recognition. Fossils of the skin show a pebbly texture. Like many hadrosaurs, *Corythosaurus* probably chewed tough vegetation including woody twigs and conifer needles.

CARING PARENTS

AMAZING FOSSILS OF THE DUCKBILL *MAIASAURA*
SHOW HOW THEIR BOWL-SHAPED NESTS, EACH
ABOUT TWO METERS (6½ FEET) ACROSS, WERE
SCOOPED OUT OF EARTH. THE MOTHER LAID UP
TO 20 ELONGATED EGGS, AND PERHAPS COVERED
THEM WITH VEGETATION, WHICH DECAYED AND
PRODUCED WARMTH FOR INCUBATION. REMAINS
OF BERRIES AND TWIGS, AND WEAR MARKS ON THE
TEETH OF THE TINY HATCHLINGS WHOSE LEGS
WERE NOT DEVELOPED ENOUGH FOR THEM TO
WALK, SUGGEST THAT A PARENT EVEN BROUGHT
THEM FOOD.

RIGHT A colony of *Maiasaura* shows various stages of the
breeding process including preparing the nest, laying the eggs,
turning them, guarding them from marauders such as small
theropod dinosaurs, and taking care of the hatchlings.

HYPACROSAURUS

DINO FACTFILE

Hypacrosaurus

Meaning: Near-topmost reptile

Pronunciation: High-pah-kroe-sore-uss

Period: Late Cretaceous

Main group: Ornithopoda

Length: 9 meters (29½ feet)

Weight: 2–3 metric tons (2–3 tons)

Diet: Plants

Fossils: USA (Montana), Canada (Alberta)

In many respects, *Hypacrosaurus* was similar to *Corythosaurus* (see page 299). It was a typical Late Cretaceous hadrosaur, with a curved neck and bulky body; large rear limbs with three stout "hooves" on each foot for walking and running; smaller but substantial front limbs with four "fingers" on each hand (which could bear body weight for four-legged trotting or galloping); and a long but rapidly tapering tail. The front of the mouth lacked teeth and was flat from top to bottom and expanded from side to side, like a duck's bill. Ridged teeth formed 40 rows or "batteries" in the rear regions of the jaws, providing a powerful chewing action for the toughest vegetation. Most hadrosaurs were relatively large eyed, and probably had keen senses of sight and smell, to detect the huge predators of their time and region, such as *Albertosaurus* and *Tyrannosaurus*. There are tall upward extensions, like straps or spines, from the tops of the vertebrae, as in other hadrosaurs. These may have formed a long ridge, or a low sail or fin, along the back and upper tail.

The bony crest of *Hypacrosaurus* was not quite as tall, or as narrow from side to side, as that of *Corythosaurus*. But it was hollow. It contained convoluted air passages that led from the nostrils at the front of the snout, through the crest, and then down into the head and throat. (The many suggestions on the functions of hadrosaur head crests are described through this chapter.) *Hypacrosaurus* was named in 1913 by Barnum Brown, an American dinosaur expert and fossil-hunter. Its remains, including skulls, partial skeletons of adults and young, and eggs with embryos, come mostly from the Canadian province of Alberta and the US state of Montana.

BELOW *Hypacrosaurus* skull and skeleton at the Royal Tyrrell Museum, Drumheller, Alberta in Canada.

GRYPOSAURUS (KRITOSAURUS AND OTHERS)

Gryposaurus – "curved nose reptile" – was named for the distinctive shape of the front of its snout, which seems to have very curved nostrils and an upward projection, giving in profile a prominent and angular "nose." The head was long and narrow from side to side. In most other respects, *Gryposaurus* was a typical medium-sized hadrosaur, about 9 meters (29½ feet) in length and weighing a couple of metric tons, from 75–70 million years ago. Most of its skull fossils, which may represent more than ten individuals, plus other bones and also skin impressions, were found in Alberta, Canada. *Gryposaurus* was named in 1914 by Lawrence Lambe, a Canadian paleontologist renowned for his many hadrosaur discoveries (see page 298).

The fossilized impressions of the skin show small polygonal scales, only 5–8 millimeters (¼–⅓ inch) across, with varying numbers of straight sides. These probably covered most of the body, but the tail may also have had taller, larger, more cone-like plates, more than 10 millimeters (⅓ inch) across and spaced out around 50–70 millimeters (2–3 inches) apart.

There has been considerable debate about *Gryposaurus* and several similar dinosaurs, including *Kritosaurus* ("noble reptile," originally named in 1910), *Trachodon* (1856), *Naashoibitosaurus* (1993) and others, and about the species that each of these genera are supposed to contain. At various times, the fossils of each of these dinosaurs have been said to represent one or more of the others. For example, *Kritosaurus* remains from North America known as the species *Kritosaurus navajovius* ("of the Navajo") – there being only one partial and poorly preserved skull – may be assigned to *Gryposaurus*. On the other hand, those from Argentina, named *Kritosaurus australis* ("of the south"), may be a distinct species, and may not even be *Kritosaurus*. Many of these matters await further study and clarification.

DINO FACTFILE
Gryposaurus
Meaning: Curved-nose reptile
Pronunciation: Grip-owe-sore-uss
Period: Late Cretaceous
Main group: Ornithopoda
Length: 9 meters (29½ feet)
Weight: 2–3 metric tons (2–3 tons)
Diet: Plants
Fossils: Canada (Alberta), Argentina

0	1	2	3	4	5	6	7	8	9

LEFT Fossilized skin showing the scale patterns allows a fairly detailed reconstruction of the outer appearance (although not coloring) of *Gryposaurus*.

BELOW This specimen from Cretaceous rocks in Patagonia, Argentina, is named *Kritosaurus australis*, but future studies may change this designation.

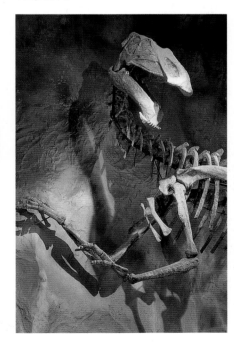

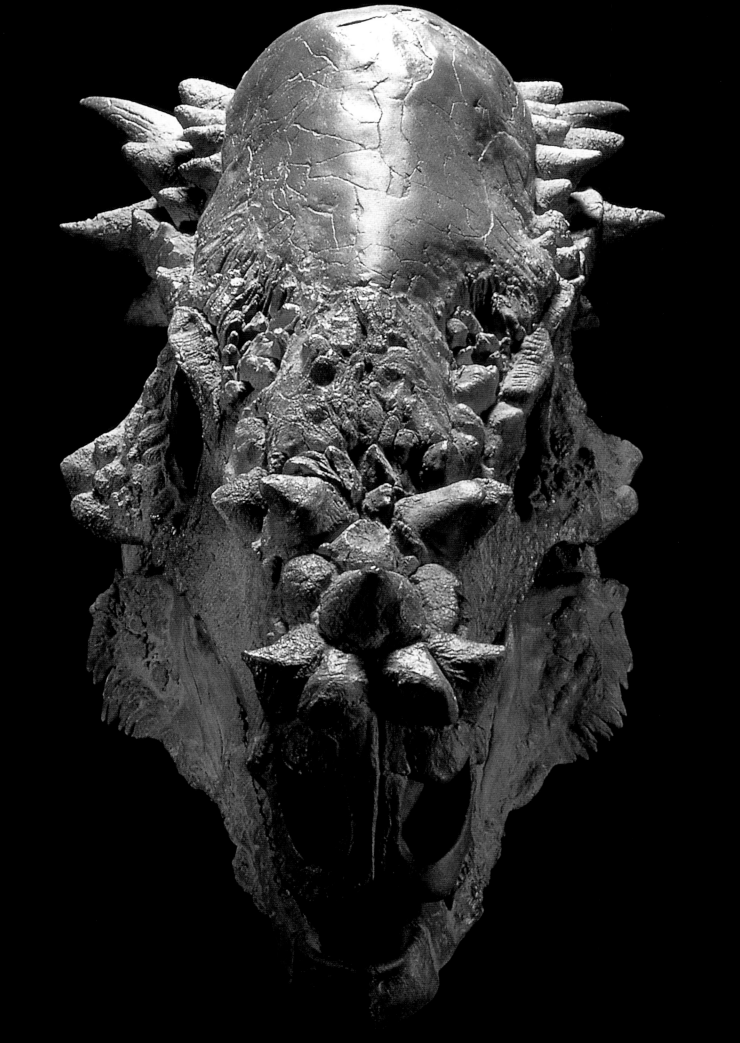

CHAPTER TEN

THE
BONEHEADS

THE PACHYCEPHALOSAURS WERE "BONEHEADS," WITH EXTREMELY
THICK LAYERS OF BONE ON THE TOP OF THEIR SKULLS.

CRASH AND BASH

AT CERTAIN TIMES OF YEAR, HILLY REGIONS AROUND THE WORLD ECHO TO THE THWACKS AND CRACKS OF RUTTING SHEEP AND GOATS. THE MALES LOWER THEIR HEADS AND HURL THEMSELVES AT EACH OTHER, CLASHING THEIR FOREHEADS AND HORNS WITH SO MUCH FORCE THAT THEY ARE SOMETIMES KNOCKED OUT. PACHYCEPHALOSAURS – "THICK-HEADED REPTILES" – MAY HAVE ENGAGED IN SIMILAR HEAD-BUTTING CONTESTS. THESE COULD HAVE TAKEN PLACE BETWEEN RIVALS AT BREEDING TIME, TO DEMONSTRATE THEIR STRENGTH AND FITNESS, AND SO SHOW THEIR SUITABILITY TO BECOME MATES AND PARENTS. PACHYCEPHALOSAURS ARE ALSO NICKNAMED "BONEHEADS," "HELMETHEADS" OR "DOMEHEADS," ALTHOUGH ONLY SOME TYPES HAD SKULL ROOFS WITH ROUNDED OR DOMED SHAPES.

WHY THE THICK SKULL?

Head-bashing is the main suggestion for the greatly thickened top or roof to the skull of pachycephalosaurs. In some types, the bony layer was more than 25 centimeters (10 inches) thick – the span of an adult human hand. This was not the only adaptation to exerting and absorbing great shocks and pressure to the head, while protecting the small brain within the skull. The neck bones were also sturdy and the neck itself was short, to withstand stress. The backbone and rear limbs were also strong, to help resist and also transmit the force of impact down through them to the ground.

LACK OF FINDS

In the rest of the skeleton, pachycephalosaurs seem to have been fairly unremarkable. Their teeth were small and weak, suited to eating soft vegetation. The tail was stiffened by bones and tendons lying alongside the caudal vertebrae (backbones). Toward the end of the tail was an expanded area of bone containing a chamber. The function of this feature is a mystery. An enlarged nerve cord, or muscle supports for tail spikes, have been suggested – but not convincingly – or the chamber may have been a store or repository for high-energy substances such as body fat or glycogen (animal starch), as seen in some birds today. Another problem stems from the extent of the fossil finds. Most pachycephalosaurs are known mainly, or solely, from their preserved skulls, or even just the thickened skull roof. Parts of the rest of the skeleton are rare or absent, with the notable exception of *Stegoceras*, which has been used as a basis or model for reconstructing most of the others.

PROBLEMS WITH HEAD-BANGING

In *Stegoceras* and *Pachycephalosaurus*, the skull roof was curved or domed. This means that, when two heads clashed, unless they did so exactly in line, the domes would easily slip past each other and jerk the animal's necks sideways. Most sheep and goats have flattened foreheads, which help them to avoid such slippage. Perhaps the domeheaded pachycephalosaurs did not butt head to head, but rammed opponents on other parts of the body. Another proposal is that these dinosaurs used their heads to bash predators, in the same way that a bull or ram or rhino lowers its head and charges at an enemy.

SMALL AND LATE

With fewer than ten well-known types, the pachycephalosaur group was among the smallest of the main dinosaur groups. They appeared during the Early Cretaceous period, probably in Europe although perhaps in East Asia, but most are known from the Late Cretaceous period, and were spread across all the northern continents. They are placed along with the horned dinosaurs or ceratopsians, such as *Triceratops*, in the larger dinosaur group known as the marginocephalians or "margin heads" (see page 353).

PREVIOUS PAGE In this front-on head view the hugely thickened, smoothed "bone dome" of *Pachycephalosaurus* shines brightly amid the various small spikes, lumps and nodules which decorated the ridge around the upper head. The whole skull is about as large as a medium-sized suitcase.

LEFT A pair of *Stegoceras* finally come to blows, perhaps after a lengthy period of strutting and posturing. Perhaps they would try to win the contest by visual threats, such as standing tall to emphasize their height and then lowering heads to show their "bone domes," before engaging in the much riskier stage of physical battle.

STEGOCERAS

DINO FACTFILE

Stegoceras

Meaning: Roofed horn, horny roof

Pronunciation: Steg-owe-sair-ass

Period: Late Cretaceous

Main group: Pachycephalosauria

Length: 2–2.5 meters (6½–8 feet)

Weight: 50–70 kilograms (110–155 pounds)

Diet: Plants

Fossils: USA, Canada (Alberta)

| 0 | 1 | 2 | 3 |

Stegoceras is the best-known of the pachycephalosaurs or "bonehead" dinosaurs. It had a total length of some 2 meters (6½ feet) and is often likened in size to a goat – the head-butting habit of goats aids the comparison. *Stegoceras* is also one of the boneheads for which fossils other than the skull are known, comprising one partial skeleton and additional fragments. As a result, it is often used as the model for reconstructing other pachycephalosaurs (see page 307). Lawrence Lambe described and named *Stegoceras* in 1902, from Late Cretaceous remains recovered from the Belly River region of Alberta, Canada. Teeth associated with these skull remains resembled those of *Troodon*, a meat-eating dinosaur named almost 50 years before, so the fossils that we now know as *Stegoceras* were first called *Troodon* too. The link between the teeth and the skull fragments was called into doubt following studies of fossil finds at other sites, however, and in 1924 the find of a skull and part of a skeleton confirmed that *Stegoceras* was distinct from *Troodon*.

Stegoceras had a large skull with the typical bony roof up to 8 centimeters (3 inches) thick, forming a helmet-like dome (its functions are discussed on page 307). Rimming the dome around the rear of the head, and curving around and over each eye, forward to the snout, was a bony edging or "shelf." The teeth were tiny and curved with serrated edges; the brain and eyes were relatively large; the neck was stout; and the front limbs were small and unsuitable for carrying body weight. The rear limbs were larger, and sturdy rather than slim, their proportions suggesting a strong, deliberate mover rather than a fleet-footed sprinter. The tail was long and evenly tapered, and was probably not flexible. The base of the tail had an enlarged or expanded "chamber" (this is discussed on page 307).

LEFT The skull of *Prenocephale* is adorned with various small lumps and nodules of bone, arranged in rows or lines. It is difficult to propose a physical function for these projections, so perhaps they were visual symbols, possibly of sex (male or female) or age (immature or sexually mature).

PRENOCEPHALE

In the 1970s, scientists from Poland and Russia, accompanied by Mongolian experts, mounted several expeditions into the Gobi, which yielded many fascinating fossils, including *Prenocephale*. Perhaps more of an "egghead" than a "bonehead," this pachycephalosaur is known from a fine upper skull described and named in 1974 by Teresa Maryanska and Halszka Osmólska. It was excavated from the finely grained sandstone of the Nemegt Basin, where excellent fossilization conditions preserved parts of the skull's inside, even showing small openings where nerves and blood vessels passed into and out of the brain. Similar fossils have also been identified in North America, in Montana, and in Alberta, Canada. The remains are scarce, however, and even at the original Mongolian site there are very few other parts of the skeleton.

While *Prenocephale's* head is very similar to that of *Stegoceras*, there are small variations, such as the slight angular prominence just above the nasal openings in *Prenocephale*, when seen from the side. There is also evidence of several sets or chain-like rows of small bony lumps. On each side, one runs from the nostril rearward, partway along the side of the snout. There are two more rows above and below the eye, and another to the lower rear of the eye, which merges with a larger series. This stretches around the back of the head, angling upward and then across at the rear. These lumps or studs seem to have been more decorative than functional. The teeth are generally small, with a few slightly larger ones at the front of the upper jaw (which possibly bit down on a horny pad at the tip of the lower jaw) and examples of smaller teeth toward the cheek region. The type specimen of *Prenocephale* (from which it was originally named) is *Prenocephale prenes*, meaning "sloping sloping head." The Canadian representative has been dubbed *Prenocephale edmontonensis*.

DINO FACTFILE

Prenocephale

Meaning: Sloping head

Pronunciation: Pren-owe-seff-ah-lee

Period: Late Cretaceous

Main group: Pachycephalosauria

Length: 2.5 meters (8 feet)

Weight: 100 kilograms (220 pounds)

Diet: Plants

Fossils: Mongolia, USA (Montana), Canada (Alberta)

HOMALOCEPHALE AND GOYOCEPHALE

DINO FACTFILE

Homalocephale

Meaning: Level head, even head

Pronunciation: Hom-ah-low-seff-ah-lee

Period: Late Cretaceous

Main group: Pachycephalosauria

Length: 1.5–3 meters (5–10 feet)

Weight: 40–90 kilograms (88–200 pounds)

Diet: Plants

Fossils: Mongolia

Yet another pachycephalosaur or "bonehead" dinosaur, similar to *Stegoceras*, was *Homalocephale*. These dinosaurs had similar overall body proportions: large head on a sturdy neck; shorter front limbs, perhaps with four digits; much larger rear limbs for walking and running, with three weight-bearing digits and one high off the ground on each foot; and a long, evenly tapering, not very flexible tail. Reconstruction is based on fossils of a fine skull and almost complete skeleton from the Nemegt region of Omnogov, Mongolia. *Homalocephale* was named in 1974 by Teresa Maryanska and Halszka Osmólska.

Homalocephale had a thickened bony roof or top to the skull, but this was not quite enough to be called a dome. When seen in profile its skull was noticeably flatter than in similar types, such as *Stegoceras* and *Prenocephale*. But like *Prenocephale*, it had several sets of chainlink-like rows of small bony studs or lumps. These seem to have formed patterns that adorned the head, rather than served a useful, physical purpose. The teeth of *Homalocephale* were small, as in other pachycephalosaurs, and leaf-like. This group of dinosaurs probably ate soft plants, chewing and shredding the foliage before swallowing it. Other parts of the skeleton show that the tail was stiffened by bony rods, and that part of the socket in the hipbone, which was the "bowl" for the "ball" or rounded head of the thighbone, had an unusual flange – different in shape to that of any other dinosaur. A similar dinosaur, *Goyocephale* (meaning "elegant or decorated head"), from the same region, was named in 1982. It also had a flat forehead. Along with other discoveries in the pachycephalosaur group, it suggests that these dinosaurs had two or four curved teeth, almost large enough to be called "tusks," near the front of the mouth.

DINO FACTFILE

Goyocephale

Meaning: Elegant head, adorned head

Pronunciation: Goh-yo-seff-ah-lee

Period: Late Cretaceous

Main group: Pachycephalosauria

Length: 2 meters (6½ feet)

Weight: 60 kilograms (130 pounds)

Diet: Plants

Fossils: Mongolia

ABOVE *Homalocephale* is shown in its "charge" posture, head lowered and stiff tail out behind as it runs at an enemy or rival.

ABOVE The reconstructed skull of *Pachycephalosaurus* from Montana, described in 1940, showing the tiny teeth.

RIGHT *Pachycephalosaurus* could probably move on all fours, or on its two rear legs. It may have munched at water plants with its very small, relatively weak teeth.

PACHYCEPHALOSAURUS

Well known as the largest bonehead discovered to date, "thick head reptile" may have reached a total length of 5 meters (16^1/$_2$ feet). It was also one of the last members of the group, perhaps surviving up to the great extinction that signaled the end of the dinosaurs, around 65 million years ago. But, like many members of the bonehead group, its body is almost unknown from fossils, and instead is modeled on those of smaller types, such as *Stegoceras*, and then scaled up in the expected dinosaur proportions.

Only one good fossil skull is known for *Pachycephalosaurus*. It was found near Ekalaka, Montana, sometime in 1938–40 by William Winkley as he herded cattle on the family ranch. It differed in various ways from the already-known *Stegoceras*, and was much larger, so in 1943 it was named as a new dinosaur by Barnum Brown and Erich Schlaikjer. (The name *Pachycephalosaurus* had in fact been coined earlier, in 1931, in association with the small meat-eater

Troodon, but that usage was abandoned.) Remains have been located in Wyoming and South Dakota as well as Montana.

Despite the lack of complete skulls, there are many parts that show the enormously enlarged roof of *Pachycephalosaurus*'s head, a mass of bone up to 25 centimeters (10 inches) thick. In addition, there are small bony spikes on the snout, and scattered lumps and nodules running around the side of the face, above and below each eye and out to the ridge or "shelf" that curves around the rear of the head. The eyes are relatively large, but the teeth are tiny and almost spiky, probably suited to soft plant food such as leaves and fruit. The main fossil of the skull is some 60 centimeters (24 inches) in length, and some scaled-up estimates of the snout–tail length of *Pachycephalosaurus* have exceeded 8 meters (26 feet), but modern versions are lower. The Pachycephalosauridae were named in 1945 by George Sternberg, when it was agreed these dinosaurs should have their own separate family.

DINO FACTFILE
Pachycephalosaurus

Meaning: Thick-head reptile

Pronunciation: Pack-ee-seff-ah-low-sore-uss

Period: Late Cretaceous

Main group: Pachycephalosauria

Length: 4–5 meters (13–16^1/$_2$ feet)

Weight: 400–500 kilograms
(880–1100 pounds)

Diet: Plants

Fossils: Western USA (Wyoming, South Dakota, Montana), possibly Canada

STYGIMOLOCH

In ancient Greek mythology, the River Styx separated the land of the living from the realm of the dead and demonic – Hades or Hell. With horns, spikes and bumps all over its skull, *Stygimoloch* – "demon of the Styx" – certainly resembles the usual image of a demon. It helps that its fossils were unearthed from the Hell Creek or "River of Hades" region of Montana. Its fossils have also been identified in Wyoming. *Stygimoloch* has been compared to a mixture of pachycephalosaur (bonehead), and ceratopsian (horned dinosaur) – especially the ceratopsian

known as *Styracosaurus* (see page 367). Some of the spiky horns of *Stygimoloch* were up to 10 centimeters (4 inches) long. A discovery reported in 1998 shows a much more complete skull of *Stygimoloch*, allowing firmer ideas of the horn pattern around the head. On each side, three or four horns project at a low angle from the squamosal – the bone that forms the "shelf." There are also many groups of small bumps or nodules along this region. This new evidence supports the view that such bonehead features were used for visual display, rather than head-butting (see page 307). *Stygimoloch* was named by Peter Galton, a British paleontologist, and Hans-Dieter Sues, a German fossil expert, in 1983. It was probably a medium-sized pachycephalosaur, up to 3 meters (10 feet) in total length. In the absence of other evidence, it is usually reconstructed with the body shape and proportions of *Stegoceras* and other better-known boneheads. It is dated, like other members of its group, to the Late Cretaceous period, right at the end of the dinosaur age.

LEFT The extraordinary headgear of *Stygimoloch* was probably for show, rather than for physical battles when the spikes and horns might easily be snapped and broken.

DINO FACTFILE
Stygimoloch

Meaning: Demon of the Styx

Pronunciation: Stij-ee-moll-ock

Period: Late Cretaceous

Main group: Pachycephalosauria

Length: 2–3 meters (6½–10 feet)

Weight: 70–90 kilograms
 (155–200 pounds)

Diet: Plants

Fossils: USA (Montana, Wyoming)

YAVERLANDIA

Some dinosaurs are named from many complete fossilized specimens. Others are not. *Yaverlandia* takes its name from Yaverland Point, a promontory near Sandown on the Isle of Wight in southern England. Known among fossil-hunters as Dinosaur Island, this small piece of England has produced a wealth of fossils, including dinosaurs such as *Hypsilophodon*, and many Jurassic marine reptiles, such as ichthyosaurs. But only part of a skull of *Yaverlandia* has been recovered. It resembles the thickened skull roof of other boneheads, but it has two distinctive bulges to the dome. It was found by Frank Abell and has been mentioned in the scientific literature since the 1930s. It was named as a new kind of pachycephalosaur in 1971 by Peter Galton (see also *Stygimoloch*, opposite). Another view, however, is that it may represent part of an armored dinosaur or ankylosaur (see *Hylaeosaurus*, page 324).

The fossil dates from the Early Cretaceous period, 125–120 million years ago, and so is much earlier in time than other bonehead dinosaurs. It is also from a very different region, since most pachycephalosaur remains are known from North America and East Asia. Also, *Yaverlandia* is small for a bonehead. From the skull parts, and using *Stegoceras* and others types as models, it is estimated to have been only about 1 meter (39 inches) long. But the evidence for other small pachycephalosaurs is growing. *Wannanosaurus*, named in 1970 from the Chinese province of Wannan, was perhaps 70 centimeters (27½ inches) long. *Micropachycephalosaurus*, also from China, was named in 1978 and, if it existed as conjectured, it, too, was probably less than 1 meter (39 inches) long, and weighed just 10 kilograms. *Micropachycephalosaurus* is often cited as one of the shortest dinosaurs with the longest of all dinosaur names.

DINO FACTFILE
Yaverlandia
Meaning: Of Yaverland (its discovery site)
Pronunciation: Yav-er-land-ee-ah
Period: Early Cretaceous
Main group: Possibly Pachycephalosauria (see also page 311)
Length: 1 meter (39 inches)
Weight: 20 kilograms (44 pounds)
Diet: Possibly plants
Fossils: Southern England

LEFT The "double-dome" head of *Yaverlandia* is shown in this reconstruction. This is the only pachycephalosaur with twin bulges on the roof of the skull, but the fossil evidence is very limited and not accepted by some experts.

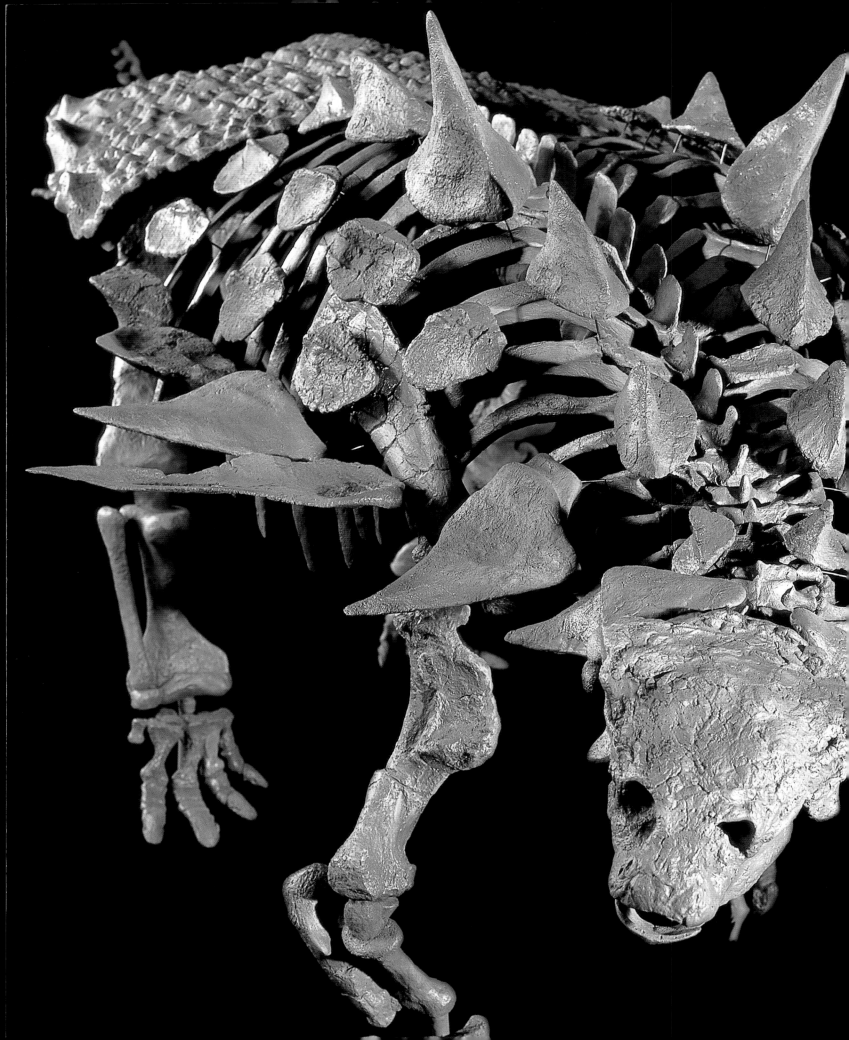

CHAPTER ELEVEN

ARMORED DINOSAURS

NICKNAMES SUCH AS "WALKING TANKS" AND "DINOSAURS IN SUITS OF ARMOR" GIVE SOME IDEA OF THE SIZE, WEIGHT AND BONY PROTECTION OF THE PROBABLY PEACEFUL, PLANT-EATING ANKYLOSAURS.

THICK-SKINNED

ANKYLOSAURS – "FUSED REPTILES" – WERE THE BEST PROTECTED OF ALL DINOSAURS. THE GROUP NAME
REFERS TO THE SLABS AND OTHER PIECES OF BONE THAT WERE JOINED OR FUSED OVER THEIR HEADS
AND EMBEDDED IN THE SKIN OF THE NECKS, BACKS, FLANKS AND TAILS. ALMOST EVERY IMAGINABLE
KIND OF BONY BARRIER – LUMPS, KNOBS, PLATES, SHIELDS, SPIKES, SPINES, SCALES – WAS USED AGAINST
THE CLAWS AND TEETH OF MEAT-EATING DINOSAURS AND OTHER LARGE PREDATORS OF THE TIME, SUCH
AS CROCODILES. ANKYLOSAURS ARE PLACED IN A LARGER DINOSAUR GROUP, THE THYREOPHORANS OR
"SHIELD-BEARERS," ALONG WITH THE STEGOSAURS OR PLATED DINOSAURS.

GROUPS OF ARMORED REPTILES

There were two main subgroups of anyklosaurs.
The most obvious distinction between them was
that the earlier subgroup, the nodosaurids, lacked
the massive lump of bone at the end of the tail
that was possessed by members of the other
subgroup, the ankylosaurids, and is usually known
as the "tail club." Nodosaurids appeared in the
Middle Jurassic period and are known from finds
on all the northern continents as well as possibly
Australia and Antarctica. Some of their kind
persisted into the Cretaceous period and became
very large: these included *Edmontonia* (see page
324). The ankylosaurids began to spread during
the Early Cretaceous period and overlapped in
range and time with several nodosaurid cousins.
They had complex, folded air passages in their
snouts and heads, and they lacked the sharp
shoulder spines possessed by most nodosaurids.
The ankylosaurids tail-clubbed their way into the
very Late Cretaceous, mainly in North America
and Asia. They also reached considerable sizes,
some being even larger than the nodosaurids.
Some classification schemes recognize additional
subgroups, such as the polacanthids, based on
Polacanthus (see page 327).

ARMOR GALORE

Some ankylosaurs had two or three layers of bone
over certain parts of the head – overlapping layers
of the real skull, and an extra layer on top of that.
The bony parts covering their bodies were not, in
general, joined to the skeleton beneath. They were
dermal ossifications – units of bone that grew in,
and were held on very firmly by, their thick, tough,
stiff, leathery skins or hides. Some of these bony
masses were set entirely within the thickness of
the hide, so they were covered by skin too. Others,
especially the sharper spines and spikes, had bony
centers or cores that, in life, were covered with
horn. This made them larger and probably sharper
than they appear in the fossils, since the horn

disintegrated before preservation. It is tempting
to make a comparison between ankylosaurs and
another group of slow, well-protected reptiles, the
tortoises, but the nature of the armor in the two
groups was very different (see page 93).

SLOW AND PONDEROUS

Such substantial protection made ankylosaurs stiff,
heavy, ponderous and slow. Their main defense
against large carnivores, like the tyrannosaurs,
was probably to crouch down, lowering their squat
bodies the short distance to the ground, to protect
their more vulnerable undersides. With weights
of several tons, they would be extremely difficult
for an opponent to topple over. Alternatively,
they may have gone on the attack. Nodosaurids
might have charged and jabbed with their long,
sharp shoulder spines, while ankylosaurids could
have swung around to bring their tail clubs into
the battle as leg-breaking weapons. For most of
the time, however, these dinosaurs roamed woods
and forests, probably on their own rather than in
herds, searching for soft plant food (see pages
322–323).

PREVIOUS PAGE *Gastonia* was an early Cretaceous ankylosaur
whose fossils come from Grand County, Utah. It shows the
heavily armored body and assorted spikes and spines which
gave formidable self-defense. This specimen is a juvenile and
its back would be about chest-high to an adult human.
Gastonia was a cousin of *Polacanthus* and was named in
1998 to honor paleontologist Robert Gaston.

LEFT *Polacanthus* turns to face an enemy, its large neck and
shoulder spines providing excellent defense. However the exact
positions of the spines, and the angles at which they were
attached to the body, are subjects of much discussion.

RIGHT *Scelidosaurus* was probably both bipedal and quadrupedal, moving with ease on two or four legs. Its teeth were most similar to those of stegosaurs. However due to finds in 1980 and especially 1985 this dinosaur has become better understood as probably the first true ankylosaur.

DINO FACTFILE

Scelidosaurus

Meaning: Limb reptile, lower hind-limb reptile

Pronunciation: Skell-eye-doe-sore-uss

Period: Early Jurassic

Main group: Scelidosauria

Length: 3–4 meters (10–13 feet)

Weight: 200– 250 kilograms (440–550 pounds)

Diet: Plants

Fossils: England, Portugal, USA (Arizona)

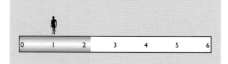

SCELIDOSAURUS

Scelidosaurus may have had a pivotal place in dinosaur evolution; it certainly presents a problem of grouping. It has been classified as an ornithischian, and, within this huge category, as a thyreophoran or "shield-bearer" and probably ankylosaur – but then the disagreements start. Some experts regard it as an early type of ankylosaur (hence its inclusion in this chapter); others regard it as a stegosaur, or as an ancestor of both groups; still others argue that it is a distinct type with its own family, the Scelidosauridae, perhaps along with *Scutellosaurus* (opposite) and *Emausaurus*, named from fossils found in Germany in 1990.

Scelidosaurus had a small head with a horny, beak-like front to its mouth. Its neck, body and tail were studded with small pebble-like scales and larger bony plates, some shaped like low cones or slim triangles. It walked on all four limbs, with the rear ones longer and stronger, so that the back sloped up toward the hips. All these features were developed and exaggerated in the stegosaur group later in the Jurassic period, although *Scelidosaurus* also had distinctive features in its teeth and skull, which link it more to the ankylosaur group.

Richard Owen, the British anatomist and paleontologist who established the whole dinosaur group, Dinosauria, in 1841, named *Scelidosaurus* in 1868. Owen had been examining specimens of *Scelidosaurus* since 1859, mainly from Early Jurassic rocks at Charmouth on the south coast of England. In 1863 a fairly complete skeleton was unearthed. More than a century later, in 1985, also near Charmouth, three amateur fossil-hunters, Simon Barnsley, David Costain and Peter Langham, discovered a specimen, from a juvenile. Between these finds had come remains from Portugal (a piece of skull there is also known as *Lusitanosaurus*) and Arizona. The tail of *Scelidosaurus* was probably quite stiff due to tendons that lay alongside the backbones and became ossified with bony minerals. Current opinion favors *Scelidosaurus* as one of the first true ankylosaurs.

SCUTELLOSAURUS

Scutellosaurus was named in 1981 by Edwin "Ned" Colbert, from the bony plates, called scutes, embedded like small, raised shields in its skin. Its main fossils are two partial skeletons, with pieces of skull, from Arizona, plus many detached scutes. This was a small and early dinosaur, dating to 208–200 million years ago, with a mix of primitive and slightly more advanced features. It was once included in the ornithopod group with *Lesothosaurus* (see page 269), but then considered as an early thyreophoran or "shield-bearer". Like *Scelidosaurus* (opposite), it has been touted as the kind of dinosaur that may have evolved into one of the later, better-known groups of thyreophorans, such as the armored ankylosaurs or the plated stegosaurs; or it could have resembled the common ancestor of both these groups.

Scutellosaurus was small, slim and long, probably weighing not much more than 10 kilograms (22 pounds), despite its light armor of scutes of – triangular wedges, low cones, lopsided limpets and curved "thorns." Hundreds of fossilized scutes have been found, but their exact pattern over the neck, elongated body and even lengthier tail are unknown. The mouth had a narrow, beak-like front and the head was also protected by low, bony plates. *Scutellosaurus* could probably run fairly rapidly on all fours, since its front limbs bear broad and sturdy paws. Perhaps it could rear up to race along on its two larger, longer hind limbs, but the long body and armor probably made it front-heavy. Estimates for the number of individual scutes on one *Scutellosaurus* range from less than 200 to more than 400.

DINO FACTFILE
Scutellosaurus

Meaning: Little-shield reptile

Pronunciation: Skoo-tell-owe-sore-uss

Period: Early Jurassic

Main group: Possibly Scelidosauria

Length: 1.2 meters (4 feet)

Weight: 10 kilograms (22 pounds)

Diet: Plants

Fossils: USA (Arizona)

0	I	2	3	4	5	6

LEFT *Scutellosaurus* had small, simple cheek teeth and probably could only eat soft vegetation. In life the body scutes would have been covered or sheathed with horn and perhaps also leathery skin.

SAUROPELTA

DINO FACTFILE

Sauropelta

Meaning: Shielded reptile, reptile with shield

Pronunciation: Sore-oh-pell-tah

Period: Early Cretaceous

Main group: Ankylosauria

Length: 7–8 meters (23–26 feet)

Weight: 3 metric tons (3 tons)

Diet: Plants

Fossils: USA (Montana, Utah, Wyoming)

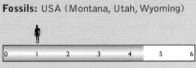

This is one of the earliest nodosaurids (armored dinosaurs without tail clubs) known in North America, where its fossils were found in Montana, Wyoming and Utah. It was named in 1970 by John Ostrom, the paleontologist also associated with *Deinonychus*. The remains are fairly abundant compared to those of other nodosaurids, consisting of parts of several skeletons, isolated skeletal bones, a skull (found in a crushed state) and the usual collection of bony plates and other pieces of "armor." Most of these plates became detached and jumbled up during the preservation process. One specimen in particular, however, now displayed at the American Museum of Natural History, is one of the most complete for any nodosaurid. It shows the layout and pattern of the armor over the body, as well as much of the skeleton, notably the bones of the massive, weight-bearing, pillar-like limbs and the feet, each with four digits.

Sauropelta was an Early Cretaceous nodosaurid, and the plating on its body had not evolved to the degree seen in later types such as *Edmontonia* (see page 324). *Sauropelta* had large spikes on either side of the neck, which continued along the sides of the body but diminished, disappearing toward the tail. The back was covered in scattered bony lumps, which were sheathed in horn in life to form low cone shapes, spaced among hundreds of much smaller bony "pebbles" that formed a semiflexible protective layer of "armor." This arrangement was extended along the upper side of the tail. The undersides of the neck, body and tail, and legs, probably bore reptile scales and thick skin. Another indication that *Sauropelta* was an early nodosaurid is the presence of teeth at the front of the upper jaw, on the premaxillary bone. Later nodosaurids had no front teeth, just horn-covered "beaks."

RIGHT The arrangement of the protective scales and nodules of *Sauropelta* is well known from an exceptionally well-preserved specimen. Another find shows the tail in detail, with its rate of taper and the lack of a bony club at the end.

NODOSAURUS

This dinosaur has given its name to the family Nodosauridae, one of the main groups of the armored dinosaurs known as ankylosaurs (see page 317) – those without a "hammer" or "club" at the end of the tail. *Nodosaurus*'s fossils are scarce and fragmentary. Remains of *Nodosaurus* are known from Early and mid-Cretaceous rocks, about 110–100 million years old, in Wyoming and Kansas. There are only the partial remains of three skeletons, without their skulls, plus various bony slabs and plates that formed the "armor." These remains were found early enough in the scientific history of dinosaurs to become the basis for establishing a family. This was in 1889, when Othniel Charles Marsh, a prolific American dinosaur-hunter, named the heavily-built armored beast. It was not until 1921, however, that a detailed description of

Nodosaurus was produced by Richard Swann Lull, just a year before he took charge of the Peabody Museum at Yale.

The length of *Nodosaurus* is estimated at between 4 and 6 meters (13 and 19½ feet). It may have had spikes as well as plates in its armor, but this is not clear. The tail was long and narrow, and its short, pillar-like legs – with five digits on each foot – were designed to carry its heavily protected body. The neck was short and powerful, and extending the evidence from other members of its family, such as *Edmontonia* and *Panoplosaurus*, the head was heavily protected with plates of bone over the narrow-snouted mouth. The mouth probably had a beak-like front, and contained leaf-like cheek teeth with vertical ridges for chopping plant food. However most of this is supposition and *Nodosaurus* remains poorly known.

DINO FACTFILE
Nodosaurus

Meaning: Nodular reptile, reptile with knobs or lumps

Pronunciation: Node-oh-sore-uss

Period: Early to mid-Cretaceous

Main group: Ankylosauria

Length: 4–6 meters (13–19½ feet)

Weight: 2–3 metric tons (2–3 tons)

Diet: Plants

Fossils: USA (Wyoming, Kansas)

BELOW The armor of *Nodosaurus* was probably arranged in rows or bands, from the back down each side of the body. It's likely that the underside was not so heavily protected, although the hide and smaller reptiles scales there would still have been very tough.

LONELY LIFESTYLE

IN GENERAL, THE REMAINS OF ARMORED
DINOSAURS OCCUR AS SINGLE INDIVIDUALS,
RATHER THAN AS GATHERINGS IN GROUPS OR
HERDS. PERHAPS EACH ONE LIVED MORE OR
LESS ALONE, PLUCKING VEGETATION WITH ITS
TOOTHLESS BEAK AND CHOPPING IT SLOWLY
WITH ITS RELATIVELY TINY, RIDGED CHEEK
TEETH, BEFORE SWALLOWING. ONE TYPE OF
HULKING, WELL-PROTECTED HERBIVORE FOLLOWS
A SIMILAR LONESOME PATTERN OF BEHAVIOR
TODAY – THE RHINOCEROS. ALSO, ARMORED
DINOSAUR FOSSILS ARE NOT ESPECIALLY COMMON
OVERALL, PARTICULARLY WHEN COMPARED TO
THE HUGE "BONE BED" FOSSIL ACCUMULATIONS
OF DINOSAURS SUCH AS HADROSAURS. SO
PERHAPS, WHEN THEY WERE AROUND, THEY
WERE NATURALLY SCARCE.

RIGHT This Late Cretaceous scene contrasts a solitary
ankylosaur with the much more numerous, herd-dwelling
and probably social hadrosaurs or duckbill dinosaurs. On the
African savanna today, similar contrasts could be made among
mammalian herbivores, between herds of zebra and wildebeest,
and the mainly solitary and much more scarce rhinos.

HYLAEOSAURUS

DINO FACTFILE

Hylaeosaurus

Meaning: Woodland or forest reptile,
Wealden reptile

Pronunciation: High-lay-oh-sore-uss

Period: Early Cretaceous

Main group: Ankylosauria

Length: 4–6 meters (13–19½ feet)

Weight: 2–3 metric tons (2–3 tons)

Diet: Plants

Fossils: Southern England

This armored plant-eater has a special place in the scientific history of dinosaurs. It was one of the three "founding members" of the group when Richard Owen coined the name Dinosauria in 1841. *Hylaeosaurus* had itself been named earlier, in 1833, by Gideon Mantell, who also described another original member, *Iguanodon*, before that (see page 261). *Hylaeosaurus* is known mainly from one specimen, a frontal part-skeleton that is still unprepared today – that is, it is still embedded in its rock or matrix, as are most fossils when they are found in the ground. It was recovered from the Tilgate Forest, in Sussex in southern England, and it may have been this site that gave rise to the name which means "woodland reptile" or "forest reptile." A few years earlier, however, another British geologist, Peter Martin, had coined the term "Wealden" for the rocks and clays of the Weald (itself an old word for "woodland"), a geological region covering parts of the counties of Sussex and Kent, and including the discovery site. Mantell and others later translated the dinosaur name to mean "Wealden reptile." Either version is acceptable.

Due to their partial and still partly enclosed state, the main fossils of *Hylaeosaurus* are difficult to reconstruct into a complete animal. Usually its bodily features are borrowed from similar nodosaurids, especially *Polacanthus* (see page 327). It has been suggested that these two are really the same type of dinosaur. *Hylaeosaurus* is certainly an early nodosaurid of the Early Cretaceous period. It was of medium size, up to about 5 meters (16½ feet) in length, and there seem to be several, large, curved ovals or "bands" of bone, perhaps reminiscent of an armadillo, arching over its back. The rest of the beast, including the arrangement of any spikes or spines, remains largely conjectural.

EDMONTONIA

DINO FACTFILE

Edmontonia

Meaning: Of Edmonton (from discovery site)

Pronunciation: Ed-mon-tone-ee-ah

Period: Late Cretaceous

Main group: Ankylosauria

Length: 6–7 meters (19½–23 feet)

Weight: 4 metric tons (4 tons)

Diet: Plants

Fossils: Canada (Alberta), USA (Montana,
South Dakota, Texas)

The great thickness and supportive strength of *Edmontonia*'s four legs – even sturdier than those of today's elephant, with massive, spreading feet and four splayed digits tipped with hoof-like nails – show that this ankylosaur was indeed a heavy creature. It was one of the biggest and the last of the nodosaurids (armored dinosaurs lacking bony tail clubs), living about 75–70 million years ago in western North America. Its first remains were excavated in 1924 by George Paterson from the Red Deer River near Morrin, in the Canadian province of Alberta. The rock layers in this region are known as the Edmonton formation, so the dinosaur was named *Edmontonia* in 1928 by Charles M. Sternberg. Later finds have come from American states including Montana, South Dakota and Texas. They add up to about four specimens, including most of the skull and skeleton, and plenty of "armor." A similar dinosaur, named *Denversaurus* in 1988, may be another specimen of *Edmontonia* but the fossil evidence is not complete enough to make a firm judgment.

Edmontonia had a comparatively long, low, wide, flat-topped head. The front of the mouth was beak-like. The small, weak teeth were set inward, with jawbones curved away from the outer edge of the skull. This suggests that the spaces on the outer sides of the jaws and teeth were occupied by cheek pouches, which retained food as *Edmontonia* chewed at length. There were large, sharp, fearsome-looking spikes on the shoulders that probably pointed forward, and could have caused terrible wounds if jabbed into an enemy as *Edmontonia* charged, then swerved and dipped its shoulder before impact. Other reconstructions show the frontal shoulder spikes facing forward to just behind the eye, and those behind sticking out sideways. More ridged, thorn-like bony spines covered the back and continued, diminishing in size, along the upper surface of the long, narrow tail.

ABOVE This front view shows the massive bulk, thick armor plating and fearsome shoulder spines of *Edmontonia*.

MINMI

DINO FACTFILE

Minmi

Meaning: Minmi (from its discovery site)

Pronunciation: Min-mee

Period: Early Cretaceous

Main group: Ankylosauria

Length: 3 meters (10 feet)

Weight: 300–500 kilograms
(660–1100 pounds)

Diet: Plants

Fossils: Australia (Queensland)

This dinosaur's name, given in 1980 by Ralph Molnar, may seem to reflect its size: at just 3 meters (10 feet) in total length, it was one of the smallest of the ankylosaurs (armored dinosaurs). In fact, the name has nothing to do with "minimum," but comes from the discovery site of Minmi Crossing, near Roma, in the southeast of the Australian state of Queensland. The remains, chiefly two partial skeletons, are dated to about 120–110 million years ago. One of the specimens was discovered in 1964 by Ian Ievers.

Minmi had a long, low head with a beak-like snout and small, leaf-like chewing cheek teeth. The short neck widened to a hump-backed body, with the front legs slightly shorter than the rear pair. Spiky plates, or scutes, protected the shoulders, with lower bony lumps scattered over the main body and taller, sharper, thorn-like spikes on the hips

and in two rows along the upper tail. In addition, *Minmi* had small bony plates, hardly as big as shirt buttons, on its underside. Also, beside each vertebra of the backbone was a small plate, called a paravertebra, about the size of a human thumb, with a bony prong or rod projecting from it, which may have helped to strengthen the whole backbone. The tail was wide-based, thick and heavy. At first it was thought to possess a "hammer" or "club" at the tip, which would place *Minmi* in the subgroup Ankylosauridae (see page 305). However, this may be a misleading feature formed independently during fossilization, and so *Minmi* has been included among the Nodosauridae (armored dinosaurs lacking tail clubs). A third and more recent opinion is that this far Southern Hemisphere dinosaur was an ankylosaurid after all, but an early type that had not yet evolved a tail club.

LEFT Fossil evidence suggests that *Minmi* lived in open woodlands, but after death, the carcass was washed out to sea, since the rocks entombing its remains were originally marine sediments.

POLACANTHUS

"Many spikes" complements *Hylaeosaurus* (see page 324) in several ways. It lived at about the same time, the Early Cretaceous period, some 130–120 million years ago, and in the same general region, what is now southern England. The main fossil specimens of *Polacanthus* make up the back part of the animal, while *Hylaeosaurus* is known mainly from its front end. There have been suggestions that these are really the same kind or genus of dinosaur, but the evidence either way is inconclusive. *Polacanthus*, like *Hylaeosaurus*, is usually regarded as an early example of a nodosaurid (an armored dinosaur without a tail club), but a recent report suggests that it may belong to the other subgroup of ankylosaurs, known as the ankylosaurids, which did have tail clubs. The long spines of *Polacanthus* may have been along the neck

and flanks, with the more curved "shark's fin" projections along the upper tail. It was a low-slung, heavy dinosaur, probably with a beak-like mouth for cropping plant food.

William Fox discovered the first fossils of *Polacanthus* in 1865. They were being eroded from a cliff on the Isle of Wight, the island off the southern coast of England that has produced many dinosaur remains over the years. There were parts of the hips, rear legs, vertebrae (backbones) from the back and tail, and assorted spines and "plates" of armor. It is possible that the front part of the skeleton and even the skull had been preserved for more than 120 million years, but lost before the discovery because of cliff falls or the erosive effects of wind, waves and rain. Richard Owen named the dinosaur in 1867. Since then, further partial fossils have been found.

DINO FACTFILE
Polacanthus
Meaning: Many spikes or spines
Pronunciation: Pole-ah-can-thuss
Period: Early Cretaceous
Main group: Ankylosauria
Length: 4–5 meters (13–16½ feet)
Weight: 1–2 metric tons (1–2 tons)
Diet: Plants
Fossils: Southern England, elsewhere in Europe

| 0 | 1 | 2 | 3 | 4 | 5 | 6 |

RIGHT The head of *Polacanthus* is mostly guesswork, and recent studies of the fossils suggest that this armored dinosaur may have had a tail club.

PANOPLOSAURUS

DINO FACTFILE

Panoplosaurus

Meaning: Totally armored reptile,
all-armor reptile

Pronunciation: Pan-oh-ploh-sore-uss

Period: Late Cretaceous

Main group: Ankylosauria

Length: 7 meters (23 feet)

Weight: 3–4 metric tons (3–4 tons)

Diet: Plants

Fossils: Canada (Alberta), USA (Montana)

One fossilized skull of *Panoplosaurus* is an especially fine specimen, and it is often used as a model to fill in for other nodosaurids for which skulls have been only partially preserved or not preserved at all. Such extrapolation is part of the science and art of paleontology. In this case, justification comes from the evidence that most of the partial skulls of other nodosaurids resemble that of *Panoplosaurus* in many details. *Panoplosaurus* shows the small, simple chewing teeth set into jaws that curve toward the midline, allowing plenty of room for fleshy cheek pouches. The rear skull is wide but the snout is fairly long and narrow, the "beak" at the front is toothless in both upper and lower jaws, and there are no horn-like or spiky projections from the rear sides of the skull bone – all typical nodosaurid features. But

there are thick, extra plates of bony "armor" covering most of the actual skull.

Fossils of this armored dinosaur were discovered in 1917 in the Judith River rocks of Alberta, Canada. The dinosaur was named in 1919 by Lawrence Lambe, a Canadian dinosaur expert who gave names to some nine other important dinosaurs during the same decade of the 1910s. *Panoplosaurus* seems to have been typically low, heavy and stumpy-legged, around 7 meters (23 feet) long and 3-plus metric tons (3 tons) in weight, and lived near the end of the Cretaceous period, 75–70 million years ago. Its fossils have also been identified in the neighboring American state of Montana. A dinosaur named *Palaeoscincus* in 1856 on the evidence of one tooth from Montana may be *Panoplosaurus* or *Edmontonia*.

RIGHT *Panoplosaurus* has provided a fine fossil skull that is used as a model for the heads of ankylosaurs. This reconstruction shows the shoulder spikes facing to the side, but the ones nearer the neck may have pointed forward.

RIGHT *Shamosaurus* squats down in self defense and switches its tail from side to side, a sequence of behavior showing it might bring this formidable weapon into play if attacked.

SHAMOSAURUS

Shamosaurus is one of the first known ankylosaurids (armored dinosaurs with tail "clubs") in Asia. It is regarded as the earliest known member of this group, possessing some features of its ancestors but lacking those features that appear in later types such as *Euoplocephalus*. The name *Shamosaurus*, given by Tatyana Tumanova in 1983, reflects the discovery site and means "desert reptile" or an adapted version of "Gobi reptile." Three sets of fossils are known from the Dornogov and nearby regions of Mongolia. One set has an almost complete head with skull and jaw; the others are part of a skeleton and detached pieces of armor-plating. The species is named from these protective bony plates, or scutes, as *Shamosaurus scutatus*.

The skull shows that *Shamosaurus* had a beak-like front to the mouth, but this was narrow from side to side. Also, the beak was not heavily protected by the plates of bone

in the skin, called dermal ossifications, that appear in later ankylosaurids. The length of the whole dinosaur is estimated at about 7 meters (23 feet), which groups it with the much later *Euoplocephalus* of North America as one of the larger of the ankylosaurids, though perhaps not as big as *Ankylosaurus* itself (see page 332). In diet and behavior it probably resembled other ankylosaurs: it was most likely a slow-moving herbivore, cropping low-growing vegetation, living alone or in a small group, and relying on its spikes and armor to protect it against the big meat-eaters of the time. The fossils of *Shamosaurus* are dated to the Aptian-Albian part of the Cretaceous period (two of the subdivisions of this time span), about 120-90 million years ago. Several other isolated fossils consist of isolated bits of ankylosaur body armor, but without further evidence it is not possible to link these to *Shamosaurus*.

DINO FACTFILE
Shamosaurus
Meaning: Gobi reptile, desert reptile
Pronunciation: Sham-oh-sore-uss
Period: Early Cretaceous
Main group: Ankylosauria
Length: 7 meters (23 feet)
Weight: 2–3 metric tons (2–3 tons)
Diet: Plants
Fossils: Mongolia

THE TAIL CLUB

THE ANKYLOSAURID TAIL CLUB WAS A FORMIDABLE
WEAPON INDEED. IT WAS SWUNG ON THE END OF
A TAIL THAT WAS STIFF TOWARD THE TIP, WITH
THE MAIN MUSCULATURE AND FLEXIBILITY NEARER
THE BASE (THE HIP END). EACH LUMP OF BONE
ON EITHER SIDE OF THE TAIL WAS AS LARGE AS
A BASKETBALL, AND THE WHOLE HAMMER-LIKE
STRUCTURE COULD EASILY CRACK THE FOOT OR
LEG OF AN ATTACKER SUCH AS TYRANNOSAURUS.

RIGHT A tyrannosaur-type theropod is on the receiving end of
a counterattack by the ankylosaurid *Pinacosaurus*. The meat-
eater was probably more than 10 meters (33 feet) long and
weighed as much as the armored herbivore, but a quick tail-
flick from the latter could mean a broken leg or foot – followed,
in the harsh natural world, by infection and/or starvation.

ANKYLOSAURUS

DINO FACTFILE

Ankylosaurus

Meaning: Fused reptile, joined reptile, stiff reptile

Pronunciation: Ann-kye-low-sore-uss

Period: Late Cretaceous

Main group: Ankylosauria

Length: 7–10 meters (23–33 feet)

Weight: 3–4 metric tons (3–4 tons)

Diet: Plants

Fossils: USA (Montana), Canada (Alberta)

The large group of armored dinosaurs are known by the general name ankylosaurs, after one of its biggest types of dinosaur. Within this main grouping is the subgroup known as ankylosaurids, which have several distinctive features, including the shape and structure of the skull, the twisted pathways of the air passages inside the skull, and the large club- or hammer-like end to the tail.

Although *Ankylosaurus* was used to establish the group, its fossils are less complete than those of similar types in the group, such as *Euoplocephalus*.

Ankylosaurus owes its name to Barnum Brown, an American paleontologist who in 1908 noted the stiff or fused nature of the backbone. Remains have been found in Montana and Alberta, and include two skulls; parts of the front limb; various vertebrae (backbones) from the neck, main body and tail; strongly curved ribs; osteoderms (bony plates from the skin); isolated teeth and of course the famous tail club.

Ankylosaurus was one of the last ankylosaurs, and one of the last of all dinosaurs, living less than 70 million years ago. It was not only long, it was also wide, at almost 2 meters (6¹/₂ feet), and very low-slung, probably standing no taller than 1.2 meters (4 feet). Its great weight was carried on four short, stumpy legs, with the rear pair being slightly longer. The neck was short and powerful, to support the wide, heavy head, and the tail was long but narrow. The bony armor of plates in the skin, two series of spikes along the body, larger horn-like spikes on the neck and hammer-like tail club were presumably used for self-defense. (Possible uses of the tail club, and the behavior patterns of ankylosaurs, are discussed over the following pages.) In North America less than 70 million years ago there was great need for some kind of self defense for a large slow herbivore, since large predators such as *Albertosaurus* and the great *Tyrannosaurus* would be on the prowl. It's thought that even the eyelids of *Ankylosaurus* were protected.

RIGHT *Euoplocephalus* may have carried its heavy tail club off the ground to minimize wear and being pulled back by dragging friction.

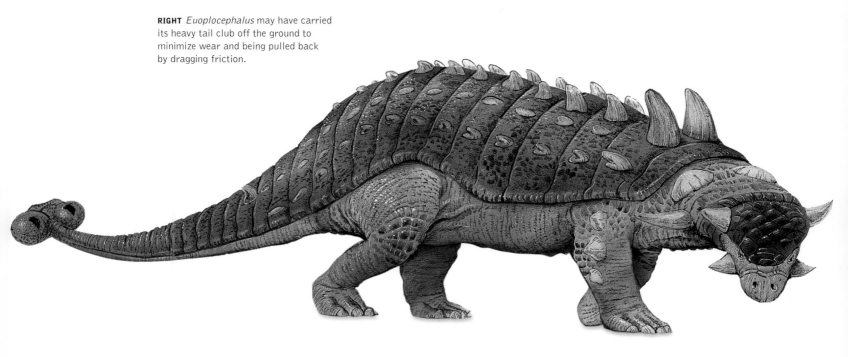

EUOPLOCEPHALUS

The fossils of *Euoplocephalus*, which are unusually plentiful for an armored dinosaur, suggest that it was one of the more common members of this group during Late Cretaceous times in North America, around 70 million years ago. It was so well-protected that even its eyelids had bony reinforcements, and flipped up and down like shutters. Bone-thickened scales were stuck over the skull, and small "horns" rose from the rear of the skull – one of the features that distinguishes ankylosaurids from nodosaurids. There were low bony lumps over the neck, higher ones across the shoulders, and more lumps along the body, set in crosswise bands arching from side to side over the back. The legs were sturdy and well muscled, and each foot had three short, wide digits tipped with hoof-like nails. *Euoplocephalus* cropped food with its broad beak, but like other armored dinosaurs, it had peg-shaped teeth that seem undersized

and insubstantial, so most mashing and digestion probably occurred inside the gut. The end of this dinosaur's tail had two huge lumps of bone, one on each side, with a pair of smaller bony bulges behind. The main length of the tail was stiff, so it must have been swung at the base, perhaps to be smashed into the legs of enemies such as tyrannosaurs.

Fossils of more than 40 specimens of *Euoplocephalus*, including some 15 skulls – more than for any other ankylosaur – have been found in Alberta, Canada, and in Montana, USA. Lawrence Lambe named the dinosaur in 1910. Since then, *Scolosaurus* and *Dyoplosaurus* and several other poorly known ankylosaurids have been reclassified as *Euoplocephalus*, following further studies showing they did not warrant separate genus status. Currently there is only one accepted species within the genus, *Euoplocephalus tutus*, as originally named.

DINO FACTFILE
Euoplocephalus
Meaning: Well-armored head
Pronunciation: You-oh-ploe-seff-ah-luss
Period: Late Cretaceous
Main group: Ankylosauria
Length: 6–7 meters (19½–23 feet)
Weight: 2 metric tons (2 tons)
Diet: Plants
Fossils: Canada (Alberta), USA (Montana)

PINACOSAURUS

DINO FACTFILE

Pinacosaurus

Meaning: Plank reptile

Pronunciation: Pin-ah-coe-sore-uss

Period: Late Cretaceous

Main group: Ankylosauria

Length: 5.5 meters (18 feet)

Weight: 1–2 metric tons (1–2 tons)

Diet: Plants

Fossils: Mongolia, China

Fossils of this ankylosaurid (armored dinosaur with a lumpy "club" at the end of the tail) have been found at several sites in China and Mongolia. There are remains of many individuals, of various ages and sizes. Since 1988, two sets of fossils representing many *Pinacosaurus* have been uncovered in "bone beds." One group numbers around 12, while the other contains more than 20 individuals, mostly juveniles, preserved together. The scientific history of *Pinacosaurus* stretches back to the 1920s, however, when remains were first excavated by American-led expeditions to the Gobi headed by Roy Chapman Andrews, the legendary fossil-hunter who became director of the American Museum of Natural History. These expeditions recovered many other dinosaurs, such as *Protoceratops* and *Oviraptor* with eggs, and the meat-eater

Velociraptor. Pinacosaurus was named in 1933 by Charles Whitney Gilmore. The dinosaur once known as *Syrmosaurus* is now considered to be the same as *Pinacosaurus*.

Pinacosaurus was armored, but perhaps not quite so heavily as other ankylosaurs. There were bony spikes along the back and club-ended tail, but no armor on the front end of the head. The main skeleton is sturdy but not particularly massive, with slim legs compared to those of other armored dinosaurs. There were five digits on each front foot and four on each rear foot, each tipped by a blunt claw that resembled a hoof or nail. The finding of the mass "grave" of mostly young *Pinacosaurus* has led some experts to suggest that ankylosaurs may have associated in groups when young, but then split up and led solitary lives when adult (see page 322).

BELOW *Pinacosaurus* was relatively slim and long-legged for an ankylosaur, and also one of the smaller types (apart from *Minmi*). In life it was about as large as a medium-sized rhinoceros, but with its main weapon at the rear rather than front end.

SAICHANIA

Saichania had a wide, blunt head, bony plates over the snout and forehead, horns rising from each rear upper corner of the head, and more cone-shaped low spikes over the neck, and along the sides and back of the body. Perhaps it is not easy to see why it has a name that means "beautiful one" in Mongolian, but some of its fossils are beautifully preserved, and some of the details offer intriguing insights into the general structure of ankylosaurids. Ankylosaurids differ from their nodosaurid cousins (which lacked tail-clubs) in several respects, one being the twisted or convoluted structure of the breathing passages inside the skull. In *Saichania* these follow an even more complex route, leading to suggestions that they were capable of humidifying and cooling the hot, dry external air before it reached the lungs, or that the breathing passages were associated with an unusual sense of smell or glands that got rid of excess salt from the body,

as in some reptiles and birds today. *Saichania* may have been unusual among ankylosaurs in that its underside or belly was also armored with bony plates (see also *Minmi*, page 326). Its total length was 7 meters (23 feet), which is average for the group.

One main specimen of *Saichania*, from Khulsan (Chulsan), consists of the head and front part of the body in what is called "natural articulation" – that is, with the parts still situated next to each other as in life, rather than separated and jumbled, as are so many dinosaur remains. It was excavated by members of a joint Polish-Mongolian expedition into the Gobi in 1971, and named in 1977 by Teresa Maryanska. The specimens include two relatively complete skulls and many pieces of detached "armor." (Ankylosaurid behavior and the nature and uses of tail clubs are discussed on various pages in this chapter.)

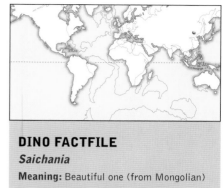

DINO FACTFILE
Saichania
Meaning: Beautiful one (from Mongolian)
Pronunciation: Sye-kahn-ee-ah
Period: Late Cretaceous
Main group: Ankylosauria
Length: 7 meters (23 feet)
Weight: 2–3 metric tons (2–3 tons)
Diet: Plants
Fossils: Mongolia

0	1	2	3	4	5	6

LEFT "Beautiful" it may not be, but the well-preserved and detailed fossils of *Saichania* help to throw light on the nature of its fellow ankylosaurids. Its skull measures about 45 centimeters (18 inches) in length, but its width is greater, at 48 centimeters (almost 20 inches).

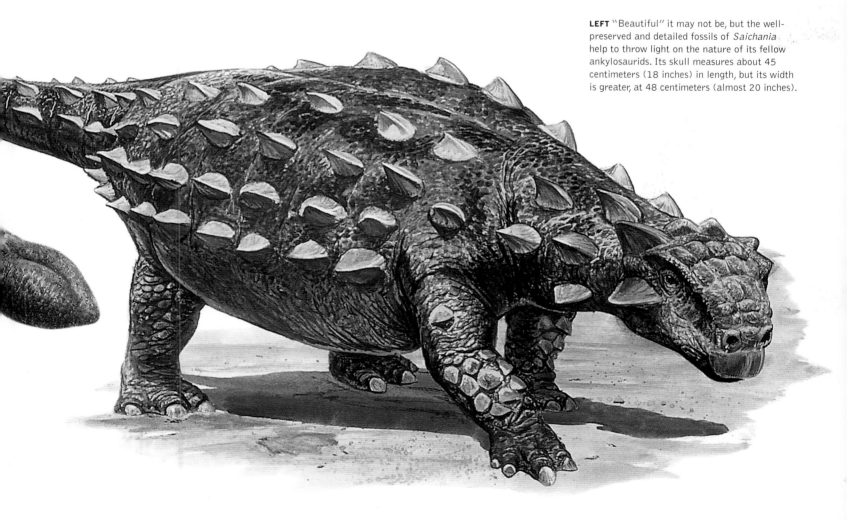

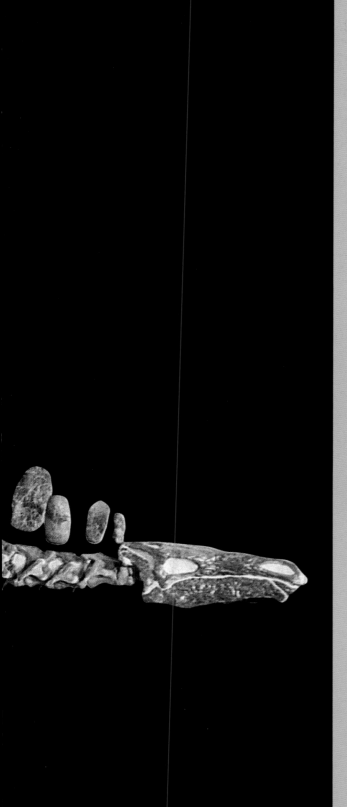

CHAPTER TWELVE

PLATED DINOSAURS

STEGOSAURS ARE FAMOUS FOR THEIR TINY BRAINS AND SUPPOSED
STUPIDITY, YET THEY WERE SUCCESSFUL FOR TENS OF MILLIONS OF YEARS.

PLETHORA OF PLATES

THE TALL PLATES OF BONE ON THE BACKS OF STEGOSAURS HAVE LONG BEEN A PUZZLE TO PALEONTOLOGISTS. *STEGOSAURUS* ITSELF HAD THE HIGHEST AND WIDEST PLATES, EACH ONE THINNER THAN A HUMAN ARM. THEY WERE PROBABLY ARRANGED VERTICALLY IN TWO ROWS, STAGGERED OR OFFSET SO THAT A PLATE ON ONE SIDE OVERLAPPED TWO IN THE ADJACENT ROW. THE PLATES WERE LARGER FROM THE NECK TO THE HIPS, THEN SMALLER AGAIN DOWN TO THE TAIL-TIP. AT LEAST, THIS IS THE PATTERN SHOWN IN MOST RECONSTRUCTIONS. BUT, DESPITE RECENT AND EXCITING FINDS (SEE "SPIKE," PAGE 340) NOT ALL EXPERTS AGREE. THE ARGUMENTS ABOUT PLATE POSITION AND FUNCTION CONTINUE TODAY AS THEY HAVE SINCE THE 1870s.

PLATED PROTECTION

Did the stegosaurs' plates give them physical protection? This is unlikely, since they were not solid but honeycombed with cavities and relatively fragile. Also, they probably stood vertically rather than lying flat to cover the body. Were they principally for camouflage among the trees and general surroundings? Again, this seems unlikely – it seems odd for so large structures to have evolved if their main function is to help an animal become inconspicuous. Camouflage, however, might have been a secondary consideration. Were the plates used for some kind of visual display? They might have been brightly colored and patterned, perhaps differently in males and in females, and in juveniles compared to mature adults, and even in different species that otherwise resembled each other closely in size and form. The colors of certain lizards and other reptiles today change as they grow and mature, and depending on their sex and breeding condition.

TEMPERATURE

The widely accepted theory for how *Stegosaurus* used its plates concerns body temperature control. Stegosaurs and most other dinosaurs were probably "cold-blooded," or, to use a more precise term, ectothermic. They absorbed heat from their surroundings, rather than generating it inside their bodies as "warm-blooded" or endothermic creatures, principally birds and mammals, do today. Warmth was important because as a reptile's body temperature rises, then up to a point the animal can move about faster, feed more efficiently and escape from danger more rapidly. The plates of *Stegosaurus* may have worked as two-way heat-exchangers, in a similar way to the "sails" on the backs of dinosaurs such as *Spinosaurus* and *Ouranosaurus*, and on other reptiles such as *Dimetrodon* (all shown in this book).

WARM AND COOL

At sunrise, after the cool night, *Stegosaurus* may have stood at a right angle to the sun, so that the back plates would receive maximum exposure to the warming rays, heating the blood flowing through their honeycomb cavities and back into the body. In this way, the dinosaur would have warmed up more quickly than it could have without its plates. The staggered arrangement of plates seems to fit this idea, since the gap between two plates in one row would have allowed solar heating to the plate between them in the other row. If *Stegosaurus* became too hot, on the other hand, it might have stood in the shade at a right angle to the breeze, which would carry away body warmth for a maximum cooling effect. The temperature regulation idea of dual heating-cooling functions seems to fit *Stegosaurus*, with its broad, leaf-shaped plates. But, it is much less convincing for other stegosaurs, whose more pointed, spike-like plates had much smaller surface areas (see pages 341 and 346).

PREVIOUS PAGE This reconstructed stegosaurid skeleton shows the tiny size of the skull and how the plates were arranged along the back but not joined to any of the other skeletal bones.

LEFT A stegosaur swishes its spiked tail at an approaching *Allosaurus*-type predator. The back plates of the plant-eater were probably not for protection – in fact, with their lightweight construction, they would be vulnerable to attack.

STEGOSAURUS

DINO FACTFILE

Stegosaurus

Meaning: Roof reptile, tile reptile

Pronunciation: Steg-owe-sore-uss

Period: Late Jurassic

Main group: Stegosauridae

Length: 8–9 meters (26–29½ feet)

Weight: 2–3 metric tons (2–3 tons)

Diet: Plants

Fossils: USA (Colorado)

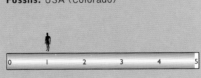

Stegosaurus has given its name to a distinctive and recognizable major group of dinosaurs with tall plates or spines on their backs. These creatures have also become famous as the "dumbest" dinosaurs, because of the relatively small size of their brains. Such topics are discussed throughout this chapter. *Stegosaurus* was named by Othniel Charles Marsh in 1877, and fossil remains have since been reported from sites in several western states in the USA with close cousins from numerous other sites around the globe. In 1992 a well-preserved and almost complete *Stegosaurus* skeleton, later named "Spike," was discovered near Canyon City, Colorado (in the same state as the very first discovery), showing in more detail the pattern of the 17 plates on its back.

Stegosaurus was the largest known member of the group, being 9 meters (29½ feet) long – equal to today's elephant with its trunk and tail stretched out lengthwise. But, *Stegosaurus* was perhaps slightly lighter than a modern elephant, and had four long tail spikes.

Stegosaurus lived during the main time-span of its group, the Late Jurassic period, 150–144 million years ago. Its back plates were huge in area: thin triangles more than 75 centimeters (30 inches) at their peaks, jutting up from the back. In the early reconstructions of this dinosaur, the plates were pictured lying flat on the back, like tiles on a roof (hence the group name). Later versions showed the plates projecting from the back in two rows, each pair of plates side by side. More recent reconstructions have the two rows of plates staggered, with one side half a plate in front of the other. At least ten functions have been suggested for the uses of these plates but the front-runner is body temperature control (see page 339).

LEFT Most modern reconstructions show the back plates in two upright rows, one slightly behind the other. The tail spikes would pose a formidable defensive weapon.

LEFT The tallest spike-like plates on the back of *Kentrosaurus* were 60 centimeters (24 inches) in height. The very large, powerful rear legs of stegosaurs suggest they may have reared up to reach higher-growing plant food.

KENTROSAURUS

Kentrosaurus is often regarded as the African equivalent of North America's *Stegosaurus*, from the same period, the Late Jurassic, around 155–144 million years ago. But, in some respects it is more similar to *Tuojiangosaurus* from East Asia (as shown on page 343). Most *Kentrosaurus* fossils were recovered from the large German-supervised expeditions to the quarries and hills of Tendaguru in the Mtwara region of what was then, in 1908–12, German East Africa (later Tanganyika, now the larger portion of Tanzania). These arduous trips yielded many tremendous discoveries – see, for example, *Brachiosaurus* (page 232). *Kentrosaurus* was named by Edwin Hennig, a German paleontologist, in 1915. Many fossils of *Kentrosaurus* stored in the Humboldt Museum in Berlin might have provided valuable extra knowledge, but some of these were sadly destroyed during bombing raids in World War II. Fortunately, however, other

Kentrosaurus fossils survived and are still located at the Museum.

Kentrosaurus had the typical stegosaurid body shape, with a tiny head containing a minuscule brain, front limbs shorter than its rear limbs, an arching back that curved steeply up and then slightly down to the long rear limbs, and a tapering tail longer than the length of the rest of the creature. The front of the head had a toothless beak for snipping off plants, and the teeth were shaped like their probable food – leaves – but were very small and had vertical ridges. The back plates of *Kentrosaurus* were much narrower than those of *Stegosaurus*, and became progressively more so from the neck along the back, changing shape around halfway along the body to become much narrower spikes, which then continued to the end of the tail. It is difficult to propose that such thin, pointed structures helped with the process of thermoregulation.

DINO FACTFILE
Kentrosaurus

Meaning: Spiked reptile, pointed reptile

Pronunciation: Ken-troe-sore-uss

Period: Late Jurassic

Main group: Stegosauridae

Length: 5 meters (16½ feet)

Weight: 2 metric tons (2 tons)

Diet: Plants

Fossils: Africa (Tanzania)

WUERHOSAURUS

DINO FACTFILE

Wuerhosaurus

Meaning: Wuerho reptile

Pronunciation: Woo-air-hoe-sore-uss

Period: Early Cretaceous

Main group: Stegosauridae

Length: 8 meters (26 feet)

Weight: 2 metric tons (2 tons)

Diet: Plants

Fossils: China, Mongolia

While the heyday of the stegosaurids was the Late Jurassic period, around 160–144 million years ago, some members of the group have been dated to after this time. *Wuerhosaurus* was one of these, for its fossils were found in Early Cretaceous rocks, around 140–130 million years old. It was almost as large as *Stegosaurus*, but it came from a different region, East Asia rather than North America. The two regions were connected by land bridges at various periods (see page 26). The main remains of *Wuerhosaurus*, probably of several individuals but sparse in nature, are known from the Wuerho region of China, and the name was provided in 1973 by Dong Zhiming, a leading Chinese fossil expert.

The back plates of *Wuerhosaurus* were probably lower and less pointed or pentagonal than those of *Stegosaurus*. Also, the main body may have been shorter. The great contrast between the front and rear legs was similar, so that the hips were twice as high as the shoulders. This allowed the head to touch the ground easily and naturally, with very little effort compared to other herbivorous dinosaurs, which had to stoop down actively, using their muscle power and balance, to feed on low-growing vegetation. Alternative theories propose that the huge, wide-set hips and back legs allowed *Wuerhosaurus* and other stegosaurids to rear up, lifting the smaller and relatively lighter head and front of the body, perhaps to browse on taller vegetation. The limited flexibility, however, of the various hip, back and neck joints, and the small, weak tooth design do not seem to support this notion.

RIGHT The lower, flatter-topped, almost rectangular back plates of *Wuerhosaurus* are distinctive among the stegosaurs. However as in other members of the group, the plates extend from the neck, enlarge along the body and diminish along the tail. This consistency of design has not clearly been explained.

TUOJIANGOSAURUS

It is probable that the stegosaurid group of dinosaurs first appeared in East Asia, in the Middle Jurassic period (see *Huayangosaurus*, page 347). *Tuojiangosaurus*, from the Late Jurassic, may represent a continuation of this evolutionary path in the same region. It was a sizable stegosaurid, 7 meters (23 feet) in total length, and probably weighed more than 1 metric ton (1 ton). As in many stegosaurids, the large bony plates, which are thought to have projected upward from the neck, back and tail, were embedded in the skin but were not firmly joined to other bones of the skeleton. Remains may yield many such plates, but they have become detached during fossilization, as the skin and flesh rotted, and the fossils became mixed and jumbled. As a result, their original positions, angles and patterns on the body are uncertain.

Tuojiangosaurus has the tiny head, stooped neck, shorter front limbs, arched back and longer rear limbs of other stegosaurids. There were around 15 pairs of back plates. The tail was not quite as lengthy or so substantial as in *Kentrosaurus*, but it was still impressive, with upward projections called neural spines, lower ones known as chevrons, and two pairs of caudal spikes near the tip. Several other stegosaurids also possessed these four tail spikes, so they were presumably an effective feature – probably as weapons for self-defense. The tail was muscular along its length and could be swung with great force. One specimen of *Tuojiangosaurus* was the first nearly complete skeleton of any dinosaur to be discovered in China. It was named in 1977 by Chinese paleontologists, including Zhou Shiwu, Dong Zhiming and Zhang-Yang Li.

DINO FACTFILE
Tuojiangosaurus

Meaning: Tuo River reptile

Pronunciation: Too-oh-jee-ang-oh-sore-uss

Period: Late Jurassic

Main group: Stegosauridae

Length: 7 meters (23 feet)

Weight: 1–2 metric tons (1–2 tons)

Diet: Plants

Fossils: China

ABOVE It is unlikely that *Tuojiangosaurus* could lift its head much higher than shown in this reconstruction.

The spread of the stegosaurs

Plated dinosaurs first crop up as fossils from the Early Jurassic period, in East Asia. Through the period they diversified, spreading to Africa, Europe and North America, enjoying their greatest success at the end of the Jurassic. By the Early Cretaceous they had faded drastically, perhaps in the face of competition from newer large plant-eaters such as the ornithopods. It was thought that a few types survived to the Late Cretaceous period, chiefly *Dravidosaurus*, whose fossils come from India. However the identity of these remains has recently been challenged, partly because they are so isolated in both place and time from other stegosaur remains, as explained later in this chapter.

RIGHT A stegosaur adult and juvenile demonstrate two of the proposed postures for feeding in this type of dinosaur. The youngster is rearing up against the tree trunk to reach its meal, while the grown-up sniffs near the ground for low vegetation.

LEXOVISAURUS

DINO FACTFILE

Lexovisaurus

Meaning: Lexovian reptile, reptile of Lexovix

Pronunciation: Lek-soe-vee-sore-uss

Period: Middle Jurassic

Main group: Stegosauridae

Length: 5 meters (16½ feet)

Weight: 2 metric tons (2 tons)

Diet: Plants

Fossils: England, France

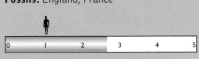

Several stegosaurids are thought to have possessed shoulder spines, jutting out from the upper rear part of the front limb, below the characteristic twin rows of bony plates along the top of the neck and back. Most are also believed to have sported two pairs of long spikes near the end of the tail, although it is not clear whether these were horizontally opposed (sticking out sideways), or angled upward to form two V shapes (see page 339). A European member of the group, *Lexovisaurus*, provides good evidence for the shoulder spines. This dinosaur was one of the smaller stegosaurids, around 5 meters (16½ feet) long, but its shoulder spines may have been 1 meter (39 inches) or more in length – formidable-looking weapons. If the spines really were one on each shoulder, that is perhaps what they were – formidable in visual display, but not so effective if it came to a

physical battle. Other views place these spines on the hips. In other ways, *Lexovisaurus* was fairly typical of the stegosaurid group, although its back plates were tall and narrow, rather than broad and angular.

Fossils of *Lexovisaurus* have been found at several sites in Europe, chiefly in Northamptonshire in England, and also in northwestern France. The dinosaur was named by Robert Hoffstetter in 1957, and recalls the Lexovix people, one of the ancient Gallic groups from the area around what is now the city of Lyons in France. There are parts of perhaps three individuals, as well as isolated bits of bones, plates and spikes, probably representing both adults and juveniles. Fossilized plates once thought to come from *Lexovisaurus* are now believed to be parts of the gills from a large prehistoric fish (see also *Dravidosaurus*, page 348).

RIGHT *Lexovisaurus* probably possessed two long spines positioned on the sides of the body. Some authorities suggest these were on the shoulders and faced sideways. Others propose the spines were more forward-pointing, or perhaps were even on the hips.

RIGHT *Huayangosaurus* is shown here with a long spike on each shoulder, pointing sideways, although this position is not certain. (See *Lexovisaurus*, opposite.) The back plates of this stegosaur are varied in different specimens, some being leaf-shaped or triangular and others more pointed.

HUAYANGOSAURUS

The general name of "stegosaur" usually covers two subgroups, or families. One is the Stegosauridae, which includes *Stegosaurus* itself and the others shown on previous pages. The second and smaller family is the Huayangosauridae, based on *Huayangosaurus*. Compared to stegosaurids, huayangosaurids tend to have lived earlier, around the Middle Jurassic period, and their remains have been found only in East Asia rather than in several regions. It is possible that the huayangosaurids were the ancestors of the later and more widespread stegosaurids. *Huayangosaurus* was named for the fossil discovery site, in 1982, by Dong Zhiming, a pre-eminent Chinese dinosaur specialist, and colleagues.

Huayangosaurus fossils come from rocks known as the Lower Shaximiao Formation in the Sichuan province of southwestern China. They probably date to 170–160 million years ago and include one almost complete skeleton with skull, another skull, and parts of the skeletons of several other individuals. They show a fairly small stegosaur-like dinosaur, around 4 meters (13 feet) in length. There were around nine pairs of tall, leaf-shaped bony plates sticking up from the neck and back along the midline. At the hips, these changed shape to become narrower spikes, which continued along the upper surface of the tail. There were probably two pairs of spikes at the tail end, as in the stegosaurids. In contrast to stegosaurids, however, *Huayangosaurus* had a longer head and snout – not so low or flat; small teeth in the front of the upper jaw, rather than an entirely toothless beak; and relatively long front limbs, although these were still shorter than the rear pair. Like other stegosaurs, *Huayangosaurus* was reputed to have a "second brain" in its hip region, but this was just a widened group of nerves connecting to the rear legs and tail, not a brain at all.

DINO FACTFILE
Huayangosaurus
Meaning: Huayang reptile
Pronunciation: Hoo-ah-yang-oh-sore-uss
Period: Middle Jurassic
Main group: Huayangosauridae
Length: 4–4.5 meters (13–15 feet)
Weight: 400–600 kilograms (1100–1320 pounds)
Diet: Plants
Fossils: China

0	1	2	3	4	5

CRATEROSAURUS AND DRAVIDOSAURUS

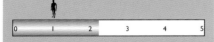

DINO FACTFILE
Craterosaurus

Meaning: Crater or cup (bowl) reptile

Pronunciation: Kray-ter-oh-sore-uss

Period: Early Cretaceous

Main group: Stegosauridae

Length: Estimated 4 meters (13 feet)

Weight: Estimated 500 kilograms
(1100 pounds)

Diet: Plants

Fossils: England

0	1	2	3	4	5

Craterosaurus was possibly a stegosaurid, but it is difficult to tell from its single fossil – one preserved vertebra (backbone) – and even this is not complete. It is probably from the Early Cretaceous period, 140–135 million years ago. At first, this specimen, found in Bedfordshire in southern England, was thought to be from the cranium (braincase) and was named as *Craterosaurus* in 1874 by Harry Seely, who devised the partitioning of the whole dinosaur group into ornithischians or "bird hips" and saurischians or "lizard hips." But the fossil is now thought to be the upper, curved part of the vertebra, known as the neural arch, from a stegosaurid. It has an unusual pitted texture on its upper surface. Most of the rest of the description of *Craterosaurus*, as a stegosaurid around 4 meters (13 feet) long, is informed guesswork based on this one fossil.

Dravidosaurus ("Dravidanadu reptile") was formerly believed to be a stegosaur-type dinosaur from the Indian subcontinent. It was thought to be a late representative of its group, since it lived during the Late Cretaceous period, long after most other stegosaurids had disappeared. It was also held up as an example of how stegosaurids had spread to many regions, since in its time the Indian subcontinent was not joined to southern Asia, but was far to the south, nestling against Antarctica (see map on pages 26–27). More recent studies, however, are possibly changing all this, and *Dravidosaurus* fossils, including the narrow head with the pointed beak-like snout and the assorted bony plates, have been reinterpreted. Some experts now propose that they come not from a stegosaurid, or even from a dinosaur, but from a swimming reptile – a type of plesiosaur (see page 393).

RIGHT *Dravidosaurus* is traditionally reconstructed as a typical stegosaur. However, a reappraisal of its fossils has led some experts to suggest that they do not represent a dinosaur at all, but a type of seagoing reptile called a plesiosaur (see page 393).

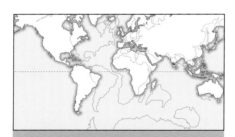

DINO FACTFILE
Dravidosaurus

Meaning: Dravidanadu (place name) reptile

Pronunciation: Drav-id-oh-sore-uss

Period: Late Cretaceous

Main group: Controversial. Stegosauridae
(dinosaur) or Plesiosauridae (plesiosaur)

Length: 3 meters (10 feet)

Weight: 350 kilograms (770 pounds)

Diet: Soft plants

Fossils: Southern India

0	1	2	3	4	5

LEFT Apart from the skull shape, reconstructions of *Paranthodon* are based on relatives such as *Kentrosaurus*. The relevance of this stegosaur is its discovery region, South Africa, and that it is reconstructed from the first dinosaur fossils from that area to be formally studied.

PARANTHODON

The only known fossil of *Paranthodon* is part of a skull with some teeth. It was possibly the first dinosaur fossil to be discovered and studied in South Africa. The remains were found in 1845 by Andrew Bain and William Atherstone between Grahamstown and Port Elizabeth, in the Eastern Cape. Bain was a supervisor for military units constructing roads in the area and developed a great knowledge of minerals, rocks and fossils as part of the then new science of geology. Bain and Atherstone recognized a reptilian likeness and proposed that the original animal was a South African version of *Iguanodon*, which four years earlier had been used by Richard Owen to establish the entire group Dinosauria (see page 261). The fossil was sent to London where Owen examined it and named it *Anthodon*, due to its "flower-shaped teeth," in 1876.

Unfortunately, Owen mistakenly included in the description of *Anthodon* some additional remains – more than 100 million years older –

of another reptile from the Karoo of South Africa. In 1929, Franz Nopsca recognized the mix-up and saw that the original skull and teeth were from a stegosaur-like dinosaur, to which he gave a new name *Paranthodon*. To add to the confusion, the original *Anthodon* fossils were re-examined and recognized as being from a type of reptile called a pareiasaur, and given yet another name, *Palaeoscincus*. These pareiasaur remains had already been named by Owen as *Anthodon*, however, and so it was finally agreed that the pareiasaur would be called *Anthodon* and the dinosaur *Paranthodon*.

Reconstructions of *Paranthodon* are based on *Kentrosaurus*, a stegosaurid whose fossils come from East Africa (see page 341). The teeth of *Paranthodon* and *Kentrosaurus* share several features, and are more similar to each other than either is to other stegosaurids, such as *Stegosaurus* itself. *Paranthodon* thus remains a fascinating and mysterious find.

DINO FACTFILE
Paranthodon

Meaning: Beside, or in addition to, *Anthodon*

Pronunciation: Parr-ann-thoe-don

Period: Early Cretaceous

Main group: Stegosauridae

Length: Estimated 5 meters (16½ feet)

Weight: Estimated 1 metric ton (1 ton)

Diet: Plants

Fossils: South Africa

| 0 | 1 | 2 | 3 | 4 | 5 |

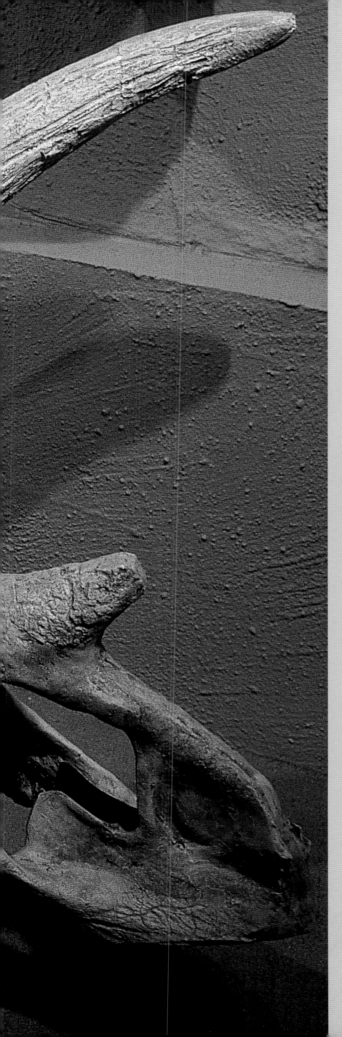

CHAPTER THIRTEEN

HORNED DINOSAURS

FROM THE SIZE OF A SMALL PIG, TO TWICE THE LENGTH AND WEIGHT OF THE
LARGEST OF TODAY'S RHINOCEROSES, THE CERATOPSIANS WERE SUCCESSFUL
AND DRAMATIC NEWCOMERS AT THE END OF THE DINOSAUR AGE.

THE CERATOPSIAN GROUP

HORNED DINOSAURS ARE KNOWN AS CERATOPSIANS, OR "HORNED FACES." THEY WERE SMALL, THEN MEDIUM-SIZED, THEN LARGE PLANT-EATERS, IN TURN, FROM THE EARLY, MID- AND THEN LATE CRETACEOUS PERIOD. MOST LIVED FROM 80 TO 65 MILLION YEARS AGO, IN ASIA AND THEN IN NORTH AMERICA. THE BIGGEST AND BEST-KNOWN OF THEIR KIND, TRICERATOPS, WAS ONE OF THE VERY LAST DINOSAURS OF THE WHOLE MESOZOIC ERA OR AGE OF DINOSAURS. THE CERATOPSIAN GROUP CAN BE DIVIDED INTO SEVERAL MAIN SUBGROUPS, WHICH IN DIFFERENT CLASSIFICATION SCHEMES ARE CALLED THE PSITTACOSAURS; THE PROTOCERATOPSIDS; AND THE CERATOPSIDS THEMSELVES, WHICH APPEARED LAST.

PARROT-BEAKS

The psittacosaurs were once regarded as types of ornithopod dinosaurs, but further studies, especially of their skulls, showed that these fleet-footed runners were the earliest kinds of horned dinosaurs. There are around ten different types or genera, the best-known being *Psittacosaurus* itself (see next page). This is named for the "parrot beak" at the front of its mouth, which was toothless, and suited to tearing and raking in vegetation. Other types sometimes classified in this group include *Chaoyangsaurus*. All these dinosaurs are known from fossils in Asia, and many well-preserved remains have been found in the Gobi Desert in Mongolia. They did not have the face horns characteristic of later ceratopsians, but, like them, they did show a ridge at each cheekbone, drawn out into a low point.

MARGIN-HEADS

A general feature of all ceratopsians were the shelf-like ridges or expanded areas around the edges of the skull, from the cheek region up to the rear of the top of the head. They are present to differing degrees in all specimens, as occasional lumps or points here and there, or longer ridges, or more complete shelves, or extended frills, over the whole neck and shoulders. These skull-edging or marginal extensions are also known from another plant-eating dinosaur group, the pachycephalosaurs or "boneheads." This has led paleontologists to group ceratopsians and pachycephalosaurs together as cousins to the larger dinosaur group called the marginocephalians ("margin-heads" or "edge-heads").

DEATH IN THE SEMIDESERT

The protoceratopsians are based on another very well-known dinosaur from the Gobi, *Protoceratops*. Extensive finds of adults, juveniles, babies and nests have allowed scientists to build up a picture of this dinosaur's behavior and breeding patterns. This treasure trove of fossils for just one kind of dinosaur is due in part to the dry, semidesert habitats in which it roamed some 80 million years ago. It seems that windblown sand or toppling dunes covered some specimens in seconds. Protected from the elements and from crunching, or even disturbance by scavengers, these individuals gradually dried out or desiccated within their sandy "tombs," leaving many details of their bones and general anatomy remarkably well preserved.

SMALL HORNS TO BIG

Protoceratopsians had the parrot-like beak at the front of the mouth, and many chewing teeth in the rear of the jaws; they also showed the beginnings of the neck frill and face horn. These head extensions rapidly became larger in the next and last major horn-face group, the ceratopsians. These were all North American, and in turn comprised two subgroups, the centrosaurines and chasmosaurines (see pages 363 and 370).

PREVIOUS PAGE A fine fossil of *Anchiceratops* showing the small eye socket or orbit at the base of each long brow horn, the pointed cheekbone extending out sideways below it, and the gaps or "windows" in the neck frill. This specimen came from Late Cretaceous rocks in Alberta, Canada.

LEFT A charging *Styracosaurus* would intimidate most predators, with its huge frill edged with long spikes, its massive feet pounding the ground and its sharp beak snapping fiercely.

PSITTACOSAURUS

DINO FACTFILE

Psittacosaurus

Meaning: Parrot reptile

Pronunciation: Sit-ah-coe-sore-uss

Period: Early to mid-Cretaceous

Main group: Ceratopsia

Length: 2 meters (6½ feet)

Weight: 25–40 kilograms (55–88 pounds)

Diet: Plants, possibly omnivorous

Fossils: Mongolia, China, Thailand

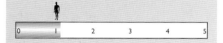

"Parrot reptile" was named in 1923, by Henry Fairfield Osborn, from its very powerful, toothless, hooked "beak" which resembles that of a modern bird such as a parrot or macaw. Its remains were recovered by one of the American-led fossil-hunting expeditions to the Gobi in Mongolia in the early 1920s, during which the preserved parts of many other dinosaurs were discovered, including *Protoceratops* (opposite). *Psittacosaurus* is now well known from more than 120 fossil specimens, and its kind seems to have survived for more than 30 million years, almost a record among dinosaurs.

Psittacosaurus was about 2 meters (6½ feet) long and would have been waist-high to an adult human, if standing bipedally, on its two rear legs, which were longer and stronger than the front limbs. But *Psittacosaurus* may also have walked or trotted on all fours, with the head much nearer the ground. The skull was tall-snouted and box-like, with large gaps for the nasal openings and big eye sockets. The skeleton was generally slender and lightly built, indicating a fast runner. The tail had a wide base and formed about one-third of the dinosaur's total length. In some features, *Psittacosaurus* resembled small ornithopod dinosaurs like *Hypsilophodon* (see page 273), and at first it was grouped with them. But, it had a bone called the rostral at the front of the upper jaw, which forms the top part of the beak, and only ceratopsians had this feature. The rostral bone and the beak itself mean that *Psittacosaurus* is regarded as an early type of horned dinosaur. It did not have the face horns or neck frill characteristic to the rest of the group, although it had a small projection from each cheek, which in later types became longer and spike-like.

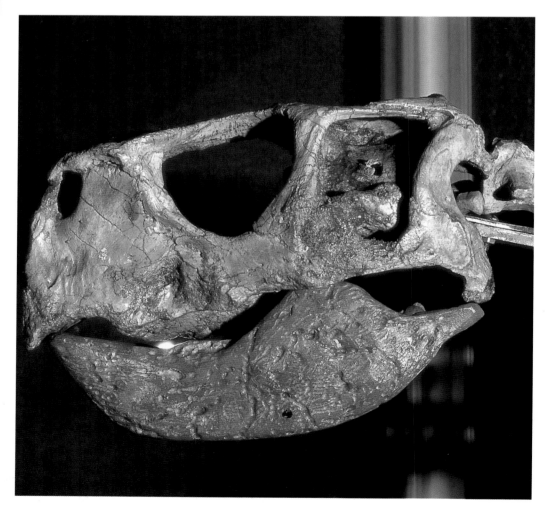

RIGHT Side view of a *Psittacosaurus* skull emphasizes the great height of the head and the massively deep jaws.

ABOVE The skeleton of *Protoceratops* shows the openings or fenestrae in the neck frill, and the four-legged gait, with rear legs larger and more powerful than the front pair.

LEFT A *Protoceratops* hatchling, about 20 centimeters (8 inches) long, from snout to tail-tip, greets the world.

PROTOCERATOPS

Protoceratops was about the size of a modern pig, and lived some 85–80 million years ago in what is now the Gobi Desert. The first *Protoceratops* fossils were found in the early 1920s by one of the American expeditions to the Gobi (see opposite). The dinosaur was named in 1923 by Walter Granger and William Gregory. *Protoceratops* – "first horned-face" – is well named, too, since it seems to represent a midway stage between small, mainly two-legged ancestors, perhaps somewhat like *Psittacosaurus* (opposite), and the much larger ceratopsians (horned dinosaurs), near the end of the Cretaceous.

Protoceratops had low bumps on its face, rather than tall horns, and a relatively small, plain neck frill or ruff, compared to the huge, elaborate frills of later ceratopsians.

Protoceratops is remarkable in other ways. It was once said to be the first dinosaur whose fossil eggs were found and recognized as such – not only eggs, but the nests where they

were laid. There are also specimens of young or juvenile *Protoceratops* in various stages of growth, so it is possible to see how features such as leg length and frill width changed in comparison to the whole body size, and perhaps with the male or female sex, as the dinosaurs grew. In one find, a *Protoceratops* seems to have perished in the act of battling against the meat-eating dinosaur or theropod, *Velociraptor* (see page 154). Fossils of other animals and plants help to build up a picture of habitat and the various dinosaurs there. Some *Protoceratops* specimens, on re-examination, have been reclassified as a new genus, *Breviceratops* (see page 358).

However recent studies have changed expert views on what were thought to be the eggs of *Protoceratops*. It is now proposed that the eggs were probably those of *Oviraptor*, (see page 160). But the evidence for the many hatchlings and juveniles of *Protoceratops* remains firm.

DINO FACTFILE
Protoceratops

Meaning: First horned-face
Pronunciation: Proe-toe-serra-tops
Period: Late Cretaceous
Main group: Ceratopsia
Length: 1.8 meters (6 feet)
Weight: 150–250 kilograms (330–550 pounds)
Diet: Plants
Fossils: Mongolia

LEPTOCERATOPS

DINO FACTFILE

Leptoceratops

Meaning: Slim or slender horned-face

Pronunciation: Lep-toe-serra-tops

Period: Late Cretaceous

Main group: Ceratopsia

Length: 1.5–3 meters (5–10 feet)

Weight: 50–70 kilograms (110–150 pounds)

Diet: Plants

Fossils: USA (Wyoming), Canada (Alberta), possibly Australia

Leptoceratops may seem an unusual ceratopsian (horned dinosaur), since it had some of the features of its ornithopod-like ancestors. Its rear legs were longer and more powerful than the front ones, so that it could move on all fours or rise up to run on two legs. It did not have the large horns and the sweeping neck frill of most of the later ceratopsians. Instead, it had only a low snout lump and a small peak-like "hat." Nevertheless, the internal structure of the skull, and the teeth and main skeleton show that this was definitely a member of the ceratopsian group, though it was distinctive in two more ways. First, the fossils of most early types, including *Protoceratops* itself (see page 355), were found in Asia, but *Leptoceratops* lived in North America. Second, if *Leptoceratops* had been a forerunner of *Protoceratops*, as its features might suggest, it should date from

before 80 million years ago, but it dates from well after, closer to 68–66 million years ago. The answer could be that *Leptoceratops* was a late-surviving but "primitive" ceratopsian, meaning that it retained many of the group's earlier features.

This plant-eating dinosaur, with its hooked, beak-like mouth and powerful, ridged, chewing cheek teeth, probably grew to about 2 or 3 meters (6½–10 feet) in total length. The five digits of its front limbs had some grasping ability and may have pulled foliage to its mouth when feeding. Fossils of *Leptoceratops* have been discovered in Alberta, Canada, and in Wyoming, and include about five skulls and other parts of skeletons in varying states of completion. The name was given in 1914 by Barnum Brown. (See also the very similar *Montanoceratops*, page 359.)

BELOW *Leptoceratops* seems to have been a "throwback" type of horned dinosaur, retaining many features of its distant ancestors while living at the same time and in the same region as much more recent or advanced cousins, such as *Triceratops*.

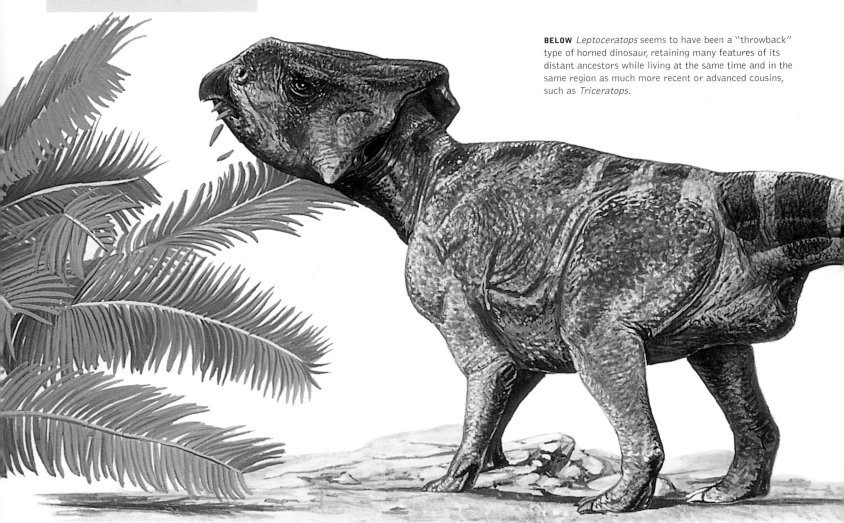

MICROCERATOPS

"Micro" indeed, compared to other dinosaurs – this horned dinosaur was tiny, probably less than 1 meter (39 inches) in total length when fully grown. Its femur (thighbone) was about the size of a human forefinger. It is the smallest known ceratopsian, and in overall structure resembles *Protoceratops* (see page 355), which lived in the same general region of East Asia. However, *Microceratops* was smaller overall, and much more lightly built, with thinner legs. The rear pair were longer than the front limbs, so *Microceratops* could perhaps balance over them – front pair off the ground and body held horizontal, balanced by the tail at the rear of the hips – for bipedal movement. The neck frill is short, but definitely present, and it has openings or fenestrae ("windows") like those of *Protoceratops*. These may have been to save weight or to allow more stable, better-aligned attachments for the muscles

that worked the jaws. Possible functions of the ceratopsian neck frill are discussed throughout this chapter.

Microceratops was named in 1953 from fossils located in Mongolia. Since then, further fossils have been discovered elsewhere in that country and in China, and attributed to it, although their identity is disputed. One strong view is that certain specimens of *Microceratops* are simply young *Protoceratops*. They look different because they have the slimmer build and altered limb proportions to be expected from a juvenile, compared to an adult of the same kind. Another and very different opinion is that some specimens of *Microceratops* should be attributed to another, entirely new genus which may be proposed as *Graciliceratops*. What is known is that *Microceratops* died out some 70 million years ago.

DINO FACTFILE
Microceratops
Meaning: Micro (very small) horned-face
Pronunciation: My-croe-serra-tops
Period: Late Cretaceous
Main group: Ceratopsia
Length: 80 centimeters (31 inches)
Weight: Estimated 10 kilograms (22 pounds)
Diet: Plants
Fossils: Mongolia, China

| 0 | | 1 | 2 | 3 | 4 | 5 |

LEFT *Microceratops* is currently the smallest known ceratopsian or horned dinosaur, although some of its fossils may be youngsters of another genus. It had a slim, lightweight build and a much reduced neck frill.

BELOW *Bagaceratops* was about the same length as a medium-sized pet dog, but heavily built. There have been proposals that it laid eggs in nests and looked after its young, but these are based on scanty evidence which may have been left by other dinosaurs or reptiles of the Mongolian Omnogov region.

BAGACERATOPS

DINO FACTFILE
Bagaceratops

Meaning: Small horned-face
Pronunciation: Bag-ah-serra-tops
Period: Late Cretaceous
Main group: Ceratopsia
Length: 1 meter (39 inches)
Weight: 30 kilograms (66 pounds)
Diet: Plants
Fossils: Mongolia

| 0 | 1 | 2 | 3 | 4 | 5 |

Bagaceratops was a small type of horned dinosaur, or ceratopsian, only about 1 meter (39 inches) in total length. It had a little lump-like horn on its snout, and a small neck frill. Its powerful rear legs were longer than its front pair, although it probably walked and ran on all fours rather than on the two rear limbs. The front of the mouth was shaped like a parrot's curved beak or bill, with teeth in the upper part. In all these respects, *Bagaceratops* resembled a smaller version of *Protoceratops*. The two are usually grouped together in the family Protoceratopsidae, along with others such as *Montanoceratops* (see opposite).

Fossils of *Bagaceratops* have been excavated from rocks that are part of the "Red Beds" of the Barun Goyot Formation in the Omnogov region of Mongolia. They are dated at around 70 million years old. The dinosaur was named by Teresa Maryanska and Halszka Osmólska in 1975. The same rock formation has also

yielded fossils of a very similar, but larger, dinosaur known as *Breviceratops*. This was about 2 meters (6½ feet) in total length and probably weighed more than 100 kilograms (220 pounds). It was described and named in 1990 by Sergei Mikhailovich Kurzanov (see *Avimumus*, page 164). *Breviceratops* may have been a distinct type of dinosaur from *Bagaceratops*, or the two may have been the same genus, even the same species: the classification depends on which features of the fossils are used to ascertain relationships. The same proposals have been made for merging or distinguishing other types of protoceratopsids, as described in these pages (for example, *Leptoceratops*, *Microceratops*, see pages 356–357). Fossils attributed to Bagaceratops include five almost complete skulls and parts of more than 15 other skulls, and various bits of limbs and other skeletal parts, showing growth from juvenile to adults.

MONTANOCERATOPS

Named after the state of Montana, where its fossils were found, *Montanoceratops* is known mainly from parts of two skeletons. Fossils were originally excavated by Barnum Brown, and they were named in 1951 by Charles M. Sternberg. Further remains have been found in Alberta, Canada. *Montanoceratops* lived toward the end of the Cretaceous period, 72–66 million years ago. (Some fossils originally attributed to *Montanoceratops* have been re-studied and are now included among those for *Leptoceratops*, see page 356.)

Montanoceratops bears a striking resemblance to *Protoceratops*, although it was slightly more advanced in many features. It may have been larger in overall size, but the proportions of the head, body, four squat limbs and short tail are all *Protoceratops*-like. So is the frill extending from the upper rear of the skull over the neck. What was once thought to be a low, cone-shaped horn on the nose of *Montanoceratops* was later identified as a projecting cheekbone, so the noses of this dinosaur and *Protoceratops* were also similar. Both dinosaurs are included in the protoceratopsids or "preceratopsian" group of horned dinosaurs (see page 353), since they have "old-fashioned" features, including teeth in the upper "beak" or front of the upper jaw, and claws on the toes. More advanced ceratopsians lost the teeth and had more hoof- or nail-like claws – although "advanced" may be a misleading word, as many of these lived around the same time as *Montanoceratops*.

DINO FACTFILE
Montanoceratops

Meaning: Montana horned-face

Pronunciation: Mon-tan-owe-serra-tops

Period: Late Cretaceous

Main group: Ceratopsia

Length: 2–3 meters (6½–10 feet)

Weight: 400–600 kilograms (880–1320)

Diet: Plants

Fossils: USA (Montana), Canada (Alberta)

| 0 | 1 | 2 | 3 | 4 | 5 |

ABOVE *Montanoceratops* was strikingly similar to the much better-known Asian *Protoceratops*, although larger in overall dimensions, and its remains date from 15 million years later. Its main fossil site is rocks known as the St. Mary River Formation of Montana.

WHY THE NECK FRILL?

THE FUNCTION OF THE CERATOPSIAN NECK FRILL
IS MUCH DEBATED. IN MOST TYPES, APART FROM
TRICERATOPS, IT WAS NOT SOLID BONE AND
WOULD HAVE BEEN OF LITTLE USE AS A PROTECTIVE
SHIELD. ONE PROPOSAL IS THAT THE FRILL
PROVIDED A LARGE AREA TO ANCHOR POWERFUL
HEAD AND JAW MUSCLES. ANOTHER IS THAT ITS
GREAT SURFACE PRODUCED AN IMPOSING VISUAL
DISPLAY, ESPECIALLY WITH THE HEAD LOWERED
SO THAT THE FRILL TIPPED UP ALMOST VERTICAL
– EVEN MORE SO IF IT WAS BRIGHTLY COLORED.

RIGHT A young *Triceratops* stands its ground, with its herd in
the background. It seems that in juveniles the head horns and
frill were smaller, relative to the overall size of the body, than in
the adults. During growth these head adornments enlarged at a
faster rate, to become proportionally bigger in the adult.

MONOCLONIUS

Monoclonius may have been a large horned dinosaur, some 5 meters (16½ feet) long and a couple of metric tons in weight – or it may not. When the remains of huge ceratopsians were dug up in North America during the latter half of the 19th century, there was great rivalry among the fossil-hunters about who could discover most. Edward Drinker Cope named *Monoclonius* in 1876, from some partial bits of head frill, bones and teeth, some of which had been discovered near the Judith River in Montana in 1855. These specimens were probably the first ceratopsian fossils to be described in North America, by Joseph Leidy. The name *Monoclonius* refers not to the single horn on the nose, but to the single row or series of cheek teeth in each jaw. Cope contrasted these with the supposed double row of teeth in each jaw for another dinosaur of the time.

Monoclonius has been through ups and downs since then. As a genus, it has contained more than ten species or, alternatively, none, with different forms of *Monoclonius* said to be variants of other ceratopsians, principally *Centrosaurus* and *Styracosaurus*. The neck frill was not as expansive and elaborate as other types – from nose-tip to rear of frill was "only" 1.8 meters (6 feet) – although it probably had a pair of down-curled spikes at the top, and a larger spike-like horn on the snout. The body was typically ceratopsian, with a wide and powerful neck, four stout limbs with spreading, hoof-capped digits, and a short tail. The hook-tipped beak cropped plant food, which was ground up by the numerous cheek teeth.

DINO FACTFILE
Monoclonius

Meaning: Single stem or one stick (often quoted as "one horn")
Pronunciation: Mon-owe-clone-ee-uss
Period: Late Cretaceous
Main group: Ceratopsia
Length: 5–6 meters (16½–19½ feet)
Weight: 2–3 metric tons (2–3 tons)
Diet: Plants
Fossils: USA (Montana), Canada (Alberta)

CENTROSAURUS

This horned dinosaur has given its name to one of the subgroups of big horned dinosaurs, the centrosaurines. They are often called short-frilled dinosaurs, but *Centrosaurus* itself had a relatively long, sweeping neck frill. The distinction lies more in the nose horn being longer than the eyebrow horns, and the front of the face being fairly deep and short-snouted, compared to the other subgroup known as the chasmosaurines (see page 370). *Centrosaurus* was a medium-sized ceratopsian, some 6 meters (19½ feet) long. It was named by Lawrence Lambe, a Canadian dinosaur expert, in 1940.

The brow horns of *Centrosaurus* are hardly more than low, pointed lumps of skull bone, but the nose horn can be up to 75 centimeters (29 inches) in length. In some individuals it is almost straight, while in others it seems to have curved back toward the eyes or forward over the beak-tipped snout. Nevertheless, this horn is not the source of the name, which means "well-horned" or "pointed" reptile.

The name comes from a pair of curved "hooks" of bone, which face each other near the middle of the upper edge of the frill, at the top. But, whether these "hooks" were uncovered and visible, or covered in skin and flesh to make a smooth frill edge, is not clear. Remains of many *Centrosaurus* have been found in bone beds in Alberta, Canada, including skulls, bits of horns, teeth, parts of skeletons and even fossilized impressions of scaly skin. There have been suggestions that these creatures were a herd, perhaps on migration, plodding some 100 kilometers (62 miles) each day (see pages 364 and 368).

LEFT This convincing restoration of *Monoclonius* shows a single nose horn, smaller down-spikes on the upper frill, and extended cheekbones (jugals) – all features that may be from other ceratopsian dinosaurs. The proposed head-down stance, swaying the nose from side to side to display the long sharp horn, was meant to intimidate the enemy – modern rhinos do the same.

DINO FACTFILE
Centrosaurus

Meaning: Well-horned reptile, pointed reptile
Pronunciation: Sen-troe-sore-uss
Period: Late Cretaceous
Main group: Ceratopsia
Length: 6 meters (19½ feet)
Weight: 3 metric tons (3 tons)
Diet: Plants
Fossils: Canada (Alberta)

PACHYRHINOSAURUS

DINO FACTFILE
Pachyrhinosaurus
Meaning: Thick-nosed reptile
Pronunciation: Pack-ee-rhine-owe-sore-uss
Period: Late Cretaceous
Main group: Ceratopsia
Length: 5.5–7 meters (17–23 feet)
Weight: 3–4 metric tons (3–4 tons)
Diet: Plants
Fossils: USA (Alaska), Canada (Alberta)

One giant bone bed in Alberta, Canada, contains the jumbled fossils of hundreds of *Pachyrhinosaurus* individual, as well as fossils of other animals and plants of the region from some 70 million years ago. Further finds in 2002 of more *Pachyrhinosaurus* bone beds far to the north, in Alaska, have led to suggestions that this horned dinosaur migrated in huge herds, moving north, nearer to the Arctic, in the summer, and south to warmer regions for the winter. But, the seasons then were different from those today (see page 26). This dinosaur was named in 1950 by Charles M. Sternberg.

Pachyrhinosaurus was a medium-sized horned dinosaur of the centrosaurine subgroup. It had the usual features a ceratopsian: bulky body, pillar-like legs with hoof-shaped nails, a thick-based but short and abruptly tapering tail and a massive neck to support its huge head.

The toothless, sharply hooked, macaw-like beak at the front of the mouth was efficient as a foliage-gatherer and a defensive weapon. The neck frill curves up and back, and may have had two or more pairs of spikes or "hornlets" along its top edge. The major distinctive feature of *Pachyrhinosaurus* is the "thick nose" that gives it its name. It is thought that there was a large bony lump or mound, termed a boss, on the front part of its nose. This could have been used as a battering ram against enemies or in shoving contests with rivals, perhaps at breeding time; or the boss could have served as a pedestal for a very tall horn. Another proposal favored by some paleontologists is that one sex, perhaps males, had larger convex (bulging) bosses while the female had smaller, almost concave (bowl-like) bosses.

ABOVE *Pachyrhinosaurus* remains from Alberta's Royal Tyrrell Museum.

RIGHT This reconstruction shows the nose with a large mound or boss of bone, rather than this being surmounted by a horn.

RIGHT The vast neck frill of *Pentaceratops* reached almost halfway along the body when this dinosaur tilted its head back, and tipped up to form a huge fan-like shield area when the head was dropped for feeding or as a threat, much as shown here.

PENTACERATOPS

For many years the horned dinosaur *Torosaurus* (see page 371) held the record as the longest skull of any known land animal (see also page 396). A recent discovery of an enormous skull has led scientists to hand the title to *Pentaceratops*. From the name, this ceratopsian might be expected to sport five horns on its face and forehead, but there are only three: a short one on the nose and a longer one on each eyebrow, much like *Triceratops*. The other two projections, thought to be horns when this dinosaur was first studied and named in 1923 by Henry Fairfield Osborn, are actually drawn-out points for the jugals, or cheekbones, angled down and sideways below each eye. Indeed, most ceratopsians have these "false horns." Nevertheless, *Pentaceratops* has a distinctive long, wide, upswept frill over the neck, studded almost all the way around its edge with more than 20 small bony nodules, called epoccipitals.

Pentaceratops fossils come from New Mexico. It was a member of the long-frilled subgroup of horned dinosaurs, the chasmosaurines. (The general structure and uses of these frills are discussed on page 360.) It was a massive beast, shaped vaguely like a rhinoceros of today, and as long as, and heavier than, an elephant. Almost one-third of its length, about 3 meters (10 feet), was the skull, from snout-tip to the rear of the frill. Feeding equipment was of the standard ceratopsian type, with a hook-like beak composed of the rostral bone, unique to ceratopsians, in the upper jaw and the predentary bone in the lower jaw, both covered by sharp, horny material. To the rear of the jaws were many sharply ridged cheek teeth and there was plenty of room for powerful chewing muscles. Fossils of *Pentaceratops* include eight skulls, some complete and others partial, along with a relatively complete skeleton, and skeletal fragments.

DINO FACTFILE
Pentaceratops
Meaning: Five-horned face
Pronunciation: Pen-tah-serra-tops
Period: Late Cretaceous
Main group: Ceratopsia
Length: 8 meters (26 feet)
Weight: 7–8 metric tons (7–8 tons)
Diet: Plants
Fossils: USA (New Mexico)

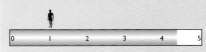

TRICERATOPS

DINO FACTFILE

Triceratops

Meaning: Three-horned face

Pronunciation: Try-serra-tops

Period: Late Cretaceous

Main group: Ceratopsia

Length: 9 meters (29½ feet)

Weight: 5–8 metric tons (5–8 tons)

Diet: Plants

Fossils: USA (Colorado, Wyoming)

0 | 1 | 2 | 3 | 4 | 5

"Three-horned face" was one of the biggest of the ceratopsians and, judging from its plentiful fossil remains, one of the most common roaming North America during the Late Cretaceous. *Triceratops* fossils, along with those of its deadly enemy *Tyrannosaurus*, have been dated to the very end of the dinosaur age, 65 million years ago. Some estimates give *Triceratops* a shoulder height of 3 meters (10 feet), a total length of 10 meters (33 feet) and a weight of 10 metric tons (10 tons), although others are 10 to 20 percent less. *Triceratops* was named in 1889 by Othniel Charles Marsh from remains found near Denver, Colorado, that were first thought to be those of an extinct species of giant buffalo. The year before, John Bell Hatcher had begun extensive excavations in Niobrara Country, Wyoming, which yielded many specimens. Parts of well over 50 individuals are now known. Some frills have large gouges in them, which fit the teeth of *Tyrannosaurus*. At one stage there were said to be 15 species within the single genus *Triceratops*, but much of the variation may be due to sex (males and females) and age (juveniles to adults). Current opinions vary between one, two and three species;

meanwhile one dinosaur previously thought to be a species of *Triceratops* may represent a different genus, provisionally named *Diceratops*.

Big-horned dinosaurs are usually divided into the long-frilled type, called chasmosaurines (page 370), and the short-frilled type, known as centrosaurines (page 363). *Triceratops* seems to be a mixture of both, but it is usually regarded as a chasmosaurine, with its shorter, solid frill. Its narrow, fiercely hooked, toothless beak could exert tremendous pressure when gathering food or slashing and pecking at enemies. Uses of the horns and frill include visual intimidation of enemies and rivals, and are discussed on page 360.

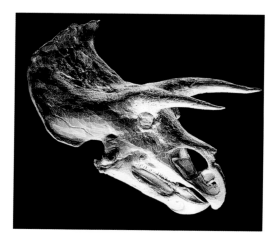

FAR RIGHT The sweeping neck frill of solid bone and long eyebrow horns are clearly shown in dozens of fossil *Triceratops* skulls.

RIGHT A side view of *Triceratops* emphasizes the length of the eyebrow horns compared to the nose horn.

BELOW Due to their elaborate headgear and sturdy neck joints, ceratopsians like *Styracosaurus* could probably not raise their heads very high. They were limited in feeding to relatively low-growing plant matter – anything below the height of an adult human.

STYRACOSAURUS

Styracosaurus had a very tall nose horn, 60-plus centimeters (24-plus inches) in length, and the two topmost parts of the frill were spikes that were even lengthier – they were fossilized as bony cores but probably sheathed in horn in life, so they would have looked even longer and sharper. On each side of the frill's upper middle edge or margin, two or three more spikes of decreasing size flanked the topmost, tallest one. Beyond this, along the side of the frill and down toward the eye, was a row of small bony nodules or nubbins that gave a scalloped effect. Similar low lumps decorated the frills of many other ceratopsians, too. They and the bony cores of the spikes were formed from outgrowths of epoccipital bones which rimmed the edge of the frill. In addition, there may have been two smaller spikes at the top of the frill, inboard of the two tallest ones and near the central notch of the frill's heart-like upper outline. The limited nature of the fossil evidence unfortunately

makes such details of the spike arrangement difficult to confirm.

Like several other horned dinosaurs, *Styracosaurus* was named by Canadian fossil expert Lawrence Lambe, in 1913. Its fossils come from Alberta, Canada, and Montana. It lived toward the end of the dinosaur age, around 73–70 million years ago. There are two fairly well-preserved skulls along with three partial skeletons, and also many jumbled bits and pieces of bones and horns, in bone beds in Arizona, some or all of which could have been from *Styracosaurus*. This led to the proposal that *Styracosaurus*, like other ceratopsians, roamed in herds and perhaps migrated to seasonal food sources. In overall dimensions *Styracosaurus* was medium-sized for the ceratopsians, standing about 1.8 meters (6 feet) tall at the shoulder, with a total nose to tail length of up to 5.5 meters (17 feet). It cropped low plants with its hooked beak – ceratopsians could not lift their heads very high.

DINO FACTFILE
Styracosaurus

Meaning: Spike lizard

Pronunciation: Sty-rack-owe-sore-uss

Period: Late Cretaceous

Main group: Ceratopsia

Length: 5–5.5 meters (16½–17 feet)

Weight: 2–3 metric tons (2–3 tons)

Diet: Plants

Fossils: USA (Montana, possibly Arizona), Canada (Alberta)

LIVE TOGETHER, DIE TOGETHER

HORNED DINOSAURS ARE OFTEN FOUND IN "BONE BEDS," WHERE THE VOLUME OF THE ROCK CONSISTS MORE OF PRESERVED FOSSILS THAN OF THE SURROUNDING STONE. SOME OF THESE SITES MIGHT CONTAIN THOUSANDS OF INDIVIDUALS. PERHAPS GREAT HERDS ON REGULAR MIGRATION ATTEMPTED TO CROSS A RIVER AND WERE SWEPT TO THEIR DEATHS BY UNSEASONABLY FAST, SWOLLEN WATERS. AN ALTERNATIVE EXPLANATION IS THAT THE DINOSAURS PERISHED WHILE SPREAD OUT OVER A WIDER AREA AND DURING A LONGER TIME PERIOD, PERHAPS AN ENTIRE SEASON, AND THEN A SUDDEN FLOOD WASHED THEIR ROTTING CARCASSES OR PICKED-CLEAN BONES TOGETHER INTO A GULLEY.

RIGHT A tyrannosaur menaces a herd of *Styracosaurus* during twilight – a favorite time for hunters to attack their prey. Evidence for herd dwelling in horned dinosaurs is well established from various sources, including large collections of fossils in "bone beds" and preserved sets of footprints.

CHASMOSAURUS

DINO FACTFILE
Chasmosaurus

Meaning: Chasm, ravine or gorge reptile

Pronunciation: Kaz-moe-sore-uss

Period: Late Cretaceous

Main group: Ceratopsia

Length: 5–6 meters (16½–19½ feet)

Weight: 2–3 metric tons (2–3 tons)

Diet: Plants

Fossils: Canada (Alberta) to USA (Texas)

The chasmosaurines were one subgroup of the horned dinosaurs or ceratopsians. These differed from the second subgroup, the centrosaurines, in having eyebrow horns that were longer than their nose horns; longer, lower skulls and snouts; and generally longer neck frills. *Chasmosaurus* was a medium-sized member of the chasmosaurine subgroup, at up to 6 meters (19½ feet) long – approximately the same length from snout-tip to tail-end as the largest living rhinoceros, the white or square-lipped rhino. The bony parts of the frill were reduced to the parietal strut in the center, and two narrow, angular arches that formed the upper and side edges or margins, enclosing a large gap or fenestra on each side. These wide-open gaps were larger in *Chasmosaurus* than in almost any other ceratopsian, and led

to its name. In life they were probably filled in with skin that covered thin layers of muscle and connective tissue. This means that the frill was not an especially strong structure, and its use probably lay in visual displays rather than physical protection (see page 360).

In its body size and proportions, *Chasmosaurus* was a fairly typical ceratopsian, from the parrot-like, toothless beak at the snout tip, to massive, pillar-like legs and smallish, pointed tail. *Chasmosaurus* seems to have been common and widespread some 75–70 million years ago, as indicated by its plentiful fossils found in several parts of North America, from the province of Alberta, Canada, south to the state of Texas. The name *Chasmosaurus* was coined in 1914 by Lawrence Lambe.

LEFT This skull of *Chasmosaurus* from the Royal Tyrrell Museum, Alberta, shows the huge gaps (fenestrae) in the frill, which would make it lightweight but relatively fragile.

RIGHT This restoration shows the facial horns of *Chasmosaurus* as relatively long and pointed. The actual material horn, which their outer coverings are made of, rarely fossilizes and so their length is guessed from the bony center or core.

LEFT Most restorations of ceratopsians like *Torosaurus* show the animals colored in drab greens and browns. But it is possible that the colors, especially on the frill, were bright with vivid patterns, perhaps even stripes or "eyespots" as in several modern lizards.

TOROSAURUS

The name of this dinosaur is often said mistakenly to mean "bull reptile," but it is *Torosaurus*, not "*Taurosaurus*," and its name actually means "perforated reptile." *Torosaurus* was one of the largest of the ceratopsians. Weighing 7 or 8 metric tons (7 or 8 tons), and perhaps 2 meters (6½ feet) tall at the hips, it rivaled *Triceratops* in size. *Torosaurus* is often also cited as having had the biggest head, or more accurately the longest skull, of any land animal. One partial skull has been restored to give a total length, from snout to rear of frill, of 2.8 meters (9 feet). A recent discovery of *Pentaceratops*, however, challenges this record. At one stage there were said to be more than 25 species in the genus *Torosaurus*, but many of the differences are probably the result of natural variation within just a few species.

Like the frill of *Chasmosaurus* (opposite), the neck frill of *Torosaurus* was mostly skin and connective tissue. The bone inside was reduced to thin struts, one along the center

and the others around the edges or margins. This would have saved a great deal of weight compared to a solid bone frill like that of *Triceratops*, but it would also have made the frill less useful as a protective shield over the neck and shoulders. This suggests that its main use was display (see page 360). There were two large brow horns and a smaller lump-like horn on the snout, as in other chasmosaurines. The mouth had a toothless beak at the front and strong chewing teeth in the cheeks, worked by powerful jaw muscles. Like other ceratopsians, *Torosaurus* had a thick neck, heavy body, sturdy elephant-like limbs, and relatively short tail. Associated fossils show that it lived on coastal plains, especially those bordering the seaway around what is now the coast of Mexico, some 70 million years ago.

The first-studied remains of *Torosaurus* were discovered by John Bell Hatcher and it was named in 1891 by Othniel Charles Marsh.

DINO FACTFILE
Torosaurus

Meaning: Pierced, perforated or punctured reptile

Pronunciation: Torr-owe-sore-uss

Period: Late Cretaceous

Main group: Ceratopsia

Length: 6–8 meters (19½–26 feet)

Weight: 7–8 metric tons (7–8 tons)

Diet: Plants

Fossils: Canada, USA, Mexico

ANCHICERATOPS

DINO FACTFILE

Anchiceratops

Meaning: Near horn face

Pronunciation: Ann-key-serra-tops

Period: Late Cretaceous

Main group: Ceratopsia

Length: 4.5–6 meters (15–19½ feet)

Weight: 2–3 metric tons (2–3 tons)

Diet: Plants

Fossils: Canada (Alberta)

0	1	2	3	4	5

In many respects, including size and body proportions, *Anchiceratops* was similar to *Chasmosaurus* (see page 370). As in most long-frilled ceratopsians, the major differences lay in the size of the neck frill, with its associated bony lumps and spikes, and in the proportions of the face horns. *Anchiceratops* had very long eyebrow horns and a much shorter nose horn, which was probably angled forward toward the beak-like front of the mouth. The frill had gaps or windows in its bony structure, but these were not as large as in *Chasmosaurus*. The upper rear edge of the frill probably had three pairs of short spikes, made from elongated epoccipital bones, and there may have also been two low, limpet-like bony projections just below them, on the middle of the upper front of the frill.

Several ceratopsians were named in 1914, described by Barnum Brown, and *Anchiceratops* was among them. Its name reflects its similarity to other large-horned dinosaurs such as *Monoclonius*, *Centrosaurus* or *Triceratops*. Fossil experts of the time suggested that the neck frill and nose horns could be seen developing in size and complexity in these dinosaurs, forming an evolutionary series through time that ended with the great *Triceratops*. It is now known, however, that many of these dinosaurs coexisted rather than living one after the other in sequence. Fossils of *Anchiceratops* are dated at 73–70 million years old. They come mostly from Alberta, Canada, and include as many as six skulls in varying states of completeness, plus eyebrow horns, and most of a skeleton.

ABOVE A fossil *Anchiceratops* skull shows the smallish gaps or fenestrae ("windows") in the frill bones.

RIGHT *Anchiceratops* was about the size of today's rhinos. The pointed beak would crop even tough vegetation efficiently.

RIGHT This version of *Arrhinoceratops* has the brow horns facing more sideways than forward. The precise angle is difficult to discern from the fossils. The parrot-like "beak" mouth is especially prominent in this pose and would be a fierce weapon giving a powerful "peck" in self-defense.

ARRHINOCERATOPS

This dinosaur's name was coined in 1925, by William Parks, to fossils discovered in the Red Deer River region of Alberta, Canada two years earlier. The fossils are around the same age, and come from the same place as those of *Anchiceratops* (opposite), so these two types of ceratopsians probably coexisted. Only one skull, however, is known for *Arrhinoceratops*. Parks proposed that there were long, sharp horns on the eyebrows, but that the bony lump on the nose of *Arrhinoceratops* was not a true horn. The horn should exist as a separate piece of bone, but this was not found, so Parks coined a name that means "without nose-horn face." It is now believed that *Arrhinoceratops* did have a nose horn, so today the name seems extremely inappropriate.

The neck frill of *Arrhinoceratops* was similar in size and proportions to that of *Triceratops*, but it had parietal fenestrae, or "windows," while that of *Triceratops* was solid bone. There are low, rounded epoccipital bones fringing the edge of the frill, giving the scalloped effect seen in many ceratopsians. The toothless, hooked beak at the front of the mouth was ideal for cutting and cropping tough plant food, which was chewed by the rows of large cheek teeth while being retained in the mouth by fleshy cheek pouches. No other fossils of *Arrhinoceratops* have been found but it is reasonable to assume that it was similar to other ceratopsians from western North America during the Late Cretaceous period. They were, in general, a group that underwent relatively little evolution, as is evident from the many thousands of specimens that have been found in hundreds of sites. They show that the horned dinosaurs were relatively "conservative," a term used to describe a group that does not change very much from its original basic shape and form, despite a long time for evolution to occur (see page 10).

DINO FACTFILE

Arrhinoceratops

Meaning: Without nose-horn face

Pronunciation: Ay-rye-no-serra-tops

Period: Late Cretaceous

Main group: Ceratopsia

Length: 6 meters (19½ feet)

Weight: 3.5 metric tons (3½ tons)

Diet: Plants

Fossils: Canada (Alberta)

| 0 | 1 | 2 | 3 | 4 | 5 |

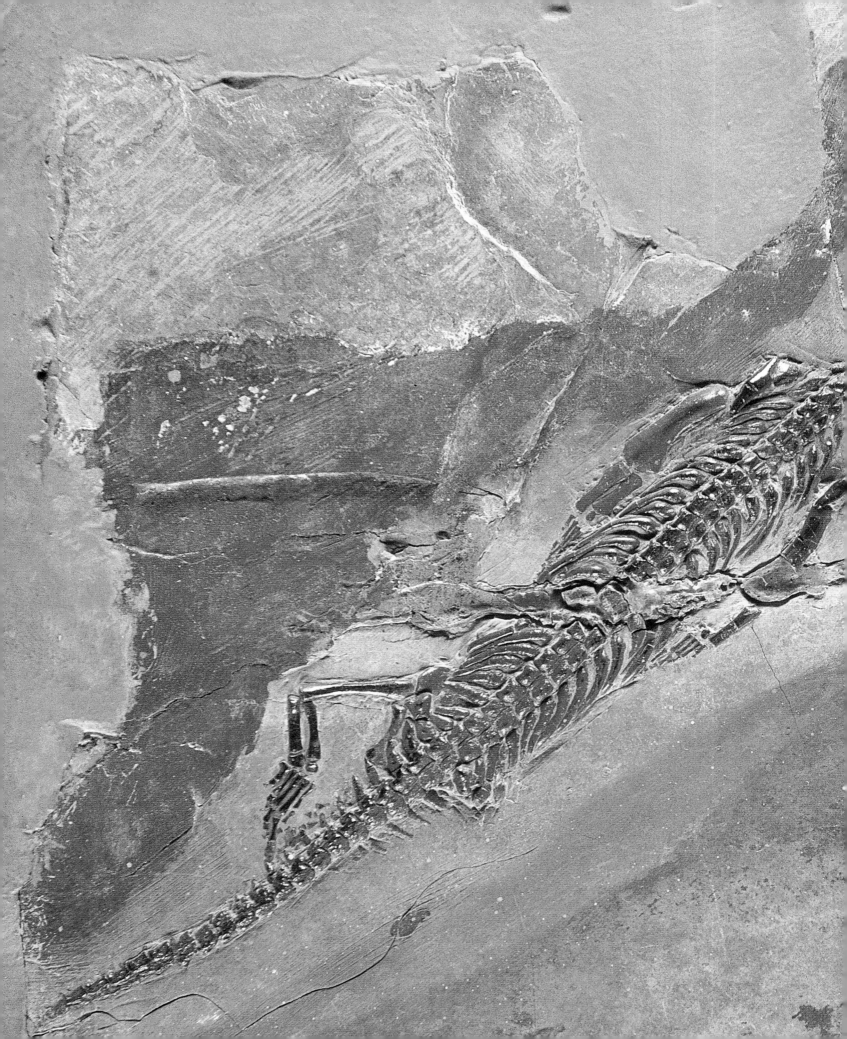

CHAPTER FOURTEEN

OTHER CREATURES OF THE DINOSAUR AGE

DINOSAURS HAD MASTERY OF THE LAND DURING THE MESOZOIC ERA, BUT THEIR NON-DINOSAUR COUSINS SHARED THEIR WORLD BY DOMINATING THE SKIES AND SEAS. THIS REPTILE-DOMINATED EARTH ALSO SAW THE FIRST APPEARANCES OF MAMMALS AND BIRDS.

ANIMALS ALL AROUND

SO OFTEN IS THE MESOZOIC ERA (250–65 MILLION YEARS AGO) CALLED THE AGE OF DINOSAURS THAT THE PRESENCE OF OTHER ANIMALS IS SOMETIMES IGNORED. YET THROUGH THE WHOLE OF THIS GREAT TIME SPAN THERE WERE INNUMERABLE OTHER REPTILES ON LAND, IN THE SEAS AND IN THE SKIES, AS WELL AS OTHER VERTEBRATES SUCH AS FISH AND AMPHIBIANS. EVEN LESS NOTICED WERE THE TEEMING HORDES OF INVERTEBRATE CREATURES IN ALMOST EVERY NOOK AND CRANNY – BUZZING INSECTS, PROWLING SPIDERS, WORMS AND SLUGS IN THE SOIL AND ENDLESS VARIETIES OF CRUSTACEANS, MOLLUSCS, STARFISH, CORALS AND JELLYFISH IN AQUATIC ENVIRONMENTS.

MAMMALS AND BIRDS

Two major absentees at the start of the dinosaur age were mammals and birds. Mammals appeared very quickly, in the Late Triassic, but stayed small and insignificant throughout the era. Birds, such as *Archaeopteryx*, flapped through the air from the Late Jurassic period, about halfway through the Mesozoic. They probably evolved from small meat-eating dinosaurs known as maniraptorans.

EXTRAORDINARY "REPTILES"

Some of the most extraordinary Mesozoic animals were pterosaurs. They are sometimes called pterodactyls, but *Pterodactylus* was only one genus among dozens, and the name pterosaur, meaning "wing reptile," is used for the whole group. It is regarded as an equivalent group to Dinosauria, the dinosaurs, and the crocodiles and alligators, Crocodylia. All three – pterosaurs, dinosaurs and crocodiles – are placed in the supergroup known as the archosaurs or "ruling reptiles." Whatever the exact relationships of the pterosaurs, they had a unique anatomy, the like of which has never been seen before or since.

FURRY FLIERS

Fossils show that some pterosaurs were scaly but others were furry or hairy. Most were able fliers, and the general demands of their aerial lives meant that they were probably warm-blooded. The time span of the pterosaurs mirrors that of the dinosaurs. They evolved in the Triassic period, probably from small ground-dwelling reptiles, and enjoyed great success during the Jurassic and Cretaceous periods, before perishing in the mass extinction. Earlier pterosaurs are known as rhamphorhynchoids. They had long, trailing tails and many had teeth in their beak-like mouths. Later pterosaurs are called pterodactyloids. Most of these were short-tailed, and their beaks lacked teeth. Some pterodactyloids had curious head crests of bone. A few later types reached giant size, becoming the largest flying animals of any age.

FINGER-WINGS

A pterosaur's body was wonderfully adapted to flight, being compact and lightweight, with hollow bones and large chest muscles with which to flap the wings. The strong feet had five clawed digits; some pterosaurs could run or hop, while others may have roosted hanging upside down like bats. The wing structure was quite unlike that of birds, and perhaps superficially more similar to a bat's wing. It was made of a very thin, stretchy flight membrane held out partly by the arm bones, but principally by the hugely elongated bones of the fourth digit. (A bat's wing is held out by four digits, from the second to the fifth.) The first three digits formed short claws on the wing's leading edge. Pterosaurs, however, were neither ancestors nor descendants of birds or bats. Meanwhile, an entirely different route was being taken by other reptile groups of the Mesozoic era: their limbs evolved into flippers as they entered the water and became fully aquatic (see pages 382–383).

PREVIOUS PAGE Sedimentary rocks were usually laid down in layers or strata, which were gradually compressed by the weight of more strata on top, squashing any animals or other remains "flat," like this marine reptile *Pachypleurosaurus*.

LEFT The pterosaur *Criorhynchus* swoops to seize a fish which was also being targeted by the hugely long-necked plesiosaur (sea reptile) known as *Elasmosaurus*. *Criorhynchus* lived during the Early Cretaceous period and had a wingspan far greater than any bird today, at 5 meters (16 feet).

RHAMPHORHYNCHUS

PTEROSAUR FACTFILE

Rhamphorhynchus

Meaning: Beak snout

Pronunciation: Ram-for-ink-uss

Period: Mid to Late Jurassic

Main group: Pterosauria
(Rhamphorhynchoidea)

Wingspan: Up to 1.8 meters (6 feet)

Weight: Up to 5 kilograms (11 pounds)

Diet: Fish, squid, similar sea animals

Fossils: England, Germany, possibly East
Africa and Portugal

0	1	2	3	4	5	6	7	8	9	10	11	12	13

Rhamphorhynchus is one of the better-known pterosaurs, with many fossils from sites such as the Solnhofen region of Germany, the Oxford area of England, perhaps in East Africa, and possibly Portugal. It has given its name to one of the two major pterosaur groups, known as the Rhamphorhynchoidea. These mostly lived in the Triassic and Jurassic periods, and had long, trailing tails, contrasting with the later, short-tailed Pterodactyloidea. Various species of *Rhamphorhynchus*, of different sizes, came and went over more than 30 million years. The larger ones tended to live later, near the end of the Jurassic. The whole skull measured up to 20 centimeters (8 inches) in length, and the body and long, stiff, tail, tipped with a diamond-shaped rudder, added another 1 meter (39 inches). The smallest members of the genus had skulls only the size of a human thumb, and wings that spanned only 40 centimeters (16 inches). Weight-saving features of the skeleton included many long bones shaped like hollow tubes, with walls almost as thin as paper.

This pterosaur's apt name means "beak snout." The thin, sharp teeth stuck out at forward-facing angles from the sides – an ideal arrangement for spearing and trapping writhing fish. *Rhamphorhynchus* probably caught food from the shallow, salty lagoons that were abundant in its home regions during the Late Jurassic, skimming its beak through the surface of the water. When a fish touched the sensitive mouth, this would snap shut in an instant, probably with a flick of the head to jerk the fish out of the sea.

ABOVE *Rhamphorhynchus* trailed its long tail as a combination of rudder and stabilizer.

RIGHT A detailed specimen of *Rhamphorhynchus* from the fine-grained limestone rocks of Solnhofen, in Germany – a site which has also yielded fossils of the early bird *Archaeopteryx* and several kinds of dinosaurs. The skull looks down to the left, with its characteristic angled teeth.

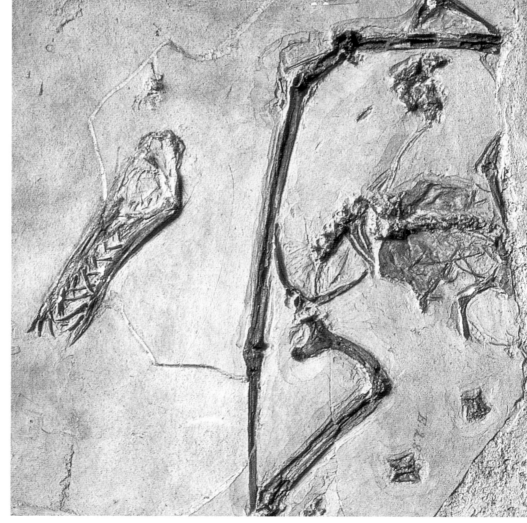

ABOVE After flying out to sea, *Tropeognathus* would swoop down low and arch its neck downward so that its head was almost upside down and facing backward, compared to the pose here. Its beak would then trail "base-first" in the water's surface — similar to the feeding posture of a modern bird, the flamingo.

TROPEOGNATHUS

Tropeognathus was a pterosaur of the Early to mid-Cretaceous period. Its remains were discovered in the astonishingly fossil-rich rocks known as the Santana Formation in northeastern Brazil. Its specimens are scarce and, as usual, much of the body is "filled in" with evidence from similar but more completely known pterosaurs from other localities. One of these is *Criorhynchus* ("ram snout") (see page 376), whose fossils come mainly from the Cambridge area of England, and whose remains were studied and named by Richard Owen, who also coined the name Dinosauria. *Criorhynchus* lived around 130–110 million years ago, while *Tropeognathus* has a more precise dating at 115 million years ago.

Tropeognathus was a sizable reptile with a 6-meter (19½ feet) wingspan. The name, meaning "keel jaw," comes from the ridge-like crests on its very narrow beak. These were at the front end on the midline, almost at the

beak's tip. They were curved into a crescent, very thin from side to side, and roughly the same size and shape on both the upper and lower jaws. *Tropeognathus* also showed signs of a small crest at the rear of the head, just above the nape of the neck. The crest size of *Tropeognathus* varies among the few individuals found. It may have distinguished females from males. Also, or alternatively, the ridges may have had a hydrodynamic function and worked in a way similar to the keel under a yacht. They would have helped to steady and stabilize the beak, and prevent sudden sideways jerks as *Tropeognathus* flew just above the surface of the water and trailed its beak in the water to feed.

There were around 26 slim, pointed, evenly spaced teeth in its upper jaw, and 22 or so in the lower jaw. There may be a second species of this genus, with more triangular beak crests.

PTEROSAUR FACTFILE
Tropeognathus

Meaning: Keel jaw, flange mouth
Pronunciation: Trop-ee-og-nay-thuss
Period: Early to mid-Cretaceous
Main group: Pterosauria (Pterodactyloidea)
Wingspan: 6 meters (19½ feet)
Weight: 12–14 kilograms (26½–31 pounds)
Diet: Oceanic surface prey, fish or squid
Fossils: South America

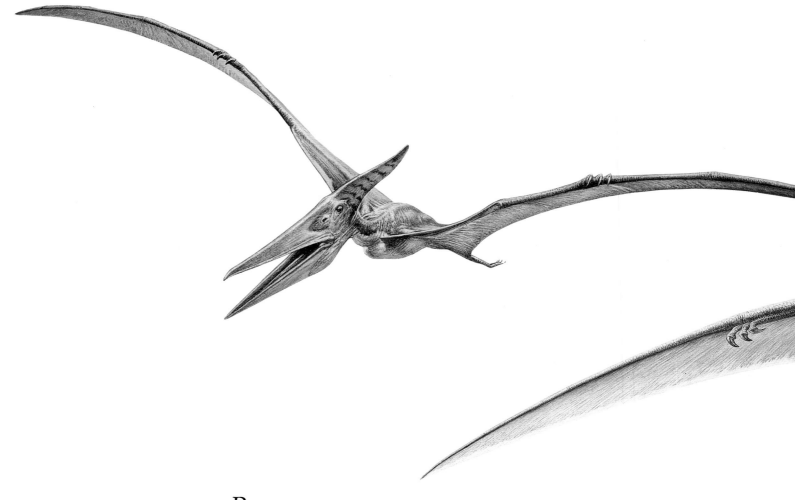

PTERANODON

PTEROSAUR FACTFILE
Pteranodon

Meaning: Toothless wing, no-toothed flier

Pronunciation: Tear-ann-owe-don

Period: Late Cretaceous

Main group: Pterosauria (Pterodactyloidea)

Wingspan: 9 meters (29½ feet)

Weight: 18 kilograms (40 pounds)

Diet: Oceanic surface prey, fish or squid

Fossils: USA

Pteranodon is the genus name for several species of large, long-beaked, head-crested pterosaurs from the Late Cretaceous period. Most of their fossils have been found in the midwestern and southwestern USA. The first specimens were named by Othniel Charles Marsh in 1876, between his numerous dinosaur finds. The larger species of *Pteranodon* were massive beasts with wings stretching almost 10 meters (33 feet) from tip to tip. The lower jaw alone was 120 centimeters (47 inches) in length. The slim, beak-like mouth was entirely toothless, and the whole pterosaur was finely structured, making it capable of lightweight agile flight. Most estimates of its air speed are in the range 40–50 kilometers (25–30 miles) per hour.

Different species of *Pteranodon* were distinguished, not only by size, but by the varied shapes of their head crests. All these crests were narrow from side to side, and projected back and up from the top of the skull, but some had a reversed "P" profile while others were more like a pointed witch's hat. Aerodynamic studies suggest that the crest counterbalanced the long beak to equalize the weight of the whole skull over the neck. Perhaps the crest acted as a rudder, too, for stability and steering in flight. Another suggestion is that the crest was brightly colored, like the beaks of toucans and puffins today, as a visual marker of maturity and readiness to mate. In the rest of its body, *Pteranodon* was a fairly typical pterodactyl-type pterosaur, although very large, with a short and sturdy neck, compact body, reduced legs and almost no tail. It probably lived along coasts and fed at sea.

ABOVE This version of *Pteranodon* has the head crest brightly patterned as an aid to recognition, perhaps by potential mates at breeding time. The long, pointed crest belonged to the species *Pteranodon ingens*. In some individuals it was slightly S-shaped, in others a straight point.

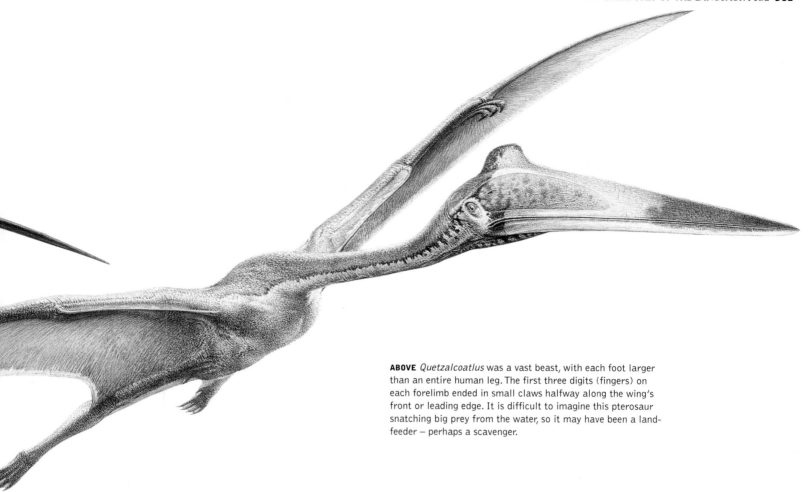

ABOVE *Quetzalcoatlus* was a vast beast, with each foot larger than an entire human leg. The first three digits (fingers) on each forelimb ended in small claws halfway along the wing's front or leading edge. It is difficult to imagine this pterosaur snatching big prey from the water, so it may have been a land-feeder — perhaps a scavenger.

QUETZALCOATLUS

This immense flier is known from fragments of fossils found in the border areas of northeastern Mexico and southern Texas. There is no complete or even partial skeleton, but there are sections of bones from the wing, skull parts, and other remains that indicate its huge size. *Quetzalcoatlus* was one of the largest flying animals known to have lived on earth. Its wingspan was at least 12 meters (39 feet), and could have been 14 or more, while its weight estimates range from 70 kilograms (154 pounds), similar to a well-built adult human today, to more than 100 kilograms (220 pounds). The neck alone was 3 meters (10 feet) in length, and the head, with its long, slim, entirely toothless beak and short, lumpy bony crest projecting behind, was 2 meters (6^1/$_2$ feet) in length.

Quetzalcoatlus was a pterodactyloid pterosaur (see page 377). It was named in 1975 for Quetzalcoatl, the feathered serpent god of the Aztec and other peoples of Mexico. It is doubtful whether *Quetzalcoatlus* had feathers – it may have been furry, as many pterosaurs were. It lived at the end of the Age of Dinosaurs, around 70–65 million years ago, and so may have swooped over the last of the North American dinosaurs, such as *Tyrannosaurus* and *Triceratops*. Other fossils found near those of *Quetzalcoatlus* suggest that it lived, or at least died, in fairly flat lands with meandering rivers, plains and swamps. One theory is that it was a giant scavenger, although it was more than four times larger than any scavenging bird of today, such as a condor or vulture. *Quetzalcoatlus* might have swooped down to a dinosaur carcass and poked in its long, slim beak, with its horn-rimmed jaw edges, to slice off pieces of meat.

In recent years fossils have been discovered of even larger pterosaurs, such as *Arambourgiana*, which could have wingspans in excess of of 15 meters (50 feet).

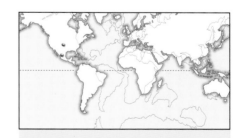

PTEROSAUR FACTFILE
Quetzalcoatlus

Meaning: After Quetzalcoatl (Mexican feathered serpent god)
Pronunciation: Kett-zal-coe-at-luss
Period: Late Cretaceous
Main group: Pterosauria (Pterodactyloidea)
Wingspan: 12–14 meters (39–46 feet)
Weight: 70–100 kilograms (154–220 pounds)
Diet: Scavenged meat, or fish and shellfish
Fossils: USA (Texas), Mexico

0 1 2 3 4 5 6 7 8 9 10 11 12 13

REPTILES OF LAKES AND SEAS

REPTILES GAINED THE INDEPENDENCE FROM WATER NEVER ACHIEVED BY THEIR AMPHIBIAN ANCESTORS, WITH FEATURES SUCH AS WATERPROOF EGGSHELLS AND SCALY SKINS. THEN, ALMOST AT ONCE, VARIOUS TYPES DIVED BACK INTO LAKES AND OCEANS, AS THEIR LEGS BECAME ADAPTED INTO PADDLES. AT LEAST 20 MAJOR REPTILE GROUPS REVERTED TO AQUATIC LIFESTYLES DURING THE AGE OF DINOSAURS. ONLY A FEW SURVIVE TODAY, INCLUDING TURTLES AND SOME TYPES OF CROCODILIANS.

RIGHT Mosasaurs were huge, long-fanged, powerful-bodied predators from the Late Cretaceous period. Despite their size and strength, they could not survive the mass extinction at the period's end. Some mosasaurs were twice the length and five times the weight of the biggest predatory fish today, the great white shark.

NOTHOSAURUS

REPTILE FACTFILE
Nothosaurus

Meaning: False reptile

Pronunciation: Noe-thoe-sore-uss

Period: Triassic

Main group: Nothosauria

Length: Up to 3 meters (10 feet)

Weight: Up to 250 kilograms (550 pounds)

Diet: Fish and similar sea animals

Fossils: Europe, Middle East, Asia

| 0 | 1 | 2 | 3 | 4 | 5 | 6 | 7 | 8 | 9 | 10 | 11 | 12 | 13 |

The nothosaurs were one of the first groups of reptiles to take up life in the sea. This was during the Triassic period, more than 240 million years ago, before the dinosaurs had appeared. The whole nothosaur group had just about disappeared by the end of the Triassic period, when the dinosaurs were achieving land domination.

Nothosaurs were long and slim, with long, narrow skulls and necks; long sharp fangs mainly in the front of the jaws near the snout tip; slim bodies, with long and flexible tails; and limbs partly modified as flippers. But, nothosaurs also retained some body features from living on land – their limbs were not totally flipper-like, as in the later ichthyosaurs, but each had five digits, which were possibly webbed.

Nothosaurus was a fairly typical genus of the group, with most species at around 1 meter (39 inches) in total length, with one up to 3 meters (10 feet). Various fossils have been found at sites right across Europe, as well as in the Middle East and in Asia. Fossils of a smaller "dwarf" species of *Nothosaurus* have recently been found in Israel. The long teeth and jaws in the arrow-like head suggest a fish-eater that darted and jabbed after prey using its long neck, swimming with its legs, and perhaps swishing its tail for extra propulsion. Once caught by the sharp teeth, which fitted together when the two jaws closed to form a "cage," the prey would have been swallowed whole. The limbs also indicate that *Nothosaurus* could move on land, if not very rapidly, with a waddling or sprawling gait. Perhaps it behaved like seals today, pursuing food such as fish and squid at sea, and then emerging onto land – "hauling out" – to rest and possibly to breed.

ABOVE *Nothosaurus* would appear sleek and streamlined in the water, swimming rapidly by powerful kicks of its webbed feet. Its group may have taken advantage by evolving as aquatic predators in a shallow sea that appeared in Triassic times, over what is now southeast Europe and the Middle East.

PLACODUS

The placodonts, like the nothosaurs (see opposite), were among the first reptiles to take to the sea. Also like the nothosaurs, they lasted only through the Triassic period. At a glance, *Placodus* resembles a giant newt, some 2 meters (6½ feet) long, or perhaps a crocodile. But placodonts were a distinct group of reptiles. They are named for the flattened teeth in the rear of their upper and lower jaws, which were broad and therefore suited to crushing hard food, probably shellfish. Some sharks today, such as the Port Jackson shark, have similar "table top" teeth. Even the palate (roof of the mouth) had hardened, tooth-like plates. The fronts of the jaws, however, bore teeth shaped more like pegs, and angled forward. These may have been used to lever shellfish off rocks, or scoop them out of mud and seaweed.

Placodus could swim by swishing its long tail from side to side, in the manner of a crocodile. There may have been a low flap or fin along the top of the tail for increased propulsion. *Placodus* may also have kicked with its webbed feet, to steer or for extra speed. It could probably move on land reasonably well, although its legs would have sprawled out sideways, like those of most non-dinosaur reptiles. It has been suggested that *Placodus* lived in shallow coastal lagoons and swamps, where an ability to move on land and water was more helpful than would be a specialized adaptation to just one of these media. There was probably "armor" of knobs and plates over parts of the body. In some later placodonts, such as *Placochelys* and *Henodus*, these plates became much enlarged, resembling the shell of a turtle.

REPTILE FACTFILE
Placodus
Meaning: Flat plate tooth, flattened tooth
Pronunciation: Plack-owe-duss
Period: Early and Middle Triassic
Main group: Placodontia
Length: 2 meters (6½ feet)
Weight: 100 kilograms (220 pounds)
Diet: Shellfish
Fossils: Europe

| 0 | 1 | 2 | 3 | 4 | 5 | 6 | 7 | 8 | 9 | 10 | 11 | 12 | 13 |

BELOW The entire mouth of *Placodus* was designed for crushing, with flattened teeth covering the upper jaws and mouth roof, and similar slab-like teeth in the lower jaw. The overall body shape suggests a compromise design for swamp-style survival, whether swimming in shallow water or slithering across soft ground.

METRIORHYNCHUS

REPTILE FACTFILE
Metriorhynchus
Meaning: Medium snout, moderate nose
Pronunciation: Met-ree-owe-rink-uss
Period: Late Jurassic
Main group: Crocodilia
Length: 3 meters (10 feet)
Weight: 200 kilograms (440 pounds)
Diet: Fish and similar sea animals
Fossils: South America, Europe

0	1	2	3	4	5	6	7	8	9	10	11	12	13

Only one crocodile today habitually ventures into the sea – the estuarine or saltwater crocodile of the Indo-Pacific. It is also the largest living reptile. Crocodilians are one of the smallest reptile groups today, with only 23 species, but they have had a long and varied history, beginning around the same time as the dinosaurs, during the Triassic period more than 200 million years ago. Some lived on dry land, almost like lizards, while others lived in rivers and freshwater swamps, like their descendants today.

Metriorhynchus was one of the dinosaur-age crocodiles most adapted to the sea. Its fossils have been found as far apart as Chile in South America, and England and France in Europe. It was half the size of the modern saltwater crocodile, but better adapted to swimming and catching fish. The snout was long and slender, with rows of small but very sharp teeth – in these features it resembled one crocodilian alive today, the gharial (or gavial) of the Indian subcontinent. The rear of the skull, bearing the eyes and ears, was broad and boxy, and the neck was short and thick. The front limbs could be used as steering rudders or rise-and-dive hydrofoils. The rear limbs had longer feet and may have assisted with forward power or maneuvering. The tail end was probably expanded into a fin with fleshy upper and lower lobes, the backbone curving down into the lower one – similar to the tails of some sharks. *Metriorhynchus* probably did not have the large, protective bony scales or plates typical of many other crocodilians through the ages, and relied on speed and agility in the water to catch food and avoid enemies.

LEFT The living crocodile known as the gharial has a long, slender snout studded with small but sharp teeth.

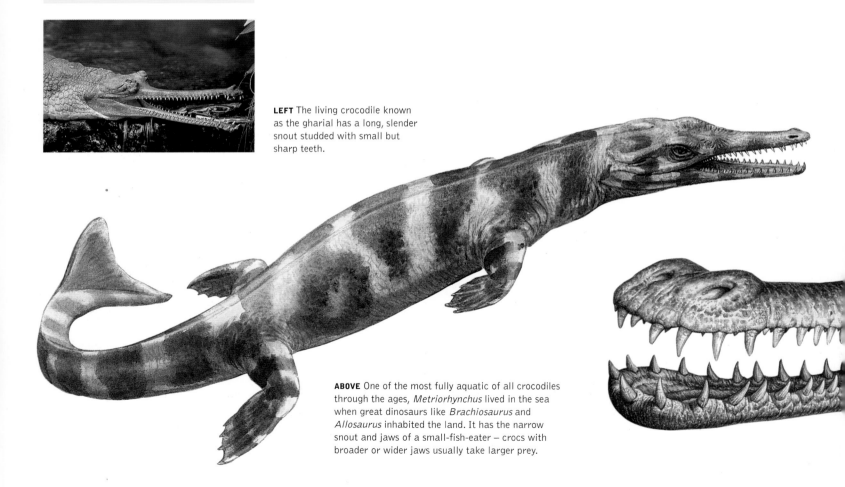

ABOVE One of the most fully aquatic of all crocodiles through the ages, *Metriorhynchus* lived in the sea when great dinosaurs like *Brachiosaurus* and *Allosaurus* inhabited the land. It has the narrow snout and jaws of a small-fish-eater – crocs with broader or wider jaws usually take larger prey.

SARCOSUCHUS

This monster crocodile was over twice the length and more than five times the weight of any crocodilian (or any other reptile) alive today. Recently its remains have been excavated from the fossil-rich rocks in the Tenere Desert, part of the great Sahara in northern Niger, Africa. These sites have already yielded many exciting discoveries of dinosaur remains, mostly during the 1990s, such as the vast sauropod *Jobaria*; another sauropod, *Nigersaurus*; the sail-backed ornithopod *Ouranosaurus*; and the massive meat-eaters *Carcharodontosaurus* and *Suchomimus* – all described in this book.

Sarcosuchus remains include a fairly complete skull and also parts of a skeleton, dated to 110 million years ago. The skull is almost 2 meters (6½ feet) long and the jaws bear more than 100 very sharp teeth. The upper jaw overbit

the lower, and long incisor teeth impaled the victim. There is a bony lump on the top of the snout, as possessed by older males of the crocodile today known as the gharial (or gavial). There were scutes (bony plates) that protected much of the body. The genus *Sarcosuchus* was founded in 1964 with the discovery of fossils by Albert-Félix de Lapparent, a French paleontologist. It was named two years later by France de Broin and Philippe Taquet. The find of a larger specimen in Niger by American dinosaur expert Paul Sereno was announced in 2001. *Sarcosuchus* rivals another huge crocodile, *Deinosuchus* (*Phobosuchus*), from the Late Cretaceous rocks of Texas, as the largest-ever member of the crocodilian group (see page 101). It may have grabbed dinosaurs as they fed along the banks.

REPTILE FACTFILE
Sarcosuchus

Meaning: Flesh crocodile

Pronunciation: Sark-owe-sook-uss

Period: mid-Cretaceous

Main group: Crocodilia

Length: 11–13 meters (32–40 feet)

Weight: 8–10 metric tons (8–10 tons)

Diet: Large animals including dinosaurs

Fossils: Niger, Brazil

BELOW *Sarcosuchus* remains come from a fossil-rich area known as Gadoufaoua in Niger. About 110 million years ago this was crisscrossed by rivers, and *Sarcosuchus* probably lay in the water, almost unnoticed, or lurked among fringing vegetation.

ICHTHYOSAURUS

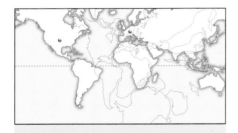

REPTILE FACTFILE

Ichthyosaurus (many species)

Meaning: Fish reptile

Pronunciation: Ick-thee-owe-sore-uss

Period: Jurassic

Main group: Ichthyosauria

Length: Average 2 meters (6½ feet)

Weight: Around 80–100 kilograms
(176–220 pounds)

Diet: Fish, shellfish, other marine animals

Fossils: Mainly Europe

There are several species in the genus *Ichthyosaurus*, meaning "fish reptile" or "fish lizard." These common and widespread creatures were not fish, or lizards, or dinosaurs: ichthyosaurs formed a distinct group of reptiles that appeared in the seas at around the same time that dinosaurs were spreading across the land. Ichthyosaurs are very well known from hundreds of remains at dozens of sites in Europe. They were the most water-adapted of all reptiles, with swimming flippers rather than walking limbs. The ichthyosaurs were named in 1818, before any dinosaurs had been named, by Charles Koenig. The various species of *Ichthyosaurus* and its cousins lived from the Early Jurassic period to the Early Cretaceous, a span of more than 60 million years.

A typical *Ichthyosaurus* was around 2 meters (6½ feet) long. Fossils of exceptional quality show the softer body parts, such as flesh and skin, allowing a complete "snapshot" of the animal. It bore a striking outer resemblance to a fish or a dolphin, due to what is known as "convergent evolution," where living things from different groups come to look like each other outwardly due to their similar patterns of behavior and similar environments. *Ichthyosaurus* had four paddle-limbs, allowing maneuvering control; a back or dorsal fin, used for stability at speed; and a two-lobed tail, which was thrashed from side to side to provide the main push for swimming. Recent reviews of the huge genus *Ichthyosaurus* propose that various species within it are assigned to other genera, in one of the "splitting" or rearrangement exercises which occasionally happens in paleontology. In dinosaurs the opposite usually happens as several species are "lumped" into one.

ABOVE *Ichthyosaurus*'s many small, sharp teeth were suited to catching fish and squid or biting through an ammonoid's shell, as in this illustration.

SHONISAURUS

A few fossils of early ichthyosaurs (see opposite) from near the start of the Triassic period show how this reptile group evolved from land-based ancestors through to wriggling, eel-like types with legs that were turning into flippers. By the Late Triassic period, the giant *Shonisaurus* had appeared. It is known from an almost complete skeleton unearthed in Nevada. It shows how the ichthyosaurs had become completely at home in the water, even though, being reptiles, they were air-breathers. The nostrils of *Shonisaurus* were just in front of its eyes, on the forehead. This allowed the animal to break the surface of the water with only this small part of the body, to take in fresh air and perhaps look around, before diving back under the waves.

Shonisaurus was one of the largest ichthyosaurs, with an overall length of some 15 meters (49 feet) – exceeding that of the biggest meat-eating dinosaurs such as *Giganotosaurus*. *Shonisaurus* also had a number of unusual features that show that it was not a typical member of the ichthyosaur group but perhaps a member of a specialized "side branch" of evolution. Its paddle-like limbs were very long and narrow compared to those of other ichthyosaurs, and all four were around the same length, while in other types the front two were longer than the rear pair. The snout was also exceptionally long and pointed, and it had fish-seizing teeth only near the front of its jaws. The body was massive, more comparable in size to a whale than a dolphin. But, there were basic differences between ichthyosaurs like *Shonisaurus* and aquatic mammals like whales and dolphins. Ichthyosaurs had four flippers and upright tail fins, while aquatic mammals have two flippers and horizontal tail flukes.

REPTILE FACTFILE

Shonisaurus

Meaning: Shoshone reptile

Pronunciation: Shon-ee-sore-uss

Period: Late Triassic

Main group: Ichthyosauria

Length: 15 meters (49 feet)

Weight: 20 metric tons (20 tons)

Diet: Fish and other sea creatures

Fossils: USA

RIGHT Almost the size of a modern great whale, *Shonisaurus* was the largest known ichthyosaur until discovery of 20-meter-plus (66-feet) specimens in Canada. It was named after the region where its fossils are common, the Shoshone Mountains of Nevada, especially near the old mining town of Berlin. *Shonisaurus* is the state fossil animal of Nevada.

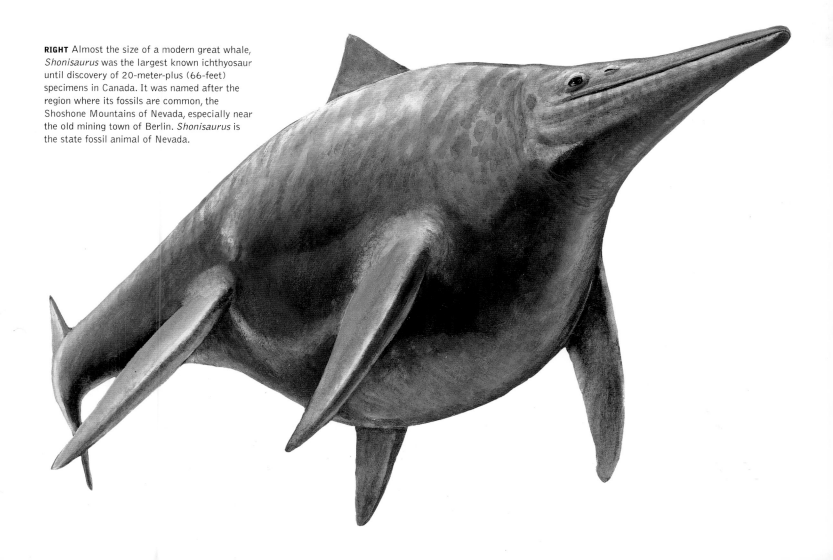

BREATHING AND SWIMMING

As some reptiles took to lakes and seas, their weight-bearing legs were converted into paddle-like flippers, and their bodies became streamlined, reducing water resistance. However, the gills that their distant ancestors had used for breathing underwater did not reappear. Like marine mammals today, such as dolphins and whales, they had to visit the surface regularly to breathe air through their nostrils or "blowholes."

RIGHT "Long and short" during the Late Cretacous period. In the background, the long-necked plesiosaur *Elasmosaurus* cruises the surface waters, while in the foreground, a pliosaur (short-necked plesiosaur) holds its breath to hunt the curly-shelled mollusc called an ammonoid. Another reptile, the huge turtle *Archelon*, swims off to the left.

OPHTHALMOSAURUS

REPTILE FACTFILE
Ophthalmosaurus

Meaning: Eye reptile, sight reptile

Pronunciation: Op-thal-moe-sore-uss

Period: Late Jurassic

Main group: Ichthyosauria

Length: 3–5 meters (10–16½ feet)

Weight: 500 kilograms (1,100 pounds)

Diet: Squid, fish

Fossils: North and South America, Europe

The largest eyes of any animal today, being almost the size of soccer balls, belong to the giant squid. The ichthyosaurs challenge this record for prehistoric creatures, and certainly for the record of largest eyes in any vertebrate (animal with a backbone). The eyeballs of *Ophthalmosaurus* were almost 10 centimeters (3 inches) across – around the size of an adult human fist. (Those of *Temnodontosaurus*, another Jurassic ichthyosaur, were twice as big.) *Ophthalmosaurus* remains are known from several fossil sites, in particular in Argentina, where a range of specimens seem to show how this reptile grew and developed from baby to adult. Fossils of other ichthyosaurs, especially *Ichthyosaurus* itself, show that the babies did not hatch from eggs; they were born, small but fully formed, emerging from the mother. Unlike most other marine reptiles in this

chapter, ichthyosaurs seem to have been so fully water-adapted that they could not come ashore to lay eggs.

Ophthalmosaurus probably had huge eyes for the same reason that the giant squid has them – to hunt prey in the dark ocean. The bulging eyeball had a circle of bones around it, called the sclerotic ring, providing support and protection. This skeletal feature is also seen in some dinosaurs. Other fossils found in rocks associated with *Ophthalmosaurus* include fish scales, and also the curly shells of ammonoids and the bullet-like internal shells of belemnoids – both prehistoric cousins of today's squid and octopus (see page 49). All of these creatures could have been caught by *Ophthalmosaurus* after a quick pursuit and sudden sideways swipe of its long, narrow, beak-like but tooth-filled snout.

ABOVE *Ophthalmosaurus* had relatively short, rounded flippers compared to many other ichthyosaurs. Its large eyes may signify that it dived deep to find food, or that it was mainly active at night as fish and squid rose from deeper waters to feed on surface plankton.

PLESIOSAURUS

The plesiosaurs were a large and successful group of marine reptiles that lived through most of the Age of Dinosaurs. There were several subgroups, including the short-necked types called pliosaurs, such as *Kronosaurus* and *Liopleurodon* (see pages 395, 396). The group was established on the basis of *Plesiosaurus*, meaning "near reptile," because its skull and backbone were basically reptilian, but it had unusual shoulders, hips and flipper-like limbs. The name dates back to 1821, twenty years before the name "dinosaur" came into being. It was given by Henry de la Beche and William Conybeare to remains from the fossil-rich Jurassic rocks near Lyme Regis in Dorset, on England's south coast. Here the first known professional fossil-collector, Mary Anning, scoured the shore for beautiful and intricate specimens, which she sold to collectors as part of the fashion for natural history.

Plesiosaurus had a smallish head, long neck, tubby body, four limbs shaped like paddles and a short, smoothly tapering tail. The bones of the limb girdles (shoulders and hips), and the chest and abdominal area, were all strongly reinforced and linked by sturdy joints that must have been moved by very powerful muscles. The upper limb bones within the base of each flipper were short and stout, so that the elongated toe bones made up most of each flipper's area. It was once thought that the plesiosaurs rowed with a forward-backward motion of their flippers, like the oars of a rowing boat. It seems more likely however, that they flapped their limbs up and down, using them like a bird's wings to "fly" underwater. Today's sea turtles and penguins move in a very similar manner, flapping rather than rowing.

REPTILE FACTFILE
Plesiosaurus
Meaning: Near reptile
Pronunciation: Plee-zee-owe-sore-uss
Period: Early Jurassic
Main group: Plesiosauria (Plesiosauridae)
Length: Up to 2.5 meters (8 feet)
Weight: 150 kilograms (330 pounds)
Diet: Fish and similar marine prey
Fossils: Mainly Europe (especially southern England), but also most other continents

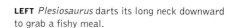

| 0 | 1 | 2 | 3 | 4 | 5 | 6 | 7 | 8 | 9 | 10 | 11 | 12 | 13 |

LEFT *Plesiosaurus* darts its long neck downward to grab a fishy meal.

BELOW The widely-splayed digits (fingers and toes) of *Plesiosaurus* are revealed within the paddles in this beautifully complete specimen.

ELASMOSAURUS

REPTILE FACTFILE

Elasmosaurus

Meaning: Plate reptile

Pronunciation: Ee-laz-moe-sore-uss

Period: Late Cretaceous

Main group: Plesiosauria (Plesiosauridae)

Length: 13–14 meters (43–46 feet)

Weight: 2 metric tons (2 tons)

Diet: Fish and similar animals

Fossils: North America

Fossils of *Elasmosaurus* have been found in North America with close cousins in Japan and elsewhere in East Asia. Toward the end of the dinosaur age, these sites were all parts of the same seabed – or at least the same system of connected seas. *Elasmosaurus* was a long-necked plesiosaur (see *Plesiosaurus*, page 393). In fact, it was the longest-necked of the group, for its neck formed about 6 meters (19½ feet) of its total length of 14 meters (46 feet). *Elasmosaurus* was also one of the last plesiosaurs: the whole group disappeared along with the dinosaurs in the mass extinction at the end of the Cretaceous period.

Elasmosaurus had a tiny head, and quite how it gathered enough food for its bulky body has long been a puzzle. It was once believed that *Elasmosaurus* probably floated or paddled at the sea's surface, its head held several meters above the water, as it peered for fish and other food below the waves. It would have darted

its neck down and snatched a victim in its mouth, either jabbing with its long front teeth, or closing its mouth around the item, its teeth coming together like the bars of a cage to prevent the prey escaping. But, since the eyes were on top of the skull of *Elasmosaurus*, looking down into the water from high above would have been awkward, with the snout and jaws in the way. Another theory is that *Elasmosaurus* flapped slowly at fish shoals and darted its neck to grab what it could. Experts are divided on whether the neck was flexible or not. Fossilized gut contents of plesiosaurs in general show they ate a mixture of fish, molluscs such as squid and ammonites, and other small sea creatures.

ABOVE *Elasmosaurus* holds the record for the largest number of cervical vertebrae (neckbones) of any animal, at around 72. (Mammals, including human beings, have only seven.)

KRONOSAURUS

This sea reptile was a pliosaur – a member of the plesiosaur group, but in the subgroup Pliosauridae, with the distinctive feature of a much shorter, thicker neck. Pliosaurs were more heavily built, more streamlined, faster and fiercer than other plesiosaurs, and were suited to catching fewer, larger meals with their massive jaws and rows of sharp front teeth up to 25 centimeters (10 inches) long. The huge head, which was mostly mouth, also had large eyes and an offset pair of nostrils that gave it its "water-sniffing" ability, as in other plesiosaurs (see page 390). A pliosaur swam with all of its four limbs, which had evolved into long, wide, strong flippers, one at each corner of the elongated body. The tail was short and tapering, as in other plesiosaurs, and was perhaps used only for steering. *Kronosaurus* was one of the largest pliosaurs and lived in the Early Cretaceous period. Most of its fossils are known from Australia, where they were first discovered in 1889 in Queensland, which was covered by shallow sea some 120 million years ago. The name was given in 1924 by Heber Longman. For many years, estimates put the total length of *Kronosaurus* at up to 13 meters (43 feet), but recent studies of its fossil skull and other parts, and comparisons with other pliosaurs, suggest that the true length was probably 9–10 meters (29½–33 feet). Other creatures preserved from the time include numerous fish and various molluscs such as squid, ammonites and belemnites. Some of their fossil shells bear tooth marks that could have been made by *Kronosaurus*, whose rear teeth were rounded and suited to crushing hard-cased victims.

BELOW By paddling opposing flippers in opposite directions, *Kronosaurus* could turn on the spot.

REPTILE FACTFILE

Kronosaurus

Meaning: Time reptile

Pronunciation: Kroe-noe-sore-uss

Period: Early Cretaceous

Main group: Plesiosauria (Pliosauridae)

Length: 9–10 meters (29½–33 feet)

Weight: 10–20 metric tons (10–20 tons)

Diet: Large sea animals

Fossils: Australia, South America

LIOPLEURODON

REPTILE FACTFILE

Liopleurodon

Meaning: Smooth-sided tooth

Pronunciation: Lie-owe-plure-owe-don

Period: Late Jurassic

Main group: Plesiosauria (Pliosauridae)

Length: 15–20 meters (49–66 feet)

Weight: 30–50 metric tons (30–50 tons)

Diet: Large sea animals

Fossils: Europe, possibly South America

When we imagine the greatest predators of the dinosaur age, *Tyrannosaurus* and the even larger *Giganotosaurus* usually spring to mind. Yet even they could not compare to *Liopleurodon*, a reptile like the dinosaurs but a denizen of the open ocean. *Liopleurodon* was a pliosaur, or short-necked plesiosaur, like *Kronosaurus* on the previous page, but probably even huger. Some of the uppermost estimates put *Liopleurodon* at 25 meters (82 feet) long and 100 metric tons (100 tons) in weight, which would mean that it rivaled the largest sauropod dinosaurs, and even today's great whales, as one of the largest creatures that ever lived on Earth. Its true size may have been only around one half of such estimates, however. If so, *Liopleurodon* would have been only slightly smaller than the creature often called the biggest hunter the world has seen, and one that we know for certain exists – the sperm whale of today. This whale can grow to more than 50 metric tons (50 tons) and lives for well over 60 years.

Fossils of *Liopleurodon* have been excavated from various sites in France, Germany, England, eastern Europe and possibly Chile, and include parts of the skull, jaws, teeth and skeletal bones. They have been known for well over a century – *Liopleurodon* was named in 1873 by Henri Sauvage, a French fossil expert – but a discovery in 1991 revealed a much larger specimen with the skull alone being 3 meters (10 feet) long. The mouth and jaws were so huge and powerful that they were probably suited to tackling the occasional single large prey, including other aquatic reptiles like plesiosaurs or ichthyosaurs, rather than gathering a host of smaller victims in the way that great whales and other "filter-feeders" do.

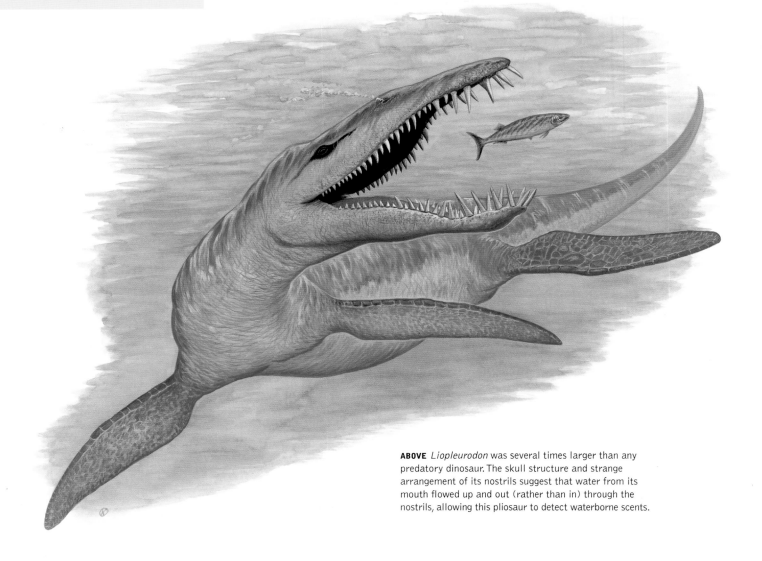

ABOVE *Liopleurodon* was several times larger than any predatory dinosaur. The skull structure and strange arrangement of its nostrils suggest that water from its mouth flowed up and out (rather than in) through the nostrils, allowing this pliosaur to detect waterborne scents.

MOSASAURUS

In the 1770s, massive and mysterious fossils of jaws and teeth were dug from a chalk mine near the River Meuse at a site now in the Netherlands in northwestern Europe. Around 30 years later, Georges Cuvier, a French biologist who was then one of the world's leading authorities on animals, noticed their similarity to the jaws and teeth of modern lizards and named them *Mosasaurus*, meaning "Meuse reptile." Cuvier believed that they had been created by God like every other animal, but had perished in a great flood, perhaps *the* Great Flood recorded in the Bible. This was how most scientists of the time viewed what we now call the fossil record. It was still many years before Richard Owen coined the name Dinosauria or Charles Darwin explained evolution (see page 10).

Cuvier was right in one respect, however: *Mosasaurus* is believed to have been an ancient but close relative of today's monitor lizards. Mosasaurs were seagoing monsters that appeared in the Late Cretaceous period,

probably evolving from small four-legged predators that lived semiaquatic lives in swamps or along seashores. Mosasaurs became spectacularly huge and fierce, some exceeding 15 meters (49 feet) in length. The head tapered via the neck into the body, which was long and slim like an eel's, with all four limbs being adapted as flippers for control in the water. Most of the pushing power came from the very long, flexible and muscular tail, which was narrow from side to side but fin-like near the end. When the ichthyosaurs faded, mosasaurs vied with pliosaurs like *Kronosaurus* and *Liopleurodon* (see opposite) as the greatest predatory reptiles of the Cretaceous seas. One of the biggest mosasaurs, *Tylosaurus*, is known from fossils found in Kansas. So many mosasaurs have been found in this state that it is famed as the "world center" for this group.

BELOW The massive head of *Mosasaurus* had sharp teeth, not only in the huge jaws but also on the bony palate (roof of the mouth).

REPTILE FACTFILE
Mosasaurus

Meaning: Meuse reptile (from its discovery site)

Pronunciation: Moe-zah-sore-use

Period: Late Cretaceous

Main group: Mosasauria

Length: 10 meters (33 feet)

Weight: 5 metric tons (5 tons)

Diet: Sea animals

Fossils: USA (Kansas), Europe

| 0 | 1 | 2 | 3 | 4 | 5 | 6 | 7 | 8 | 9 | 10 | 11 | 12 | 13 |

CRETACEOUS SKIES AND SEAS

AT SEVERAL FOSSIL SITES DATED TO THE MID-CRETACEOUS PERIOD, THE MAKE-UP OF THE SEDIMENTS, AND THE VARIOUS FOSSILS OF SMALL SHELLFISH AND OTHER MARINE CREATURES, SHOW THAT THE AREAS WERE ONCE COVERED BY WARM, SHALLOW SEAS, OR WERE NEAR THE SHORELINES. FOSSILS INCLUDE THE REMAINS OF OCEANIC REPTILES LIKE PLESIOSAURS AND MOSASAURS, AND OF FLYING PTEROSAURS WHICH PERHAPS CAME TO GRIEF BY CRASHING ONTO THE SURFACE AND WERE THEN UNABLE TO TAKE OFF AND SO SANK INTO THE PRESERVING MUD. THIS WAS A PERIOD OF GREAT DIVERSITY AMONG GREAT REPTILES AND THEIR COUSINS.

RIGHT The pterosaur *Pteranodon* banks steeply and flaps strongly to escape the huge teeth and jaws of a mosasaur surging up from the sea. To the right, the amazingly long necks of elasmosaurs arch above the waves, searching for prey such as small fish just below the surface. However recent theories have cast doubt on this method of hunting for *Elasmosaurus*, and suggest it grabbed prey while fully submerged.

MEGAZOSTRODON

MAMMAL FACTFILE

Megazostrodon

Meaning: Large girdle tooth

Pronunciation: Meg-ah-zos-troe-don

Period: Late Triassic to Early Jurassic

Main group: Mammalia

Length: 10–12 centimeters (4–5 inches)

Weight: 50 grams (2 ounces)

Diet: Insects, grubs, worms

Fossils: Southern Africa

The earliest mammals crop up as fossils in rocks from the Late Triassic period. *Megazostrodon* is one of these. A fairly complete skeleton was excavated from a site in Lesotho in southern Africa, where remains of dinosaurs from around the same time have also been found (see *Lesothosaurus*, page 269). *Megazostrodon* is included in the mammal group for various reasons, especially the detailed structure of its jawbones, some of which had become tiny earbones – one of the mammals' defining features. Its skull, hardly larger than a human thumb, contained sharp teeth that suggest that it was a carnivore – it hunted other creatures, probably small insects, worms and similar soil or leaf-litter animals. *Megazostrodon* had differentiated teeth in various parts of its mouth, unlike most reptiles, including most dinosaurs. *Megazostrodon*'s dentition included straight-edged incisors at the fronts of the jaws, pointed canines behind, then chewing premolars, and, in the cheek region, molars each with three cusps (raised points), which assign it to the ancient mammal group Triconodontia.

Megazostrodon had four walking legs and a long snout, and was probably active mainly at night, using its large eyes, acute hearing and sensitive vibrissae (whiskers) to find its way. (Whiskers are modified, extra-long hairs from the mammalian furry coat.) Being nocturnal and warm-blooded would have allowed *Megazostrodon* to move quickly at any time, including the cool of the night. This would have helped it avoid predatory reptiles and other enemies, since such cold-blooded creatures would have been unable to race about at speed in low temperatures.

ABOVE Wide-eyed, with long whiskers, *Megazostrodon* was well adapted for a nocturnal lifestyle.

MORGANUCODON

In many respects, *Morganucodon* resembles *Megazostrodon*, shown opposite – but this is partly because the fossils of each have been used to help reconstruct the other. *Morganucodon* lived during the Early Jurassic period, as the dinosaurs were spreading and diversifying. Like other very early mammals, it was probably nocturnal. It may have emerged from a burrow or crevice at dusk, and then hunted for grubs, bugs and similar small items of food, scratching at the soil or nosing in leaf litter, using its well-developed senses of hearing and smell. Fossils of the cranium (braincase) show that the parts or lobes of the brain that dealt with these senses were particularly well developed. Also, the brain was almost completely encased in bone, as it is in modern mammals. This was not the case in most reptiles or in the mammal-like reptiles called cynodonts that could have given rise to true mammals (see page 112).

Morganucodon's skull was less than 3 centimeters (1 inch) long. It reveals how the jawbones had changed from the typical reptilian pattern: *Morganucodon*'s lower jaw was made almost entirely of one bone rather than two or three fused together. Other bones had shrunk and become incorporated into the ear, for hearing. It had small incisor teeth in the front of the jaw, two long pointed canines, premolars and long three-cusped molars for chewing its food. *Morganucodon* stood almost upright on its four legs with the erect limb posture shared by dinosaurs, birds and mammals. The fossils of *Morganucodon* were first discovered in caves in South Wales and the name was bestowed in 1941 by F.W. Parrington. More recent finds have been made in China. Like *Megazostrodon*, *Morganucodon* is sometimes regarded as a member of the early mammal group, Triconodontia, from the three mounds or cusps on each molar tooth.

MAMMAL FACTFILE
Morganucodon
Meaning: Morgan's tooth
Pronunciation: More-gan-you-coe-don
Period: Early Jurassic
Main group: Mammalia
Length: 15 centimeters (6 inches)
Weight: 80 grams (3 ounces)
Diet: Insects and worms
Fossils: China, Britain

ABOVE *Moganucodon* grabs a tasty cockroach in its tiny but sharp teeth. This early mammal probably lived a similar lifestyle to the shrews of today, energetically hunting and ferociously devouring all kinds of small creatures.

ZALAMBDALESTES

MAMMAL FACTFILE

Zalambdalestes

Meaning: Much-like-lambda robber or stealer

Pronunciation: Zall-amb-dah-less-teez

Period: Late Cretaceous

Main group: Mammalia (placentals)

Length: 20 centimeters (8 inches)

Weight: 100 grams (4 ounces)

Diet: Insects

Fossils: Mongolia

0 1 2 3 4 5 6 7 8 9 10 11 12 13

Zalambdalestes lived during the Late Cretaceous period, before the great extinction that wiped out the dinosaurs and many other forms of life. Its fossils come from Mongolia where many and varied dinosaurs thrived at the time, including meat-eaters such as *Velociraptor*, ostrich dinosaurs, and horned plant-eaters like *Protoceratops*. *Zalambdalestes* probably avoided these by hiding in a burrow by day, emerging to feed under cover of darkness. The shape and details of its skull show that it had a long, low snout, presumably with whiskers to feel the way, big eyes to see in the gloom and large ears to detect sounds of danger.

Zalambdalestes had rear limbs that were longer and stronger than the front ones, although all four limbs showed the upright posture typical of mammals. Probably it could leap well, using its rear limbs and very long feet, its calcaneus (rearmost anklebone) in

contact with the ground. Various details in the fossils – such as four premolar and three molar teeth in each side of each jaw, the shape of the molars, and the structure of the shoulder, elbow and ankle – are very similar to those found in today's placental mammals, as opposed to marsupial ones. *Zalambdalestes* is often compared to the elephant shrew in Africa today – an active, busy eater of insects and other small animals, with a long, quivering, trunk-like nose, leaping back legs and long, balancing tail.

BELOW *Zalambdalestes* received its tongue-twisting name from the shape of its teeth. The crushing or working surfaces of some teeth had raised lumps or ridges forming a pattern on each tooth similar in shape to the ancient Greek letter lambda. This dinosaur-age mammal is one of the first known with very long rear feet, probably for leaping.

RIGHT Fossils discovered and studied in the 1990s lend weight to the view that *Deltatheridium* was a type of marsupial mammal, especially from the evidence of how old teeth were replaced by newer ones, and the patterns of grooves and holes in the skull which show the routes of blood vessels and nerves.

DELTATHERIDIUM

This mammal lived at around the same time, 80 million years ago, and in the same region, Mongolia, as *Zalambdalestes* (opposite). It was smaller in size, with a total length, including tail, of some 15 centimeters (6 inches), however, it differed in many respects from *Zalambdalestes*. *Deltatheridium* was one of many mammals from near the end of the Age of Dinosaurs, showing how the mammal group had diversified and spread to various regions over the preceding 130 million years.

Deltatheridium is usually likened in overall appearance to a possum, or perhaps a weasel with slightly longer legs. Its skull was long but the muzzle was relatively tall, giving a large-nosed appearance. The tail was also fairly long. The teeth show the usual mammalian pattern of small, sharp incisors at the front, then one large, pointed, stabbing canine in each side of each jaw and, behind this, lower and wider premolars and molars in the cheeks, for chewing. The shapes of the molars, when seen from above, that is, in the opposing jaw, are triangular, rather than forming a rounded rectangle. This led to the name of the mammal, "delta" meaning a triangular shape. (Many of these small, early mammals are named after their tooth shapes – see also opposite.) The teeth are arranged so that the upper and lower molars slide past each other and interlock when the jaws close, rather than their topmost surfaces butting together. This gave a powerful shearing and chopping effect, which is also seen in the long-extinct mammal group known as creodonts, which were predators (flesh-eaters). Creodonts are considered to have been placental mammals, but other features of the skull and skeleton are more similar to those of marsupial mammals. *Deltatheridium* probably hunted insects and baby reptiles, and perhaps scavenged using its powerful chewing jaws.

MAMMAL FACTFILE
Deltatheridium

Meaning: Triangle or delta beast

Pronunciation: Del-tah-thurr-id-ee-um

Period: Late Cretaceous

Main group: Mammalia

Length: 15 centimeters (6 inches)

Weight: 80 grams (3 ounces)

Diet: Insects

Fossils: Mongolia

CHAPTER FIFTEEN

AFTER THE DINOSAURS

THE AGE OF DINOSAURS CLOSED ABRUPTLY 65 MILLION YEARS AGO,
WITH ONE OF THE GREAT MASS EXTINCTIONS THAT HAVE PERIODICALLY
DEVASTATED LIFE ON EARTH. TWO MAJOR ANIMAL GROUPS SURVIVED AND
SOON BURGEONED – THE BIRDS AND THE MAMMALS.

MASS EXTINCTIONS

IT MAY SEEM STRANGE, EVEN CONVENIENT, THAT THE TRANSITION FROM THE CRETACEOUS PERIOD TO THE TERTIARY, 65 MILLION YEARS AGO, WAS MARKED BY ONE OF THE MOST CATASTROPHIC EVENTS THE WORLD HAS EVER SEEN. BUT THIS IS SIMPLY THE CUSTOMARY SCIENTIFIC WAY IN WHICH GEOLOGICAL PERIODS ARE DEFINED – BY ABRUPT CHANGES IN THE ROCKS AND THE FOSSILS THEY CONTAIN. THIS PARTICULAR TRANSITION IS KNOWN AS THE CRETACEOUS–TERTIARY, OR K/T, MASS EXTINCTION EVENT. THE "K" STANDS FOR KRETA, THE ANCIENT GREEK WORD FOR "CHALK" THAT IS THE BASIS OF THE TERM "CRETACEOUS," SO NAMED BECAUSE MANY OF THE ROCKS FROM THAT PERIOD ARE CHALKS. MASS EXTINCTIONS WERE NOT NEW, HOWEVER. AT LEAST A DOZEN OCCURRED THROUGH PREHISTORY. THE GREATEST ONE OF ALL MARKED THE END OF THE PERMIAN PERIOD AND THE START OF THE TRIASSIC, 250 MILLION YEARS AGO, AND THEREFORE AROUND 185 MILLION YEARS BEFORE THE K/T EVENT. SURVEYS OF THE FOSSIL EVIDENCE SUGGEST THAT PERHAPS 19 OUT OF 20 LIVING SPECIES DISAPPEARED AT THE END OF THE PERMIAN PERIOD, IN WHAT HAS BEEN DUBBED THE "GREAT DYING." THIS MASSIVE SHOCK TO LIFE SIGNIFIED THE START OF A NEW ERA, THE MESOZOIC ("MIDDLE LIFE"), COMMONLY CALLED THE AGE OF DINOSAURS. THE K/T EVENT CLOSED THAT ERA, AND WITH IT THE DINOSAURS' REIGN. IT MARKED THE START OF THE CENOZOIC (OR CAINOZOIC) ERA OF "RECENT LIFE," THE SUBJECT OF THIS CHAPTER.

WHAT DIED OUT?

Dinosaurs have such a prominent reputation that reports of their demise tend to sideline coverage of all the other living things that disappeared at the same time, which included many reptiles and similar creatures – not only the dinosaurs, but pterosaurs in the air, and mosasaurs, plesiosaurs and others in the sea. Many kinds of marine molluscs and miscellaneous other sea animals also became extinct, as did various plants, especially marine algae or "seaweeds." Larger land animals seem to have suffered most, since after the catastrophe all terrestrial creatures bigger than a modern Labrador dog were gone. Overall, two thirds of all families of living things perished. Curiously, some reptile groups, such as the crocodiles, were only partly affected. Many swamp and freshwater types survived, while marine crocodiles were wiped out. Other reptiles that survived are still with us today, including turtles and tortoises, lizards and snakes.

ON THE WANE?

The K/T event might have taken a few days, several months, or hundreds of years. Looking back so far into the past, it is not possible to discern the timescale precisely. Also, opinions differ on whether the dinosaurs were already on the wane before that event of around 65 million years ago. Some surveys indicate that their overall numbers and diversity had been decreasing for up to 20 million years previously, though these depletions were regional rather than global. In addition, some major dinosaur groups had expanded during this time, such as the "duckbilled" hadrosaurs, the horned dinosaurs or ceratopsians, the great meat-eating tyrannosaurs and the ostrich dinosaurs.

DID DINOSAURS DIE OUT?

Occasional claims are made for dinosaur fossils dating from less than 65 million years ago. In many cases, these turn out to have been misidentified, or are remains of dinosaurs that have been exposed or eroded from older rocks, from before the great extinction, and later incorporated into younger rocks. The overwhelming weight of evidence points to a total mass extinction of the dinosaurs, but the reasons for the event are among the most hotly debated topics in all of paleontology (discussed on the following pages). In one sense, however, dinosaurs may be said to live on, though greatly altered, and with feathers and wings – as birds.

PREVIOUS PAGE One of the last dinosaurs, the ceratopsian *Torosaurus*, freezes to death in the sudden climate change at the end of the Cretaceous period. The change could have been due to one or several factors, including an asteroid or meteorite strike, massed volcanic eruptions, and altered weather patterns due to continental drift.

LEFT A single volcanic eruption is one of nature's most awesome events. One explanation for the end-of-Cretaceous mass extinction is a whole series of such eruptions, poisoning Earth's atmosphere with choking fumes and blanketing ash.

K/T EXTINCTION THEORIES

The current leading contender for the title of "Dinosaur Killer" is an asteroid (meteorite) impact. A giant "mini-planet" lump of rock, perhaps 10 kilometers (6 miles) across (the size of a large city), came by chance from space and slammed into earth at more than 20,000 kilometers (12,500 miles) per hour. The immense shock at the impact site vaporized everything there – soil, water, animals, plants, even the solid rock under the ground and making up the asteroid itself. This threw massive amounts of debris into the atmosphere, to spread around the globe on the winds. Some of the debris was so hot that as it fell to the ground it sparked wildfires on almost every continent. The resulting haze then blotted out the sun for days, weeks, even years. Plants withered in the cool gloom of the "asteroid winter," and so herbivorous animals starved, followed by the carnivores. Water creatures were afforded some protection from the catastrophe by their aquatic environment.

EVIDENCE

Several lines of evidence support the asteroid theory. In certain rocks formed at the time, there is a thin layer that is unusually rich in the metallic element iridium. This is generally rare on and in Earth, but relatively common in space rocks. Perhaps parts of the asteroid vaporized, floated and settled as the rocks formed. Another clue is a massive bowl-shaped crater, some 200 kilometers (125 miles) across, buried by ooze on the seabed off the Yucatán coast of Mexico. Named the Chicxulub Crater, it may be the impact site. Other events triggered by the collision could have been giant tsunamis, or "tidal waves," which flooded vast areas; a rain of terrifically hot debris that set off wildfires; and shock waves reverberating through the planet's outer, shell-like rocky layer, the crust. These seismic events might have pushed already strained parts of the crust to breaking point, allowing massed volcanic eruptions and self-perpetuating chains of earthquakes. Layers of compressed ash and soot in many areas date back to this time, especially in the Indian region.

CONTINENTS AND CLIMATE

The asteroid theory has many consequences, but some of these could have been concentrated into a relatively short time, without the extraterrestrial stimulus of the asteroid itself. At the end of the Cretaceous, continents were drifting across the globe, mountains were rising in some areas as rift valleys formed in others, and sea levels, as well as patterns of winds and ocean currents, were changing rapidly. Such events may have encouraged unusually fast climate change, combined with a series of widespread volcanic eruptions that poured ash and poisonous gases into the atmosphere. These might have frozen and/or suffocated large land animals, caused a thinning of the atmospheric ozone that protects Earth's surface from harmful solar rays, and formed acid rain that burned and corroded plants. (Two of these events concern us today.) The vast uplands of central India known as the Deccan Plateau were formed by outpourings of runny volcanic lava at around this time. They are cited as evidence of mass volcanic activity, which led to swift climate change.

DISEASE AND COMPETITION

Less refined theories about the demise of the dinosaurs include: epidemics of disease that swept the world, affecting some groups of animals more than others; small mammals beginning to gain success as they ate the eggs of the dinosaurs; "genetic stalemate" or "evolutionary dead ends" for the dinosaurs, as they evolved into highly modified forms that could no longer adapt readily to rapidly changing environmental conditions; and a burst of deadly radiation from outer space, perhaps from the Sun or a nearby exploding star (supernova). However these theories have little serious scientific support.

RIGHT Our planet's surface has long been pockmarked by meteorite collisions, forming craters which are then eroded and eradicated over millennia. This example, Wolf Creek crater from Western Australia, is over a million years old – erosion is very slow in its desert region. It is almost one kilometer (⅔ mile) across. The end-of-Cretaceous impact could have left a crater 200 times wider, now buried on the seabed.

GASTORNIS (DIATRYMA)

ANIMAL FACTFILE
Gastornis

Meaning: Stomach bird

Pronunciation: Gaz-torn-iss

Period: Tertiary

Main group: Aves
  (possibly related to wildfowl group)

Height: 1.8–2 meters (6–6½ feet)

Weight: 100–120 kilograms (220–260
  pounds)

Diet: Prey of varied sizes, carrion

Fossil sites: USA (Wyoming, New Jersey,
  New Mexico), Europe (Germany,
  France, Belgium)

Often referred to by its former name of *Diatryma*, *Gastornis* has no clear equivalent or relation among modern birds. It may have been an offshoot or cousin of the anseriforms or waterfowl group, which today includes ducks, geese and swans, or perhaps the gruiforms, such as cranes, rails or bustards. This massively built creature stood as tall as an adult human being today, and weighed nearly twice as much. Its wings were tiny and useless for flight, but its legs were sturdy and very well muscled, suited to powerful running. On each foot the four long digits, one of them smaller and rear-facing, had huge claws, and *Gastornis* probably could have kicked to death almost any other land animal of the time. The head was as big as a modern horse's, and half of it was the gigantic beak, deep and strongly constructed, which crushed bones as easily as human beings now crunch peanuts. Experts have suggested that in a landscape empty of meat-eating dinosaurs, or any other very large reptiles, rapid evolution of certain bird groups equipped them to take on the role of large land predators before some mammals also adapted to hunting. (For the suggested behavior patterns of *Gastornis*, see *Phorusrhacus* opposite.)

Fossils of *Gastornis* have been found at various sites in New Mexico, Wyoming and New Jersey, and also in Germany, France and Belgium. The oldest remains are from some 55 million years ago, in the Paleocene epoch. The first species was named as *Diatryma gigantea* in 1876 by Edward Drinker Cope, from remains found in New Mexico. More recently, the name *Gastornis* has been accepted.

RIGHT The absurdly tiny wings of *Gastornis* are held out of the way as this huge bird lowers its head to attack. The massive beak was ideally suited to shearing gristle and cracking bone. However some experts suggest it was a huge nutcracker too and that *Gastornis* was an omnivore.

RIGHT Most specimens of *Phorusrhacus* were about as tall as an adult human. With useless wings, these birds relied on their massive beaks and feet both to attack prey and for self-defense. Their cousins today may be birds called seriemas, which also live in South America, and which can fly but prefer to run.

PHORUSRHACUS

Phorusrhacids – "terror cranes" – were huge, powerful, flightless birds of the second half of the Tertiary period in South America. This continent was isolated during much of the period, and it did not drift nearer to and join North America until some time in the past few million years (see page 27). South America's animal and plant life evolved in isolation, and many strange creatures appeared there that had no close relations or equivalents anywhere else. Outwardly, the phorusrhacids resembled other big predatory terrestrial birds that have long been extinct, such as *Gastornis* (see opposite). *Gastornis* lived millions of years earlier, however, and on entirely different continents.

Nevertheless, the behavior patterns of these birds were perhaps similar. They were strong predators, striding or charging across the land on stout, heavily muscled legs. They used their massively powerful, hooked beaks

to catch smaller prey, such as mammals and other birds, or to gash and tear flesh from larger victims, perhaps holding them down with one strong, sharp-clawed foot. They may have sliced lumps from carcasses and probed within to crunch the bones, using their beaks in much the same way that the hyenas of the Old World scavenge today. In South America there were few, if any, large predatory mammals to compete with them.

Phorusrhacus appeared in the Early Miocene epoch, about 25 million years ago, and grew to about 1.8 meters (6 feet) tall. Similar members of the group came and went over following epochs. One of the last and largest was *Titanis*, some 2.5 meters (8 feet) tall, with claws on the two digits of each of its feet. Even larger birds have existed since, including giant moas over 3 meters (10 feet) tall in New Zealand, but these were not fierce predators like the "terror cranes."

ANIMAL FACTFILE
Phorusrhacus

Meaning: Terror crane

Pronunciation: Foe-roos-rak-uss

Period: Tertiary

Main group: Aves

Height: 1.5–2.5 meters (4–8 feet)

Weight: Up to 140 kilograms (310 pounds)

Diet: Prey, carrion

Fossil sites: South America

0 1 2 3 4 5 6 7 8 9 10 11 12 13 14

PLESIADAPIS

The primate group of mammals includes lemurs, bushbabies, monkeys, apes and humans. Whether *Plesiadapis* was one of the earliest primates, or a very close relative of them, is not clear. At a quick glance, it resembled the tree-dwelling lemurs of modern Madagascar. It was about the size of a very large squirrel of today, with four strong, mobile limbs equipped with long, clawed toes for a powerful grip, probably on tree boughs and trunks. It also had a long, flexible tail, which may have been bushy, and may have been useful for balance when *Plesiadapis* was running and leaping through the branches. But *Plesiadapis* had a face and teeth more like those of a modern rodent, such as a mouse or rat. Its snout was slender, and it had long, gnawing incisors at the front of each jaw, then a gap where true primates have canine

teeth, and, in the cheek region, broad molars for chewing and grinding. There are many different opinions about the diet of *Plesiadapis*, ranging from mainly insects and other small animals, to fruits and seeds, to foliage, to sap and grubs found in tree bark, to a mixture of all these items.

Many *Plesiadapis* fossils have been uncovered in northwestern France, and others have been found at sites in Colorado and other areas in and around the Rockies in North America. They mostly date from 60–50 million years ago, although some appear to date from as recently as 35 million years ago. Comparisons are often made between *Plesiadapis* and the modern ring-tailed lemur. Although the lemur is smaller, it, too, spends some time in trees and also frequents the ground, and eats a wide variety of plant foods.

ANIMAL FACTFILE
Plesiadapis

Meaning: Near to Adapis
 (another Tertiary mammal)

Pronunciation: Pleez-ee-ah-dap-iss

Period: Tertiary (Paleocene-Eocene epochs)

Main group: Mammalia (probably Primates)

Length: Head and body 80 centimeters
 (31 inches), tail 50 centimeters
 (19½ inches)

Weight: 10 kilograms (22 pounds)

Diet: Unclear (see text)

Fossil sites: France, Rocky Mountains of
 North America

0	1	2	3	4	5	6	7	8	9	10	11	12	13	14

ABOVE Strong-toed and bushy-tailed as reconstructed here, *Plesiadapis* seemed well suited to life both in trees and on the ground. Its tail would be useful for precise balance when scampering and leaping through the branches.

ANDREWSARCHUS

The fossil remains of this formidable beast consist of its skull and little else. The skull, which is almost 85 centimeters (33¹/₂ inches) long, suggests that *Andrewsarchus* was a huge creature, with a total head-and-body length of more than 6 meters (19¹/₂ feet). If so, *Andrewsarchus* would have been the largest meat-eating mammal ever to walk the earth. Its pointed front teeth, especially the canines, were massive, useful for piercing prey and ripping flesh. Its cheek teeth, or molars, were shaped for a combination of cutting and crushing. Despite so many features resembling those of today's carnivores, such as cats, dogs and, perhaps more pertinently, bears and hyenas, *Andrewsarchus* was not a member of the Carnivora group of mammals. In fact, its closer relations were deer, horses and cattle. *Andrewsarchus* was a hoofed mammal, or ungulate: it had nail-like hooves shaped like claws rather than the true claws of a cat or dog. It was a member of the ungulate subgroup called Mesonychidae (or Acreodi), which were some of the earliest large hunting mammals. It is thought to have lived during the Late Eocene epoch, some 45–40 million years ago. The mesonychids spread and thrived after the extinction of the dinosaurs, but by 35 million years ago they were becoming extinct in the face of a newer group of big predatory mammals, the creodonts.

The limited remains of *Andrewsarchus* were discovered in 1923 during an American-organized fossil-hunting expedition to Mongolia. The venture, which also discovered fossils of many dinosaurs such as *Velociraptor* and *Protoceratops*, was led by Roy Chapman Andrews, then director of the American Museum of Natural History. *Andrewsarchus* was named in his honor.

ANIMAL FACTFILE
Andrewsarchus

Meaning: Andrews's flesh-eater

Pronunciation: And-rue-sark-uss

Period: Tertiary (Late Eocene epoch)

Main group: Mammalia (Ungulata)

Length: Head and body possibly up to 6 meters (19¹/₂ feet)

Weight: 500-800 kilograms (1,100–1,760 pounds)

Diet: Meat, carrion, perhaps varied animal and plant foods

Fossil site: Mongolia

ABOVE The long, low skull of *Andrewsarchus* gave its muzzle a peculiar shape, unlike the cats and wolves of today. Only the skull of this creature is known with any certainty.

RIGHT At a glance, *Icaronycteris* would be difficult to distinguish from a small insect-eating bat of today. In this picture its mouth is open to emit pulses of very high-pitched sound, ultrasound. Its large ears detect the echoes, which are analyzed to show the location and size of nearby objects.

ICARONYCTERIS

ANIMAL FACTFILE
Icaronycteris

Meaning: Night wing of Icarus (character in Greek myth)

Pronunciation: Ick-ah-roe-nick-tur-iss

Period: Tertiary

Main group: Mammalia (Chiroptera)

Size: Wingspan 38 centimeters (15 inches)

Weight: 100 grams (4 ounces)

Diet: Insects, similar small animals

Fossil sites: North America

0 1 2 3 4 5 6 7 8 9 10 11 12 13 14

Bats are among the most specialized of all mammals, and they were also one of the earliest major mammal groups to appear after the death of the dinosaurs. By the Early Eocene epoch, more than 50 million years ago, *Icaronycteris* was flitting through the gloom as it chased small flying insects like moths, almost exactly as bats still do today (or rather, tonight). Its forelimbs were highly evolved as wings made of very thin, stretchy, skin-like flight membranes (patagia), held out by greatly elongated finger bones. Tiny ear bones, preserved as fossils in similar early bats, show that *Icaronycteris* probably used high-pitched squeaks or clicks as a form of echolocation, or sonar, to track and catch prey in midair during the hours of darkness. The sharp-clawed feet had specialized ankle joints that allowed the feet to turn around and face backward, for hanging upside down to rest. Most of these features are shown by other bats from the

Eocene epoch (53–33 million years ago) including *Palaeochiropteryx*, *Archaeonycteris* and *Hassianycteris*.

All these features are still found in bats today, but *Icaronycteris* inherited older features from its shrew-like insectivore ancestors. It still had a claw on each second digit: later, bats lost this and they now retain only one claw on each first digit ("thumb"). *Icaronycteris* had more teeth than today's insectivore bats. Its wings were comparatively short, and broad from front to back. The tail was long and "free" – it was not joined to the rearmost part of the wing membrane. The body of a modern bat is compact and rigid, while that of *Icaronycteris* was longer and flexible. Fossils of bats, as for birds, are generally rare due to their thin and fragile nature, but an exciting new discovery is the "Mahenge bat," named after its site in the Singida region of north-central Tanzania, Africa.

BASILOSAURUS

As the dinosaurs became extinct 65 million years ago, so did the large flesh-eating reptiles of the seas, such as the mosasaurs and pliosaurs. Less than 20 million years later, fully aquatic whales with flippers and tail flukes had evolved from their land-living, four-legged ancestors. One of the biggest of these prehistoric whales was *Basilosaurus* of the Late Eocene, 40–36 million years ago, which, in spite of its name, was a mammal, not a reptile. Its fossils have been discovered in rocks formed from ancient, shallow seabeds which are now far inland on several continents, including the Fayum fossil beds (layers) near Cairo, the capital city of Egypt.

The ancestry of whales is hotly debated among prehistoric mammal specialists. Some of the latest fossil and genetic or DNA evidence suggests that hoofed mammals may have been their forebears – perhaps ancient members of the hippopotamus group, or even the flesh-eating mesonychids (see *Andrewsarchus*, page 413).

Basilosaurus rivaled the length of today's great whales, such as the blue, humpback or gray, although it was probably slimmer and more eel-like, and so weighed considerably less. Also, while great whales now filter or sieve small prey from the water, using their mouthfuls of comb-like baleen plates (whalebone), *Basilosaurus* had a mouthful of fearsome teeth for attacking large victims. The front teeth were stout and pointed, like back-curved cones, while those to the rear were like wide-based blades with serrated edges, and were used for slicing. They explain why *Basilosaurus* is sometimes still known by a former name, *Zeuglodon*, meaning "saw-toothed." The front limbs had become flippers, as in modern whales. The rear limbs were still present, but only just – as tiny, three-toed legs that may have projected from the main body. The flukes at the end of the tail had no limb bones.

ANIMAL FACTFILE
Basilosaurus

Meaning: Emperor reptile (it was originally thought to be reptilian)

Pronunciation: Baz-ill-owe-sore-uss

Period: Tertiary

Main group: Mammalia (Cetacea)

Length: 25 meters (82 feet)

Weight: About 10 metric tons (10 tons)

Diet: Marine prey such as fish, squid

Fossil sites: North America, Africa, southern Asia

ABOVE *Basilosaurus* had a relatively small head and slim body, and its fossil skull shows that its brain was smaller, in comparison to overall body size, than in today's whales and dolphins. Other fossils associated with its remains show that it probably ate fish, including small sharks, and perhaps smaller whales such as *Dorudon* which was only one-quarter the length of *Basilosaurus*.

BELOW *Hyaenodon* had powerful jaws with long canine-type teeth at the front for stabbing prey, and ridged molars farther back for shearing. Its fossilized droppings, coprolites, show that it could crunch up complete carcasses including gristle and bone.

ANIMAL FACTFILE
Hyaenodon

Meaning: Hyena tooth

Pronunciation: High-een-owe-don

Period: Tertiary

Main group: Mammalia (Creodonta)

Length: Mostly 1–2 meters (39–78 inches)

Weight: Up to 50 kilograms (110 pounds)

Diet: Prey, carrion

Fossil sites: Asia, Europe, North America, Africa

HYAENODON

Edward Drinker Cope named many kinds of prehistoric animals, including birds and also extinct mammals. In 1877, he defined and described a group of mammal meat-eaters known as the Creodonta. These were certainly flesh-devourers, as shown by their sharp teeth, which are shaped like spears or daggers. They were not, however, part of the main mammal group of carnivores that survive today, known as the Carnivora (including cats, dogs and bears). The creodonts were a separate group with distinct skeletal and dental features. They appeared from about 60 million years ago, soon after the death of the dinosaurs. They spread around the world and by 30 million years ago they had evolved into many forms that parallel various types of modern Carnivora, such as wolves, foxes, mongooses, civets and

otters. But, by seven million years ago the creodonts had all become extinct, and in many cases they had been replaced by today's Carnivora.

Hyaenodon was perhaps the longest-lived, most widespread and most varied genus of creodonts. It included species similar in size to today's weasels, wolves, hyenas and big cats, some exceeding 3 meters (10 feet) in length, with a shoulder height of 1.6 meters (3 feet). Most had a hyena-like shape, with long legs for speedy running, and large, powerful jaws housing sharp-ridged cheek teeth that could slice flesh, skin, sinew and gristle. The earlier species are known from the Eocene epoch, more than 40 million years ago, while the later ones lived in early Miocene times, about 25–23 million years ago.

HYRACOTHERIUM (EOHIPPUS)

The story of horse evolution is one of the most well-known sequences from prehistory. A series of fossils shows how a small, almost rabbit-sized forest-dweller gradually increased in size, lost toes along the way, and became the familiar large, speedy, grazing herbivore of modern times. The true picture is much more complicated, however, with several offshoots and dead-end evolutionary branches, coupled with changes of habitat and continent. Even so, the earliest known horse was indeed very small, with slim running legs, and four toes on each front foot but three on each of the rear feet. (Modern equids or horses, including donkeys, zebras and horses themselves, all have just one large, weight-bearing, hoof-capped toe on each foot.) The body of *Hyracotherium* was slightly hunched, or arched, and the head was long-muzzled with a large braincase, indicating a creature with keen senses, alert to its environment. The jaws were equipped with 44 teeth, almost the full set for a typical early mammal.

When *Hyracotherium* was named in the 19th century it was thought to resemble the modern hyraxes (also called dassies or conies), small, guinea-pig-like, tail-less creatures that live in Africa and West Asia. They are interesting in terms of evolution since they are the closest living relatives of elephants. Further studies of the plentiful and widespread fossil remains of *Hyracotherium* led to a reidentification as a type of very small and early equid. Many suggestions have since been made that it should be renamed *Eohippus*, "dawn horse."

BELOW The familiar evolutionary sequence of the horse, well known from hundreds of fossils, usually begins with *Hyracotherium* and continues with *Mesohippus*, *Merychippus* and so on. However the situation is more complex, with some of these types being cousins rather than direct ancestor-descendants. Although the rear feet of *Hyracotherium* had three toes, the middle one (digit 3) was enlarged – a trend that would continue in the group, leaving this toe as the only weight-bearing digit on each foot.

ANIMAL FACTFILE
Hyracotherium
Meaning: Hyrax beast
Pronunciation: High-rack-owe-theer-ee-um
Period: Tertiary
Main group: Mammalia (Ungulata)
Length: 60 centimeters (24 inches)
Weight: Up to 10 kilograms (22 pounds)
Diet: Low-growing forest plants
Fossil sites: North America, Europe, Asia

| 0 | 1 | 2 | 3 | 4 | 5 | 6 | 7 | 8 | 9 | 10 | 11 | 12 | 13 | 14 |

RIGHT *Uintatherium* scratches its thick hide on rough bark. Despite its rhino-like horns and elephant-style small tusks, this huge herbivore was not closely related to either of those mammal groups.

UINTATHERIUM

ANIMAL FACTFILE
Uintatherium

Meaning: Uintah beast (see text)

Pronunciation: Ooo-in-tah-theer-ee-um

Period: Tertiary

Main group: Mammalia (Ungulata?)

Size: Head and body 3.5–4 meters long (11–13 feet)

Weight: 2 metric tons (2 tons)

Diet: Plants

Fossil sites: North America

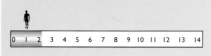

With its three sets of paired bony head knobs or "horns," and a pair of large tusks protruding from the upper jaw, *Uintatherium* generally resembles a modern rhinoceros, or perhaps a hippopotamus. Indeed, it was about the size of today's largest rhinoceros species, the white or square-lipped rhinoceros. However, *Uintatherium* belonged to a long-extinct group of huge herbivores known as the dinoceratans, "terrible horns." These appeared about 60 million years ago and peaked around 55–50 million years ago; by 30 million years ago they had all but disappeared. Their place in classification is uncertain. They are often assumed to be ungulates (hoofed mammals), while other theories regard them as massive and distant cousins of rabbits.

Uintatherium was the biggest of the dinoceratans. Its fossils have been found at numerous sites in North America, including several in Utah. The creature was named in 1872 after the Uintah, a Native American people from that area. The function of the lumpy, bony growths on the head is much debated. They may have been signs of sexual maturity to deter same-sex rivals and attract partners for breeding. Or they could have been weapons to be used in fighting rivals, in the way that male deer use their antlers to battle each other during the rutting season. The tusks, which are enlarged upper canine teeth and are found only in some specimens – probably males – could have also been symbolic, for visual display, or might have been used for physical battles too. The tusks fitted over shelf-like extensions or flanges of the lower jaw, which presumably protected them from snapping if they were knocked while the mouth was closed. The teeth were not especially large or well developed, so *Uintatherium* probably had a soft diet of young shoots and leaves. At some sites, fossils of other animals and plants found with its remains suggest a lakeside habitat.

PARACERATHERIUM

Paraceratherium is the largest land mammal known from any age. It lived mainly during the Oligocene epoch, around 30 million years ago. Fossils of this immense beast have been found at various sites in eastern Europe and in Asia, including China and the Baluchistan region of Pakistan. Remains once known as *Baluchitherium* or *Indricotherium* are now usually included in the genus *Paraceratherium* although the sub-group to which it belongs is usually known as the indricotheres or hyracodontids. Despite its resemblance to a massive horse, and its lack of facial horns, *Paraceratherium* was a member of the rhinoceros group. Today the rhinoceroses are among the most restricted and endangered of all mammal families, with just five species,

but in prehistoric times there were many widespread species, including speedy, pony-sized members (see also *Coelodonta*, page 422). The first fossils of *Paraceratherium* were found in 1910 in Baluchistan by an English paleontologist, Clive Forster-Cooper.

It seems that male *Paraceratherium* were larger than females, and they had heavier skulls with more domed foreheads, perhaps used in butting contests at breeding time. A large male *Paraceratherium* had a skull 1.3 meters (52 inches) long, and could stretch its long neck to reach leaves and other plant food 8 meters (26 feet) above the ground. This exceeds the tallest modern animal, the giraffe, by 2 meters (6½ feet). Females were a meter or two (3-6 feet) smaller all around. The front teeth of *Paraceratherium* were unusual: a tusk-like, downward-directed pair in the upper jaw and a forward-pointing pair in the lower jaw. The skull structure around the nasal area suggests that it had very mobile lips, perhaps elongated into a short but flexible trunk like a modern tapir's, for browsing.

ANIMAL FACTFILE
Paraceratherium
Meaning: Beside horn beast
Pronunciation: Para-seer-ah-theer-ee-um
Period: Tertiary
Main group: Mammalia (Ungulata)
Size: Head-and-body length 9 meters (29½ inches)
Weight: Up to 20 metric tons (20 tons)
Diet: Foliage, buds, shoots, twigs
Fossil sites: Asia, eastern Europe

| 0 | 1 | 2 | 3 | 4 | 5 | 6 | 7 | 8 | 9 | 10 | 11 | 12 | 13 | 14 |

LEFT Vast in every dimension, *Paraceratherium* stood as tall at its shoulder as the head height of a giraffe today. It belonged to probably the first subgroup of rhinoceroses to evolve, called the hyracodontids or "running rhinos."

INTERGLACIAL GREENERY

DURING THE PAST COUPLE OF MILLION YEARS, WORLD TEMPERATURES HAVE FLUCTUATED IN A SLOW CYCLE, AND ICE AGES, OR GLACIATIONS, HAVE COME AND GONE. DURING THE MOST SEVERE OF THE "BIG FREEZES," ICE SHEETS COVERED HALF OF ALL THE NORTHERN CONTINENTS. EACH TIME THE CLIMATE WARMED FOR AN INTERGLACIAL PERIOD, THE SHEETS AND GLACIERS RETREATED, AND PLANTS AND ANIMALS SPREAD NORTHWARD AGAIN. AS THE COLD RETURNED, SOME SPECIES COULD NÓT ADAPT AND SO BECAME EXTINCT.

RIGHT Deciduous and coniferous forests flank a meadow in interglacial times, some time in the past quarter of a million years. A female cave bear protects her cubs and growls at the saber-toothed cats on the opposite bank, while a giant elk grazes in the clearing, a herd of mammoths heads for the trees, and a prehistoric fox sniffs the trail of turkey-like gamebirds.

COELODONTA

ANIMAL FACTFILE

Coelodonta

Meaning: Cavity tooth

Pronunciation: Seel-owe-don-tah

Period: Quaternary

Main group: Mammalia (Ungulata)

Size: 3.5 meters (12 feet)

Weight: Up to 2 metric tons (2 tons)

Diet: Grasses and other low-growing plants

Fossil sites: Europe, Asia

0	1	2	3	4	5	6	7	8	9	10	11	12	13	14

Commonly called the woolly rhinoceros, *Coelodonta* was indeed a member of the rhinoceros group, and was also extremely furry. It had two long nose horns, humped shoulders, a stocky body, four squat limbs, a short, thin tail and long, dark, shaggy hair. This amount of detail is clear because *Coelodonta* is known, not only from fossilized bones and teeth, but also from whole bodies frozen and preserved in the ice of the far north, in Asia – especially Siberia – as well as in Europe. It can also be recognized in the cave paintings of ancient human beings, dating to less than 30,000 years ago. Some of their art appears to depict woolly rhinoceroses being hunted with spears and other weapons.

Coelodonta was as big as the larger rhinoceroses of today, but with a greater shoulder height of up to 2.2 meters (7 feet).

It lived during much of the Pleistocene epoch, from about half a million years ago and probably became extinct during the last major ice age (see previous page), perhaps as recently as 10,000 years ago. The front nose horn was longer than the rear one, and in some individuals – probably older males – it reached almost 2 meters (6½ feet). It differed slightly from a modern rhinoceros's horn in being flattened from side to side, like a thick and curved sword blade, rather than having a more circular cross-section. It has been suggested that *Coelodonta* used its "nose blade" to sweep snow aside and reveal vegetation, and perhaps even slice into semifrozen ground to loosen low-growing plants. In addition, the horn, as in modern rhinoceroses, was a visual symbol of maturity and power, used to deter enemies or attract breeding partners.

RIGHT The fur pattern of the woolly rhinoceros is known from frozen carcasses and ancient human cave art. It was probably dark brown or gray in color. There was also a shoulder hump that varied in size. This was a store of fat that accumulated in well-fed individuals but was then used up by the body in times of food shortage.

DEINOTHERIUM

There are just three living species of elephants, but the elephant group, the proboscideans, has a long and varied prehistory, with numerous subgroups and dozens of species. The earliest kinds of proboscideans, from more than 55 million years ago, were about the size of small pigs, but the trend was soon to a much larger body size, pillar-like legs, and nose and upper lip joined and extended into the characteristic flexible trunk. Some types were tuskless and had shorter legs, and probably lived like modern hippopotamuses. (See also *Mammuthus*, next page.)

The genus *Deinotherium* was one of the largest and longest-lived among the proboscideans. It first appeared in the Miocene epoch, some 20 million years ago, in Africa. Later, it also spread into Europe and Asia,

with only minor evolutionary changes. A typical *Deinotherium* was slightly bigger than the elephants of today, and its trunk was probably stubbier and thicker than that of a modern elephant. Its most distinctive feature was its tusks, which grew, not from the upper jaw as in most other proboscideans, but from the front of the lower jaw. The tusks curved down and back to emerge through the skin of the chin. The way that *Deinotherium* used its curious tusks has been much debated. It may have rooted in soil for underground plant parts, pulled down branches to snap them and reach leaves, or stripped soft bark from tree trunks. *Deinotherium* fossils have been uncovered at several of the African sites where remains of hominids, prehistoric relatives of modern human beings, have also been found.

ANIMAL FACTFILE
Deinotherium
Meaning: Terrible beast
Pronunciation: Day-noh-theer-ee-um
Period: Quaternary
Main group: Mammalia (Proboscidea)
Size: Shoulder height up to 4 meters (13 feet), head-and-body length (excluding trunk and tail) 7–8 meters (23–26 feet)
Weight: 5-plus metric tons (5 tons)
Diet: Plant material
Fossil sites: Africa, Europe, Asia

| 0 | 1 | 2 | 3 | 4 | 5 | 6 | 7 | 8 | 9 | 10 | 11 | 12 | 13 | 14 |

LEFT The biggest individuals of *Deinotherium* rivaled the largest elephants of today, the African savanna species. When its fossils were first studied in the 1820s, experts were so puzzled by the lower-jaw, down-curving tusks that they tried to reconstruct the animal with the jaw attached upside down.

RIGHT Face to face with the largest land animal of the last Ice Age, as perhaps seen by people from 500 generations ago.

BELOW The hard, ridged surface of a mammoth's molar tooth ground tough vegetation. The whole tooth surface was about the size of the sole of an adult person's shoe.

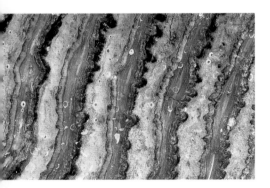

ANIMAL FACTFILE
Mammuthus

Meaning: First grown mammoth

Pronunciation: Mam-ooo-thuss

Period: Quaternary

Main group: Mammalia (Proboscidea)

Height: At shoulder 3 meters (10 feet)

Weight: 5–8 metric tons (5–8 tons)

Diet: Grasses and other plants

Fossil sites: Europe, Asia, North America

MAMMUTHUS (MAMMOTH)

Mammuthus was a genus of huge proboscideans (members of the elephant group), with as many as eight species. They were mostly large to very large, with long curving tusks. They are known from fossils, subfossils, deep-frozen bodies in the ice of the far north, and from the cave art of ancient human beings. Various anatomical and genetic comparisons – mammoth DNA was obtained and studied in the 1990s – show that mammoths were very close relatives of living elephants, compared to much more distant cousins such as *Deinotherium* (see previous page).

The ice-age woolly mammoth, *Mammuthus primigenius*, was still living less than 10,000 years ago, and some smaller or dwarf forms may have been in existence only 4,000 years ago, on Vrangelya (Wrangel Island) off the coast of the extreme northeast of the Asian continent. The woolly mammoth lived across all the northern continents. It had humped

shoulders, a markedly domed top to the head, and a very short tail. It was not the largest mammoth, but it was the hairiest: frozen specimens show that the shaggy strands of the outer furry coat were as long as 90 centimeters (36 inches). These hairs were dark, almost black: earlier reconstructions of "red-haired" mammoths were due to natural chemicals in the soil and rocks seeping into the fur and staining it red.

The steppe mammoth of Europe and Asia, *Mammuthus trogontherii*, had a shorter furry coat and was one of the largest mammoths, probably standing 4.6 meters (15 feet) at the shoulder, and weighing more than 10 metric tons (10 tons). The American or Columbian mammoth, *Mammuthus columbi*, was slightly smaller, lacked fur, and lived only in North America. The ancestor of all these forms may have been the southern mammoth, *Mammuthus meridionalis*.

MEGALOCEROS

Also known as the giant elk or Irish elk, *Megaloceros* was a member of the cervid or deer group, like the living species called the elk (in Europe) or moose (in North America). However, it was more closely related to fallow deer and was not a true elk/moose, although it rivaled the latter in size. Its remains have been found at many sites across Europe and Asia, from Ireland to China. The common name Irish elk comes from many early finds made in Ireland, including parts of up to 100 individuals in a bog near Dublin. The "-ceros" part of the scientific name means "horn," but deer antlers are different from the true horns of mammals such as cattle or antelopes. Unlike true horns, which grow continually in both sexes, antlers are shed and regrown annually, and by males only, except in one living deer species, the reindeer/caribou.

For a male *Megaloceros*, growing new antlers each year must have put a huge strain on its food resources, for it had to gather enough nutrients to build a fresh set of these massive, spreading structures. In some specimens, the antlers spanned more than 3.5 meters (12 feet) and weighed 50 kilograms (110 pounds). *Megaloceros* survived from more than 500,000 to less than 10,000 years ago. Tiny wear marks on antler fossils suggest that they were not solely for show, but were used in battle, as in deer rutting today. A popular notion is that the antlers became so big and heavy as they evolved that *Megaloceros* could no longer hold up its head. It is more likely that predation by humans during the Ice Age, and perhaps climate change, hastened this enormous deer's extinction. Cave paintings portray it as brown with a paler chest.

ANIMAL FACTFILE
Megaloceros (Megaceros)
Meaning: Mega horn [antler], giant horn
Pronunciation: Mega-low-sair-oss
Period: Quaternary
Main group: Mammalia (Ungulata)
Size: Head-and-body 2.5 meters (8 feet), height at shoulder 2 meters (6½ feet)
Weight: 400–500 kilograms (880–1,100 pounds)
Diet: Grasses, leaves
Fossil sites: Europe (particularly Ireland), Asia (mainly north)

0 | 1 2 3 4 5 6 7 8 9 10 11 12 13 14

RIGHT Remains of mostly antlered rather than non-antlered *Megaloceros* suggest that more of the huge male deer perished, probably during winter, compared to females. Despite the great size of this deer, its general body shape was of a strong, swift runner with plenty of stamina.

Ursus spelaeus (Cave Bear)

ANIMAL FACTFILE

Ursus spelaeus

Meaning: Cave bear

Pronunciation: Er-suss spell-ay-uss

Period: Quaternary

Main group: Mammalia (Carnivora)

Length: Up to 3 meters (10 feet)

Weight: Up to 500 kilograms (1,100 pounds)

Diet: Mainly plant matter, possibly small prey and carrion

Fossil sites: Europe, Asia

0	1	2	3	4	5	6	7	8	9	10	11	12	13	14

The ursids are bears, and the genus *Ursus* includes half of the eight living bear species: polar, brown/grizzly, and American and Asiatic black bears. *Ursus spelaeus* was the giant cave bear of the ice ages, surviving to just a few thousand years ago. It was similar in size to the modern brown/grizzly bear, but had a longer, more prominent muzzle. Its fur was long and shaggy, its limbs were extremely muscled and powerful, and each foot bore five digits with long, curved claws. It features in the cave art of ancient human beings, and its bones and teeth were used by them, especially Neanderthals, for carvings, in decorative items such as necklaces and in rituals (see page 432).

The cave bear is so called because many of its remains have been found in caves, especially in the European Alps. These include fossilized bones and teeth, subfossils (materials partway along the process of turning to stone), and mummified scraps of skin and other soft tissue. Other sites known for this species are spread across Europe and Asia, from Britain and Spain east to Russia. In some caves, such as the Drachenhohle (Dragon's Cave) in Austria, there are remains of many thousands of cave bears. Today's bears are solitary, even during winter. Possibly to survive such extreme winters, the ice-age cave bears adapted their social behavior and gathered in groups to sleep deeply in sheltered places, although in the Drachenhohle a flood or similar disaster overtook them. The search for ice-age shelter may well have brought cave bears and human beings into conflict, but the bear was probably mostly herbivorous.

RIGHT The cave bear and ice-age humans perhaps came face to face while searching for shelter from the bitter ice-age winter. Rearing up onto its back legs, this ursid stood more than 3 meters (10 feet) tall, about the same as a large grizzly of today.

ABOVE "Smiley's" mouth was dominated by the massive canine teeth, each longer than a human hand but slim and blade-like when seen from the front. The equivalent canine teeth in the lower jaw were tiny or non-existent, and the molars or cheek teeth were reduced in number.

LEFT The saber-toothed "tiger" *Smilodon* was slightly smaller than today's large tigers. For a catlike carnivore its skeleton was relatively robust, that is, of a sturdy and solid build.

SMILODON (SABER-TOOTHED CAT)

Probably the best known of the saber-toothed cats, the largest specimens of *Smilodon* grew to the size of today's lion. They are sometimes called saber-toothed "tigers," but, while they were certainly members of the felid or cat family, tigers are among their more distant cousins. Several species of the genus *Smilodon* are known, including *Smilodon fatalis/ californicus*, with thousands of individuals preserved in the La Brea tar pits of Los Angeles, California. They were trapped in the natural pools of sticky tar along with wolves and other predators that had presumably come to feast on the various mastodons (ancient elephants) and other large herbivores already floundering there. *Smilodon populator/neogaeus* lived in South America and was slightly larger. It probably evolved there after its predecessors crossed from North America, following the joining of the two continents by the Central American land bridge a few

million years ago. Other types of saber-toothed cats are known from Europe, Asia and Africa.

Smilodon was a powerfully built, heavily muscled cat, especially in its shoulders and front limbs. The "sabers" were upper canine teeth that reached 25 centimeters (10 inches) in length. They were sharp and had serrated rear edges, but they were also narrow from side to side, blade-like, and rather fragile. They would be unlikely to survive a strong bite that hit solid bone. More likely, the cat opened its mouth very wide (120 degrees), and used them to stab, slash and slice the skin and flesh of its victim, perhaps inflicting wounds so that the prey bled to death. Then lumps of meat could be bitten off and swallowed without the risk of damaging the teeth as the prey twisted and struggled. Likely prey included prehistoric forms of bison, camels, horses and giant ground sloths.

ANIMAL FACTFILE
Smilodon

Meaning: Knife tooth

Pronunciation: Smile-owe-don

Period: Quaternary

Main group: Mammalia (Carnivora)

Length: up to 3 meters (10 feet),

Weight: 200 kilograms (440 pounds)

Diet: Meat

Fossil sites: North and South America

EARLY HOMINIDS

HOMINID FACTFILE

Ardipithecus

Meaning: Ground ape, root ape

Pronunciation: Ard-ee-pith-ee-kuss

Period: Tertiary (Pliocene epoch)

Main group: Mammalia (Primates)

Size: Standing height 1 meter (39 inches)

Weight: 40 kilograms (88 pounds)

Diet: Probably mixed but mostly
plant material

Fossil site: Ethiopia

```
0  1  2  3  4  5  6  7  8  9  10  11  12  13  14
```

The science of "where we came from" and, in particular, where and how our distant ancestors lived, holds a special fascination – and also generates exceptional numbers of debates and arguments. The group of mammals called Primates includes lemurs, bushbabies, monkeys, apes and hominids. The hominid group is usually described as consisting of one living species – *Homo sapiens*, ourselves – and various ancestors and cousins, as far back as, but not including, the common ancestor that gave rise to us and our closest living relatives, the chimpanzees. This common ancestor almost certainly lived in Africa, and probably at least 5 million years ago.

A century ago, the notion that humans evolved from ape-like ancestors via "missing links" seemed either laughable or heretical. Today, there is almost an excess of "found links" or extinct hominids known from numerous fossils. The early types are all from Africa. One of the earliest was *Ardipithecus*, whose remains, found in the Middle Awash region of Ethiopia, date back nearly 4½ million years. This chimpanzee-like creature may have walked semi-upright but its brain capacity was probably only 400–500 cubic centimeters (24½–30½ cubic inches), while our own is nearer 1,500 (90). In some schemes, however, *Ardipithecus* is regarded as a species of *Australopithecus* (see opposite). Still older is *Orrorin*, whose 6-million-year-old fossils were discovered in 2000 in the Tugen Hills of Kenya. An even more recent find of even more ancient date is *Sahelanthropus*, from Chad. These fossils were unearthed in 2002 and date back almost 7 million years. These creatures have variously been proposed as very early hominids, or members of the chimpanzee group, or, in the case of *Sahelanthropus*, as close relatives of gorillas. Debates over them will certainly continue.

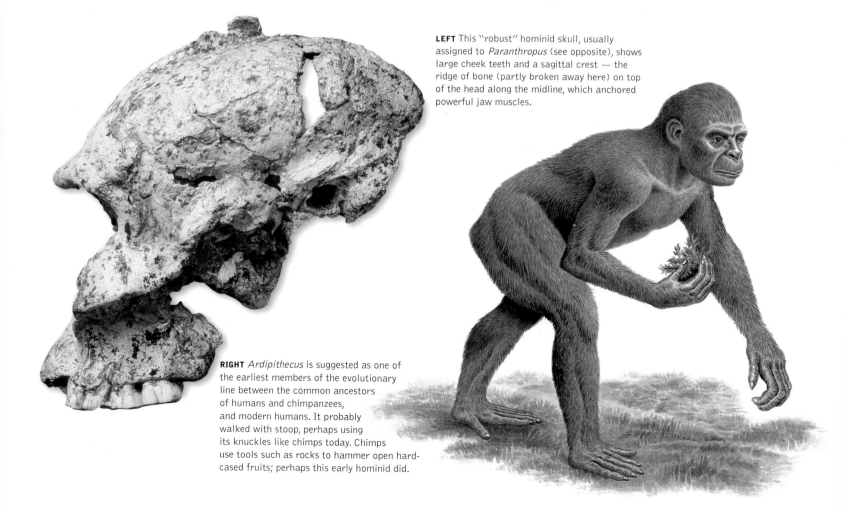

LEFT This "robust" hominid skull, usually assigned to *Paranthropus* (see opposite), shows large cheek teeth and a sagittal crest — the ridge of bone (partly broken away here) on top of the head along the midline, which anchored powerful jaw muscles.

RIGHT *Ardipithecus* is suggested as one of the earliest members of the evolutionary line between the common ancestors of humans and chimpanzees, and modern humans. It probably walked with stoop, perhaps using its knuckles like chimps today. Chimps use tools such as rocks to hammer open hard-cased fruits; perhaps this early hominid did.

AUSTRALOPITHECUS

Fossil hominids generate huge amounts of controversy (see notes about human evolution opposite). Some experts list more than ten species of the genus *Australopithecus*, while others limit themselves to three. One of the most important is specimen AL 288-1 – better known as "Lucy." Her skeleton, some two-fifths complete, was discovered in 1974 near Hadar in Ethiopia, and was named *Australopithecus afarensis* by Donald Johanson and Tim White in 1978. Her kind probably lived from about 4 million to just less than 3 million years ago. They could walk upright, after a fashion, but resembled their ape ancestors in many respects, such as their sloping foreheads, protruding noses and mouths, less angular chins, and teeth that resembled those of chimpanzees. Some experts now claim that "Lucy" was actually a male and have renamed her "Lucifer." Her ability to walk fully upright has also been recently challenged.

Australopithecus afarensis is perhaps the strongest contender to be a link between earlier hominids and later types – one of which evolved into ourselves. Another species, *Australopithecus africanus*, lived between 3 and 2 million years ago in southern Africa. It was named in 1925 by Raymond Dart, a South African paleontologist, from the fossil skull of a youngster, perhaps three to six years old, known from its discovery site as the "Taung Child." In addition, the genus *Australopithecus* was formerly said to include "robust" types – bigger, stronger, more heavily built species such as *Australopithecus robustus* and *Australopithecus boisei* (formerly *Zinjanthropus*). They had very powerful jaws and large teeth suited to efficient chewing. They mostly lived between 2½ million and 1 million years ago. However, these robust species are usually now placed in another genus, *Paranthropus*.

HOMINID FACTFILE
Australopithecus afarensis
Meaning: Southern ape from Afar
Pronunciation: Ost-rar-low-pith-ee-kuss aff-are-en-siss
Period: Tertiary (Pliocene epoch)
Main group: Mammalia (Primates)
Size: Standing height 1 meter (39 inches),
Weight: 40 kilograms (88 pounds)
Diet: Probably chiefly plant material
Fossil sites: Africa, mainly East and southern

| 0 | 1 | 2 | 3 | 4 | 5 | 6 | 7 | 8 | 9 | 10 | 11 | 12 | 13 | 14 |

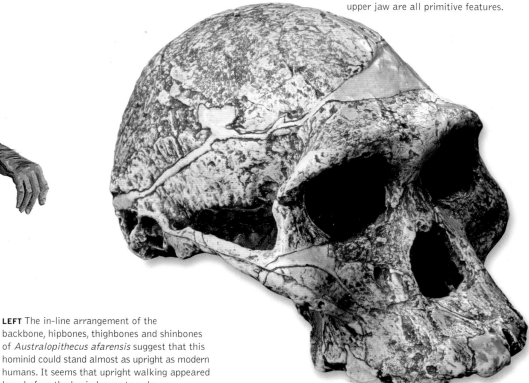

BELOW A specimen of *Australopithecus africanus* from the famous cave site at Sterkfontein, South Africa. The low braincase, pronounced eyebrow ridges and protruding upper jaw are all primitive features.

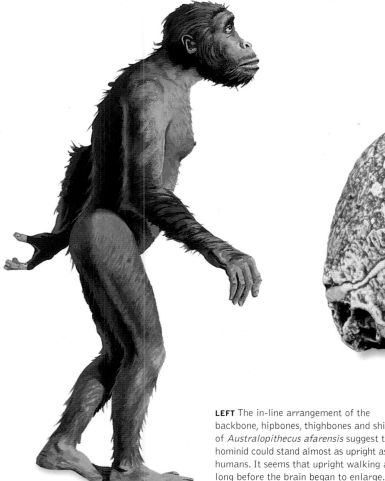

LEFT The in-line arrangement of the backbone, hipbones, thighbones and shinbones of *Australopithecus afarensis* suggest that this hominid could stand almost as upright as modern humans. It seems that upright walking appeared long before the brain began to enlarge.

Early species of Homo

HOMINID FACTFILE

Homo (Australopithecus) habilis

Meaning: Handy person

Pronunciation: Hoe-moe hab-ill-iss

Period: Tertiary

Main group: Mammalia (Primates)

Height: up to 1.3 meters (5 feet)

Weight: 30–40 kilograms (66–88 pounds)

Diet: Mixed, possibly including hunted meat

Fossil sites: East Africa

0	1	2	3	4	5	6	7	8	9	10	11	12	13	14

Our own genus, *Homo*, includes our closest relatives (see note about human evolution on page 428). Some classification schemes list eight or more *Homo* species; others have three or four. One of the earliest is *Homo habilis*, "handy person," so named because its fossils have been found associated with simple stone tools, of a type known as the Oldowan culture. *Homo habilis* fossils come from East Africa, especially Olduvai Gorge in Tanzania, and date from about 2½ million to 1½ million years ago. The species was named in 1964 by Louis Leakey, John Napier and Phillip Tobias. Reconstructions show what many people imagine as an "ape person," with a mixture of apelike and human features: It was able to walk upright but was fairly small, standing perhaps 1.3 meters (5 feet) tall.

Some experts view *Homo habilis* as a species of *Australopithecus* or as a mixture of fossils representing two or more species. One of these is *Homo rudolfensis*, named in 1986 from skull "1470," which was discovered in 1972 by a team led by Richard Leakey (Louis's son). Like the fossil sites of many other hominids, those of *Homo rudolfensis* stretch along the Great Rift Valley in East Africa. They date from about 2½ million to just less than 2 million years ago. The brain capacity of *Homo rudolfensis* is estimated to have been 750 cubic centimeters (45 cubic inches), roughly half our own, and comparable to *Homo habilis*, at 650. Other proposed but hotly debated species of *Homo* include *Homo ergaster*, also in East Africa (1.9–1.2 million years ago, see opposite); *Homo antecessor*, chiefly in Spain (almost 800,000 years ago); *Homo heidelbergensis*, mainly in Europe (600,000 to perhaps less than 100,000 years ago and the possible ancestor of neanderthals); and *Homo erectus*.

BELOW This *Homo* (*Australopithecus*) *habilis* skull from Olduvai, Tanzania, is dated at 1.8 million years old. The habiline people are often credited as the first hominids to make and use stone tools in a systematic way.

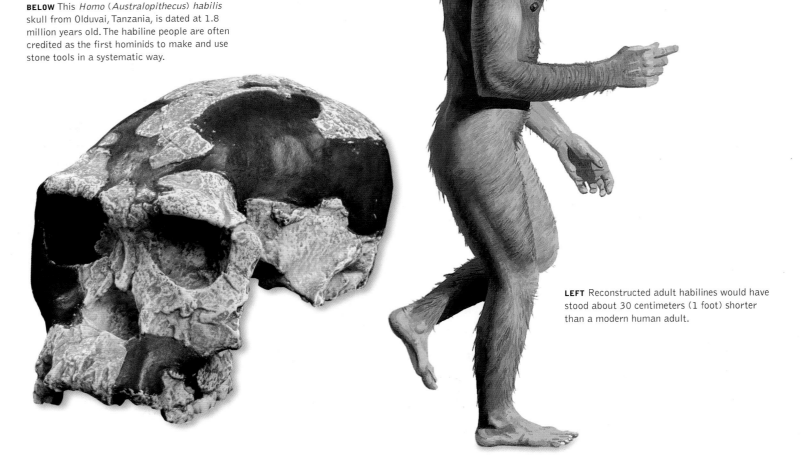

LEFT Reconstructed adult habilines would have stood about 30 centimeters (1 foot) shorter than a modern human adult.

HOMO ERECTUS

Homo erectus is generally viewed as having lived from almost 2 million to about half a million years ago, first in Africa but then gradually spreading to most parts of the Old World. One of the first discoveries was by Eugene Dubois in Java, Indonesia. He found part of a skull in 1891 and called it *Pithecanthropus erectus*. At the time, his proposal was roundly rejected by established paleontologists. In the 1920s more finds were uncovered at Zhoukoudian in China and dubbed "Peking (or Peiping, or Beijing) Man." These and many others were reclassified as *Homo erectus* in the 1960s, and the species was then regarded by some as our direct ancestor. A more recent trend has been to redefine *Homo erectus* as a mixture of species, including early fossils from Africa as *Homo ergaster*, and later ones in Europe as *Homo heidelbergensis* (see opposite and also notes about human evolution on page 428).

One of the most complete early African specimens is "Turkana Boy" or "Nariokotome Boy" (specimen KNM-ER 15000) from Kenya. The specimen dates back 1.6 million years and shows *Homo erectus* as strongly built yet slim and, as the species name suggests, standing erect at about the same height as many humans today. He was 10–12 years old when he died. Many of the remains of *Homo erectus* have been found associated with tools fashioned from stone, wood, bone, antlers and other materials, including hand axes, choppers and scrapers. These examples of what is known as the Acheulean tool culture gradually become more sophisticated with time. Many sites of *Homo erectus* finds, especially later ones in Europe and Asia, are also associated with remains of fires.

HOMINID FACTFILE

Homo erectus / ergaster

Meaning: Upright / work person

Pronunciation: Hoe-moe ee-reck-tuss / erg-ass-tur

Period: Tertiary

Main group: Mammalia (Primates)

Height: Up to 1.8 meters (6 feet)

Weight: 60–80 kilograms (132–176 pounds)

Diet: Mixed, probably including hunted meat

Fossil sites: Africa (possibly *Homo ergaster*), Europe and Asia

| 0 | 1 | 2 | 3 | 4 | 5 | 6 | 7 | 8 | 9 | 10 | 11 | 12 | 13 | 14 |

LEFT Reconstruction of a fully upright, powerfully built, weapon-wielding *Homo erectus*, based on fossils found in China during the 1920s.

RIGHT A specimen of *Homo ergaster*, sometimes regarded as an early type of *Homo erectus*, from Kenya. Compared to human-like skulls on the previous pages, the braincase is larger and the upper jaw less protruding. The teeth, in particular, identify this as from an adolescent.

HOMO NEANDERTHALENSIS

HOMINID FACTFILE
Homo neanderthalensis

Meaning: Neander Valley person

Pronunciation: Hoe-moe nee-and-er-tal-en-siss

Period: Quaternary

Main group: Mammalia (Primates)

Size: Height up to 1.7 meters (5½ feet)

Weight: 70-90 kilograms (154-198 pounds)

Diet: Mixed, probably including hunted meat

Fossil sites: Germany, Portugal

The first Neanderthal fossils known to science were discovered by quarry workers in a cave in the valley of the Neander River in Germany in 1856: "Neanderthal" simply means "Neander valley." (In modern German spelling, and often in English too, the "h," which was always silent anyway, is no longer included.) Many further discoveries showed that the Neanderthals were powerfully built, with brains as big as ours or even larger, at more than 1,700 cubic centimeters (100 cubic inches). The typical Neanderthal face had a low, sloping forehead, prominent bony ridges above the eyes, protruding jaws and a back-sloping chin. The body was long and barrel-chested, and the limbs were relatively short but well-muscled. These stocky proportions are associated with adaptation to cold climate, since they lose less warmth to the environment. For many years after remains of Neanderthals were first discovered, they were popularly

viewed as having been cave dwellers living in an ice age. In part, this was true. They appeared before 200,000 years ago, possibly descended from *Homo heidelbergensis* (see page 430), and lived in Europe and western Asia. Neanderthals are sometimes still viewed as slouching, stupid brutes, without language or culture. Yet they survived the comings and goings of several ice ages, especially in Europe, and used increasingly sophisticated axes, spears, scrapers, and many other tools and weapons, typical of what is known as the Mousterian tool culture. They probably hunted large animals such as woolly mammoths; they may have had a spoken language; and they certainly held ceremonies and buried their dead with rituals (which makes them very like modern humans and completely unlike any other known animals). By 28,000 years ago, however, it seems that they had disappeared. They may have been forced into extinction by the rapidly spreading and newest species of *Homo, Homo sapiens*. Some fossils, such as the "Lagar Velho Child" found in central Portugal and dated to around 24,500 years ago, are said by some to show a mixture of Neanderthal and modern human features, which may suggest interbreeding.

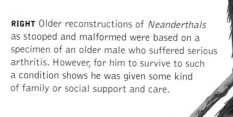

RIGHT Older reconstructions of *Neanderthals* as stooped and malformed were based on a specimen of an older male who suffered serious arthritis. However, for him to survive to such a condition shows he was given some kind of family or social support and care.

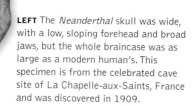

LEFT The *Neanderthal* skull was wide, with a low, sloping forehead and broad jaws, but the whole braincase was as large as a modern human's. This specimen is from the celebrated cave site of La Chapelle-aux-Saints, France and was discovered in 1909.

HOMO SAPIENS

Of the many kinds of hominids that have existed over the past few million years (see notes about human evolution on page 428), only one species is left. One scientific view of our origins, the "multiregional hypothesis," proposes that our direct predecessors were *Homo erectus*. They spread to many parts the world, and gradually evolved in these regions, with mixing and interbreeding, into the various geographic and ethnic groups of *Homo sapiens* seen around the globe today. The "out of Africa hypothesis," on the other hand, suggests that anatomically modern human beings arose in East or southern Africa some time between 200,000 and 100,000 years ago. This hypothesis is supported by fossil evidence of such beings, and also by analysis of genetic material from living humans: it is the view supported by most paleontologists today.

By 100,000 years ago modern humans were spreading north into Europe and east into Asia. Traveling overland, or perhaps along coasts in primitive boats, they colonized new regions, and adapted to local climates and conditions, resulting in the different groups that we know today. Whether they encountered members of the related species *Homo erectus*, and replaced or interbred with them, is not clear. These modern humans reached Southeast Asia and Australia by at least 40,000 years ago. The Americas were colonized by around 15,000 years ago, with recent evidence suggesting arrival long before, perhaps 35,000 years ago, from northeast Asia across what is now the Bering Straits, which was then dry land. By 40,000 years ago in Europe, "quantum leaps" were occurring in the sophistication of human beings' tools, body ornamentation, ceremonies, rituals, sculpture, and art, in what is known as the Cro-Magnon culture. This was the time of very young fossils: from this point on, archeology gradually replaces paleontology, and prehistory becomes history.

HUMAN FACTFILE
Homo sapiens
Meaning: Wise person
Pronunciation: Hoe-moe sap-ee-ens
Period: Quaternary
Main group: Mammalia (Primates)
Size: Height up to 1.8 meters (6 feet)
Weight: 50-80 kilograms (110-176 pounds)
Diet: Mixed, including hunted meat
Fossil sites: Worldwide

0 1 2 3 4 5 6 7 8 9 10 11 12 13 14

LEFT From about 100,000 years ago, humans were anatomically almost identical to people of today. Current genetic evidence suggested they arose as a smallish group in Africa and spread worldwide, with major phases of early cultural progress in Europe.

BELOW Compared to the Neanderthal skull (opposite), the modern human skull has a higher, more domed forehead and smaller jaws.

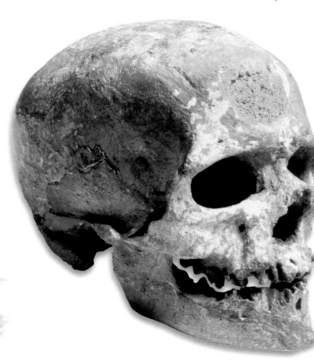

POSTSCRIPT ON EVOLUTION

The rise of our own species, *Homo sapiens*, has caused more numerous and more rapid changes than the world has ever known before. Industrial developments, plundered natural resources, exploding populations, burgeoning cities, pollution of land, sea, and air, global warming and the thinning of the ozone layer accompany frighteningly rapid loss of much of nature in all its forms, including wild areas, plants and animals. In terms of the prehistoric time scale, all of this is happening in less than the blink of an eye. What legacy might we leave as fossils for the future – if we leave any legacy at all?

RIGHT Urban sprawl as far as the eye can see in Los Angeles – which is not very far on a smoggy day, when air pollutants cloud the view. How will this area look in one million years, or even one thousand? Humans cannot continue their present rate of population increase and industrial development. The planet does not have enough space and natural resources.

MAIN FOSSIL SITES: THE AMERICAS

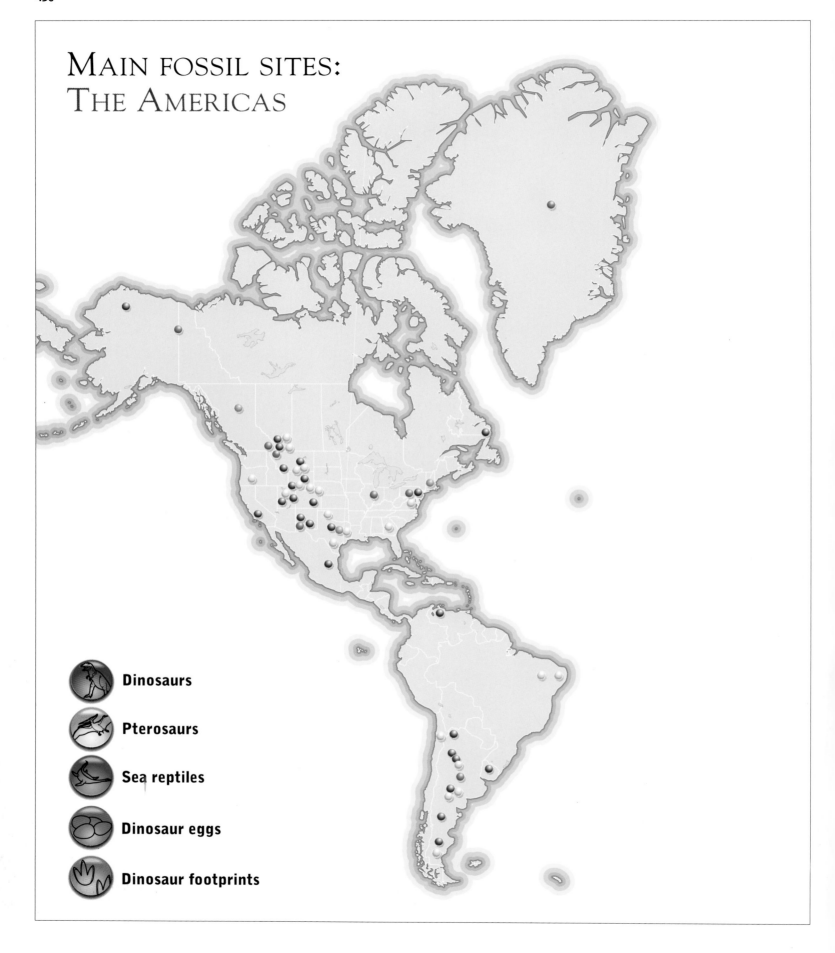

Dinosaurs

Pterosaurs

Sea reptiles

Dinosaur eggs

Dinosaur footprints

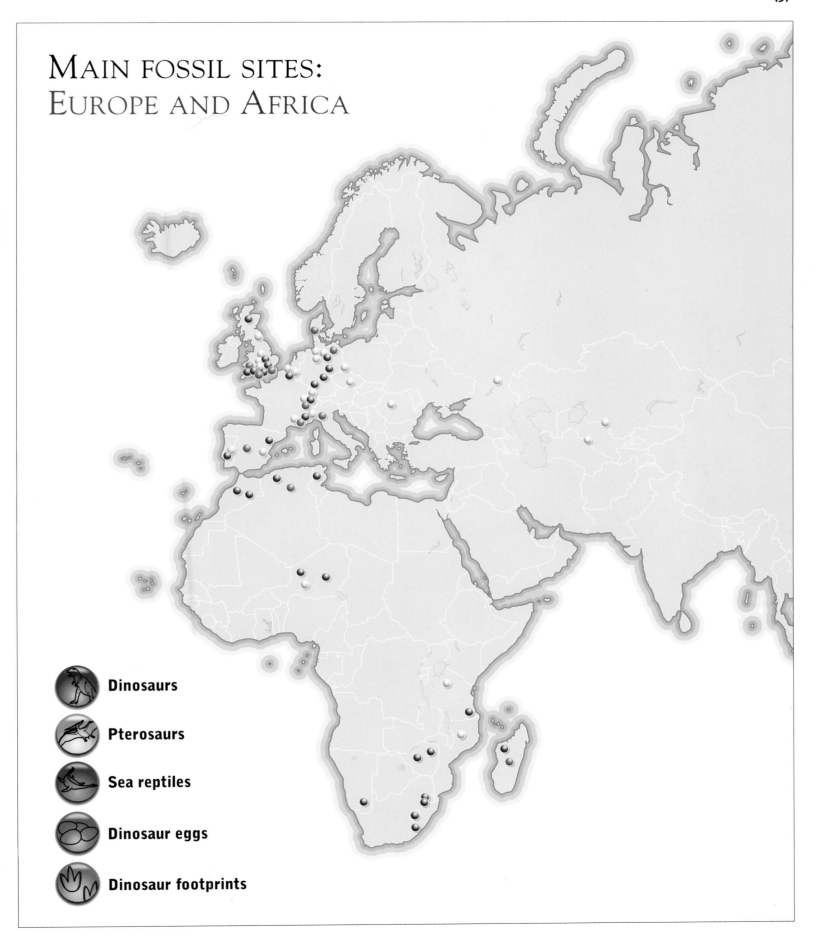

Main fossil sites:
Europe and Africa

Dinosaurs

Pterosaurs

Sea reptiles

Dinosaur eggs

Dinosaur footprints

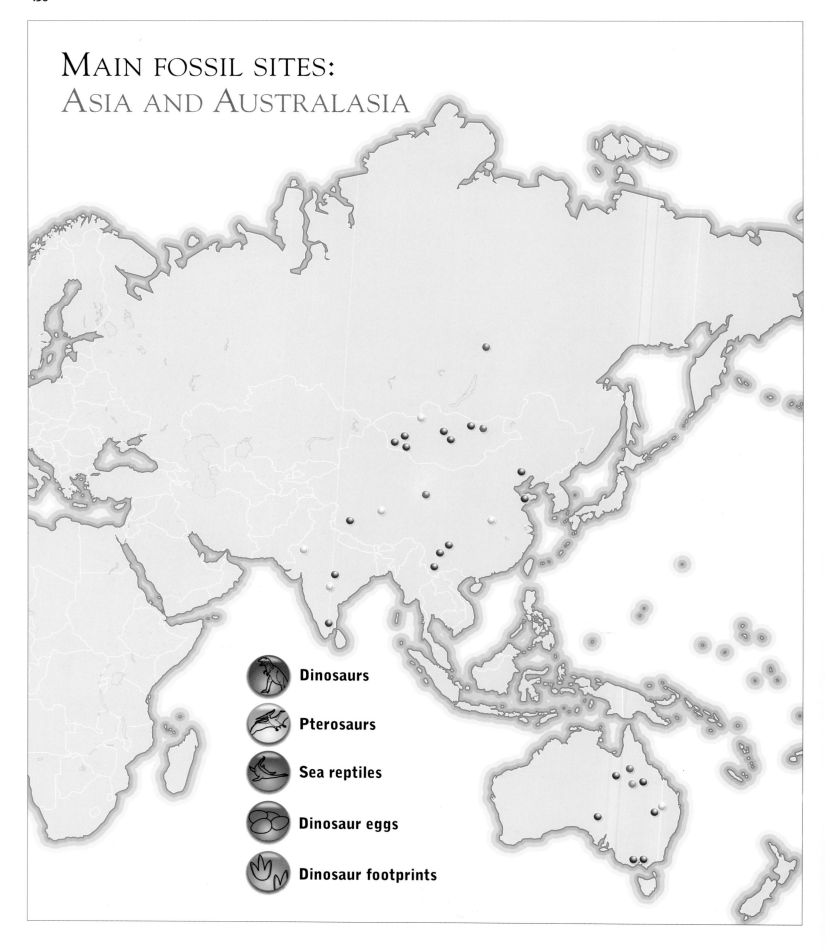

MAIN FOSSIL SITES:
ASIA AND AUSTRALASIA

Dinosaurs

Pterosaurs

Sea reptiles

Dinosaur eggs

Dinosaur footprints

WHERE TO SEE DINOSAURS

NORTH AMERICA

UNITED STATES OF AMERICA

American Museum of Natural History
Central Park West at
79th Street,
New York, NY 10024-5192
Tel. (212) 769-5100
www.amnh.org

California Academy of Sciences
Golden Gate Park,
San Francisco, CA 94118
Tel. (415) 750-7145
www.calacademy.org

Carnegie Museum of Natural History
4400 Forbes Avenue,
Pittsburgh, PA 15213
Tel. (412) 622-3131
www.carnegiemuseums.org/cmnh

Dinosaur National Monument
Located near Vernal, Utah and
Dinosaur, Colorado
4545 E Highway 40,
Dinosaur, CO 81610-9724
Tel. (435) 781-7700
www.nps.gov/dino/index.htm

Field Museum of Natural History
1400 S. Lake Shore Drive,
Chicago, IL 60605-2496
Tel. (312) 922-9410
www.fmnh.org

Museum of the Rockies
Montana State University,
600 West Kagy Boulevard,
Bozeman, MT 59717-2730
Tel. (406) 994-DINO
www.montana.edu/wwwmor

National Museum of Natural History
10th Street and Constitution
Avenue, NW,
Washington, DC 20560
Tel. (202) 357-2700
www.mnh.si.edu

Natural History Museum of Los Angeles
County 900 Exposition
Boulevard,
Los Angeles, CA 90007
Tel. (213) 763-DINO
www.nhm.org

Peabody Museum of Natural History at Yale University
PO Box 208118,
170 Whitney Avenue,
New Haven, CT 06520-8118
Tel. (203) 432-5050
www.peabody.yale.edu

Museum of Palaeontology, University of California, Berkeley
1101 Valley Life Sciences
Building,
Berkeley, CA 94720-4780
Tel. (510) 642-1821
www.ucmp.berkeley.edu

Utah Museum of Natural History
1390 E Presidents Circle,
University of Utah,
Salt Lake City, UT 84112-0050
Tel. (801) 581-6927
www.umnh.utah.edu

CANADA

Canadian Museum of Nature
Victoria Memorial Building,
240 McLeod Street,
PO Box 3443 Stn D,
Ottawa, ON K1P 6P4
Tel. (613) 566-4700
www.nature.ca

Royal Ontario Museum
Main Building,
100 Queen's Park,
Toronto, Ontario,
M5S 2C6
Tel. (416) 586-5549
www.rom.on.ca

The Royal Tyrrell Museum of Palaeontology
Highway 838, Midland
Provincial Park,
Drumheller, Alberta, T0J 0Y0

Toll free in Alberta: 310-0000
then 403-823-7707

Toll free in North America
(outside Alberta) 1-888-440-4240

Outside North America:
Tel. (403) 823-7707
www.tyrrellmuseum.com/home/

SOUTH AMERICA

ARGENTINA

Museo Argentino de Ciencias Naturales "Bernardino Rivadavia" (Argentine Museum of Natural Sciences)
Casilla de Correo 220, Avda.
Angel Gallardo 470, Suc. 5,
1405 Buenos Aires
Tel. +54-1-982-0306

EUROPE

BELGIUM

Royal Belgium Institute of Natural Sciences
Rue Vautier 29, B-1000,
Brussels
Tel. +32 (0)2 627 42 11
www.kbinirsnb.be

FRANCE

Le Musée des Dinosaures d'Espéraza
11260 Esperaza
Tel. 04 68 74 26 88
http://perso.wanadoo.fr/musee/dinosaures

Le Musée d'Histoire Naturelle
36 rue Geoffroy Saint-Hilaire,
Paris, 75005
Tel. 01 40 79 30 00
www.mnhn.fr

Le Musée Parc de Dinosaures
RN 113-3410 MEZE,
Béziers
Tel. 04 67 43 02 80
www.musee-parc-dinosaures.com

GERMANY

Naturhistoriches Forschungsinstitut Museum für Naturkunde
Zentralinstitut der Humboldt-
Universität zu Berlin
Invalidenstrasse 43,
D-10115, Berlin
Tel. +49 (0)30 2093-8591
www.museum.hu-berlin.de

Staatliches Museum für Naturkunde
Rosenstein 1,
70191 Stuttgart-Nord
Tel. +49 (0)72 1175-2111
http://www.stuttgart
museums.com/natural_history_
museum.html

POLAND

Institute of Palaeobiology, Warsaw
Instytut Paleobiologii PAN
ul. Twarda 51/55, 00-818
Warszawa
Tel. (48-22) 620-6224
www.paleo.pan.pl

RUSSIA

Paleontological Institute of Russian Academy of Sciences
117868,
Moscow, Profsoyuznaya st., 123
Tel. (059) 339-54-77

SPAIN

Museo Nacional de Ciencias Naturales
José Gutiérrez Abascal, 2
28006 Madrid
Tel. 91 411 13 28
www.mncn.csic.es

UNITED KINGDOM

Bristol City Museum
Queens Road, Bristol, BS8 1RL
Tel. 01179 223 571
www.bristol-city.gov.uk

Dinosaur Isle
Culver Parade,
Sandown, Isle of Wight
Tel. 01983 404344
www.miwg.freeserve.co.uk

Hunterian Museum
University of Glasgow,
University Avenue,
Glasgow, G12 8QQ, Scotland.
Tel. 0141 330 4221
www.hunterian.gla.ac.uk

The Natural History Museum
Cromwell Road,
London, SW7 5BD
Tel. 0207 942 5011
www.nhm.ac.uk

Oxford University Museum of Natural History
Parks Road,
Oxford, OX1 3PW
Tel. 01865 272 950
www.oum.ox.ac.uk

Sedgwick Museum of Earth Sciences
Downing Street,
Cambridge, CB2 3EQ
Tel. 01223 333 456
www.sedgwickmuseum.org

AFRICA

SOUTH AFRICA

South African Museum
Company Gardens,
Cape Town
Tel. 021 4243330
www.museums.org.za/sam

ASIA-PACIFIC

AUSTRALIA

Monash Science Centre
Building 74
Monash University
Clayton Campus
Victoria 3800
Tel. (03) 9905 1370
www.sci.monash.edu.au/msc/index.html

Queensland Museum
Grey & Melbourne Streets,
South Bank,
South Brisbane
Tel. 07 3840 7635
www.qmuseum.qld.gov.au

CHINA

Zigong City Dinosaur Museum
Dashanpu
Zigong, Sichuan
Tel. 86-813-580-1233

JAPAN

Gunma Museum of Natural History
1674-1, Kamikuroiwa,
Tomioka-shi,
Gunma-ken,
370-2345
Tel. 0274-60-1200
www.gmnh.pref.gunma.jp

The National Science Museum
7-20 Ueno Park, Taito-ku,
Tokyo 110-8718
Tel. +81-(0)3-3822-0111
www.kahaku.go.jp/english

GLOSSARY

abelisaurids
A group of theropods (meat-eating dinosaurs) from the Cretaceous, with primitive or "old-fashioned" features, based on the 29-foot-long (9-meter) *Abelisaurus* from South America.

absolute dating
Determining the age of formation of rocks in terms of actual time ago, in thousands or millions of years ago (compare **relative dating**).

acanthodians
One of the first groups of fish with jaws and paired fins, dating from the Early Silurian to the Permian periods. They are sometimes called "spiny sharks" but were not true sharks.

actinistians
Another name for the coelacanth group of lobe-fin or fleshy-fin (sarcopterygian) fish.

actinopterygians
The group name for ray-finned fish, which are fish with bony skeletons whose fins are supported by spine-like structures called fin rays; they form the great majority of fishes today (compare **sarcopterygians**).

agnathans
"Without jaws," a term usually applied to fish that do not have jaws but mouths like suckers or rasps; the two main types surviving today are lampreys and hagfishes.

alula
A small tuft of feathers part-way along the front or leading edge of a bird's wing, which adjusts the airflow, especially when flying at low speed; also called the bastard wing.

ammonoids
Types of extinct molluscs with external spirally coiled shells, large eyes and many tentacles for catching prey; related to octopus and squid.

ankylosaurids
A subgroup of the ankylosaurs (see below) which also possessed large bony lumps at the tail tip (compare **nodosaurids**).

ankylosaurs
Plant-eating armored or plated dinosaurs, well protected by many bony plates, lumps and shields in the skin.

annelids
Segmented worms – a major worm group which includes earthworms – where the body is formed of a long row of many similar ring-like sections or parts, called segments.

anseriforms
The group of birds usually called waterfowl or wildfowl, which today includes ducks, geese and swans.

anthracosaurs
A subgroup of the main group of amphibian-type animals known as labyrinthodonts, which arose early in the history of four-legged land animals during the Carboniferous period, but became extinct in the Permian.

anurans
"Without tails," a name usually applied to the tail-less amphibians or lissamphibians commonly known as frogs and toads.

apodans
"Without feet," usually applied to the worm-like amphibians or lissamphibians also known as caecilians or gymnophiones.

archosaurimorphs
Reptiles with a form or body structure resembling that of the archosaurs (see below).

archosaurs
"Ruling reptiles," a large group that arose in the Triassic period and included dinosaurs, pterosaurs and crocodiles.

arthropods
Invertebrate animals with a hard outer body casing and legs with movable joints – a massive group that includes insects, spiders and other arachnids; horseshoe crabs, true crabs and other crustaceans; centipedes, millipedes, also the extinct trilobites and eurypterids.

articulation
A joint or connection, usually between parts of the skeleton or structural framework of an animal, such as between the bones of a dinosaur's skeleton.

axis
The central line or middle band, for example, the middle lobe of the three lobes forming the body of a trilobite.

baleen plates
Long, fringe-edged strips of gristle-like baleen or "whalebone" hanging from the upper jaw of a great whale, used for filter-feeding.

brachiopods
"Shellfish" resembling bivalve molluscs such as mussels, but which form a different major group, also known as lampshells; they have a very long history and a strong claim to the description "living fossils."

belemnoids
Types of extinct molluscs with internal bullet- or spear-shaped shells, large eyes and many tentacles for catching prey; related to octopus and squid.

blastoids
Extinct sea-dwelling relatives of starfish in the echinoderm group, consisting of a cup-shaped body with two tentacle-like feeding arms, held up on a stalk.

boss
A rounded lump or mass, usually of a hard material like bone or horn.

brachiosaurids
Subgroup of sauropod dinosaurs based on *Brachiosaurus* ("arm reptile"), with front legs longer than the rear ones.

caecilians
See apodans.

calyx
Body part shaped like a bowl, cup or trumpet (a term also used to describe the shapes of certain flowers).

camarasaurids
Subgroup of sauropod dinosaurs based on *Camarasaurus* ("chambered reptile"), with weight-saving scoops and hollows in the vertebrae (backbones).

carnosaurs
A general and descriptive name (rather than the name of a specific and well-defined group) for large, predatory, meat-eating or carnivorous dinosaurs, such as *Allosaurus* and *Tyrannosaurus*.

caudal vertebrae
Backbones or vertebrae at the rear end of the spinal column, usually forming the animal's tail.

caudatans
See urodelans.

centrosaurines
"Short-frilled" subgroup of ceratopsian or horned dinosaurs based on *Centrosaurus*, where the nose horn was usually longer than the brow horns, and the front of the face was fairly deep and short-snouted (compare **chasmosaurines**).

cephalon
The front or head end, with the mouth and sensory organs like eyes, of certain animals, such as trilobites.

cephalopods
"Head-foot," a group of predatory molluscs with large eyes, big brains and many tentacles, including extinct ammonoids and belemnoids, also octopus, squid, cuttlefish and nautilus.

cephalothorax
The front or head end, with the mouth and sensory organs like eyes, combined with the middle part of the body that bears the limbs, of certain animals such as spiders and other arachnids.

ceratopsians
Horned dinosaurs, a group of plant-eaters, mostly with facial horns and sweeping neck frills or shoulder shields, such as *Triceratops*.

ceratosaurs
A group of theropods (meat-eating dinosaurs) based on *Ceratosaurus*, mainly from the first half of the Age of Dinosaurs, most of which had horns or rounded crests above the eyes and four digits on the front limb.

cervids
The family name for the hoofed mammals called deer, with antlers rather than horns.

chasmosaurines
"Long-frilled" subgroup of ceratopsian or horned dinosaurs based on *Chasmosaurus*, where the nose horn was usually shorter than the brow horns, and the front of the face was fairly shallow and long-snouted.

chelicerae
Long, sharp "biting claws" that work like fangs or jaws, in animals such as spiders, scorpions and horseshoe crabs; also the extinct eurypterids.

chelicerates
Animals that possess chelicerae (see above).

chelonians
The group name for dome-shelled reptiles commonly known as turtles, terrapins and tortoises.

chilopods
The group name for centipedes, which have strong jabbing **chelicerae** and one pair of legs per body segment.

cnidarians
Group of soft-bodied animals, including jellyfish, anemones, hydras and corals, most of which have stinging tentacles encircling a stalk-like body.

coelurosaurs
General name for small meat-eating dinosaurs, theropods, that mostly lived toward the beginning of the Age of Dinosaurs, such as *Coelophysis* and *Coelurus*, with hollow, bird-like bones.

collembolans
Small insects or insect-like animals also known as springtails, which were some of the very first land animals in the Devonian period.

coracoid
Bone in the upper or front shoulder region, especially in a bird, which braces the breastbone and front limb against the vertebral column or backbone; usually an additional bone to the collarbones or clavicles, which together form the V-shaped furcula or "wishbone" of a bird.

creodonts
Flesh-eating mammals, similar in many ways to today's wolves, cats and bears (Carnivora), but which formed a different group and died out by 5–10 million years ago.

crinoids
Animals of the echinoderm group, which includes starfish and urchins, that have a flower-like body shape and a very ancient history.

cusps
Raised, pointed or ridged surfaces on a part such as a tooth.

cycads
Plants that resemble palm trees, with a central stalk or trunk and an umbrella-shaped crown of frond-like leaves, which still survive but were much more numerous in the Mesozoic era.

cynodonts
"Dog teeth," creatures with features of both reptiles and mammals, some resembling dogs or cats – part of the group often called "mammal-like reptiles," which probably gave rise to mammals in the Triassic period but themselves became extinct in the Jurassic (see also **dicynodonts**).

decapods
Ten-limbed members of the crustacean group, such as crabs and prawns.

denticles
Small skin scales or projections shaped like cones or teeth, characteristic of the shark group.

diapsids
Major group of reptiles, identified by an opening or window in the skull behind the eye socket, that includes sea reptiles such as ichthyosaurs, snakes and lizards, and the archosaurs such as crocodilians, dinosaurs and pterosaurs.

dicynodonts
Meaning "two dog teeth," creatures with features of both reptiles and mammals, some resembling today's plant-eaters such as hippos – part of the group often called "mammal-like reptiles" (see also **cynodonts**).

dimorphism
"Two forms," usually describing the same kind or species which typically has two distinct forms, as when the male is much larger than the female, or vice versa.

dinocephalians
Meaning "terrible heads," animals in the therapsid group with features of both reptiles and mammals – many had horns, lumps and projections on their heads, and lived during the Permian period.

dinoceratans
Large plant-eating mammals from early in the Tertiary period, which had features of hoofed mammals and also other groups such as rabbits; they died out by 30 million years ago.

diplodocids
Subgroup of sauropod dinosaurs based on *Diplodocus* ("double beam"), with very long tails that had twin ski-like chevrons on the underside of each tail bone.

diplopods
The group name for millipedes, which are arthropods with chewing mouthparts and two pairs of legs per body segment.

dorsal fin
A fin or flap on the top or back (dorsal surface) of an animal such as a fish or ichthyosaur.

dromaeosaurs
Medium-sized predatory, meat-eating or carnivorous dinosaurs, based on *Dromaeosaurus*, including the well-known *Deinonychus* and *Velociraptor* – the group is sometimes known as "raptors."

echinoderms
"Spiny-skins," marine creatures with a radial or wheel-like body design, including starfish, brittlestars, urchins, sea cucumbers, sea lilies and feather stars.

echolocation
Locating objects such as prey in the surroundings, by emitting squeaks, clicks and similar pulses of sound that bounce off or reflect from the objects as echoes, and these are analyzed for the size and distance of the objects.

eurypterids
Medium to large extinct arthropods often called "sea scorpions," with large pincers for attacking prey, included with spiders and scorpions in the chelicerate group.

femur
Familiar name for the thighbone – the main bone in the upper rear limb of four-legged vertebrates.

fenestrae
"Windows," gaps or holes, usually in a plate or slab of a hard substance like bone.

fibula
Familiar name for the calf bone – one of usually two bones in the lower rear limb of four-legged vertebrates (see also **tibia**).

gastroliths
Pebbles or stones swallowed deliberately into the stomach or similar part of the gut of an animal, usually to help mash and grind up food there.

genus (plural, genera)
In the classification of living things, a group of closely related species; many dinosaurs such as *Tyrannosaurus* and *Triceratops* are referred to by their generic (or genus) names (see **species**).

graptolites
Extinct, small worm-like creatures with tentacles to sieve sea water for food; each lived in a tough, cup-shaped structure called a theca, and rows of these formed fossils like saw-teeth or chains.

gymnophiones
See apodans.

hadrosaurs
Medium to large plant-eating dinosaurs commonly called "duckbills," with wide, beak-like mouths, and many with projections or crests of bone on the head.

hallux
First or innermost digit on the rear limb – often called the "big toe."

heterodontism
Possessing teeth of different shapes and sizes, such as incisors, canines and molars, which are specialized for different purposes, rather than teeth which are all similar in shape and size.

hominids
Members of the primate group of mammals which are human-like – the "human family" including living humans (*Homo sapiens*) and our close extinct relatives such as Neanderthals.

huayangosaurids
Early group of plant-eating stegosaurs or plated dinosaurs based on *Huayangosaurus*, which lived mainly during the Jurassic period.

humerus
The main bone in the upper front limb of four-legged vertebrates.

hydrozoans
Small aquatic animals resembling sea anemones – members of the cnidarian group which includes coral creatures, anemones and jellyfish (see **cnidarians**).

hypsilophodontids
Group of plant-eating ornithopod dinosaurs based on *Hypsilophodon*, which were mainly small, slim and fast-moving, and survived during the Jurassic and Cretaceous periods.

ichthyosaurs
"Fish reptiles," marine reptiles shaped like fish or dolphins, with four limbs modified like paddles, a dorsal (back) fin and a twin-fluked tail.

igneous rocks
Major group of rocks formed when other rocks melt under great heat and pressure, and then cool and harden – like solidified lava from volcanoes.

iguanodontids
Group of plant-eating ornithopod dinosaurs based on *Iguanodon*, which were mostly fairly large and powerful, with three-toed rear feet and thumb spikes, and survived during the Cretaceous period.

incisors
Teeth with straight, sharp edges like spades or chisels, usually at the front of the jaws, for nibbling, nipping and gnawing.

index fossils
Remains of living things which were widespread, plentiful and readily fossilized, and which survived through great time periods evolving in well-documented ways, so they can be used to compare and date rocks (see **relative dating**).

invertebrates
General name for animals without a backbone (vertebrae or spinal column) – that is, not a fish, amphibian, reptile, bird or mammal.

labyrinthodonts
Early group of tetrapods or four-legged vertebrates, often called "the first amphibians," mainly from the Devonian to Permian periods.

lambeosaurs
Group of duckbill dinosaurs based on *Lambeosaurus*, with hollow head crests (see **hadrosaurs**).

lepospondyls
Relatively early group of tetrapods or four-legged vertebrates, often resembling large salamanders (and regarded as ancestors of today's amphibians), that lived mainly during the Carboniferous and Permian periods.

lissamphibians
Newer name for members of the group traditionally known as amphibians which survive today – frogs, toads, newts, salamanders and caecilians.

lobe-fins
Fish with fins that have a fleshy, muscular base (see **sarcopterygians**).

maniraptorans
"Grasping hands," large group of theropods (meat-eating dinosaurs) typified by a wrist that can swivel easily, including the dromaeosaurs or raptors.

marker fossils
See **index fossils**.

marsupials
Mammals in which the baby is born at a very early stage of development, and spends time growing in a pocket-like pouch or marsupium on the mother's front (compare **placentals**).

mesonychids
Group of hoofed mammals or ungulates from the early Tertiary period which became adapted as predators for hunting, but which had died out by about 30 million years ago.

mesosaurs
Group of water-dwelling reptiles, broadly resembling small crocodiles, that lived mainly during the Permian period.

metamorphic rocks
Major group of rocks formed when other rocks are changed by great heat and pressure, but do not melt in the process.

metatarsals
Bones between the ankles and toes which usually form the foot of an animal such as a reptile, bird or mammal.

mosasaurs
Group of extinct, large, predatory, sea-dwelling reptiles, probably related to today's monitor lizards, that lived during the Cretaceous period.

muscle scars
Roughened patches on bones, often preserved in fossils, where muscles were attached or anchored to them in life.

mutation
A change in a living thing's genetic make-up or genes, which may cause a visible effect in the living thing itself; mutations can be helpful or positive, harmful or negative, or neutral.

myriapods
Name usually applied to centipedes and millipedes (see **chilopods, diplopodas**).

nautiloids
Predatory marine molluscs of the cephalopod group, related to ammonoids, belemnoids, squid and octopus, with an external coiled shell, large eyes and many tentacles; only a few types survive.

nectrideans
Types of extinct lepospondyl amphibians shaped like newts or salamanders.

nematodes
Major group of worms that live almost everywhere and lack body sections or segments; often called roundworms.

neodiapsids
Group of diapsid reptiles which outwardly resembled lizards and lived during the Permian and Triassic periods (see **diapsids**).

nodosaurids
A subgroup of the ankylosaurs – armored or plated plant-eating dinosaurs – which did not possess large bony lumps at the tail tip (compare **ankylosaurids**).

nothosaurs
Early group of predatory swimming reptiles, that lived mainly during the Triassic period.

onychophorans
Worm-like animals with stubby tentacle-like legs, also called velvet-worms, which may show a link between true "legless" worms and the arthropods such as insects.

opisthosoma
Middle section of the body of certain animals, such as the extinct eurypterids ("sea scorpions"), between the head end and the tail.

ornithischians
Meaning "bird-hips," one of the two major groups of dinosaurs, where the lower part of the hipbone called the pubis slanted down and backward; this group includes all plant-eating dinosaurs except the prosauropods and sauropods (compare **saurischians**).

ornithomimosaurs
Group of medium-sized, slim, fast-running dinosaurs with two powerful rear legs and a bird-like beak, often called ostrich dinosaurs.

ornithopods
Main group of "bird-foot" plant-eating dinosaurs including *Hypsilophodon* and its cousins, *Iguanodon* and its relatives, and hadrosaurs (duckbills).

ornithosuchians
Reptiles that were closely related to dinosaurs and looked outwardly similar, mostly walking on their two rear legs and with sharp teeth.

osteoderms
Plates, lumps or pieces of bone that develop within the skin, rather than as part of the main skeleton.

ostracoderms
Early group of jawless fish from the Ordovician to Devonian periods, with protective plates of bone in the skin.

oviraptorids
Group of theropods (meat-eating dinosaurs) based on *Oviraptor*, with a tall, parrot-like beak.

pachycephalosaurs
"Thick-headed reptiles," a group of plant-eating dinosaurs with exceptionally thickened bone in the top or roof of the skull, variously called "boneheads" or "helmetheads."

paleomagnetism
Magnetism "trapped" in ancient rocks as they formed under the influence of the Earth's natural magnetic field; also the study of these features.

paleontology
Scientific study of fossils and the once-living things they represent.

parareptiles
Large grouping of reptiles, including some of the early land reptiles such as pareiasaurs, also mesosaurs, turtles and tortoises.

pareiasaurs
Group of early, large, squat, plant-eating reptiles mainly from the Permian period (see **parareptiles**).

parietal
One of the paired bones that form the upper rear of the cranium (braincase) or the main skull.

patagia
The thin, lightweight, elastic, sheet-like membrane that forms the main flight surface of a bat's wing.

pectoral fins
Pair of fins usually on the lower side of a fish toward the front of the body, which may have evolved into the front limbs of four-legged animals (compare **pelvic fins**).

pedipalps
Pair of limb-like parts to each side of the head, especially in arachnids – they are modified as leg-like feelers in spiders and large nipping claws in scorpions.

pelvic fins
Pair of fins usually on the lower side of a fish toward the rear of the body, which may have evolved into the rear limbs of four-legged animals (compare **pectoral fins**).

pelycosaurs
Group of large, sprawling-limbed mammal-like reptiles or synapsids mainly from the Carboniferous and Permian period, including the well-known "sail-back" *Dimetrodon*.

periods
Spans of time in the entire history of the Earth, which are subdivisions of eras, and which are themselves divided into epochs; most periods cover tens of millions of years.

phorusrhacids
Large, powerful, flightless birds of the second half of the Tertiary period, mainly in South America, and related to today's birds called cranes.

phragmocone
Front part of the shell of a belemnoid, an extinct type of mollusc that had the shell embedded within the body (like the squid today).

placentals
Mammals in which the baby is born at a relatively advanced stage of development, having been supplied with nourishment from the mother in her womb via a body part called the placenta (compare **marsupials**).

placoderms
Early group of fish with jaws, true paired fins, and protective bony plates over the head and front of the body; they originated in the Late Silurian period but went extinct after the Devonian.

placodonts
Early group of water-dwelling reptiles with flattened teeth for crushing hard food, probably shellfish; they lived mainly during the Triassic period.

platyhelminthes
Major group of simple, leaf-shaped worms also called flatworms.

plesiosaurs
Major group of swimming reptiles with tubby bodies, short tails and four legs modified as paddles, that lived through much of the Age of Dinosaurs (see also **pliosaurs**).

pleural lobes
The two side parts of the body of a trilobite, flanking the central part or axis.

pleurocoels
Scoop-shaped hollows or cavities, usually to save weight, such as in the vertebral bones of certain dinosaurs.

pliosaurs
Predatory plesiosaurs with large heads and short necks (see **plesiosaurs**).

polyplacophorans
Types of molluscs also called chitons or coat-of-mail shells.

poriferans
Group of creatures with the simplest body structure of any animal, lacking nerves, a brain, heart, digestive tract or muscles – often known as sponges.

predators
Animals that hunt and consume other creatures, their prey.

premaxillary
Bone at the front of the upper jaw, found only in certain dinosaurs.

premolars
Broad teeth for chewing and crushing, sited just in front of true molars.

preparator
Person who prepares scientific specimens, for example, extracting and cleaning fossils from their surrounding rock.

primates
Major group of mammals that includes lemurs, bushbabies, monkeys, apes and humans.

proboscideans
Major group of mammals that includes elephants and their many extinct relatives such as mammoths and deinotheres.

prosauropods
Group of medium-to-large plant-eating dinosaurs mainly from the Triassic and early Jurassic periods, typically with a small head, long neck, bulky body, pillar-like legs and long tail.

prosoma
Front body part of chelicerate animals such as eurypterids and spiders, bearing the eyes, mouthparts and walking limbs.

protoceratopsids
Early group of horned dinosaurs (certopsians) based on *Protoceratops*, where the face horns and neck frills were relatively small.

pterosaurs
Major group of flying vertebrates from the Age of Dinosaurs, sometimes included within the Class Reptilia or as an equivalent, the Class Pterosauria; they were probably warm-blooded and furry.

pygidium
The tail section of a trilobite or similar creature.

pygostyle
The lumpy mass at the tail end of the spinal column of a bird; colloquially called the "parson's nose."

quadrupedal
Walking or running on four legs.

raptors
Variously meaning "thieves," "plunderers" or "hunters," a term that refers to various predatory creatures, such as birds of prey, like eagles and hawks, and among the dinosaurs, the dromaeosaurs such as *Deinonychus* and *Velociraptor*.

rauisuchians
Reptiles resembling crocodiles and closely related to them, which lived mainly during the Triassic period.

ray-fins
See **actinopterygians**.

recombination
In sexual reproduction, when hereditary material or genes come together in various combinations, producing differences among the offspring.

relative dating
Determining the time of formation of certain rocks compared to other rocks, and which ones were formed earlier or later (compare **absolute dating**).

reptiles
General name for vertebrate animals with scaly skin that lay tough-shelled eggs; in the study of fossils and newer systems of classification, reptiles are defined by particular openings in the skull known as suborbital fenestrae, and the reptile group is sometimes taken to include birds too.

rhipidistians
"Fan-sails," a group of lobe-fin fishes related to coelacanths that were successful in the Devonian period and probably included the ancestors of land-dwelling tetrapods such as amphibians.

rhynchocephalia
A group of mainly Triassic plant-eating reptiles, mostly the size of today's pigs, fairly closely related to the archosaurs or ruling reptiles, that included the rhynchosaurs and leaves one surviving genus, the tuataras of New Zealand.

rostrum
A projecting part from the front of the head, like a beak or nose, in certain animals such as prawns, weevils and some kinds of fish.

sacral vertebrae
Backbones or vertebrae from the hip or pelvic region of the spinal column, usually joined to or forming part of the pelvis or hipbone.

sacrum
Single bony structure formed from several fused sacral vertebrae.

salientians
Name for the frog and toad group – see **anurans**.

sarcopterygians
The group name for lobe-fin or fleshy-fin fish, which are fish with bony skeletons whose fins have fleshy, muscular bases, including lungfish and coelacanths; they form a minority of fish alive today (compare **actinopterygians**).

saurischians
Meaning "lizard- or reptile-hips," one of the two major groups of dinosaurs, where the lower part of the hipbone called the pubis slanted down and forward; this group includes all meat-eating dinosaurs or theropods, and the plant-eating prosauropods and sauropods (compare **ornithischians**).

sauropods
Group of large to extremely large plant-eating dinosaurs with a small head, long neck, bulky body, pillar-like legs and long tail, most successful during the Late Jurassic and Cretaceous periods.

scaphopods
Group of molluscs or "shellfish" where the single shell is shaped like a long cone or elephant's tusk, also called tusk-shells.

scapula
A usually broad bone of the shoulder or pectoral region commonly called the shoulder blade.

scutes
Bony plates or bone-reinforced scales in the skin, especially of dinosaurs, crocodiles and similar reptiles, often covered with horn.

sedimentary rocks
Major group of rocks formed when tiny particles of sand, mud or other sediments settle as layers and are compacted and cemented; they are generally the only rocks to contain fossils.

septa
Flaps or cross-walls that divide an animal's shell or other bodily structure into segments.

siphon
In molluscs, a usually cone-shaped funnel in the side of the body, through which water is squirted at high pressure to thrust the animal along by "jet propulsion."

sonar
Sound-based system that works in a similar way to radar, for locating and navigating (see **echolocation**).

species
Group of living things that can breed together to continue their kind, but which cannot breed with members of other species; a group of closely related species forms a genus.

squamates
Group name for the reptiles commonly known as lizards and snakes.

squamosal
Bone forming the lower rear side of the skull, and which in mammals bears the jaw joint with the lower jaw or mandible.

stegosaurids
Later group of plant-eating stegosaurs or plated dinosaurs based on *Stegosaurus*, which lived from the Jurassic to Cretaceous periods.

stegosaurs
Major group of plant-eating dinosaurs, also called plated dinosaurs, with tall slabs or points of bone along the back, typified by the largest member, *Stegosaurus*.

sternum
Bone at the front of the thorax (chest), joined to the front ends of the ribs on either side – also called the breastbone.

telson
Tail part of aquatic animals, such as lobsters, prawns and eurypterids, often shaped like a flap or fan.

temnospondyls
Subgroup of the labyrinthodont group of amphibian-type animals, which appeared in the Early Carboniferous and died out by the Early Jurassic period.

tergites
One of the sections or segments of the rear body part, in animals such as eurypterids and certain insects.

tetanurans
"Stiff-tails," one of the main groups of theropod or meat-eating dinosaurs, that included allosaurs and tyrannosaurs.

tetrapods
Vertebrate animals with four limbs; a term applied particularly to the earliest of these, known as the "first amphibians" in older classification schemes, which had evolved from fish ancestors.

thecae
Body part shaped like a cup or socket, for example, the cup-shaped shells of the extinct creatures called graptolites.

thecodonts
"Socket-tooth" reptiles, one name for a group of reptiles that may have included the ancestors of dinosaurs.

therapsids
Subgroup of the synapsid group, "mammal-like reptiles," which evolved during the Permian period, and which included dinocephalians, gorgonopsians, dicynodonts and cynodonts.

therizinosaurs
Major group of dinosaurs with a beak-like mouth, perhaps fiber-like feathers, and huge claws on the forelimbs, that lived mainly in the Cretaceous period.

theropods
Major group of dinosaurs that includes all meat-eating or carnivorous types, from tiny *Compsognathus* to huge *Giganotosaurus*.

thescelosaurids
Group of medium-sized ornithopod dinosaurs based on *Thescelosaurus*, which are related to *Iguanodon* and *Hypsilophodon*.

thoracic vertebrae
Backbones or vertebrae in the chest region of the spinal column, often bearing the rib bones.

thorax
The chest region of animals, such as reptiles, birds and mammals, containing the lungs and heart.

thyreophorans
"Shield-bearers," major group of plant-eating dinosaurs that includes stegosaurs and ankylosaurs.

tibia
Familiar name for the shinbone – one of usually two bones in the lower rear limb of four-legged vertebrates (see also **fibula**).

titanosaurids
Subgroup of sauropod dinosaurs that flourished in the Cretaceous period, including *Saltasaurus* and *Argentinosaurus*.

trace fossils
Preserved signs and traces left by animals, such as fossilized footprints, eggshells and droppings, rather than actual body parts.

trackways
Rows or tracks of footprints.

trilobites
Huge group of arthropods, with a body divided lengthwise into three parts, that lived from the Cambrian to Permian periods.

ungulates
Hoofed mammals, where the digits or toes are capped by hooves rather than ending in nails or claws; the group includes horses, rhinos, deer, antelopes, cattle and many others, both living and extinct.

urodelans
Tailed amphibians or lissamphibians, commonly known as salamanders and newts.

ursids
Members of the bear family of mammals.

vertebrae
The separate bones making up the "backbone" or spinal column of a vertebrate animal.

vertebrates
Animals with vertebrae or backbones – conveniently described as fish, amphibians, reptiles, birds and mammals.

vibrissae
Long, thick, stiff hairs on the snout, used for feeling the way – usually called whiskers.

weigeltisaurs
Group of outwardly lizard-like reptiles (types of diapsids) with extendible skin flaps for gliding, that lived mainly during the Permian period.

Picture credits

American Museum of Natural History
page 44, 208, 336.

Ardea
8, 9, 12(top), 12(bottom), 15, 17, 18, 21(b), 22, 34, 50, 51, 53, 64, 84, 90(right), 106(left), 106(r), 110(t), 113, 114, 121(b), 140, 148, 152(top left), 152(l) 155(b), 170, 173, 186(l), 196(l), 202(l), 205(r), 212, 218, 223, 227, 272, 279, 282, 289(r), 303(r), 304, 311(l), 314, 350, 354, 355(l), 355(r), 370(l), 372(l), 374, 393(r), 424(l).

Richard Burgess
24–25, 26, 27, 436, 437, 438 and Factfile maps throughout.

Karen Carr
61(t), 61(b), 150, 153, 159, 179, 185, 270, 382, 390, 420.

Dinosaur Isle
36(r), 43(l), 49.

Pamela J.W. Gore
Georgia Perimeter College 82(t).

Steve Kirk
118, 120, 121(t). 133, 139, 160, 164, 191, 196(r), 217, 247, 248, 252, 273, 275, 288, 291, 309, 310, 335, 340, 343, 356, 373, 378.

Marshall Cavendish Archive
104, 174, 205(l), 220, 228, 264, 306, 308, 330, 334, 344, 360, 398.

Marshall Editions
Colin Newman 60(t), 60(b), 65(t), 66(t), 66(b), 68; *Steve Kirk* 80, 81, 82, 86, 87, 93, 101, 102, 103, 107, 126, 127, 129, 132, 137, 144, 145, 146, 149, 158, 184, 192, 204, 215, 223, 225, 236, 237, 244, 255, 263, 267, 269, 280, 290, 292, 293, 296, 298, 299, 303(l), 320, 321, 328, 341, 342, 358, 359, 365, 371, 384, 385, 386, 389, 392; *Malcolm Ellis* 411; *Andrew Wheatcroft* 412, 429(l), 430(r), 431(l), 432(l); *Graham Allen* 413, 414, 415, 416, 419, 426; *Steve Holden* 423; *Andrew Robinson* 425.

Monash Science Centre
Peter Trusler 210, 276.

Oxford Scientific Films Ltd
5(b), 122, 130, 134, 152, 165, 168, 176, 190, 206, 214, 243, 250, 274, 319, 325, 333.

Royal Tyrrell Museum
162, 294, 302, 364(l).

Science Photo Library
2, 10, 11(t), 11(b), 13(t), 13(b), 14, 15(b), 16, 19(t), 19(b), 23(l), 23(r), 25, 30, 32, 35, 37, 40, 41, 42, 43(r), 48(l), 48(r), 54, 55, 56, 62, 65(b), 69, 70, 72, 74, 75(t), 75(b), 76, 80, 87, 99(l), 112, 142, 160(l), 180, 186(r), 240, 256, 322, 332, 338, 366(t), 366(b), 378, 386(l), 393(l), 394, 395, 397, 404, 406, 409, 424(r), 427(r), 428(l), 429(r), 430(l), 431(r), 432(r), 433(r), 434.

John Sibbick
5(t), 6, 20, 21, 25, 25, 36(l), 38, 46, 78, 78, 88, 92, 94, 109, 110(b), 116, 128, 156, 172, 182, 213, 226, 253, 258, 261, 262, 284, 300, 316, 327, 364(r), 372(r), 376, 380, 381, 387, 388.

Joe Tucciarone
155(t), 166, 169, 188, 194, 197, 200, 202(r), 232, 281, 297, 352, 357, 368.

Wildlife Art Ltd
Ken Oliver 52, 67, 83, 85, 98, 100, 108, 111, 178, 198, 216, 222, 231, 233, 234, 235, 238, 239, 242, 245, 254, 287, 289, 311, 313, 318, 347, 367, 396, 401, 418, 422, 427(l); *Philip Hood* 58(l), 90, 96, 97, 119, 124, 125, 136, 138, 147, 159, 161, 163, 187, 193, 199, 207, 230, 246, 249, 260, 266, 268, 278, 286, 312, 326, 329, 346, 348, 362, 370, 379, 400, 403, 410, 417, 428(r), 433(l), 440, 441, 442, 443, 444, 445; *Myke Taylor* 91, 99(r), 203, 349, 402; *Wayne Ford* 177, 224.

Acknowledgments

Steve Parker would like to acknowledge Jane Parker for research assistance, Dr Paul Barrett of the Natural History Museum in London for valuable additions to and comments on the text, Peter Coates for freshwater reptile information and John Rush for "bringing dinosaurs to life."

The publishers thank Dr Thomas Holtz, Paleontologist and Director of the Earth, Time & Life Program at the University of Maryland, College Park, for his assistance; Sarah Whittley of Wildlife Art Ltd for organizing the production of many wonderful illustrations for this book; and Richard Burgess for all maps and for the Time Scale of Prehistory Chart on pages 24 – 25.

INDEX

FREEPORT MEMORIAL LIBRARY

3 1489 00502 4755

49.95   5-17-04

FREEPORT MEMORIAL LIBRARY
FREEPORT, NEW YORK
PHONE: 379-3274

GAYLORD M